INDIA

A WORLD IN TRANSITION

INDIA

A WORLD IN TRANSITION

REVISED EDITION

by

Beatrice Pitney Lamb

FREDERICK A. PRAEGER, *Publishers*

New York • Washington • London

FREDERICK A. PRAEGER, PUBLISHERS
111 FOURTH AVENUE, NEW YORK, N.Y. 10003, U.S.A.
77–79 CHARLOTTE STREET, LONDON W. 1, ENGLAND

Published in the United States of America in 1966
by Frederick A. Praeger, Inc., Publishers

Third printing, 1967

The original edition of this book was published in 1963.
The present edition is revised, updated, and expanded.

Library of Congress Catalog Card Number: 66-14163

Printed in the United States of America

FOREWORD TO THE REVISED EDITION

IT IS GRATIFYING to an author that a book long labored over should be in such continual demand that a revised edition becomes necessary. Having spent over twelve years preparing for and finally writing the first edition of this book, I have been especially pleased by its reception.

Often I wish, however, that its title had not been *India—A World in Transition*, but rather *India in the Light of Her Past*. For this is a book of history fully as much as it is a book about contemporary, always changing India.

My approach to history, though, is different from that of the historian who finds the past interesting per se and without reference to the swiftly changing scene of the present day that succeeds it. Rather, I am intrigued by the deep interconnections between the past and the present, and by the way a nation such as India always carries with herself deposits from long ago which explain much that would otherwise be inexplicable in the current scene. It is because of the current scene that I look to the past.

Since the first edition was published, I have made one more trip to India—my sixth—in 1965, before the outbreak of war between India and Pakistan. On the eve of that war, Indians were discouraged and depressed by the many problems their government seemed unable to solve. But as this edition goes to press, in October, 1965, the Indian mood is quite different. Although India did not inflict a major military defeat on Pakistan, her army did prevent the Pakistan army from seizing Kashmir. This victory, viewed by the Indian press as a major one, produced a new elation, a new sense of unity within the nation, and a renewed self-confidence.

Rapid and extreme changes of national mood are perhaps characteristic of India. But regardless of how the Indian climate of thought—and actual conditions—may change in the future, I hope and believe that this book will shed light on how the various aspects of India past and present are interrelated, and hence on the underlying nature of the nation, whatever the future may bring.

FOREWORD TO THE REVISED EDITION

[illegible]

[illegible]

[illegible]

[illegible]

FOREWORD

ALTHOUGH THIS BOOK attempts to be an objective study of India, it has highly personal roots. When I went to India for the first time in 1949, I had no idea that I would someday write about it. Having never before been outside North America and Europe, I was utterly unprepared for an Asian culture. At first, much of India's strangeness repelled me. Yet, at the same time, I was attracted, partly by its many beauties—of old buildings, of groups of women in colored saris, of easy graceful gestures, of the slow rhythm of bullocks pulling their creaking carts, a rhythm so good for a soul tired of the endless rush of automobile traffic. At a deeper level, I was also attracted by the Indians I came to know. They were outgoing and friendly like Americans. More than that, they had an unspoken expectancy that a friendship once established would continue indefinitely—not vanish in the busy flux of life, as Americans so often expect and allow friendships to do. And many of them had a wonderful serenity and a way of accepting quietly not only the eccentricities of a foreign friend, but also any difficulties, either minor or major, within their own lives. Being with them created in me a profound feeling of well-being.

Gradually, this liking and respect for individual Indians stimulated in me an increasing curiosity about their land, their history, their culture, and the problems that modern India is facing. My Indian friends volunteered to tell me everything, and I listened gladly. But what they said always left much that I wanted to know unexplained—quite naturally, since I especially needed to understand precisely the things they took so much for granted that they would not think of mentioning them. So, when I returned from my first trip, in 1950, I began reading voraciously about the country. And I have never stopped. The bibliography at the end of this book indicates the kind of reading I have done.

In 1956–57, in 1958, in 1960, and again in 1962, I went back to India. The more I came to understand, the less I minded any of the customs, ways, or other things that had bothered me at first. Just as one so often feels, in the case of a personal friend, that any quality one does not like is merely the reverse side of the qualities one loves, so in the case of India as a whole it came to seem to me meaningless and irrelevant to judge separately this or that aspect. India is a world in herself, with her own laws of being, and as such she commanded my respect, much as individual Indians have won my affections. I began to feel it imperative to write about India in order to convey this sense of her totality.

Having now written this book, I want above all to express my gratitude to the many Indian friends who have helped me in various ways. I am especially grateful for the time spared me by Indian officials out of their days crowded with heavy loads of work.

My thanks go also to the following persons who have read parts or all of this book in manuscript and given me valuable help and suggestions: Professor W. Norman Brown, Professor Norman D. Palmer, Professor Richard D. Lambert, Dr. Richard L. Park, Professor Milton Singer, Professor John E. Brush, Professor Amiya Chakravarty, Professor Margaret Cormack, Professor Ainslee Embree, Mr. Selig S. Harrison (Editor of *The New Republic*), Mr. Champion Ward (of the Ford Foundation), Mr. V. K. Narasimhan (Editor of *The Hindu*, Madras), Mr. S. Krishnan (USIS, Madras), Mr. S. K. Roy (Consul General of India in New York City), Professor Wilfred Malenbaum, Mr. August Maffry (Chairman of the Executive Committee of the Asia Society), and Mr. Paul Sherbert (Executive Director of the Asia Society).

The American expert who has helped me most is Dr. Phillips Talbot, now Assistant Secretary of State for Near Eastern and South Asian Affairs. Before assuming this office, he advised me on books to read, shared with me his own observations based on more than seven years in the Indian subcontinent, and encouraged me to undertake this book.

My husband, Horace R. Lamb, has shared part of my travels and supported my efforts in innumerable ways—even when the throes of composition greatly decreased my efficiency as a housewife. For all this, I am very grateful.

I owe a special debt to Mrs. Shirley Denner, whose unfailing good humor as she typed and retyped this manuscript through its many revisions helped me more than she realizes.

CONTENTS

INDIA
A WORLD IN TRANSITION

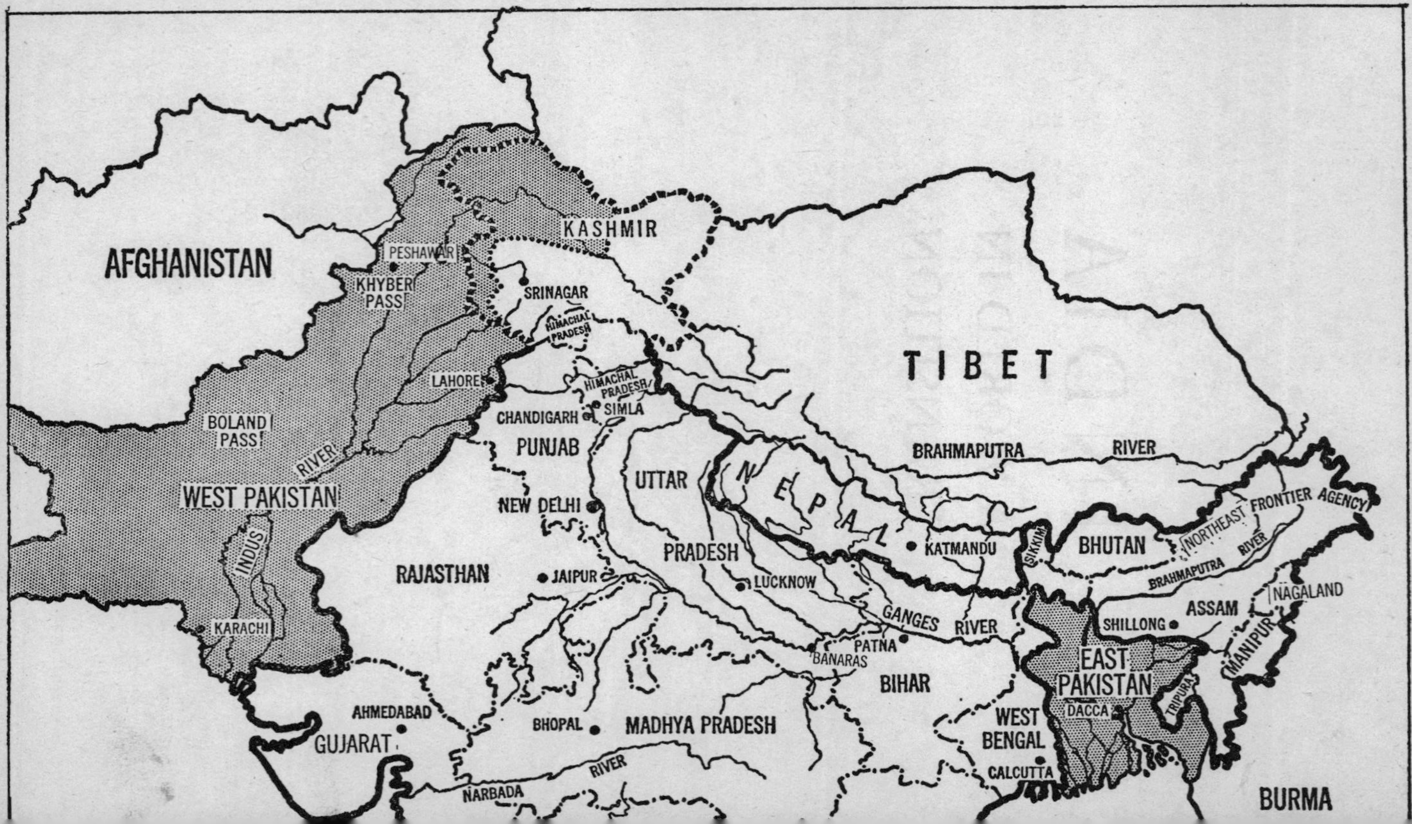
AFGHANISTAN
KASHMIR
PESHAWAR
KHYBER PASS
SRINAGAR
HIMACHAL PRADESH
LAHORE
HIMACHAL PRADESH
SIMLA
CHANDIGARH
BOLAND PASS
RIVER
WEST PAKISTAN
INDUS
KARACHI
PUNJAB
NEW DELHI
UTTAR
PRADESH
RAJASTHAN
JAIPUR
LUCKNOW
TIBET
BRAHMAPUTRA
RIVER
NEPAL
KATMANDU
SIKKIM
BHUTAN
NORTHEAST FRONTIER AGENCY
RIVER
BRAHMAPUTRA
NAGALAND
ASSAM
SHILLONG
MANIPUR
GANGES
RIVER
PATNA
BANARAS
BIHAR
EAST PAKISTAN
TRIPURA
DACCA
WEST BENGAL
CALCUTTA
AHMEDABAD
GUJARAT
BHOPAL
MADHYA PRADESH
RIVER
NARBADA
BURMA

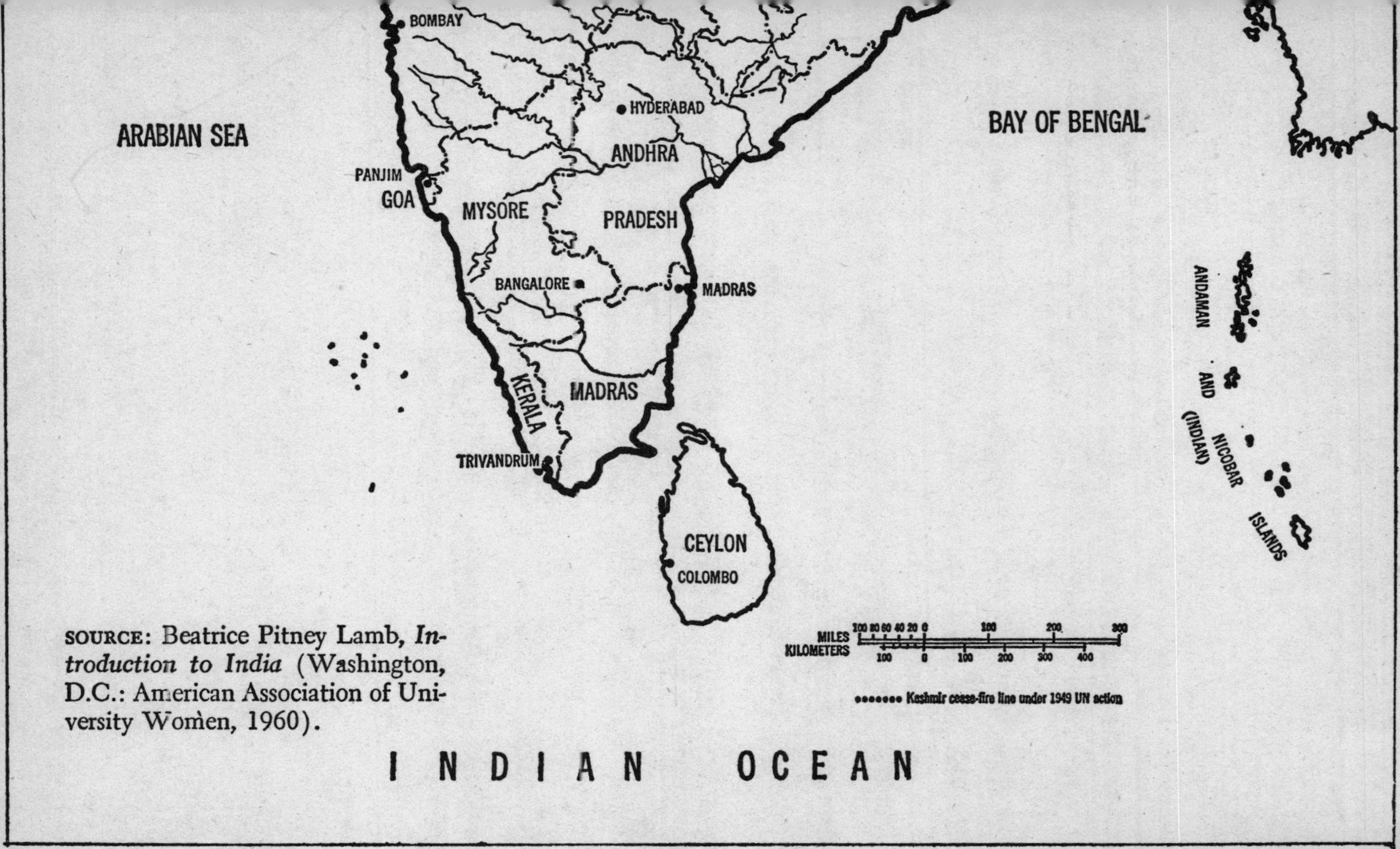

SOURCE: Beatrice Pitney Lamb, *Introduction to India* (Washington, D.C.: American Association of University Women, 1960).

1 • INTRODUCTION

A Westerner visiting India is immediately struck by the sharp contrasts he sees. Aside from the contrast between wealth and poverty, perhaps the most startling is that resulting from the close juxtaposition of elements belonging to different centuries and originating even in different continents. Ancient customs, behavior patterns, and techniques exist side by side with modern machines and ways of living that bear the clear imprint of the West.

In a steel plant equipped with the finest furnaces, rollers, and monster cranes, coal is carried in wicker baskets on the heads of women. A modern highway encounters an unbridged river over which cars, trucks, buses, bicycles, and bullock carts must cross on an ancient wooden barge rowed by sweating oarsmen. In windowless village homes with mud floors, mud walls, and thatched roofs, more than 7 million weavers work endlessly in semidarkness, slowly turning out beautiful fabrics on handlooms, while far fewer industrial workers tending power looms in large, shed-like factories turn out much more cloth—on which a special excise tax is levied to keep the handloom industry alive. Working in pairs, half-naked agricultural laborers walk all day back and forth on a high wooden seesaw-like beam to raise well water for the parched earth and thirsty crops. What they do or fail to do affects the success or failure of plans drawn up by Western-trained economists who contemplate a transformation of India unimaginable to such villagers.

Many such examples can be given, and no single one is typical of all of India. Some highways have as many bridges as may be needed. Not all the irrigation is done by human labor or alternatively by canal waters from large modern dams; many devices falling between these extremes are in use.

In the vast variety of India, few things are typically Indian—even to the degree that certain things can be said to be typical of the United States, the United Kingdom, or any Western nation. For India not only embraces a far wider variety of geographic, climatic, and economic circumstances than does any Western nation; it also includes peoples of great ethnic diversity and highly dissimilar historical origins. These peoples have tended to preserve their customs and their group identities over the centuries to an extent unthinkable in the United States, where ancestral origins, even of the children of immigrants, often can scarcely be guessed. Then, too, the patterns of the various invasions and conquests of India have overlapped or cut across one another in various ways in different parts of the country. Each region of India has its own history which has left its own distinctive mark on current attitudes and problems.

Throughout the variety of India, however, the combination of elements that seem to belong to different worlds remains characteristic. To Westerners, it is what makes India endlessly interesting—and at times entertaining. For example, the large lawn within the Red Fort in Delhi—one of the splendid remains of the Mughul* period and a prime tourist attraction—is mowed by a small reel-type lawnmower pulled by a bullock!

But the incongruities of India are not only those which lie on the surface to be seen; nor are they all as trivial as a bullock-drawn lawnmower. They extend deep into the fabric of Indian society, affect every aspect of Indian life, and constitute the pivotal problem of modern India. Modern-minded Indian leaders have been attempting to pull India quickly out of the past and place her firmly in the twentieth century. Much of India lags, resists the changes, becomes bewildered by the conflict of values.

* Often spelled "Mogul." The English spellings of certain Indian names used in the past give a misleading impression of their pronunciation. Modern scholars are attempting to introduce a spelling that more closely suggests the sounds of the words. Throughout this book, an attempt has been made to follow the spellings most widely accepted by scholars at the present time.

Modernism—in the sense of the secular, rational, scientific, technological approach to living—first came to India from the West in the period of British rule. Beginning in the nineteenth century, certain groups of Indians appropriated this modernism, developed it in their own way, modified it according to their own Indian needs. Thus, within India today, the "modern" is certainly not synonymous with the "Western." Quite distinct from any fresh importation of Western modernism, there is a truly Indian modernism as well. Yet, because modernism first came from outside and still seems alien to the vast majority, many Indians view the new values and technology as Western—as opposed to their own Indian or Asian or Eastern ideals and ways.

In each area of Indian life, the incongruous and contrasting elements lie side by side waiting for time somehow to fuse them or choose between them. In the economic sphere, Western-type concepts, goals, plans, and factories confront a predominantly agricultural peasant economy still greatly dependent on barter and the use of primitive techniques. In government and politics, a Western-type constitutional framework serves as a channel through which a wide variety of political forces, both traditional and modern, strive to affect state policy. A nationalism learned from the West has splintered, under Indian conditions, into assertive subnationalisms that continue to grow in number. In society, new ideas of equality have been superimposed on a caste system retaining the resilience of centuries. New ideas of family relations have begun to break apart the old joint families, which emphasized group welfare as against individual decision-making.

The vast majority in the countryside have as yet no inkling of the changes that lie ahead or the new concepts that will challenge them. Among the educated urban elite, however, many experience the conflict between East and West, between the traditional and the modern, as a painful inner conflict involving difficult personal decisions. How Western or modern should one become? And in what ways? In superficial matters like clothes, house furnishings, eating habits? Or in more basic matters, such as work habits, political attitudes, social behavior, religious belief, and basic goals? Which of the traditional values are worth defending at any cost? How does one best defend them? Choices such as these are never made by the mind alone, for the whole person is involved. All the most intimate ties, all the emotional roots, all the problems of character and personality inevitably tangle with the issue. As in any case of inner conflict, the alternatives never seem as clear-cut and simple from within as they may appear to an outsider.

While in prison, twelve years before he became Prime Minister of India, Jawaharlal Nehru wrote:

> I have become a queer mixture of the East and the West, out of place everywhere, at home nowhere. Perhaps my thoughts and approach to life are more akin to what is called Western than Eastern, but India clings to me as she does to all her children, in innumerable ways. . . . I am a stranger and alien in the West. I cannot be of it. But in my own country also, sometimes I have an exile's feeling.[1]

Being unusually articulate, secure, and accustomed to introspection, Nehru was able to report on the inner tug of war about which many Indians are more reticent. Later, as he progressively "discovered" India—and discovered also his own outstanding ability to speak directly to the Indian masses—he acquired a position that gave him the freedom to work out his own synthesis of the conflicting traditions in his daily life and activities.

The few Indians who reach the top in any sphere of action may thereby attain a similar freedom to synthesize. Others are hopelessly pulled or pushed by social pressures toward or away from Westernization or in both directions at once. They may therefore experience the cultural conflict primarily as personal frustration.

In any society, only a very few of the hardiest individualists, pioneers, or prophets succeed in defying the culture of their group in more than a few unimportant matters. Thus the cultural whole has a certain inertia. It comes down from the past and tends to continue into the future, accepting changes reluctantly and only as they can somehow be fitted into existing patterns of thought. When a change does occur in one area of life, it tends to lead in turn to changes in others, like ripples spreading from the spot where a stone has fallen into a pond.

It is not easy, then, to change a culture merely here and there, as one might change the detachable parts of a machine—to subtract selectively from that culture certain "irrational" attitudes, such as reverence for the cow, and to add some, but not all, Western-type values and techniques.

In mid-1965, while the long-term transition from the traditional to the modern was proceeding at its own pace, India was plunged into a war with Pakistan that could bring radical changes in her fortunes as a nation, in her economy, in the mood of her people, in the patterns of Indian politics. Fighting continued even after the formal cease-fire, soon reached in response to U.N. pressure, and the animosity exacerbated by the conflict seemed likely to remain a pivotal factor in world politics for many years to come.

Whatever the final repercussions of that war may be, this book attempts to reveal, as a living whole, the India that existed in 1965, exploring the interconnections between the past and the present, and between the various aspects of the modern scene.

Even to consider, in a preliminary way, why that war began is to sample the vitality of such interconnections. (The causes of the war will be treated more fully in subsequent chapters, especially Chapter 16.) India faced so many pressing economic and political problems in 1965 that she could ill-afford to be drawn into a war, let alone to escalate it sharply herself. Viewed in practical terms; the object of contention—the mountainous, economically backward state of Jammu and Kashmir (generally known simply as Kashmir)—was hardly worth the many risks involved. But in both India and Pakistan, the passionate hostility each harbored toward the other was too great, too deep-rooted to be checked by reason.

Some Westerners consider this a religious war, for it grew out of centuries-old animosities between Hindus and Muslims—animosities that were most recently vented at the time of partition, in 1947, when there was wholesale slaughter and millions lost their homes and possessions as they hastily fled to escape being massacred themselves. But as this book will show, these animosities stemmed originally not so much from religious differences as such, as from economic and political relations between the two groups: Hindu memories of Muslim domination, later Muslim fears of similar domination by the Hindus.

Apart from these animosities, the Indo-Pakistan war had its

roots also in the internal situation within India (as well as in Pakistan). India feared that if she agreed to the plebiscite in Kashmir so much desired by Pakistan, groups in certain other regions of India might demand plebiscites for their regions also, thus perhaps eventually fragmenting the Indian Union. More immediately, she feared that it might trigger a new wave of blood-letting, as fanatical Hindus slaughtered many of the 50 million Muslims still in India.

To try to make life tenable for her various religious minorities, India had determined to be a secular state. The resulting insistence that religion and politics be kept separate was a major irritant to religion-based Pakistan. Most Indians argued that the religion of the Kashmiris should not determine the future of their state, and moreover that religion should not have led to the creation of Pakistan itself. The continued resentment on the part of many Indians (particularly Hindus) regarding the very existence of Pakistan was one of the many long-suppressed feelings that finally found expression in the war fever that swept north India early in September, 1965. China's threatening presence—and the fact that she stood ready to invade India again—made India's predicament all the more complex, but had no lessening effect on Indian hostility toward Pakistan.

These brief introductory observations on one important issue may serve to illustrate the fact that to answer any question about India, one must try to understand the entire fabric of Indian life and history. This book will attempt to illuminate that fabric. In doing so, we will first consider the geographical, climatic, and historical background; then religious factors, social relations, education, governmental structure, political issues and parties, economic conditions and programs; and, lastly, foreign policy, which emerges out of internal factors all too seldom understood in the West.

India, with its forty-five centuries of history, its infinite diversity, and its complex contemporary problems, defies any abbreviated treatment. More questions may be raised than there is space to answer—or, indeed, can be answered. But perhaps this book will at least provide a coherent framework for further reading and some insight into the dynamics of the world's largest democracy.

2 • THE INDIAN SETTING

STRETCHING FROM A POINT in the north in the same latitude as Norfolk, Virginia, to within 550 miles of the equator, and with altitudes ranging all the way from sea level to over 28,000 feet, India embraces geographical and climatic variety and contrasts far greater than can be found even in the continental United States (which is two and a half times India's size). Great fertile plains, a desert, dense jungles teaming with wildlife—tigers, elephants, monkeys, birds of brilliant plumage, to name only a few—a number of vast rivers (including one of the longest in the world), high, dry, rolling tablelands, low-lying tropical coastal plains with palms leaning over lazy streams or inland lagoons, and the mightiest mountains in the world: Everything, it seems, is there.

The Land

Not a single range but a series of parallel ranges, together forming a wall between 100 and 200 miles in depth, the Himalayas lie partly in India and partly beyond India's northern boundary. From Kashmir in the north, they extend to the southeast and the east for 1,500 miles, with few usable passes. In most places, the barrier reaches 20,000 feet. For miles, even the passes are as high as Mont Blanc, the highest mountain peak in Europe. At least forty peaks are over 24,000 feet; and the towering, defiant Mount Everest, the highest in the world, is 29,028 feet—almost half again as high as Mount McKinley, the highest peak in the United States. Generations of daring mountain climbers sought in vain to scale the various peaks until at last, in the 1950's, the determined application of scientific thought to the problem, plus the use of modern, lightweight equipment, made their conquest possible. No wonder that Indians have looked to their lonely, inaccessible, eternally white mountains with awe and wonder, regarding them as the home of the gods.

Other ranges of mountains and spurs of ranges run through northwest Pakistan, meeting the Himalayas at an angle to the north of Kashmir, thus forming, as it were, a pitched roof over the Indian subcontinent which India shares with Pakistan. It was from the northwest, through the Hindu Kush, and through passes now in West Pakistan, that wave after wave of migrant tribes or invaders entered the Indian subcontinent over the centuries. The most famous of these passes is the Khyber, near Peshawar—low enough to provide at least a funnel into the Indian subcontinent, but not so wide as to provide easy access for large numbers. Invaders have never entered the Indian subcontinent in such numbers as to overwhelm or destroy the civilization they found in India. Each wave of invaders left its mark, but was, in time, absorbed into the complex, heterogeneous whole that is India. Just as one of the great themes in American history has been the absorption of immigrants into American life, one of the important themes in Indian history is the quite different way in which India has assimilated immigrants and invaders arriving at intervals over a far longer span of time.

Directly south of the mountain barrier lie two great river valleys. India's holiest and most important river, the Ganges, flows to the southeast, parallel with the mountains, through one of the most fertile agricultural areas in the world. Pakistan's chief river, the Indus, flows southwest and south through drier land where irrigation is crucial. Three of its five important tributaries have their source in India. The use of the waters of these rivers was a major matter of dispute between India and Pakistan until a settlement was reached in the autumn of 1960.

Only a low divide separates the valleys of the Ganges and the Indus. Together, they have historically been the great melting pot of India. Incoming races and tribes, once they had gone through the narrow northwest passes, were able to spread out over the two valleys and come in contact with the people already in north India.

The lack of barriers on the Indo-Gangetic plains has also favored at least some degree of political unification there—whereas elsewhere Indian geography tends to divide instead of unify. On several occasions, the northern plains have been brought under the control of a single ruler. Today, the states of the Punjab, Uttar Pradesh, and Bihar form the heart of the great valley area of north India. West Bengal includes part of the delta of the Ganges, although the chief mouth of the river is in East Pakistan.

Almost as impressive as the Himalayas, the Indo-Gangetic plains have a majesty of their own. Unfolding in seemingly endless flatness and monotony, they stretch on and on for over 1,500 miles from west to east, dotted with village after village of tight clusters of box-like mud huts with mud or thatched roofs (or sometimes roofs of handmade tiles). Between the villages lies the same patchwork quilt of tiny fields separated from one another by low mud banks in irregular, haphazard patterns. Along the few roads, bullock carts move with a primeval slowness that itself seems to enlarge the mighty plains. The traveler crossing the plains by car (or even by plane) almost begins to believe that there is no world but this.

South of these plains there is the rich variety of the large triangle that juts deep into the Indian Ocean, giving India its long coastline on the Arabian Sea to the west and on the Bay of Bengal to the east. This peninsula is rimmed with a narrow coastal strip —very narrow along the western side of the peninsula, somewhat wider on the east coast, especially in the area of Madras (where the British established their first main foothold in India). The people of the coastal strips turned to navigation at a very early period. Those on the west coast developed trading relations with the Arabs of the Middle East, and through them with Ancient Rome. By the beginning of the Christian era, either the Arabs or the Indians had observed the seasonal regularity of the winds blowing across the Indian Ocean and found that they could tell in advance when the wind would be right to blow their boats to the west or to the east. Indians on the east coast carried Indian culture not only to the nearby island of Ceylon, but also to much of Southeast Asia and the long archipelago now known as Indonesia. Absorbed in these overseas activities, they seem to have had little contact with the Indian kingdoms of the northern plains.

Certain portions of the coastal strips form natural subdivisions and have significant separate histories of their own. On the southeastern coast, the area around Madras early became the center of a high southern culture. Farther north, on the eastern coast, the areas that are now Orissa and Andhra Pradesh became centers of high culture perhaps as early as 200 B.C. On the west coast, two significant divisions are those occupied by the present-day states of Gujarat (to the north) and Kerala (to the extreme south). India's problem state, Kerala is the only one in the world that has voted a Communist government into power in a free election. Its abundant lushness of nature is in striking contrast to the problems of today. Kerala has the beauty of long lagoons and inland waterways presided over by a line of lovely high hills which press close to the coast. Kerala also has the problems of too much water, too little land that is dry or flat enough for food crops, and, above all, too many people. Back from the lagoons, back from the few roads, there are rows upon rows of detached wooden huts. Each hut may have as little as a quarter of an acre of land to supply the food for the family—coconuts and other fruit, and tapioca, the poor man's starch.

The interior of the large southern peninsula is a tableland known as the Deccan, or southland, which tilts up high toward the west and is fringed by a line of jagged mountain peaks close to the western coast. Although these mountains, the Western Ghats, cannot be classed with the Himalayas, they rise abruptly to 5,000 feet or more, and the sudden contrast between them and the tropical coastal plain out of which they rise is dramatic. Their ruggedness and the year-round cool, stimulating climate have bred a race of wiry, nimble fighting men, the Marathas, who have been especially vigorous defenders of Hinduism against Muslim or Christian encroachments. Their stubborn resistance to Muslim rule was one of the rocks on which the great Mughul empire finally foundered. The British conquered them only with difficulty. In the late nineteenth century, the first terrorists who began to attack the British rulers with homemade bombs came from this area, now in the state of Maharashtra, as did the fanatical Hindu nationalist who murdered Gandhi.

Though the Western Ghats fall off steeply to the west coast, they merge gently into the high Deccan tableland to the east, which in turn slopes gradually down to the east coast. Varied in appearance, with abrupt hills rising out of it here and there, the Deccan contains not only agricultural and grazing land but also forests filled with big game. The area covered by the Deccan includes the inland sections of the states of Maharashtra, Mysore, Andhra Pradesh, and Madras. The Deccan is cut by long eastward-flowing rivers—the Godavari, the Krishna, and the Cauvery. Unlike the rivers flowing out of the eternal snows of the Himalayas, these southern rivers, which frequently cause destructive floods in the rainy season, dry up almost completely in winter. Between the northern plains and the Deccan, in the states of Rajasthan and Madhya Pradesh, lies a band of hills rising to 4,000 feet which historically has tended to discourage the migrants who entered north India from penetrating the south in large numbers, thus effectively separating the north from the south. Southern India has a racial composition somewhat different from the north and has developed customs and attitudes of its own. In India today, political differences between the north and the south are fully as important as the differences in the corresponding areas of the United States, if not more so.

The political boundaries that since 1947 have divided what was previously called India into the new independent nations of India and Pakistan follow no natural geographic lines. They are purely man-made. Pakistan received the northwestern part of the subcontinent plus another, much smaller piece to the east (only one-sixth the size of West Pakistan). Nearly 1,000 miles of Indian territory lie between the two quite separate and unequal parts of Pakistan. East Pakistan, in turn, almost completely separates the bulk of India from one of its states, Assam. The boundaries were drawn in this awkward way in order to separate areas where Muslims were in the majority from areas where Hindus predominated. (Just why Muslim majorities existed in two such widely separated parts of the subcontinent will be made clear in a subsequent chapter.)

Internally, India is divided into sixteen states, including the state of Kashmir, long the subject of dispute between India and Pakistan. Drawn largely on the basis of language differences, these state boundaries are far more significant than those in the United States. As already suggested, a number of them look back with pride to their own separate histories and periods of high cultural development.

The Climate

No one can prove how and to what extent climate affects people. Yet we all instinctively feel that it does. How can one be as active and energetic when oppressed by intense heat as one can be when a cool tang in the air lifts the spirits? Who knows what India would have been like if so much of it did not suffer such great heat so much of the time? On the southern coastal plains, the thermometer seldom falls below 85° F. But hot though the coastal plains are, the most intense heat is not in the south (as many Westerners imagine) but on the northern plains. Although cool and bracing during three winter months, these plains have intense, concentrated, persistent, crushing temperatures up to 120° F. in May and early June. The heat of the south never equals that of this cruel northern furnace; indeed, much of the interior of the southern peninsula, being high, is cool all year. The northern mountains, of course, have an Alpine climate, with cool or cold summers (depending on the altitude) and severe winters.

Next to the heat, the dominant climatic fact of India is the southwest monsoon, the wind that brings the annual rains which mean life or death to millions of people. From the end of September until the middle of June, the wind blows from the north or northeast. Before it reaches India, it hits the Himalayas and deposits its moisture on their slopes and snowy peaks, so that it carries virtually no rain beyond them into India. But beginning in June, the southwest monsoon blows, coming to India across the Indian Ocean and picking up moisture on its way. When it reaches India, it deposits its moisture unevenly—heavily on the coastal strips, lightly to the immediate leeward of the hills near the coast, more heavily again on the lower Ganges valley, and most heavily of all where clouds that have come across the Bay of Bengal encounter the slopes of the eastern Himalayas and the Assam Hills.

As a result, there are extreme variations of annual rainfall in different parts of India. The west of Rajasthan is desert. Eastward, across the northern plains, the annual rainfall gradually increases. Far to the east, the soggy jungles of Assam receive at least 75 inches of rain in the summer months. At one mountainous spot in Assam, Cherrapunji, the average annual rainfall reaches the unbelievable total of about 450 inches, one of the two highest recorded averages in the world.

In most of India, virtually all the rain that falls does so within the space of the three short monsoon months, leaving the rest of the year predictably rainless. Those of us who are accustomed to the possibility that it may rain at any time can hardly realize what it means to face such a timetable. Each year, all of India awaits the arrival of the southwest monsoon with anxiety. If the wind swerves slightly out of its ordinary course, failing to deposit the water for which the land is thirstily waiting, the crops are lost, and there is hunger and famine. If, on the other hand, it deposits more than its ordinary amount, it may also ruin the crops, flood the inhabitants out of their homes, dissolve and destroy mud huts, leave people in great areas perched in any available treetop above the water, fighting off the snakes that likewise seek refuge from the floods. In July, 1960, there were disastrous floods in five states, completely cutting many essential rail and road connections, and wiping out hundreds of villages.

Engineering as well as agricultural and human difficulties result from this concentration of rain in three months. It is hard to bridge rivers that in dry months are mere trickles, but swell in the summer to wide raging torrents spread out far beyond their previous banks, moving into new channels.

There is one compensation for such climatic disadvantages. Because the temperature never drops below freezing except in the northern mountains, two or more crops can be grown each year, if moisture is available. For this reason, India has done more than any other country to develop irrigation. Irrigation works date back at least to the fourth century B.C. Hindu rulers of small southern kingdoms in the Middle Ages built reservoirs on a scale truly vast for the age in which they lived. British rulers diverted the waters of the snow-fed rivers of the north into major irrigation canals. After independence, India pushed ahead with the building of more dams and canals to bring millions of additional acres under cultivation.

The People

The ancestors of the Indians came from a number of regions outside India far removed from one another. The earliest inhabitants of the subcontinent seem to have been small, curly-haired Negritos and other peoples known as Proto-Australoids, akin to the Australian aborigines. Tribes of these types still survive, living for the most part in primitive fashion in remote hilly areas, as dissociated from the rest of Indian society as the majority of American Indians are from the rest of American society.

Apparently the dominant ethnic strains in India are of Mediterranean and Aryan origins. In this sense, Indians are more akin to Europeans than they are to the Chinese and other Asians to their east. Only along the northern boundary, bordering on China, are there many faces of the Mongoloid type.

The early Mediterranean and Aryan ethnic strains were overlaid by many other strains. A long series of later invasions brought to the Indian subcontinent a wide variety of peoples of Central Asian stock, as well as some Greeks and Arabs. Taboos on intermarriage tended to keep the various racial and ethnic strands apart. Yet some intermarriage clearly occurred. In the same family, one brother may be quite fair, another quite dark. On the whole, however, the taller, fairer types are most numerous in the north and among the upper classes of the south. Particularly in the Punjab, the classic route of entry of invaders and migrant tribes, there is a high proportion of tall, sturdy, large-boned, powerful men, probably chiefly of Central Asian ancestry. They make energetic farmers and soldiers.

Just as Americans, with or without justification, speak of "typical" southerners, New Yorkers, or New England Yankees, so Indians have mental pictures of significant character differences between different regions. The typical Punjabi is sometimes described as strong, brave, practical, and mechanically minded; the Bengali as intellectually brilliant, emotionally volatile, and artistically inclined; the Madrasi as conservative, interested primarily in religion, but often scientifically minded. Just what characteristics the typical man of any region possesses depends, of course, on the person describing him, but there is no doubt that significant regional differences do exist. The almost isolated Kashmiri peasant —carefully terracing any bit of top soil that has somehow adhered to his high, rocky mountain slopes, and wrapped to the chin in a brown wool blanket under which he perilously clutches a brazier of burning charcoal to keep himself warm—has by no means the same life, the same outlook, customs, or character as the sweating, almost naked agricultural laborer on the hot, fertile, crowded southeast coast.

But the sharp differences are not only regional. They exist also between one caste and another, and between one educational or economic level and another. Can the professional beggar—dirty, unkempt, forever whining with hands outstretched, his body broken or maimed by deliberate action of his parents so that his money-gaining power may be increased—belong to the same nation as the well-groomed Brahman, wrapped in fine flowing muslin of immaculate whiteness, who walks through filth as though it does not exist? Can the tense, nervous, anxious, belligerent Calcutta University student, memorizing dog-eared pages and discussing Marxism with fellow students as hungry and sleepless as he, really be a relative of the serene, friendly, well-knit, satisfied, religious-minded peasant family from which he comes? Do the fishermen who fish from hollowed logs and live in improvised pup tents on the very beach of Madras city bear any relation to those other Madrasis in nearby factories who tend with finest mathematical precision the most modern machines? As for the brilliant professor of comparative literature who can shame any Western intellectual with his broad and creative grasp of the writings of Western as well as Indian classical and modern authors, is he a fellow countryman of the village illiterates?

Obviously, the Indian people run every gamut imaginable. Perhaps this is one of their fascinations for Westerners. There is no uniformity either of character, personality, or even outward style, manner, and dress. One man will wrap his cloth around and between his legs as a dhoti, another will wrap it skirtwise as a lungi, still another will wear Western trousers or shorts, and another a loin cloth. These fashions and the various manners of headdress more or less correspond to differences in either region, caste, religion, or educational background. They are outward and visible signs of very great inner differences.

Another of the fascinations of the Indian people is that they seem to do almost everything in plain sight of everyone. Besides bathing, brushing their teeth, and urinating in full view, Indians will sit on the sidewalk to be shaved or have a haircut, or to make footwear or any of a variety of other articles, including the Indian-type toothbrushes cut out of twigs. Much of the selling and buying —and haggling over prices—occurs outdoors either in front of the little stalls (which are shops) or on bare ground. Vegetable dealers will spread out their wares neatly on the earth. A man who sells sugar-cane juice will grind the juice to order in the street. Clothes are washed outdoors by slapping them against flat stones; vacant stretches of land burst into riotous color when newly laundered saris have been spread out full-length upon the ground to dry. The frank, unashamed, sociable living of life in full view serves as a refreshing contrast to sidewalk life in the United States, where people so often seem to be merely pedestrians, engaged in no activity except walking past one another hurriedly and unseeing.

These are some of the elements of the endlessly varied, colorful panorama of Indian life. There is dust and dirt, squalor and disease. There is also beauty and dignity. Above all, there are people —490 million of them—engaged in their various ways of living, which, of course, seem as natural and inevitable to them as our quite different ways seem to us. If there is any generalization that can be made about such a variety of people, I would say that they include an unusually large proportion of serene, mild, friendly, gentle, sensitive, tolerant, courageous individuals, extremely hospitable to strangers and exceptionally adept at making the most of whatever life offers them.

3 • THE GREAT VISTA OF INDIA'S PAST

WITH FORTY-FIVE CENTURIES or more of highly developed civilization behind her, India has so long a history that in a book of this kind, essentially dealing with the modern scene, one might be tempted either to omit it entirely or to treat it so briefly that not even the most pivotal historical developments could be brought out clearly. But if one did so, many of the significant features of modern India would seem inexplicable.

India's problem today is not simply one of relations with Pakistan and China, of economic development, or of combatting Communism. It is essentially a problem of nation-building. In the course of those forty-five centuries, many quite different cultural elements have become implanted in Indian soil. Regional and religious rivalries have grown up from deep roots. If India is to remain a democracy, and if she is to make the best use of her economic resources, a certain inner cohesion must be created. The diverse and contrasting approaches to life must be integrated. And it is only by looking with some care at Indian history that one can begin to locate and understand the divisive forces as well as the positive potentialities.

In the tremendous upsurge of national feeling that followed the Chinese invasion in October, 1962, it seemed as though many age-old barriers had evaporated overnight. Indians of every region, religion, and economic and social level seemed ready to make any and every sacrifice in order to defend the nation. Women gave up their jewelry to the national cause; retired government employees gave up their pensions; army recruiting stations were besieged by would-be recruits. The spontaneous nationwide reaction to the emergency was beyond anything India's leaders expected. But when the external danger seemed over, the old rivalries reasserted themselves. The common struggle had not wiped out the legacy of the past. So, too, in any future emergency, old rivalries may temporarily decrease in apparent importance without at all losing their long-term force. As Nehru once wrote: "The burden of the past, the burden of both good and ill, is overpowering, and sometimes suffocating, more especially for those of us who belong to very ancient civilizations like those of India and China."[1]

To many Indians, however, the past is not a burden, but rather a glorious, very precious compensation for the problems of today. Evidences of the glories of the past are visible in stone all over the country. Never wholly unified until the consolidation of British rule in the nineteenth century, and before then seldom even partially unified, India was almost always ruled from innumerable capital cities scattered throughout the land. Although much of the art and architecture of bygone kings and dynasties has perished, so much remains that one could easily spend months touring India and still see only part of it. Rock carvings, frescoed caves, temples, forts, palaces, tombs, and mosques are dotted over the archaeological map of India—not haphazardly but in accordance with the tides of history. For example, there are no old Hindu temples in or near the capital city of New Delhi, or indeed in all of north India except one or two quite out-of-the-way spots. To realize even this is to discover one of the roots of an antagonism of immense and continuing importance. Between the eleventh and the seventeenth centuries, Muslim conquerors destroyed every Hindu temple they could conveniently reach in the areas they ruled. Therefore, to see Hindu temples of the great period of temple architecture—from the eighth to the twelfth centuries—one must go either to the far south (which the Muslims did not conquer), to Orissa on the remote east coast, or to Khajuraho in central India.

Although the kinds of structures vary from one area to another, all areas have their reminders of the past. Many of these, in idioms far removed from those of traditional Western art, are of marvelous workmanship and beauty. Today, bus-loads of Indian tourists and school children swarm around them while guides give lectures. Interest is growing in the ancient glories both of the regional dynasties and of the few dynasties, such as the Mauryas and the Mughuls, which had almost country-wide importance.

In addition to the still visible past glories of art and architecture, the wonderful ancient literature, and other cultural achievements of which educated Indians are justly proud, the Indian past includes another type of glory most tantalizing to the Indians of today—prolonged material prosperity. For well over a millennium and a half, the Indian subcontinent may have been the richest area in the world. As early as the first century A.D., a statesman in ancient Rome wrote in worried vein about the squandering of Roman wealth on Indian luxuries. In south India, large hoards of ancient Roman coins have been unearthed. Although direct relations between Europe and India were cut off by the Arabs in the Middle Ages, the legend of the wealth of the "Indies" continued to grip Western minds. A few intrepid world travelers, Marco Polo among them, confirmed it with eyewitness accounts. The power of this legend caused Columbus in 1492 to take his dangerous journey westward across the Atlantic, seeking to re-establish direct contact with India. As late as the eighteenth century, British observers were repeatedly struck by the material prosperity of the land they were beginning to conquer.

It is not known to what extent this wealth was shared by the common people. It may be that at some time before the British conquest they had a higher standard of living than today, but this is by no means certain. The idea that the common people have a right to a substantial share of national income is, of course, a very recent development in the West as in India.

To modern Indians who look back with nostalgia to the ancient wealth of India, the sheer fact of that wealth seems far more significant than its distribution, which in any case is debatable. If India could produce such great wealth and for so long, why should she not do so again? Surely what made her poor was the British conquest and rule, which has now ended. Westerners may often think of India as somehow destined to be poor. Quite naturally, Indians hope to create for themselves a different destiny.

The Earliest Civilization

Ironically, what we know of Indian history began in what is now Pakistan. Although India and Pakistan face each other today as rival nations, they were linked by a common past until 1947, the time of partition, when independence was granted to each.

In the Indus Valley, which forms the axis of West Pakistan, the earliest high Indian civilization took shape some time around 2500 B.C., or, according to some authorities, even as early as 3000 B.C. It is believed that many of the people of this civilization were of a racial type commonly found farther west, but who apparently had come to India from the Mediterranean sometime before 2500 B.C. They seem to have been of the same racial composition as the dark-skinned people known as Dravidians (referring to linguistic rather than racial features), who constitute the population in south India today. Perhaps the ancestors of the Dravidians formed the dominant strain in all of India before migrations in the north made the picture more complex. Or perhaps the people of the early Indus Valley civilization were pushed south by later invasions.

In many ways, that first early Indian civilization was fully as highly developed as such other great civilizations of the time as those in Egypt and Sumer. Two great cities have been unearthed, Harappa and Mohenjo-daro, each three miles in circumference. They had wide main streets and were magnificently laid out in grid form, reflecting careful town planning. They had sewers, municipal water systems, public baths, and well-fortified citadels. The private houses were well built, of fine solid baked bricks which have not crumbled over the centuries. Many of them were two stories high, and had seat latrines and chutes for refuse. Like so many Indian homes today, they were built around courtyards—illustrating again the tremendous continuity in Indian culture.

The people of the Indus Valley civilization had an advanced technology. They knew how to make cotton cloth and copper and bronze castings and forgings. Some of their art objects have a wonderful simple realism. The torso of one small dancing male figure is so unbelievably alive that one can almost feel the easy muscles at work under the smooth skin.

We know very little about the religion and customs of these

people. Their writing has not been deciphered. But from their statues of gods and goddesses, it seems probable that certain strands of later Hinduism stemmed from the Indus Valley civilization, including the fertility cult of the mother goddess and worship of the dancing god Shiva.

Mohenjo-daro and Harappa seem to have been the capitals of a state that was highly organized politically and that appears to have lasted at least 900 years—longer than any subsequent dynasty or empire in India. Certainly it was a far higher civilization than any that emerged in Europe until the rise of the Greeks and the Romans.

Aryan Invasions

It is generally believed that the Indus Valley civilization was destroyed by Aryan invaders, though there is no proof of this. In any event, the Aryans, related to the European Aryans, entered India in a series of folk migrations beginning around 1500 B.C. They were a warlike people, not given to city life. They had flocks of cattle and sheep, and they fought from chariots drawn by horses. In their language, Sanskrit—akin to Greek, Latin, and the Germanic and Slavic languages—they composed a great mass of religious literature, passed down carefully by word of mouth for many centuries before it was committed to writing.

Unlike the fertility cults of the Indus Valley civilization, the religion of the Aryans involved the worship of the great external forces of nature. Some of their early hymns, the Vedas—composed some time between 1500 B.C. and 1000 A.D.—had a quality of religious vision that foreshadowed the deep speculations that were to come. The Vedas are still of major importance in living Hindu tradition. Some of the revivalist neo-Hindu cults of north India today, such as the Arya Samaj, claim that the Vedas contain intuitions of the discoveries of even the most modern science, including the airplane and the atomic bomb! However surprising such claims may be, they illustrate the vitality of ancient history in India and the Indian tendency to invoke the past in current situations.

Hardy nomadic tribesmen, the Aryans referred disparagingly in their literature to the darker-skinned, more urban inhabitants they found in the country. The collision between the two races is thought to have been one of the factors leading to the formation of the peculiarly Indian institution of caste—although occupational distinctions clearly played a part as well.

In traditional Hindu theory, Hindu society is divided into four castes. At the top are the Brahmans, who are teachers and priests. Next come the Kshatriyas, who are warriors and rulers. Merchants and traders form the third level, the Vaishyas. Finally, there is the great mass of peasants and workers, the Shudras. Below the hierarchy of caste are the outsiders—the "untouchables," who perform various functions considered polluting, like the disposal of carcasses and the tanning of leather. As we shall see, the caste system as it exists today, consisting of some 3,000 castes, is far more complex than this simple scheme might suggest. Here it is important merely to note the early racial antipathy between the lighter-skinned Aryans and the darker-skinned original inhabitants.

A certain amount of intermarriage undoubtedly occurred over the centuries, despite caste restrictions. Yet there remains today a surprisingly strong sense of color distinctions—a heritage of the old Aryan attitude. Although all skins darken in the course of time under the hot Indian sun, skins that are relatively light continue to be preferred. The many marriage advertisements in Indian newspapers often stress the light complexion of the young man or woman in question. Dark skins are never mentioned in these advertisements.

From northwest India, the Aryans spread eastward. Gradually, throughout north India, there evolved a society and a culture that was a synthesis of Aryan and native elements, hence Indo-Aryan. It was only later, and then in lesser numbers, that Indo-Aryans penetrated the south. Those who went to the south seem to have been chiefly Brahmans, bent on cultural rather than military conquest. They introduced a strong Sanskritic element into the culture of the south, particularly in the upper layers of society. But underneath, the Dravidian strain remained intact. Today there is still a pronounced racial and cultural contrast between the Indo-Aryan north and the Dravidian south. A significant southern political movement plays on the hostility of the southern Dravidians toward the Indo-Aryans, raising the cry of domination and exploitation of the south by the north. It also turns against the Brahman upper classes of the south who are Indo-Aryan in origin. Though these Brahman families may have lived in the south for 2,000 years, they are called "outsiders" and "foreign exploiters."

In the north, the fusion of cultures had progressed far by the sixth century B.C. The nature gods of the Vedas had, for the most part, disappeared or had been merged with indigenous deities. Vishnu and Shiva, the great gods of later Hinduism, had emerged. The specifically Hindu concepts of rebirth, of fate (karma) as the consequence of acts, and of duty (dharma) had taken form. These had been linked to a particular social organization, the caste system. Thus Hinduism had begun to take form both as a religion and as a social framework. It was dominated by the Brahmans, who required the performance of costly animal sacrifices and elaborate ritual.

Buddhism and Its Influence

In the sixth century B.C., there occurred two great movements of religious revolt directed particularly against these last aspects of the orthodox Hinduism of the time—both originating in Bihar in the eastern valley of the Ganges. The religious reformers who led them were Mahavira, the great teacher of the Jain sect, and his far better known younger contemporary the Buddha, who lived probably from 563 to 483 B.C. (Buddha is a religious title like Christ, meaning Enlightened One.)

Neither Mahavira nor the Buddha offered a god for worship. Nor did they challenge the gods of Hinduism. The Buddha's teachings ring out as a clear call to strenuous moral effort in this life, as opposed to preoccupation with useless speculation about gods and otherworldly paths to salvation.

For almost a thousand years, from the third century B.C. until the fifth or sixth century A.D., Buddhism seems to have overshadowed Hinduism, particularly in northwest India, Bihar, and Bengal. Outside India, it had tremendous influence, claiming many converts in China and later in Japan, and becoming the dominant religion of Tibet and of Southeast Asia. To faraway peoples, India came to be regarded as the "holy land," the objective of long and difficult pilgrimages, the place where the gospel could be studied at first hand and where the holy spots of Buddha's enlightenment and his teaching could be visited. Through Buddhism, India had far-reaching cultural influence throughout Asia from the first through the tenth centuries A.D. The religion of the Jains never had so wide an appeal outside India as did Buddhism, but within India many local rulers at one time or another adopted it as their religion.

Today, only a small proportion of the population of India are Jains or Buddhists, but many of the teachings of these two minority religions have been absorbed within the majority religion, Hinduism. Thus they have had a profound affect on Indian attitudes. The Indian ideal of nonviolence received special impetus from the teachings of Mahavira and the Buddha. Vegetarianism, which is practiced by some but not all Hindu castes, also probably stems from these sources.

The taking of life in any form has always been especially abhorent to Mahavira's followers, the Jains. The strictest Jain monks carry this abhorrence so far that they brush the ground where they intend to step lest they tread on any form of life, and wear gauze masks lest they inhale and destroy an insect. The most important modern disciple of the old doctrine of nonviolence was Mahatma Gandhi, whose mother had been profoundly influenced by the Jains.

The feature of the Buddha's teachings most generally known in the West is that he stressed the sorrowful and transient nature of life and considered the goal of man to be the progressive detachment from desire and finally the extinction of the self—nirvana (literally, a blowing out). This is only one part of his message, which focused above all on personal everyday morality, self-control, integrity, and love. These were preoccupations quite different from the stress on ritual in early Hinduism.

A few quotations from the early collection of Buddhist sayings, *The Dhammapada*, will illustrate the quality of the Buddha's thought:

> Let a man overcome anger by love, let him overcome evil by good; let him overcome the greedy by liberality, the liar by truth. . . .

The fault of others is easily perceived but that of one's self is difficult to perceive; a man winnows his neighbor's faults like chaff, but his own fault he hides, as a cheat hides the bad die from the player. . . .

Rouse thyself by thyself, examine thyself by thyself. Thus self-protected and attentive will thou live happily. . . . For self is the lord of self, self is the refuge of self; therefore curb thyself as the merchant curbs a noble horse.[2]

Over the course of time, Buddhism changed greatly. The quality of the Buddha as a unique and outstanding human being was no longer stressed. He who had urged men not to look to the gods but rather to be self-reliant came to be worshiped as a god himself. Throughout Asia, Buddhism branched into a number of different sects, each with its own theology. In India, it became greatly altered through the incorporation of various superstitions and magical practices which probably were current in popular tradition.

Meanwhile, Hinduism took over much of the Buddha's moral message and recognized him as one of the many gods of the Hindu pantheon. Thus the original sharp contrast between Hinduism and Buddhism became blurred. This tendency to absorb and appropriate, to engulf by toleration, is one of Hinduism's main features. In the late twelfth century A.D., the destruction of a few Buddhist monasteries in Bihar and Bengal by Muslim armies was enough to eliminate from India the remnants of Buddhism as a distinct religion, although its influence lived on within Hinduism.

Early Empires and the Mauryas

During the thousand or more years when Buddhism was expanding and then losing its separate identity within India, many kingdoms and dynasties rose and fell.

In the closing years of the sixth century B.C., while the Buddha was teaching and preaching in eastern India, the northwest region of the subcontinent (now part of West Pakistan) was conquered by the Persian King Darius the Great and incorporated into the Persian Empire. This conquest established links between India and the Greek world, with which the Persian Empire was also in contact.

Two centuries later, in 326 B.C., the great conqueror Alexander of Macedonia, after attacking Persia, brought his army over a pass into northwest India, fought a few victorious battles there, and then sailed down the Indus and off to Babylon, where he died in 323 B.C. His invasion of India was so brief that it left no lasting effects, except perhaps to stimulate the concept of an all-embracing empire.

Until then, north India had been divided politically into many small kingdoms. In 322 B.C., shortly after Alexander's invasion, an Indian empire-builder, Chandragupta Maurya, succeeded in placing himself on the throne of Magadha, the principal kingdom in what is now Bihar. From there, he gradually conquered many of the small princedoms of north India, extending his power as far to the northwest as Kabul, in Afghanistan.

The Maurya Empire he founded was a highly centralized and efficient bureaucracy. He kept his large realm under tight control with the help of a strong standing army, secret police, and the use of torture to extract confessions—in short, by police-state methods. He also carried on a large program of public works, including road building and irrigation. Chandragupta's son conquered much of southern India, probably as far south as Mysore, thus effecting one of the few approximations of political unity the Indian subcontinent has experienced. However, some of the areas within the empire were not administered directly by the central government, but consisted of vassal kingdoms allowed to retain autonomy.

Chandragupta's grandson was the great Ashoka (273–232 B.C.), one of the outstanding rulers of all time. While subduing the people in the area that is now Orissa, Ashoka became appalled by the horrors of war and either turned Buddhist or was strongly influenced by Buddhism. He renounced war and became the earliest and most eloquent royal exponent of the philosophy of nonviolence. His support of Buddhism helped to spread that religion throughout the country and far beyond India, to Ceylon and many other countries where he sent missionaries. He gave up the royal sport of hunting, built hospitals and rest houses, and dug wayside wells for travelers and animals along the dusty roads. Instead of using the police-state methods of his father and grandfather, he tried to win the obedience of his subjects by kindness. In order to popularize the Buddhist moral principles in which he believed, he had a series of proclamations engraved on rocks and pillars in different parts of the empire. These preached religious tolerance and kindness to all living things, and they warned against envy, lack of perseverance, harshness, impatience, and laziness (all of which would have been lapses from the Buddhist moral law). If there is an Indian ruler whom most modern Indians can agree to revere, it is Ashoka. The state seal of the Government of India today depicts the capital of one of his pillars, and the biggest, most luxurious government-owned hotel of modern New Delhi is named after him.

Soon after the death of Ashoka, the Maurya Empire fell apart. Over the northwest passes came a succession of new waves of migrating peoples, bringing into India new foreign influences and new physical types—on the whole, probably larger and more heavily boned than earlier arrivals. First came the Greeks from the Greek kingdom north of the passes which had survived since the conquest by Alexander. The Greeks were followed by the Sakas (or Scythians), then by a Central Asian people known in India as the Kushans.

The Kushans established a great kingdom in north India which reached its height in the second century A.D. It straddled the northwest passes, ran down the Ganges as far as Banaras, but also extended far to the north and east in Central Asia. Being thus in contact with the great trade routes that ran across Central Asia, the kingdom served as a meeting ground for the four great cultural traditions of the time—those of India, China, Persia, and the Greco-Roman world. The Kushans were patrons of Buddhist learning and helped spread Buddhism to China, Korea, and Japan. It was during the period of Kushan rule that the concept of the Buddha as a god rather than a man first came into prominence.

The contrast between the Buddhist art that preceded their arrival and the Gandhara Buddhist art near their capital city of Peshawar is an interesting illustration of the contrast of cultures brought about by successive invasions of India. In earlier Buddhist sculptures, done in the first century B.C., the figure of the Buddha was never portrayed. Stories of his life were told with the aid of a set of fixed symbols: A horse, whose rider is invisible, was the symbol of the Buddha's renunciation of his princely status and his departure on horseback from his father's royal palace; a group of men sitting on the ground reverently facing an invisible person under a tree was the symbol of the Buddha's first sermon preached under a tree. In contrast, Gandhara art specialized in figures of the Buddha carved in Greek style with Greek features, closely resembling a Greek Apollo.

While the Greeks, Sakas, and Kushans were bringing new influences into north India, peninsular India had its own separate history—or histories, for the south was divided into a number of separate kingdoms. The Pandyas occupied the southern tip of the peninsula; the Cholas established themselves in the region that is now Madras; and the Cheras controlled the southwestern coast, now Kerala. These were Dravidian kingdoms, and the southerners were racially, culturally, and linguistically different from the Indo-Aryans of the north. In the Dravidian Tamil language, a high literature had developed in the first three centuries A.D., or perhaps earlier. As has been mentioned, the southern port cities were involved at a very early period in highly profitable trading relations with the Western world. These kingdoms also sent their sailing vessels eastward to Southeast Asia, carrying Indian culture to Cambodia, Thailand, and Indonesia (which means Islands of India).

On the Deccan and the east coast, another powerful local dynasty, the Satavahanas, ruled a people called the Andhras from about the second century B.C. until the third century A.D. Today, the people of the area, who speak the Telugu language, still take pride in their past. When state boundaries were altered in 1953 so as to give Telugu-speaking people a state of their own, the ancient name of Andhra was chosen for the new state—only one example of how ancient history serves in India as the emotional foundation for modern loyalties of a regional rather than a national nature.

In the north, in the fourth century A.D. (about a century after the fall of the Kushan Empire), there arose a new dynasty of importance, the Guptas. This dynasty centered around Magadha, the old capital of the Mauryas. It regarded its rule as a continuation of the glorious Maurya Empire, which had terminated over 500 years earlier. Two of the Gupta emperors even took the name of the founder of the Maurya dynasty, Chandragupta. Between 320 A.D. and the middle of the following century, the Guptas expanded their territory until it included all of north India. Unlike the Mauryas, they did not succeed in penetrating the Deccan and the southland. Toward the end of the fifth century, the Gupta Empire was destroyed by invading Huns. After a brief confused period, one more great ruler, King Harsha, pulled the empire together during his long reign (606–647 A.D.). His death was followed by further movements of peoples and rivalries of kingdoms.

The Golden Age

The Gupta period and its extension under King Harsha are generally considered the "golden age" of ancient Indian history. A wonderful flowering of every art and science took place. Like the Italian Renaissance, it was one of those rare periods when every faculty of man seemed to come alive at once. Kalidasa, who has been called the Indian Shakespeare, lived at this time, as did a number of other outstanding authors. Gupta sculpture has a classic simplicity and rhythm that have never been surpassed. Hindu philosophy, which had begun its development many centuries before, now moved toward classic expression and clear systematization. The science and technology of the time surprises us by mastery of principles and techniques the West learned much later. By the fifth century A.D., Indian surgeons were performing plastic surgery to repair mutilated faces. An iron pillar over 23 feet high, now standing just outside the capital city of New Delhi, was cast at the time but has not yet rusted—a remarkable achievement. During this golden age, some unknown Indian had the brilliantly simple idea that every conceivable number could be formed by arranging only nine digits and a zero in different positions relative to one another—and this Indian decimal and digit system was later learned by the West from the Arabs. To hear, across time and space, of such many-sided cultural achievements is to sense how much energy and exuberance of spirit the Indians of the period must have had.

Although the Guptas were Hindus, Buddhism still flourished. Fa-Hsien, one of the Chinese Buddhists who made a pilgrimage to India during this time, has left a most favorable account of what he saw. According to his report, there appears to have been much more personal freedom than there had been under the earlier Maurya Empire. Capital punishment was rare. The government took only one-sixth of the gross produce of the land. Travel was safe, the countryside was peaceful and prosperous, and there were a number of wealthy commercial towns. Indians were gentle and generally abstained from both meat and liquor.

More Invasions and Disintegration

After the death of Harsha in 647 A.D., a new series of invasions and incursions from the northwest took place, bringing into India more people of Central Asian, Turkish, and Mongol blood. Society was greatly reorganized. Although the multiplication of castes had begun before this time, many more new castes now came into being. According to one theory, the Brahmans (who still dominated Indian life, religion, and society) responded to the confusion caused by the arrival of large foreign tribes by evolving a way of protecting Hinduism while absorbing the newcomers into Hindu society. They recognized the chiefs of the tribes as members of the Kshatriya caste. They honored the priests as Brahmans, though of lower status than native Brahmans. So, too, they assigned the priests' followers some caste status, thus splitting each incoming tribe into three or four sections in accordance with the Hindu caste hierarchy. If the effective units of Indian society had ever been the four main castes that Indians still stress today, this now ceased to be the case.

Among the peoples who first appeared in India during the confusion of the seventh, eighth, and ninth centuries and who later played distinctive roles in Indian life were the Marathas of the Western Ghats and the Rajputs, a military aristocracy classed as Kshatriyas. High-spirited fighting men reared in traditions of courage and chivalry somewhat like those of the knights of medieval Europe, the Rajputs established a number of small personal kingdoms in north India, but proved unable to unite. It was they who bore the main brunt of the Muslim invasions in the eleventh and twelfth centuries. Under Muslim pressure, they retreated to the dry, rocky hillsides of Rajasthan. This uninviting area, where little grows except tortured thorn trees almost bare of foliage, was easier to defend than the plains; its rugged hills are still capped by the Rajputs' forts and crenelated walls. When the Rajputs faced certain defeat, their wives and children committed the awful rite of *jauhar*, placing themselves on a common funeral pyre, while the men fought to the end without surrendering. Never completely subdued by the Muslims, the Rajput princes retained the status of autonomous rulers until 1948 or 1949, when their princedoms were gradually integrated into the Indian state now known as Rajasthan.

The early center of northern power had been in the Ganges Valley, in present-day Bihar. But after the eighth century A.D., there seems to have been a shift of power westward because of the growth of trade with the Western world through the ports of what is now Gujarat. The new trade routes passed through Delhi, which first began to rise in importance in the ninth and tenth centuries A.D.

Many dynasties and kingdoms with fluctuating boundaries continued to exist in the south. The Pallava Dynasty, which dominated southeast India from the sixth to the eighth century, was apparently Brahman and northern in origin. Significantly, it promoted the introduction in the south of the northern Indo-Aryan Sanskritic culture, as opposed to the local Tamil culture, thus lessening the cultural gap between north and south.

The Hindu period of Indian history came to an end sometime between 1000 and 1200 A.D.—to be succeeded by the Muslim period and later by the British period, for whose beginnings it is not easy to fix exact dates. Before turning to the arrival of the Muslims, it may be well to consider certain political and economic features of the India they encountered.

Absolute monarchy was the characteristic form of political organization and was often associated with governmental ownership of such key industries and enterprises as mines, forests, spinning and weaving establishments—and particularly the all-important irrigation works. In fact, it may have been the monopoly of the water supply that provided the economic basis for absolutism.

The king was regarded as being imbued with divine power, but was considered to be bound by a special kingly duty not only to protect his land from invasion, but also to promote the "right" way of life as set forth in the sacred texts. How the kings behaved in practice was not adequately recorded.

The boundaries of the many kingdoms were in constant flux. Kings who were successful in territorial expansion controlled their various outlying provinces either by appointing governors or by requiring the submission and vassalage of the local rulers whom they had conquered. When the central power became weak, the appointed governors tended to pass their position on by heredity and vassals again became independent.

Although substantial political unity existed only for a few brief periods before the coming of the British, the unifying effect of Hinduism and Sanskritic culture was great. Records dating from the early centuries of the Christian era indicate that shrines regarded as sacred to all Hindus were located at widely separated points in all directions. Clearly, some concept of religious or cultural unity already existed. Long pilgrimages to such shrines created for many a connection with peoples in areas under different sovereignties. Then, too, the great body of Sanskrit literature provided a significant bond. Although the sacred literature was virtually the monopoly of the Brahmans, it set the standards of a common culture that the lower castes often sought to imitate and adopt. Other Sanskrit classics were available to all who could either read or listen to itinerant storytellers. Legends and traditions stemming from the Sanskrit matrix were handed down by word of mouth from generation to generation all over the country. The fact that kings tended to rely on Brahman advisers no doubt greatly aided the process of cultural unification also.

In the villages, from very early times, there was a hereditary village headman, normally one of the wealthier peasants. The village headman still survived until very recently. In some places, there were also village councils. Just how important a role they played is not clear. In any event, one of the beliefs dear to many modern Indians is that village self-government was strong until the coming of the British.

Despite absolute monarchy, taxation does not seem to have been oppressive. The basic tax was the land tax, usually a fixed proportion of the crop, from one-sixth to one-quarter or sometimes even one-third of the actual grain gathered. Apparently it was levied with flexibility, depending on the special problems of the peasants.

Dr. A. L. Basham, a leading authority on Indian culture before the coming of the Muslims, has summarized his general impressions as follows:

> Our over-all impression is that in no other part of the ancient world were the relations of man and man, and of man and the state, so fair and humane. In no other early civilization were slaves so few in number, and in no other ancient law book are their rights so well protected as in the *Arthashastra*. . . . In all her history of warfare, Hindu India has few tales to tell of cities put to the sword or of the massacre of noncombatants. . . . To us the most striking feature of ancient Indian civilization is its humanity. . . . Our second general impression of ancient India is that her people enjoyed life, passionately delighting both in the things of the senses and the things of the spirit. . . . India was a cheerful land, whose people, each finding a niche in a complex and slowly evolving social system, reached a higher level of kindliness and gentleness in their mutual relations than any other nation of antiquity. For this, as well as for her great achievements in religion, literature, art, and mathematics, one European student at least would record his admiration of her ancient culture.[3]

4 • THE NATURE AND LEGACY OF THE MUSLIM PERIOD

ONE OF THE FOUR great turning points in Indian history was the beginning of the Muslim invasions in the eleventh or twelfth century A.D. These invasions rank in importance with those of the Aryans some twenty-six centuries earlier and with the later arrival of the European conquerors. (The fourth great turning point was the achievement of independence.)

The Muslim invasions had an effect quite different from the many other invasions that the subcontinent of India had experienced since the coming of the Aryans. For centuries, Hinduism, with its broad tolerance, had succeeded in overcoming and absorbing all invaders and their faiths—once the actual fighting was over—by simply assigning to them and to their gods places in the Hindu scheme of things. But Hinduism could not overcome the Muslims in this way. Islam—the clear-cut, coherent, articulate, and self-confident religion of the Muslims—was not at all ready for absorption into the vast, complex, subtle, many-sided, self-contradictory agglomeration of Hinduism.

In Islam, God is one and indivisible. His name is Allah (Arabic for God). The monotheism is complete and absolute. Allah has revealed himself in history through a line of prophets—including Adam, Noah, Abraham, Moses, and Jesus (who, in early Muslim thought, ranked close to Muhammad himself in importance). The last and greatest prophet was Muhammad. None of the earlier prophets had so perfect a revelation of God's will as did he.

The word Muslim means "he who submits," and it is the duty of a believer to submit completely to the Faith. Muslims do not call their religion Muhammadanism—believing that this would suggest a sharing of Allah's divinity with the Prophet, as the Christian God's divinity is shared with Christ; instead, they call it simply Islam (the Faith).

The messages from Allah that Muhammad received are recorded in the holy book, the Koran, which Muslims regard as the pure, undistorted, final word of God. The injunctions of the Koran must be controlling not only in personal life, but also in law and government. A secular state is thus theoretically out of the question. For Muslims, government should be an extension into the political field of the overriding will of Allah.

If the Koran is unclear on points of current importance, the tradition of the Muslim community may be consulted. This tradition rests especially on the earliest recorded memories of the words or deeds of the Prophet. On points where he did not express himself, other traditional opinions may be used as a basis for decisions. The legalistic citation of early authorities became an important feature of Islam on the intellectual plane.

For the more simple-minded, religious duties were straightforward. The submitters must constantly repeat their creed—that there is no God but Allah and that Muhammad is his prophet. They must pray five times a day, facing toward Mecca, the holy city where Muhammad was born and where he had his first revelations of Allah. Once during their lifetime, if possible, they must make a pilgrimage to Mecca. They must take no food or water from sunrise to sundown one month of the year, Ramazan, which starts ten days earlier each year. (Muslims do not use the Western solar calendar.) Otherwise, Islam avoids the asceticism that was a prominent feature of both Hinduism and also of the early Christianity with which Muhammad had been in contact and to which he had reacted.

Congregational worship, which occurs on Friday, is simple, consisting essentially of prayer and readings from the Koran. There are no special priests. Any educated Muslim may conduct the service. Music in connection with worship is prohibited. So also are pictures, figures, or other symbolic representations of the deity. No religion, not even Judaism, has been so strict and uncompromising in its opposition to visual representations of God.

The Muslim abhorrence of idolatry was one of the chief factors that placed Islam squarely in opposition to Hinduism. Also, the Muslim concept of the brotherhood of man was the antithesis of the Hindu hierarchical organization of society.

Especially in its early days, Islam was a strenuous, intolerant faith. Each Muslim had the duty to convert infidels. Wars against nations or people who did not submit to the Faith were holy. It was clear from the start that a cultural synthesis involving Hindus and Muslims would not be easy to achieve. As time went on, religious differences were reinforced by educational differences and political rivalries.

The First Muslim Invasions

The prophet Muhammad died in what is now Saudi Arabia in 632 A.D. Within a decade, Arabs who had embraced his religion had captured the great cities of Jerusalem and Damascus, then all of Palestine, Syria, and Egypt, and had defeated armies of the two powerful states of the day, the Persian and Byzantine empires. Within a century, conquering Muslim armies had spread westward across North Africa to Spain and France, where their menacing drive was finally checked in the Battle of Tours in 732 A.D. Also within a century, other Arabian armies had pushed eastward to Baghdad and into Central Asia. In 711 A.D., a young Arabian General, Muhammad bin Qasim, with the aid of several thousand soldiers and a heavy stone-throwing catapult (which he lovingly called the "Bride"), fought his way up the Indus Valley in what is now West Pakistan. No religion has ever energized its converts more dramatically or caused a more sudden change in the political map of three continents.

Later Muslim armies, from the eleventh century on, penetrated far deeper into India than did that first Arabian General, but influential contacts of a more peaceful nature preceded these major invasions. After the death of the Prophet Muhammad, a series of caliphs (successors) served as the religious leaders of the sprawling new Muslim dominions. In 660 A.D., their capital was moved from Mecca in Arabia north to Damascus in Syria. In 762 A.D., it was moved again, this time eastward to Baghdad and thus nearer to India. Under the caliphs, Baghdad became a great intellectual center and clearinghouse, transmitting culture from East to West and vice versa. The learned men of Baghdad absorbed the thought and culture not only of classical Greece and the Mediterranean area, but also of Persia and India. They took particular interest in Indian mathematics, astronomy, and other natural sciences. It was by way of Baghdad that the Indian system of numerals was transmitted to the West, as "Arabic numerals." This fertile cultural contact between India and Baghdad is an aspect of Indo-Islamic relations often overlooked.

Meanwhile, in the ports along the southwest coast of India—where there were Arab traders who had become converts to Islam soon after Muhammad had received his revelations from Allah in the seventh century—personal contacts between Hindus and Muslims had become routine. The Muslim traders enjoyed the patronage, support, and aid of the Hindu kings, who welcomed the prosperity these traders brought to their kingdoms, and they converted many Hindus to Islam.

The chief Muslim invaders and conquerors of north India were not Arabs, but Central Asian converts to Islam. Beginning in the eleventh century, these Central Asians—Turks, Afghans, Persians, Mongols—entered India in successive waves through the northwest passes, the traditional route of all invaders. About 1000 A.D., a Central Asian chief named Mahmud of Ghazni received the sanction of the Caliph of Baghdad for a series of holy wars in India. Between 1000 and 1026 A.D., his armies swept through north India during the cool, pleasant winter months, destroying one temple after another, demolishing the hated idols, and assembling loot to be carried home to Ghazni on camels before the hot weather started. The records of the old chroniclers describing this loot remind us of the fabulous wealth of India in former days: "jewels and unbored pearls and rubies shining like sparks of iced wine, emeralds as it were sprigs of young myrtle, diamonds as big as pomegranates."[1]

After Mahmud's death, there was an interval of more than a century and a half before another Afghan ruler, Muhammad Ghuri, began another series of invasions. Divided into many rival kingdoms, principalities, clans, tribes, and castes, the Hindus were no match for the zealous crusading Muslims, who occupied Delhi in 1193 A.D. and most of the important cities in north India thereafter. In Bihar, then the chief center of Buddhism, they destroyed Buddhist shrines and monasteries. The Buddhist monks fled to Nepal, and Buddhism virtually disappeared in north India. The Muslims pressed on eastward into Bengal.

The Sultanate of Delhi

While Muhammad Ghuri lived, these conquered areas in India were directed from his capital beyond the northwest passes in Afghanistan. After he died in 1206 A.D., his General, Qutb-ud-din Aibak, detached the conquered areas within India from the parent kingdom and set up an independent Sultanate of Delhi with himself as the first Sultan. He was a typically ferocious Central Asian—merciless, fanatical, brave, profusely generous to his comrades, ruthless in his suppression of revolts, insistent on humble submission on the part of Hindus. Like Mahmud of Ghazni, he destroyed Hindu temples right and left; to build the Qutb Mosque, outside Delhi, he took materials from twenty-seven Hindu temples.[2]

As Sultan of Delhi, he was the first of a line of thirty-four sultans, who ruled—from that new capital city—an empire that was small at first, then large, then small again. The Sultanate lasted from 1206 to 1526 A.D., when it was supplanted by the Mughul Empire. Its history is filled with bloodshed, tyranny, and treachery. There was no definite rule of succession. Sometimes the sultan was succeeded by a relative, sometimes by a usurper. The decision rested in the hands of the nobles and generals. At a sultan's death, there was usually a general and bloody scramble for power. Occasionally, the nobles disposed of a sultan by poison or other means, setting up another sultan in his place. It was not unusual for the sultan himself to execute as many as possible of the strongest of the nobles to ensure his position. For all members of the ruling class, survival—let alone the transmission to heirs of property or power—was uncertain.

The ranks of the nobles were constantly augmented by foreigners—Turks, Afghans, Pathans, Persians, and other Muslim adventurers from beyond the northwest passes. The group in power thus tended to retain its vigor and also to remain foreign.

In spite of the absence of true hereditary succession, the thirty-four sultans fell into five groups, sometimes called dynasties. A visitor to Delhi can scarcely fail to encounter the tombs, mosques, and palaces built under these dynasties. The five groups, and a few of their outstanding sultans, were: (1) the "Slave" Kings (1206–90)—Qutb-ud-din Aibak, Iltutmish, and Balban; (2) the Khaljis (1290–1320)—Ala-ud-din; (3) the Tughluqs (1320–1413)—Ghiyas-ud-din Tughluq, Muhammad Tughluq, Firuz Shah Tughluq; (4) the Sayyids (1414–51); and (5) the Lodis (1451–1526).

For almost a century, the sultans were fully occupied in establishing their position in north India. By the beginning of the fourteenth century, their control of the north was secure. In 1310, Sultan Ala-ud-din sent an army into the far south. Nine years after his death, another Sultan, Muhammad Tughluq (1325–51), pursued the southern conquests. By 1335, he ruled from Lahore in the Punjab to the northern part of what is now Kerala, a wider area than had ever been united in Indian history up to that time. Muhammad Tughluq was a brilliant man, but capricious, arbitrary, and lacking in the judgment or statesmanship to hold together so large a realm. By the time he died, there were clear indications that his great empire could not last.

Under the Sultanate, conquest usually did not involve the administration or direct control of the conquered areas but rather the exaction of tribute from local princes or chiefs who became the sultan's vassals, retaining autonomy. Whenever the Sultanate weakened, this autonomy tended to change again into independence—a situation much like that during the earlier Hindu period and also during the Middle Ages in Europe. In some cases, provincial governors were appointed directly by the sultan. They, too, tended to assert their independence whenever the sultan was weak, indolent, or debauched—as many were.

As for the villagers, they had little contact with either the central power or the provincial governors, except through the agents sent to collect taxes. The land tax paid by the villagers continued to be the principal source of imperial revenue, but whereas Hindu rulers had normally collected about one-sixth of the gross product of the land, the levy of the Muslim rulers was considerably higher. Under Ala-ud-din, for example, it was half of the yield.

A classic description of village indifference to central rule and to changes of dynasties is that written in 1832 by Sir Charles Metcalfe, a close student of Indian history who later became Governor-General of India:

> The village communities are little republics, having nearly everything they want within themselves, and almost independent of any foreign relations. They seem to last where nothing else lasts. Dynasty after dynasty tumbles down; revolution succeeds to revolution; Hindu, Pathan, Mughul, Mahratta, Sikh, English are masters in turn; but the village communities remain the same. In times of trouble they arm and fortify themselves; a hostile army passes through the country; the village community collect their cattle within their walls, and let the army pass unprovoked; if plunder and devastation be directed against themselves and the force employed be irresistible, they flee to friendly villages at a distance, but when the storm has passed over they return and resume their occupation. If a country remains for a series of years the scene of continual pillage and massacre, so that the villages cannot be inhabited, the villagers nevertheless return whenever the power of peaceable possession revives.[3]

Some authorities hold that Sir Charles may have overstated both the democracy and the autonomy of Indian villages, but his description is vividly suggestive of the resilience of the peasantry as the Muslim armies marched up and down the land. In any event, it has served as a foundation for the idealization of the Indian village so important in the policy-making of modern India.

While the peasants endured what they had to endure, Muhammad Tughluq's cruelties, eccentricities, and lack of personal stability encouraged the revolt of both Hindus and Muslim nobles. In 1336, a strong new Hindu state was organized south of the Krishna River to offer a united front against Muslim advance. A European traveler of those days who saw its capital city, Vijayanagar, reported that it was larger and more magnificent than even Rome. Vijayanagar successfully defended south India against Muslim conquests until 1565, when it was defeated by a coalition of Muslim states to the north.

Meanwhile, the Sultanate had lost province after province. In 1347, a general established an independent Bahmani kingdom on the Deccan which itself split into five kingdoms after 1482. To add to its troubles, the Sultanate of Delhi was also subjected to a brief invasion in 1398–99 by Timur (Tamerlane), the great Central Asian conqueror who had already swept through Persia and into Asia Minor.

By the early sixteenth century, the map of India was greatly fragmented. In addition to a shrunken Sultanate, it contained a number of independent Muslim kingdoms in north India, such as Gujarat, Malwa, and Bengal; five Muslim kingdoms in the Deccan—Bijapur, Golconda, Bidar, Ahmadnagar, and Berar; various defiant Hindu princedoms in Gwalior, Orissa, Rajasthan, and elsewhere; and one big and important Hindu empire in south India, Vijayanagar. Thus the same tendency toward disintegration that had plagued the period of Hindu rule operated under Muslim rulers.

Besides destroying idols and temples, the Muslim conquerors had attempted in a number of other ways to suppress Hinduism as a religion. For example, under the rule of Firuz Shah Tughluq, one of the most zealous of the sultans, a Brahman was burned alive for practicing his rites in public.[4] But as time went on, some moderation of the severity toward Hindus occurred. The reasons were practical. It is hard to rule a large population that has been thoroughly antagonized, and Muslim rulers needed Hindus to fill the lower positions on their staffs.

Attempts at conversion continued and were highly successful. It has been estimated that of the Muslims of the Indian subcontinent today, probably as many as 90 per cent are descendants of converts from Hinduism, rather than of Muslim invaders. To stimulate conversion, discriminatory taxes were imposed on non-Muslims. Other incentives existed. For the educated Hindus, conversion might lead to high position in government services. Lower-caste Hindus were often attracted by the doctrine of the universal brotherhood of man. In order to escape their position of inferiority within the Hindu hierarchy, entire lower castes sometimes went over to Islam. This occurred especially in Bengal, where caste discriminations were particularly onerous. In time, the converts formed the majority in eastern Bengal. Thus, there is an understandable basis to the curious fact, often puzzling to Westerners, that Pakistan today has an eastern section separated by 1,000 miles from West Pakistan. Muslims came to be in the majority in both areas, but for different reasons. In the west (first entered by the Muslim invaders), they sought converts more vigorously than they did later in other parts of the country. In the east, social conditions were such that they acquired converts almost without effort. In the areas in between, Muslims never exceeded half the population, and in some places were as few as 5 per cent.

It is noteworthy that Hinduism did not collapse completely under the pressures exerted by the conquerors. In many areas outside India that were occupied by Muslim armies, scarcely a trace remains of the original religion of the people conquered. The explanation surely lies in the nature of Hinduism, which made it peculiarly invulnerable to a frontal attack. Islam could destroy Buddhism in India by destroying a few major monasteries. But there was no single place or group of places, no man or group of men whose capture or destruction would harm Hinduism. It was everywhere and nowhere. Yet, despite its lack of an ecclesiastical framework or center, it contained its own unique form of organization. The essential discipline of Hinduism took place and still takes place today within the many separate cells of the caste system. These units were small enough to provide an intimacy and a sense of belonging which must have greatly strengthened the resistance of their members to conversion.

The Mughul Empire

Into the disintegration and confusion of sixteenth-century India, there entered a new and highly significant Muslim dynasty, again from the north—the Mughuls. The word Mughul, the Indianized version of Mongol, is applied only to this particular dynasty. Babur, its founder, was descended on his mother's side from the famous Mongol Genghis Khan, who swept across Asia in the thirteenth century from his home on the fringes of China as far west as Hungary, leaving behind him a trail of terror and destruction.

On his father's side, Babur was descended from another, later scourge of Asia, Timur, whose capture of Delhi in 1398 enabled Babur to claim that India was his by right of inheritance.

Far more civilized and cultured than his wild forebears, Babur had adopted the religion of Islam and had absorbed the high culture of medieval Persia. He was invited into India by a group of Afghan nobles who were dissatisfied with the Delhi Sultan of the moment, hence in search of allies and military support. But after defeating the Sultan in 1526 in the First Battle of Panipat, Babur took the throne himself with the title of Padishah (Emperor).

How foreign he was to India, how different his culture and taste from that of the land he and his successors ruled for more than three centuries can be judged from many homesick passages in his charming and warmly human autobiography. For example:

> Hindustan is a country that has few pleasures to recommend it. The people are not handsome. They have no idea of the charms of friendly society. . . . They have no good horses, no good flesh, no grapes or muskmelons, no good fruit, no ice or cold water, no good food or bread in their bazaars, no baths or colleges or candles or torches—never a candlestick![5]

But despite these adverse thoughts, Babur's attitude toward his conquered subjects was humane and tolerant. He even urged his son to respect the religious beliefs of the Hindus—an extraordinary attitude for a man of his century and religion.

It may be convenient at this point to list the first six Mughul emperors—an unusually able succession of rulers commanding finally the largest and most glorious empire that had yet been put together in India: Babur (1526–30), Humayun (1530–56), Akbar (1556–1605), Jahangir (1605–27), Shah Jahan (1628–58), and Aurangzeb (1659–1707). Although their successors remained on the throne of Delhi until 1858, those who came after 1707 are of little individual significance. Toward the end, they were mere puppets in the hands of various powers (finally the British).

Before his death in 1530, Babur was able to conquer part but not all of north India. This small empire was lost temporarily by his son, Humayun. Driven from his throne, Humayun wandered homeless for fifteen years in the deserts of Rajasthan and Sind, until finally the Shah of Persia helped him regain his lost throne. He died shortly thereafter. His great tomb in Delhi interestingly foreshadows the style of the more famous Taj Mahal at Agra, built some eighty years later by his great-grandson.

It was Humayun's son, Akbar, who effectively established the Mughul Dynasty in India. A contemporary of Queen Elizabeth I of England, he stands out as a great ruler and statesman, an extraordinarily capable, many-sided, interesting man. During his long reign of forty-nine years, he laid the foundations of Mughul power and splendor—a splendor that was to continue undiminished for a hundred years after his death and not to lose its grip on men's minds until long after its actual power had vanished.

When Akbar inherited the title of Emperor in 1556, he was only twelve years old and had, in effect, no empire. Even to gain access to the capital city of Delhi, he had to fight a hard battle—the Second Battle of Panipat, in 1556. (Panipat was a natural battlefield because it guarded the northern approach to Delhi and the junction of important trade routes from the southwest and southeast.) By the time he died a half-century later, his territory extended clear across north India and also included Afghanistan. He did not undertake the conquest of the south, but his grip on the north was solid and substantial—the result of his own hard work and ability, not only military but also administrative. Most of the independent rulers of north India were successively overcome by this dynamic man, with his clear, powerful will and his ability to combine swift campaigns and firm administration. No detail was too small for him to investigate personally; yet he knew how to delegate work and command the loyalty of able ministers. Quick and severe in his punishment of wrong-doing or treachery, he was never cruel for cruelty's sake, as many of the earlier Muslim rulers had been.

Like them, however, he was a complete despot, and would not permit even a hereditary aristocracy to exist lest it question the will of the ruler. He made himself the heir of the possessions of the nobles, and he alone chose the fortunate few who, during their good behavior, occupied the various points below him on the narrow pinnacle of power.

Akbar divided his empire into provinces and organized a carefully graded bureaucracy along disciplined military lines. Each officeholder carried a military title. In addition to his civilian duties, he was supposed to supply a given number of troops on request by the Emperor.

The salaries paid were very high and attracted the ablest men from western Asia. Akbar's predecessors and his successors tended to pay salaries by the granting of temporary estates, jagirs, from which the officers could raise revenue to pay themselves. Akbar preferred cash payments because he rightly feared that the holder of a jagir might be too difficult to control.[6]

As always in India, the main source of taxation was the land revenue. The original system of levying taxes was to divide the actual produce of the land at harvest time between the state and the cultivator. Akbar attempted to secure payments in cash instead of in grain. He made his collections directly from the cultivator through salaried officials, rather than through the traditional tax farmer or zamindars (intermediaries who paid themselves by squeezing the peasants as much as they could).

So solidly did he build the administrative machine of his empire that more than two centuries later, after Mughul power had crumbled at the center, the machine was still running in the provinces. Parts of it were taken over virtually intact by the early British empire-builders, who tried to grope their way back to Akbar's orderly method of assessing and collecting revenue.[7]

But the Emperor's abilities as a general and administrator were only one side of this complex, brilliant man. Full of zest, ebullience, and mental as well as physical energy, he possessed a large library, enjoyed having books read aloud to him, experimented with various mechanical inventions such as a bigger and better cannon and a device for loading several guns at once.

His outstanding characteristic was his religious tolerance. As part of a policy of winning the loyalty of his Hindu subjects, Akbar married two Hindu princesses, the daughters of Rajput princes who had long resisted Muslim rule. He also repealed the much-hated *jizya*, the discriminatory tax levied on Hindus by his Muslim predecessors. Although in practice he employed few Hindus, in theory he opened the public service to Hindus and

Muslims alike. The new capital city he built at Fatehpur Sikri, 20 miles outside Agra, reveals in stone his interest in absorbing the ideas native to the land he ruled. For it relies chiefly on the post and lintel construction and the carved brackets typical of Hindu architecture, rather than on the arches and domes brought to India by the Muslims.

If Akbar's policy of religious tolerance and his acceptance of things Indian had been pursued by his successors, the history of modern India would certainly have been quite different. Perhaps the partition of India in 1947 would not even have taken place. But such tolerance was vigorously resented by the Muslim nobles. It required an unusually strong statesman to maintain it as a policy, and as we shall see, no subsequent emperor had Akbar's statesmanship. The next two were, above all, great patrons of the arts. Under them, the flowering of Mughul culture occurred.

Akbar's son and successor, the heavy-drinking Jahangir, took a keen interest in miniature painting and maintained large workshops of painters who turned out exquisite, colorful portraits of proud, jeweled nobles and of the dissolute Emperor himself, scenes of luxurious court life and its oriental pageantry, and (in a different key) lovely and simple naturalistic studies of flowers, birds, and animals.

It was to the Emperor Jahangir that England first sent an ambassador in 1615. This harrassed gentleman, Sir Thomas Roe, failed to gain the rights and privileges his monarch, James I, had sent him to secure, and he was constantly subjected by Jahangir to practical jokes. The self-assured Mughul court of the time had small regard for the distant, insignificant, and little-known island of England.

Both architecture and luxury of living reached their peak during the reign of the next Mughul, Shah Jahan (1627–58), best known to the West as the ruler who built the Taj Mahal as a tomb for his wife. The beauty of the Taj Mahal lies not only in its proportions and the lovely curves of its marble dome, but also in the exquisite attention to detail, the varied designs wrought upon its surfaces, the colored inlays in floral patterns or in stylized writings from the Koran (all of them done with costly semiprecious stones carefully cut by hand). It is said to have taken 20,000 workmen over 15 years to complete the Taj. Yet this was only one of Shah Jahan's architectural achievements. He was also responsible for most of the lovely palaces within the Red Fort at Agra and for the entire Red Fort in old Delhi, including all its palaces, audience halls, baths, and gardens.

The splendor and opulence of life as it was lived within these palaces was beyond anything known in Europe at that time. The interiors were hung with silks from China and carpeted with rugs from Persia. Niches in the walls contained gold and silver vases of flowers in the daytime and white wax candles at night. Various methods of cooling the palaces in the hot summers were evolved—by the evaporation of water from many fountains and by the use of moistened reed mats kept in motion by servants. In winter, ice was brought from the Himalayas and stored deep underground for use during the summer. In his audience hall, the Emperor sat upon his Peacock Throne made of costly jewels.

Shah Jahan's great building program and his luxurious living were expensive. But he could afford it. It has been estimated that the value of his treasure exceeded £337 million (in present monetary terms—a risky business to translate—it was probably equivalent to at least $3–4 billion). All of this money came, of course, out of taxes, which the Emperor collected even in periods of famine, when his people were starving. During his reign and subsequently, the gulf between the rich and the poor became progressively wider. Meanwhile, the nobility that clustered around the court grew weak and effete. In terms of strength, if not of wealth, the empire had passed its peak.

In other ways also, Shah Jahan's policies were to prove disastrous. Although he was three-fourths Hindu by birth, he reversed Akbar's liberal policy toward Hinduism and ordered a wholesale destruction of Hindu temples. In the district of Banaras alone—the holiest city of Hinduism—seventy-six temples were destroyed.[8] Moreover, Shah Jahan sent his armies south to conquer the Deccan. The armies succeeded in absorbing one of the independent Muslim kingdoms of the Deccan, Ahmadnagar. Two others, Golconda and Bijapur, withstood his operations. The attempt to subdue the Deccan—a central focus of the next reign also—proved to be too big a task. By the end of the seventeenth century, it had led to hopeless difficulties.

In his old age, Shah Jahan was overthrown and imprisoned by the third of his four sons, who also exterminated his brothers in order to secure the throne for himself—a bloody succession of events not at all unusual in the annals of Muslim rule in India. The Emperor who thus came to the throne was Aurangzeb, who had been the General in charge of his father's armies during the campaign in the Deccan. During his own reign, Aurangzeb pushed the southern extension of Mughul rule to its greatest limits, conquering various independent Muslim kingdoms that controlled the Deccan. The year 1691 may be taken as the date of the largest territorial conquest.

But Aurangzeb's extreme bigotry and religious intolerance proved to be his undoing. He reimposed the discriminatory tax on Hindus, and he pursued the wholesale destruction of Hindu temples. Only a few Hindu temples on the east coast in Orissa, in central India at Khajuraho, and in the far south remained standing. By his intolerance, Aurangzeb alienated the Hindu Rajput princes who had given allegiance to Akbar, and he aroused the antagonism of two other groups who were to figure prominently in Indian history thereafter. One of these was the Sikhs, a minority religious group stemming from the teachings of the fifteenth-century religious leader Nanak, who had sought to combine the best of Islam with the best of Hinduism. Aurangzeb summoned to his court the ninth Sikh Guru (leader) and killed him. From a semipacifist religious group owning much to the Muslim religion, the Sikhs were thereafter transformed into a fighting body implacably hostile to the Muslims. In the eighteenth century, they established a kingdom in the Punjab in north India and successfully defied Muslim rule; they were one of the last independent Indian powers conquered by the British. Today, they are of major political significance in the Punjab.

The most troublesome group that rose to face Aurangzeb, however, proved to be the Marathas, staunch Hindus who lived in the Western Ghats, the rugged mountainous area near the western coast, behind Bombay (now in the state of Maharashtra). The

Marathas continually harried the Emperor's baggage trains on his march toward the south. At first, Aurangzeb thought of them as a mere nuisance and continued to regard the Muslim kingdoms of the Deccan as his real opponents. But the Marathas grew in strength until it became necessary for the Emperor to turn the full strength of his army upon them.

Shivaji, the Maratha leader who became their King, seems to have been a very unusual person. The British, who had acquired Bombay in 1662, had repeated trouble with him. One British official recorded that Shivaji had "courage, deftness, and mobility, to a degree never surpassed in the world's history."[9] Sometimes he pressed the British for money; sometimes he made friendly overtures, hoping to get their support against a Mughul admiral who liked to use Bombay harbor as his port. One of his great exploits was the murder, singlehanded, of a Mughul general who came to him under a flag of truce.

A military genius, a good organizer, and a born leader of men, Shivaji stirred new feelings of Hindu regeneration and resistance. He welded together the Maratha people scattered through the Deccan and made alliances and conquests farther south so that his vast territory finally included much of the area of the present-day states of Mysore and Madras, as well as Maharashtra. The Marathas whom he galvanized into a nation were to be the chief power in India throughout the eighteenth century.

Shivaji died in 1680. Aurangzeb captured and executed his son and carried off to court his grandson to bring him up as a Muslim. But even this did not check the Maratha menace. Fired by strong Hindu religious feeling, they continued to make war on the imperial forces. With light cavalry and no baggage to encumber them, they attacked Aurangzeb's large and unwieldly army wherever he least expected them. When he tried to seize them, they climbed the steep, wild hills like monkeys and escaped. Year after year, in his old age, the Emperor used up his best contingents against them in vain. Finally at the age of 80, after 48 years of rule, he died in his military camp, still fighting the Marathas. On his deathbed, he wrote bitterly that his whole life's work had failed.

Disintegration and Chaos

After Aurangzeb's death in 1707, the mighty and magnificent empire quickly fell to pieces. It had become overripe. Luxury had sapped the virility of the nobles. No strong leadership existed at the center capable either of conciliating or of holding in check the Rajputs, Sikhs, and Marathas. The imperial territory had become too large and unwieldy. Wars of succession and a series of short reigns by debauched or inefficient rulers undermined imperial power. In a short space of time, the treasury became depleted, allies were lost, provincial governors broke away. There set in the same process of disintegration that had previously broken up the great empire of the Sultanate of Delhi and the still earlier empire of Ashoka.

The nobles were now paid by the grant of supposedly temporary land tenures and thus became increasingly strong, each in his own jagir. In 1724, the chief minister of the Emperor set himself up virtually as an independent ruler in the large province of the Deccan, thereby becoming the first Nizam of Hyderabad. (The last Nizam lost his status as a ruling prince only in 1948.) The province of Oudh, in the Ganges plain to the east of Delhi, likewise became independent under a line of nawabs (governors) who were later recognized as kings. Still farther to the east was the Nawab of Bengal, who ruled Bengal, Bihar, and much of Orissa. His successor was the first strong Indian ruler whom the British defeated. Other parts of the empire also slipped out of central control.

The most troublesome problem continued to be the Marathas. Throughout the eighteenth century, a line of hereditary prime ministers (peshwas) were the real Maratha leaders, while Shivaji's descendants retained an empty title. During much of this century, the Marathas, who had started in such a small way as local guerrillas, seemed likely to bring all of India under their control and to become the effective successors of the Mughul Empire. Maratha armies foraged far and wide, exacting tribute or plunder from many distant areas which they made no attempt to govern. Various Maratha chiefs also carved realms for themselves out of the Mughul Empire. Until 1802, they remained loosely united in a confederacy headed by the peshwa. One of these chiefs, Sindhia of

Gwalior, pushed close to Delhi, defeating an imperial army in 1738. Another, the Bhonsle of Nagpur, drove clear across the subcontinent and seized central India and the east coast just below the little British trading post of Calcutta, which anxiously prepared to resist him. He turned away in search of richer gain elsewhere.

In 1739, the weakened Mughul Empire failed to check a new invasion from across the northwest passes by Nadir Shah of Persia. The Shah defeated the imperial armies, plundered Delhi, and carried off the crown jewels, the famous Peacock Throne, and all the transportable wealth on which Mughul glory had been based. The remaining remnants of imperial power were further destroyed by court intrigues and civil war. In 1753, the armies of two rival factions of nobles cannonaded each other from two sections of the city of Delhi. In 1756, Delhi was again invaded and sacked, this time by an Afghan chief, Ahmad Shah Durrani. Certain nobles asked the Marathas for help to drive him back. This request gave the Marathas the opportunity to occupy Delhi and the Punjab to the north. They now controlled virtually all of India from the Himalayas to Tanjore in the deep south. Growing alarmed at this resurgence of Hindu power, various factions formed a coalition against the Marathas, who were decisively defeated in the Third Battle of Panipat (1761). This ended their chances of consolidating a new empire. But the Mughul Emperor was too weak to take advantage of their defeat, and no other single leader emerged to fill the resulting power vacuum. Thus the British, far to the east in Bengal, gained time to establish control over the lower Ganges Valley. It was the mounting chaos of the late eighteenth century that opened the way for the rapid extension of British power.

Shah Alam II, the Mughul Emperor during the last half of the century (1759–1806), was a titular ruler only, a pensioner supported and controlled first by one power, then by another (including for a while the Maratha chief, Sindhia of Gwalior). In 1803, he came under British control. In dilapidated palaces, his successors continued to hold court for half a century, keeping up the pretense of splendor and protesting against the ever-increasing encroachments on their dignity by their real overlords, the British, who finally sent the last Mughul Emperor into exile in Burma in 1858.

Thus the Mughul dynasty finally came to an end. It was the last independent Indian dynasty, and certainly the greatest since that of the Mauryas in the fourth and third centuries B.C., which in turn represented the highest peak of political organization since the Indus Valley civilization of the second and third millennium of the era before Christ. To say this is to remind ourselves how long is the corridor of Indian history and from what remote distances come the echoes of the past. We must now consider the curious circumstances under which this ancient land was conquered by a handful of people from a small Atlantic island, whose wild tribes had been given their first glimpse of civilization by Julius Caesar as late as 55 B.C.

5 • THE RISE AND CONSOLIDATION OF BRITISH RULE

An old engraving now hanging in the museum of Fort St. George in Madras depicts an early landing there of a group of British traders. The square riggers in which they have arrived are anchored far off the sandy beach, and the passengers have been transferred to rowboats, two of which are having trouble with the surf. An Indian woman, with a baby astride her hip, gravely watches the landing. A group of Indian fishermen sit on their own tiny boats made of hollowed logs (like the boats that Madras fishermen still use skillfully in that same surf). From one rowboat, several Britishers in waistcoats, cutaway coats, and high black silk hats are wading to shore, unhappily lifting their trousers in the vain hope of keeping them dry. A lady in a long dress with ruffles, a feathered hat on her head and a parasol in her hand, is being carried over the waves by two coolies, naked except for their loincloths and the rich brown of their skins. Nothing could more vividly suggest how alien to the land were the newcomers—two cultures meeting in the midst of salt spray!

The facts as to when the Europeans first came to India and how the British gained an empire serve as the framework within which began the most profoundly disturbing cultural confrontation India had experienced since the coming of the Muslims—or perhaps even since the earlier Aryan invasions.

The first European conquerors to arrive were the Portuguese. Indeed, they came some thirty years before the founding of the Mughul Empire. In 1498, Vasco da Gama landed with three small ships at Calicut, on the southwest coast. Another Portuguese,

Albuquerque, seized Goa on the west coast in 1510; this became the most important Portuguese outpost, remaining in Portuguese hands until its seizure by India in December, 1961. Although the Portuguese succeeded in establishing trading posts on both the east and west coasts and also in Indonesia, their power decreased toward the end of the sixteenth century. They were too small a nation to maintain a maritime empire far away, and their oppressive policy of trying to force Indians to become Christians required military and naval strength, as did the appearance on the scene of new European rivals.

In the early 1600's, the command of the Indian Ocean passed to the Dutch, who in 1602 had formed a strong trading company under government patronage. They seized many of the Portuguese settlements on the west coast of India, and drove the Portuguese from Ceylon in 1658. But their chief activities were in the islands that now form Indonesia, where the quickest profits could be made.

In 1600, during the reign of the great Mughul Akbar, a private commercial company in London received a charter from Queen Elizabeth. Although it was later to be known as the East India Company, it first bore the name The Governor and Company of Merchants of London Trading into the East Indies. It was granted the monopoly of British trade with the "Indies," which included India, China, and Indonesia. After a resounding defeat by the Dutch in Indonesia in 1623, it confined its attentions to India and China. The conquest of India was achieved by this private company, sometimes aided after 1685 by ships of the Royal Navy and after 1754 by Royal regiments sent to India to fight alongside Europeans and Indians whom the Company itself hired and trained. The Company continued its trade with China until 1853, but never gained political control there comparable to that in India.

There were other European arrivals in India. A Danish company, established in 1620, founded a few settlements which it sold in 1845 to the East India Company. More significantly, a French company, La Compagnie des Indes Orientales, was formed in 1664 under the strong patronage of King Louis XIV. Pondicherry, on the southeast coast below Madras, became the chief

French post, and it remained in French control until 1954, when (unlike Goa) it was voluntarily ceded to India.

Empire-building was not yet the fashion in the seventeenth century. During its first 150 years in India, the British Company focused on commercial profits, hiring armed guards or soldiers only as needed to protect warehouses and other property. The trade was largely in luxuries such as silks, gems, indigo—and especially pepper and other spices (for which England was ready to pay high prices).

Throughout the seventeenth century, the company operated only on a small scale. In 1647, it had only twenty-three trading posts and ninety employees in India. Its first outright territorial acquisitions were tiny and gave little promise of what lay ahead. In 1639, by agreement with a local governor, it acquired four miles of sandy beach on the southeast coast at Madras. In 1662, Charles II of England, by marrying a Portuguese princess, acquired as part of his dowry the fine port of Bombay, on the west coast, which the Portuguese had conquered earlier. Three years later, he leased Bombay to the Company for the modest sum of £10 a year. In 1690, the Company secured from Emperor Aurangzeb permission to settle on certain muddy, seemingly worthless flats near the mouth of the Ganges. The location became Calcutta.

At each of these three ports—Madras, Bombay, and Calcutta—the Company erected a fort. Gradually, there grew up around each a city that attracted increasing numbers of Indian residents as agents or servants of Company officials. These "Presidency cities" became the three legs of the tripod on which British power rested. But in each, until the second half of the eighteenth century, the British community consisted of no more than a few hundred Europeans (most of them men who had come to India without their wives). Clinging to their own culture as people everywhere tend to do, the merchants at first lived together within the forts and dined at one table. The gates were shut at night. There was little recreation, a shortage of women, and much boredom. The greatest excitement occurred when some Mughul official visited their fort; in deference to Mughul power, processions, the exchange of presents, feasting, fireworks, and gun salutes marked the honor of such a visit. Gradually, the merchants succumbed to the lure of the land around them. They began to imitate Indian customs, wear Indian clothes, eat Indian food, keep Indian women, and live in Indian luxury whenever they could afford it.

Until the death of Emperor Aurangzeb in 1707, there was no attempt by any of the European companies to extend power inland or to control more than a few ports and trading stations. Then, early in the eighteenth century, when the Mughul Empire collapsed into anarchy and disintegration, a power vacuum was left that inevitably had to be filled. But by whom? On the continent of Europe, the English and the French were locked in warfare. They were rivals also in North America. How natural that they should fight each other in India as well. Natural, too, that they should look for allies among the many rival Indian powers that had splintered off from the Mughul Empire. The French took the first step. In 1746, during the War of the Austrian Succession, they seized and held Madras until forced by a European peace treaty to return it. A few years later, the Nizam of Hyderabad, the central state in the Deccan, died. The succession to his throne was disputed, as was also the succession to the Nawabship of the Carnatic, the coastal plain behind Madras. The French gave support to one contender in each case and began new military operations. The English Company, allied with the other contenders, at first suffered reverses. But a bold, resourceful young Company clerk named Robert Clive got up from his desk, gathered together 200 British soldiers and 300 sepoys (Indian soldiers), and seized Arcot, the capital of the Carnatic, while the French-supported army was off foraging in other directions. When this army of 10,000 returned, he withstood a lengthy siege until additional forces came to his rescue. A hero overnight, he became the indispensable man, to be called on in any new emergency.

How Conquest Began

Such an emergency occurred in 1756. The British in Calcutta encountered trouble when the Nawab of Bengal seized the city. Several ships of the British Navy, plus Clive and a small army, were sent from Madras to recapture Calcutta. After having done so, the expedition then went on to seize a neighboring French post, Chandernagore, with which the Nawab was in contact. Clive, who had few scruples and never failed to take the main chance, began to connive with one of the Nawab's generals, Mir Jumla, who agreed to allow Clive to defeat the Nawab's forces if Clive would make him Nawab. The result was the great "Battle" of Plassey (1757), in which Clive's army of 3,000 men, including only 950 Europeans, defeated the Nawab's forces of 68,000 men. Really a transaction rather than a battle, Plassey nevertheless laid the foundation for British political power in India, and gave the Company virtual control over the rich valley of the Ganges and access to wealth as yet undreamed of.

Having deposed the Nawab and installed Mir Jumla in his place, Clive received from the latter a present of £234,000, plus a land grant worth £30,000 a year—a fortune worth many millions of dollars today. When later impeached in Parliament for the acquisition of this wealth, Clive coolly stated that, in view of the wealth of Bengal, he was astonished at his own moderation! Although acquitted, he later committed suicide. A brilliant, ambitious, and lonely man, Clive was truly a tragic figure.

For the next fifteen years, following Clive's example, lesser men within the Company's service joined in an unabashed, greedy scramble for wealth, taking bribes from Indians and utilizing for their private gain the Company's right to trade duty-free. Their activities ruined normal internal trade and undermined the rich economy of Bengal. The Company's employees amassed great fortunes, while the finances of the Company itself dwindled.

Lord Cornwallis, who served as Governor-General from 1786 to 1793, cleaned up this corruption. Best known to Americans as the British general defeated at the Battle of Yorktown, Lord Cornwallis was the most outstanding public figure yet to enter Company service—a man of great integrity and sufficient prestige to push through effective changes. He made a sharp distinction between the administrative and commercial functions of the Company, organized a separate civil service to handle the administration, required civil servants to covenant or promise that they would not engage in trade, raised salaries so that irregular profits were no longer a necessity, and severely disciplined any infractions of his rules. From his time on, corruption within the Company was the exception rather than the rule.

As part of his program of reform, Lord Cornwallis excluded Indians from the higher posts of government, believing that the corruption stemmed from them. This separation of Indians from governmental service had repercussions that became increasingly important in the second half of the nineteenth century.

But to speak of Cornwallis at this point is to anticipate the sequence of events. He did not arrive in India until almost thirty years after the pivotal Battle of Plassey. For seven years after that battle, it was not clear whether the real power in Bengal was the British Company or the Nawab, whom the British regarded as their puppet. This crucial question was settled at the hard-fought Battle of Buxar in 1764, when the British defeated the Nawab. A year later, the powerless Mughul Emperor granted the Company the right to collect revenues in Bengal, Bihar, and Orissa. Since the Emperor was still the titular overlord of this area, the grant in a sense legalized the British position. In 1772, under Warren Hastings, then Governor of Bengal, the Company for the first time assumed direct control of the whole civil administration instead of working through a puppet government.

After the great political changes that followed the battle of Plassey, the British settlements grew rapidly in size with the influx of professional soldiers and others. The merchants, now transformed suddenly into politicians, no longer had to approach Indian officials with deference and could now mix with them as equals. Although both Indians and English might disapprove of particular customs of the other, they still looked on one another with curiosity, interest, and respect. Some Englishmen knew several Indian languages and had many close Indian friends. Warren Hastings was one of these and, indeed, was a great patron of Indian learning and art.

But in a few short years, as the political balance shifted further, the British turned away from things Indian. British settlements began to resemble English towns. Fashion dictated that, instead of the wide, shady verandas so fitted to the climate, the houses of Britishers must have Ionic columns going up two flights, though such columns allowed the sun to bake the open porches below. It became no longer quite the thing to keep Indian women or to appreciate Indian textiles or other products. British amusements (dancing, theater, etc.) were introduced. Having acquired political power, the new Western rulers absorbed many of the autocratic tendencies of the Oriental despots whom they had displaced. A horde of retainers and ostentatious luxury became desirable. Despotic tempers seemed appropriate to their new status. In this sense, Englishmen lived like the Nawabs they had dispossessed.

Parliament Regulates the Company

In England, there were increasing political demands that the government should take over the Company's possessions. Because of shifting alignments in British politics, this was not done. But in 1773, Parliament for the first time asserted the right to regulate the Company. It decided that the three "Presidencies" should be subjected to more unified control. The position of Governor-General was therefore created, and Warren Hastings was selected to fill it. A new Regulating Act in 1784 went further. Although it allowed the Company's own directors to continue to appoint Company officials and employees and to control purely commercial matters, it set up a new governmental agency under the Crown, the Board of Control, and gave to this Board the power to "superintend, direct, and control all acts . . . which in any wise relate to the civil or military government, or the revenues of the British territorial possessions in the East Indies."[1] The Board of Control could recall a Governor-General, though it could not appoint one. This curious system of double government—by Company and Crown—lasted until 1858 without major modification. But before then, three acts were passed—in 1813, 1833, and 1853—which progressively curtailed the powers of the Company. In 1813, influenced by the free-trade ideas of the time, Parliament ended the Company's monopoly of Indian trade; and in response to the new resurgence of Christian evangelicism in England, it required that the Company freely admit Christian missionaries into Company lands (hitherto barred). In 1833, Parliament deprived the Company of trading rights in India, leaving it as the political agent of the Crown. In 1853, Parliament stripped the directors of their power to make appointments to the Company, requiring that entry to the service be on the basis of competitive examinations; at the same time, it also ended the grant to the Company of trading rights in China.

Expansion: Intentional or Accidental?

The East India Company had clearly become a political power in Bengal by the early 1770's, and was therefore faced with new and difficult problems of foreign policy. Perched precariously on the edge of a large land full of potential enemies, its only security lay in the rivalries among other Indian powers. Which of the contending rulers were the more dangerous? Would alliances with one or another increase or decrease the Company's security? Should it remain neutral in the wars that were continually occurring beyond its territories—or should it choose sides? None of these questions was easy to answer. Policy fluctuated under successive governors-general.

For a quarter of a century, sheer survival was the main preoccupation, but even so the Company was constantly pulled deeper into the morass of Indian politics. For example, by reason of a defensive alliance entered into in 1765 with Oudh, just west of Bengal, the Company became involved nine years later in a war with an Afghan enemy of Oudh 800 miles inland from Calcutta. Such were the problems of diplomacy in the turmoil of eighteenth-century India. The Presidencies of Madras and Bombay soon became embroiled in wars also. At one time, while Warren Hastings was serving as Governor-General (1774–85), it was necessary to face three enemies at once: the state of Mysore, which had fallen into the hands of an able and ambitious Muslim usurper; the Nizam of Hyderabad, just to the north; and the always dangerous Marathas, still farther to the north. After eight years of war and skillful diplomacy, Hastings managed to prevent any loss of territory, but expansion was out of the question.

In any event, the directors of the Company back in England were at first explicitly opposed to expansion. They preferred to keep down military expenses in order to protect profits. Moreover, Parliament, in the Regulating Act of 1784, stated: "To pursue schemes of conquest and extension of dominion in India are measures repugnant to the wish, honor, and policy of this nation."[2] The Act forebade the Company to declare war or enter into treaties without specific permission of the Board of Control. But it took many months for letters to reach India by sailing vessels. Decisions had to be made by men on the spot, and a man who firmly believed in conquest could take advantage of the great distance separating him from London.

Such a man was Lord Wellesley, Governor-General from 1798 to 1805, whose policy was frankly annexationist. Decisive, strong-willed, vigorous, and energetic, he was a man thirsty for honor and scornful of his Indian subjects, whom he considered "vulgar, ignorant, rude, familiar, and stupid."[3] But then he was cold and haughty toward Britishers, too, and wrote that his favorite leisure-time activity was to be alone "in this magnificent solitude where I stalk about like a Royal Tiger."[4] He was haughty even toward his own younger brother, who was one of his ablest generals and later became the Duke of Wellington.

An excellent pretext for aggressive action existed. At the moment that Wellesley arrived in India, Napoleon was in Egypt with an army and a plan to weaken England by waging a campaign in India. And French officers or agents were at work in several Indian states. Wellesley considered himself faced by the double menace of French aggression and French penetration.

The three chief powers in India were still those whom Warren Hastings had faced: the Nizam of Hyderabad in the center, the Sultan of Mysore to the south, and the Maratha confederacy to the north and west. Preying on the Nizam's fears, Wellesley persuaded that unwise monarch to disband and disarm his entire French-trained army in return for the promise of English support against his enemies. From England, Henry Dundas, President of the Board of Control, wrote Wellesley to praise him for this stroke and at the same time to try to restrain him from aggression: "It would be too strong for me to state that under no given circumstances our own forces were to go beyond our own provinces . . . but the temptation must be very great and the advantage very evident to induce us to do so. . . . Preserving the general peace of India . . . is certainly our wisest system."[5]

But Wellesley had not waited for a war to be sanctioned. Before the letter was written, he had launched an attack on Mysore. Before the letter was received, the Sultan of Mysore had been killed in the Battle of Seringapatam, in May, 1799. Next to Plassey, this battle stands out as probably the most significant military event in the history of British conquest. It showed clearly that the Company was a power to be feared.

Annexing the coastal areas of Mysore and giving the Nizam another slice of territory to confirm him as an ally, Wellesley handed over the rest of Mysore to a five-year-old prince who could be easily controlled.

There remained the Marathas. In 1802, Wellesley succeeded in dividing them by diplomacy. Their Peshwa, the titular head of their confederacy, was jealous of the growing power of the unruly Maratha chiefs supposedly under his authority: Sindhia, Holkar, the Bhonsle of Nagpur, the Gaekwar of Baroda, and others. Wellesley persuaded the Peshwa to accept the same kind of "subsidiary alliance" by which the Nizam of Hyderabad had been previously disarmed. This alliance provided for the stationing of Company troops within the Peshwa's territory and the Company's guarantee of his position. It precipitated war between the Company and the Maratha chiefs. Brilliant campaigns in 1803 and 1804 against Sindhia, who had been in control of the two old capital cities of Delhi and Agra, placed the Mughul Emperor in British hands. Like the Marathas, however, the Company found it convenient to leave the Emperor, with his empty title and pomp, in full sovereignty over the narrow confines of Shah Jahan's Red Fort in Delhi. Subsequently, one of Wellesley's forces was annihilated by another Maratha chief, Holkar. Thereupon, both the directors and the Board of Control decided that their aggressive Governor-General should be recalled. His disregard of directives from London had been tolerated while he was victorious. Defeat was a different matter.

Besides waging these wars, Wellesley had quietly annexed the territory of several nawabs and rajahs too weak to resist him, and had forced on others subsidiary alliances like those with the Nizam and the Peshwa. By this device, large areas that still remained under the control of native princes were effectively subordinated to British policy. Wellesley's seven years of rule had completely changed the political picture of India. At his arrival, the Company had been only one of many contending powers on the subcontinent. When he left, it was unquestionably the strongest power in India.

Wellesley's wars left the Company's resources depleted. There was a pause of eight years before the extension of territory was again pursued. Then, from 1813 to 1818, another Governor-General, Lord Hastings (not to be confused with the earlier Warren Hastings), finally broke Maratha power completely and spread British control across central India, linking together the three sections of Company territory that had expanded inland from the three ports of Madras, Bombay, and Calcutta. Thus, by 1818, the British controlled directly or indirectly all of India east and south of the Punjab.

Lord Hastings also waged a war with the mountain kingdom of Nepal to the north and annexed its western part. Most of the mountainous area of north India, except Kashmir, was thus acquired. Many lovely mountain resorts ("hill stations") were built in former Nepalese territory—including Simla, perched on a mountain slope so steep that the top floors of many houses can be entered directly from a higher level of the same vertical street that provides access also to their ground floors and basements. After 1830, the British rulers of India began to take refuge in Simla from the heat of the plains. Although Calcutta remained the capital of India until 1912, when Delhi took its place, Simla became the headquarters of the Governor-General and later of the Viceroy, except during the brief winter period of cool weather. Between the ruling race in their cool retreat and their subjects on the sweltering plains, the distance increased.

How Much Westernization?

As the East India Company pushed forward its boundaries, it faced, of course, the problem of how to govern this alien land. From the Battle of Plassey until the coming of Lord Cornwallis (1786), the basic policy was to build on what was already there—the remnants of the Mughul administration—using many Indians in government and making as few changes as possible.

Having inaugurated the policy of keeping Indians out of the higher governmental positions, Lord Cornwallis took an even more significant step in 1793, one that profoundly affected land tenures, a matter of major importance in a predominantly agricultural country. He made a "permanent settlement" with the Mughul revenue agents (zamindars) in Bengal, whereby in return for a fixed annual payment thereafter to the Company's government, these men were given ownership rights in the land from which they had formerly merely collected taxes. This settlement created a new class of large landlords at the expense of the peasants, who had previously had substantial rights in the land. It also limited in perpetuity the amount of taxes the government could collect from these landlords, while leaving the latter free to increase at will the amounts they in turn collected from the peasants. Viewed from the vantage point of the twentieth century, the entire transaction seems so strange that one wonders how Lord Cornwallis could have blundered into it. Part of the explanation seems to lie in the fact that the Indian concept of land ownership was so different from the English concept that it was hard to determine exactly who had been the actual "landowners" (as the English understood the word). Cornwallis believed that it was desirable to create a landed aristocracy, like the squires of England. In any case, his administration was too understaffed to make a careful investigation of tenures and land values. The holdings of some of the very large absentee landowners, against whom the land-reform measures of independent India have been directed, can be traced back to the settlement made by Cornwallis.

After Cornwallis' time, a number of extremely able Company servants emerged who took a profound interest in studying India closely and in making very careful assessments and revenue settlements. The permanence of the arrangement made by Cornwallis in Bengal was recognized as a mistake. Subsequent settlements in territory conquered later were made subject to periodic revision. In some places, whole villages were made responsible for the payment of taxes. In others, peasants were assessed individually.

There was a brief return to the old policy of respecting native institutions and customs and of attempting to make as few changes as possible. But, as a later Company servant, General Mountstuart Elphinstone, was to observe, it was not always possible to avoid innovating, and the British often did not even realize when they were introducing change: "Our assumption of the government is so great and radical an innovation that there is scarcely any institution in the country into which it does not necessarily introduce great changes."[6]

At any rate, the policy of avoiding Western innovations did not last long. Lord Bentinck, Governor-General from 1828 to 1835, embarked on a series of drastic Westernizing reforms, tried to stamp out certain Hindu customs and abuses, and took the momentous decision to make English the official language. (Some of these reforms and the important repercussions will be considered in detail in subsequent chapters.)

There was also a reversal of policy in 1841 regarding the acquisition of territory. The Court of Directors in London expressly turned away from the principle of nonaggression, which had seldom in fact curbed an energetic Governor-General. The new directive was to abandon "no just and honorable accession of territory."[7] More annexations followed. Between 1842 and 1848, the British conquered the westernmost province of Sind (now in West Pakistan) and the Punjab, where the hardy Sikhs, the minority religious group that had been persecuted by Aurangzeb, had succeeded in establishing a kingdom in the early nineteenth century. As a result of the wars with the Sikhs, the British acquired not only the Punjab but also Kashmir, which they placed in the hands of a subservient prince. Without war, the Company also annexed several of the small Maratha states that still retained independence—and even the great state of Oudh, on the upper Ganges, whose capital, Lucknow, still conveys through the splendor of its late Mughul buildings a sense of how dramatic it must have been for the British to humble so easily such a kingdom.

By 1857, the British Company was in complete control of India. It ruled about three-fifths of the subcontinent directly and the remaining two-fifths indirectly through subservient Indian princes. The British believed themselves able to annex at will any of these princely states, as they had just annexed Oudh.

The "Mutiny" and Crown Rule

Suddenly, on a scorching Sunday in May, 1857, there broke out what the British call the great Indian Mutiny and what some Indians refer to as the First War of Indian Independence. Whatever it is called, though, the revolt was probably the most pivotal event in the history of British rule in India. It began in the army post at Meerut, some 30 miles north of Delhi. There, on that Sunday in May, the Company's sepoys killed every European—man, woman, or child—on whom they could lay their hands. Then they raced to Delhi and announced to the aged, bewildered, long powerless Mughul Emperor that he was their leader. The sepoys at Kanpur, Lucknow, and certain other army posts also mutinied.

The causes of the revolt were many. The cartridges for a new rifle that had been introduced involved the use of animal grease, taboo to Hindus and Muslims alike. The soldiers had been required to serve overseas in Burma and elsewhere, even though travel across black waters was regarded as wrong by upper-caste Hindus. The new innovations of the railroad and telegraph were disturbing. There were rumors of enforced conversion to Christianity.

Once started by the Company's own soldiers, the revolt received the support of many discontented elements in north India —dispossessed princes, their former soldiers (now unemployed), and many others made anxious by the pace of change and the departure from old Indian customs. Certainly, it had a wider basis than the word "mutiny" tends to suggest. Yet it was not a truly national uprising. Southern India remained untouched by it. Even in the north, there were many who stayed loyal to the British, including the newly conquered Sikhs, who were delighted to fight against the Mughul Emperor, descendant of their oppressor Aurangzeb.

The revolt was put down only with great difficulty after a year of hard fighting, and with the help of Royal British troops rushed in from abroad. The British suppression of the revolt was fully as violent and barbaric as the Indian sepoys' inauguration of it had been. Many Indians were hanged for no reason other than the fact that they looked as though they might have been hostile; some Indians were even shot from the mouths of cannons.[8] It is no wonder that the mutiny left an aftermath of racial bitterness and suspicion on both sides that was never completely forgotten.

When the revolt had finally been put down, the British Government decided to take over the Company's empire once and for all. In 1858, Queen Victoria issued a proclamation to that effect and promised that there would be no more annexations of princely territory. This promise was not broken, and the map of India remained unchanged from 1858 until after independence. The various provinces and territories of British India occupied about three-fifths of the total area; 562 native states, scattered irregularly over the subcontinent, occupied the remainder. The states ranged in size from Hyderabad, as large as France, to tiny states of only a few hundred acres each.

Although annexation ceased, the Crown gradually asserted rights over the princely states far greater than those the Company had exercised. A system of overlordship or "paramountcy" was worked out, and in many cases this went far beyond the rights the states had specifically yielded in their treaties with the Company. The British government of India not only controlled the foreign affairs of the states and their relations with one another, but also asserted the right to superintend their internal affairs as well, deposing several native rulers for reasons of bad government, and choosing new princely successors. The claim of overlordship was made explicit by the Act of Parliament of 1876, which declared Queen Victoria the Empress of India and suzerain of the Indian princely states, as well as of British India. The completeness of British control over the princes is illustrated by the fact that Lord Curzon, in the early twentieth century, forbade the princes to take trips outside India without his permission. Yet, despite the assertions of paramountcy, the princes remained loyal, content with the guarantee of their thrones. When the nationalist movement arose in the late nineteenth century, it drew support not from them, but from the Westernized, middle-class intellectuals who had received an English-type education.

The Administrative Machine

The transfer of power from the Company to the Crown was smooth, but it brought significant changes. A highly efficient, impersonal bureaucratic machine was organized. Until the gingerly introduction of partial parliamentary self-government in the twentieth century, British rule in India was fully as autocratic as any to which the Indians had been accustomed in the past. Administration, justice, and lawmaking alike centered in the hands of the all-powerful Governor-General, now given the additional title of Viceroy. Although he governed with the help of executive and legislative councils, these were appointive and consisted largely of British officials. The Viceroy was responsible only to a member of the British cabinet, the Secretary of State for India, and to Parliament, which took little interest in India for some time after 1858.

The chief posts in government service were filled by members of an elite corps, the Indian Civil Service (ICS), which grew to be probably the most efficient civil service in the world, with a tradition of proud integrity and of selfless dedication to carrying the "white man's burden." The ICS was recruited in England by open competitive examination and remained almost entirely British in composition during the nineteenth century. As late as 1935, only one-third of its members were Indian. British authorities tended to believe that the participation of Indians in government would benefit the bulk of the people far less than would efficient government, which seemed to them axiomatically to require direction by British personnel. Although, theoretically, Indians could take the competitive examinations, it was made extremely difficult for them to do so.

The social distance between the British and the Indians greatly increased after the mutiny. This was partly a result of the strong racial hostility the mutiny itself aroused. It was also caused by the arrival of increasing numbers of British wives after the opening of the Suez Canal in 1869, which greatly shortened the travel time from England to India. Having little in common with Indian women, who were still largely uneducated and unable to speak English, the English wives formed exclusive little English social groups wherever they were posted. (Perhaps another reason was to divert or shield their men from the lures of Indian women.) Social contacts between Britishers and Indians became rare. The British attitude toward things Indian changed from disapproval to contempt. Descriptions like "irrational," "superstitious," "barbaric," and "inferior" filled the letters that went home to England. The superiority complex grew, and so did rudeness of bearing. British life centered around clubs open to any European, but closed to any Indian no matter how distinguished. When Westerners become critical of the Indian caste system, it is worth remembering that the British themselves fell into the trap of acting like a separate and superior caste within that system.

In his *Discovery of India* (written in 1943), Nehru recorded how humiliating he had found it always to see posted in railway carriages, in station waiting rooms, on park benches, and in other places the exasperating sign "For Europeans Only." He added:

> The idea of a master race is inherent in imperialism. There was no subterfuge about it; it was proclaimed in unambiguous language by those in authority. More powerful than words was the practice that accompanied them, and generation after generation, and year after year, India as a nation and Indians as individuals were subjected to insult, humiliation, and contemptuous treatment. . . . The memory of it hurts, and what hurts still more is the fact that we submitted for so long to this degradation.[9]

Because of the good grace with which England finally relinquished power, Indians today harbor little rancor against their former rulers. But the reactions of Indians to the old humiliations explain the vigor with which India has pressed the cause of colonial countries in the United Nations. Anticolonialism is, indeed, one of the strongest political passions in India. The West was both surprised and shocked when peace-loving India invaded the Portuguese territory of Goa on the western coast of India in December, 1961, but so compelling were the emotions associated with colonialism that many Indians could not see this as an act of aggression. They insisted that Goa was Indian territory which quite naturally had to be liberated from the tyranny of a colonial power.

The Impact of British Rule

Except for the limited autonomy of the princes, British rule brought complete unification to India—and for the first time. On the other hand, the British (through policies to be discussed in the next chapter) perhaps intensified the rivalries between Hindus and Muslims, thus paving the way for the partition of 1947. British rule gave India a common language for the educated minority, and a common cause—opposition to foreign rule. It introduced the concept of equality, especially before the law; previously, punishment had varied according to a man's class, caste, and status. It made profound changes in governmental forms, in political ideas, and in the economic and educational systems of the country.

Many Indians believe that the root cause of India's present poverty is the fact that the British drained much wealth out of the country and used the Indian economy for British, rather than Indian, purposes. British writers, on the other hand, argue that the "drain" was more than counterbalanced by the positive benefits of British rule—that the law and order established by the British saved India more wealth than the entire "drain." They point to a number of other concrete improvements: the best railroad system in Asia, a telegraph system, roads, a partially effective famine-relief system, public-health measures, and an extensive system of irrigation. By the time of independence, India had more irrigated land than any other country in the world. Except for the railways, however, these benefits were paid for entirely by the Indian taxpayers themselves. Even the railways, though built mostly by private companies, received subsidies out of Indian governmental revenues. Indian taxpayers also had to pay for the upkeep of the Indian army, thus shouldering the entire cost of their own subjugation, and also had to bear the cost of various military expeditions outside India in which the Indian army participated.

Leaving aside the old issue of praise or blame, it is clear that profound changes in the very shape of the economy took place during the period of British rule—changes that are of continuing significance today. Vast forests were cut down, and the amount of land under cultivation greatly increased. This led to a fourfold increase in agricultural production, but also intensified the tragic problem of soil erosion. The death rate was lowered through efficient attacks on cholera, smallpox, and other major epidemics —resulting in a great increase in population. On balance, there seems to have been little, if any, net rise in the general standard of living during the period of British rule. Some economic historians hold that there was an actual decline. Whereas seventeenth-century India had been far wealthier than England, the relative positions were sharply reversed by the end of the nineteenth century. While the cottage industries of eighteenth-century England and other Western countries were rapidly transformed into mechanized factory industries in the early nineteenth century, a similar transformation could not occur in India under British rule. The cottage industries of India suffered from the competition of machine-made British goods and from the declining fortunes of their many former patrons—Mughul Emperors, local governors, and others. This was especially true of the weavers, whose inherited skills had placed India in the forefront of the textile nations of the world, but who were ruined after 1815 when British textile goods began flooding the Indian market. Although the British textile industry had earlier protected itself by tariff from Indian textile exports, the Indian textile industry was not allowed tariff protection until 1921.

The trend toward a commercial economy stimulated by British rule created a revolution in almost every aspect of Indian life. Previously, the taxes paid by landowners had usually depended on the condition of the harvest, often consisting of a stated percentage of the actual crop. In the areas where they collected the revenue directly, the British made the taxes payable in cash, regardless of whether the harvest was good or bad. Now when a landowner failed to pay, he found himself before an implacably impersonal law court which might decree the forfeiture of his entire holding. One year of bad crops could ruin him. As money transactions in the villages increased, they began to undermine the old stable interrelationships between castes, based on hereditary, almost permanent arrangements for the exchange of goods and services. The transition to a money economy, not yet complete, is still changing intercaste relationships progressively.

Throughout the nineteenth century, a new commercial class was growing up around the three great ports where British power was centered. This resulted in a shift of the Indian economy from the inland to the seaboard. The new class worked closely with the

Company in the early trading days and profited greatly by the expansion of the demand for the goods the Company created. In this way were founded the fortunes of the Indian capitalists who later in the nineteenth century joined with British enterprise and capital in laying the small foundations of an Indian industrial revolution. In the second half of the nineteenth century, textile factories, jute factories, tea and indigo plantations, shipping, and banking developed increasingly, using Western technical skills and business enterprise. With these changes went the growth of great new cities with appalling slums.

More profound than the impact of such economic changes was the effect of modern Western education upon India. Previously, the Brahmans had the exclusive right to study the Sanskrit sacred texts. The sons of traders had access to limited practical schooling, including reading, writing, and arithmetic. For women and the lower castes, there was no education at all. (But it must be remembered that even in the West the idea of education for all classes alike did not gain acceptance until the late nineteenth or early twentieth century.) The new schools and colleges started in India in the nineteenth century by the government, by missionaries, and by private enterprise were sufficient to educate only a tiny minority of the population. But to this minority they brought ideas that challenged many basic Indian assumptions. Western thought led to the reform movement within Hinduism (to be considered in a subsequent chapter). Furthermore, Indians educated in Western-type schools absorbed the new ideas of nationalism, democracy, and socialism. They also learned to condemn British imperialism with quotations from British writers.

6 • TOWARD INDEPENDENCE—AND AFTER

Unlike the African nations, which attained independence with only brief prior training in the use of representative institutions, India's preparation for independence was long and gradual. In 1862, the Viceroy appointed three Indians to his legislative council, the first Indians to be associated with the lawmaking process during the British period. But they were in the minority, and the Viceroy, in any case, had veto power over the council's decisions. Gradually, more Indians were added to both the central and the provincial legislative councils. In 1892, various Indian groups—religious communities, municipalities, universities, and chambers of commerce—were invited to recommend the names of Indians for such appointments, and their recommendations were accepted. In this indirect way, the first Indian elections occurred.

Before the achievement of full independence in 1947, the three chief steps toward self-government were taken in the years 1909, 1919, and 1935, when the British Parliament enacted new laws relating to the Government of India. (The British actually gave the Indians far more experience in self-rule prior to independence than the French, the Dutch, the Belgians, and the Portuguese gave their colonies. This is undoubtedly one reason for the stability of India since independence.)

The Gradual Constitutional Steps

The Morley-Minto Reforms of 1909 for the first time gave Indians a majority in the provincial legislative councils (though not in the central legislative council). It accorded full recognition to the principle of election, but the constituencies were still limited to particular kinds of groups. However, the legislatures were given no real responsibilities, and remained purely advisory. The ultimate power, even in law-making, was retained by the Viceroy. The Secretary of State for India, Lord Morley, who was responsible for these reforms, specifically indicated that he did not regard them as milestones toward parliamentary government: "If it could be said that this chapter of reforms led directly or necessarily to the establishment of a parliamentary system in India, I for one would have nothing at all to do with it."[1]

Eight years later, a new Secretary of State for India, Samuel Montagu, took a radically different view, announcing that the official British policy in regard to India would be "the gradual development of self-governing institutions with a view to the progressive realization of responsible government as an integral part of the British Empire." Following this announcement, the Government of India Act of 1919, known as the Montagu-Chelmsford Reforms, increased the degree of self-government in the provinces through a dual system of government known as "dyarchy." The provincial legislatures, in which Indians were in the majority, were given the right to enact laws in certain areas. The list included education, agriculture, and health, but did not include finances, taxation, or the police, which remained under the control of British officials. "Safeguards" by which the governors or the Viceroy could block any undesirable action by the Indian legislators were retained. The Act extended the franchise to more than 5 million voters, whereas only 33,000 had been eligible in previous elections.[2] This was still, of course, a small minority of the adult population.

A far greater step toward self-government was the Government of India Act of 1935, which extended the franchise to 35 million voters, while retaining a property qualification.[3] It gave the provincial legislatures control over *all* legislative matters in the provinces, thus ending the system of dyarchy, or dual rule. It provided also for responsible government at the Centre, except that defense and foreign affairs were to be left in the hands of the Viceroy. Both British India and the princely states were to be represented in the central legislature. This portion of the Act was to come into effect, however, only when half of the ruling princes agreed, and their agreement was never secured. Indeed, if the federation contemplated in the Act of 1935 had come into effect, it would have been a strange one—a federation joining together an increasingly democratic British India with the autocratic princely states.

Nationalism Before Gandhi

These intermittent progressive steps toward independence were taken under the constant prodding of an increasingly vocal and active independence movement. The roots of this movement go back to the pioneering ideas of an outstanding early-nineteenth-century religious and social reformer, Rammohun Roy (1772–1833), who has been called the "father of Indian nationalism." By his lifelong effort to synthesize the best of Indian traditions and the best that the West had to offer, Rammohun Roy created the beginnings of a new intellectual climate which grew in importance as time passed. Perhaps he was the father of Indian modernism even more than of Indian nationalism.

Toward the end of the nineteenth century, the chief organ for the expression of Indian public opinion became the Indian National Congress, called together for the first time in 1885. Its first meeting, held in Bombay, was attended by only seventy delegates. Thereafter, it adopted the custom of meeting annually, and the attendance rapidly increased. Until 1916, it remained under the control of moderates who pressed for the reform of British rule rather than its elimination. The Congress repeatedly passed petitions asking for wider employment of Indians in the public services, civil-service examinations to be held simultaneously in India and England, the spread of education, the reduction of military expenditures, and the development of self-government by means of legislative councils in the central as well as in the provincial governments.

Partly outside the Congress and partly within it, there developed a new extremist movement, impatient with the politeness of the moderates. The extremists urged incessant agitation and, if necessary, the use of physical force and terrorism.

The first great leader of the extremists was Bal Gangadhar Tilak (1856–1920), a Maharashtrian Brahman from Poona in the

Western Ghats (the area from which Shivaji had harassed the Mughul armies two centuries before). Tilak brought to the extremist cause the fire of religious revivalism. He organized great politico-religious festivals to honor the elephant-headed deity, Ganesh, and other festivals to honor the militant Shivaji. Like Gandhi later, Tilak believed in noncooperation with British rule. Unlike Gandhi, he did not frown on violence. In the newspapers he founded, he exhorted direct action. Accused and found guilty of having instigated the murder of certain British officials, he was imprisoned from 1908 to 1914.

The leader of the moderates during this period was Gopala Krishna Gokhale (1866–1915), whom Gandhi was to regard as his guru (teacher)—a dedicated man whose profound concern for social welfare left a clear imprint on the Congress movement and helps to explain the welfare-state orientation of the government of independent India.

In the early years of the twentieth century, the extremist movement that Tilak had started in western India flamed up also in Bengal, in eastern India. Lord Curzon, Viceroy from 1899 to 1905, had antagonized the Bengalis by partitioning Bengal. This action may have been in the interest of administrative efficiency, but as the nationalists saw it, the real purpose was to create a rift among Bengalis, decrease their influence, and stifle the intellectual renaissance that had flowered in Bengal throughout the nineteenth century.

In 1905, Japan's defeat of Russia in the Russo-Japanese War created a new surge of confidence among Indians that Asians need not be subject to Europeans. Between 1906 and 1909, there was much agitation, violence, and terrorism. The government responded to this in 1909 with the Morley-Minto Reforms and in 1911 by repealing the partition of Bengal, thus illustrating to the Indians that political terrorism could force the British to retreat. In 1915, Tilak, out of prison, was once again active. The extremists secured control of the Indian Congress movement the following year, and adopted the principle of home rule advocated by Tilak and by the British theosophist Mrs. Annie Besant, a strong admirer of Hinduism and a nationalist leader in her own right.

Again, in 1919, the British sought to appease the mounting nationalist feeling—this time with the Montagu-Chelmsford Reforms. But at the same time that this limited change in constitutional government was being worked out, new laws restricting civil liberties were being adopted. These seemed necessary because the police had encountered increasing difficulty in protecting life and property in the face of terrorist movements. Then, in March, 1919, there occurred an event almost as pivotal in Indo-British relations as the revolt (or "mutiny") of 1857. At Amritsar, in the Punjab, a British general ordered his men to fire without warning on an unarmed crowd, killing 379 Indians and wounding at least 1,200. This massacre profoundly shocked many Indians who had not previously taken an interest in politics. It led a number of distinguished moderates to revise their beliefs, and it brought to the forefront a new leader, Mohandas K. Gandhi, (known as the Mahatma or Great Soul).

Gandhi—The Man and the Leader

Gandhi completely transformed the national movement in at least three ways. First, he introduced highly successful techniques of nonviolent noncooperation and civil disobedience. It is worth remembering, however, that he himself did not regard nonviolence merely as a technique, as did many of his followers, but as a fundamental principle to be applied to every aspect of life.

Secondly, he transformed Indian nationalism from a small movement led by the Western-educated elite into a mass movement supported by the uneducated millions. Although he himself was Western-educated, had even spent three years in London as a student, and had laboriously aped British manners while young, he later progressively discarded Western borrowings and found new truth for himself in the best of the old Hindu tradition. Retaining only the most meager possessions, wearing nothing but a loincloth (made from yarn spun with his own hands), going often on foot from village to village, meditating and fasting, he was recognized by the simplest villagers as a man to be revered—a man different from the ordinary, less socially minded Hindu holy man, but certainly springing from the very soil of India. Because the villagers could follow him without question, Gandhi's lieutenants were able to effect an efficient organizational network down to the village level.

Thirdly, Gandhi brought into the nationalist movement the concept of social justice, as well as other ideals. He made it clear that it would not be enough to attain freedom from British rule. The relation of rich man to poor man within India must change also. The rich man must think of himself as his brother's keeper, and must use his wealth as a trust for the benefit of the poor. Within the nationalist movement, there were both conservatives and radicals who did not agree with this doctrine of the trusteeship of wealth. Many conservatives preferred to regard what they owned as strictly their own. The radicals regarded his paternalistic approach to social justice as reactionary in comparison with the Marxian approach which was gaining currency. Yet, because of Gandhi, conservatives thereafter had to pay at least lip service to social justice, and radicals had to confront an anti-Marxian social idealism which today still retains strength within the nation.

Gandhi was born in 1869 in western India, in one of the many tiny princely states that are now part of Gujarat—an area relatively untouched by Westernizing influences, where the petty princes ruled their tiny states with absolutism. Gandhi's father was the diwan (chief administrative officer) of two such princely states—first Porbunder, then Rajkot. These positions of dignity were somewhat above the family's status as determined by caste. The Gandhis belonged to a caste of grocers and moneylenders (the word Gandhi means grocer), and as such they fell within the third of the four main orders into which Hindu society is divided. Compared with the other leaders of the Indian National Congress with whom he was to work so closely, Gandhi was a low-caste man, though still far above the untouchables whose position he sought to improve.

Gandhi's mother was a devout, simple, selfless woman, though almost illiterate and in many ways superstitious. "Her life was an endless chain of fasts and vows."[4] Gandhi wrote in his autobiography that she was a major influence in his life and gave him his first understanding of love and sacrifice. To his own boyish and adolescent misdeeds, Gandhi reacted with intense moral seriousness. When he conspired with some friends secretly to eat meat and smoke, and when he told a lie, he suffered agonies of guilt that forced him into resolutions he did not break. Apart from this moral seriousness, Gandhi may have seemed like an unpromising boy. He was inarticulate, diffident, passive.[5]

When he was thirteen, he was married to a girl about his own age in an ordinary arranged marriage. He fell passionately in love with his child-bride and enjoyed the sexual relationship with her with an intensity that made him feel guilty. He tried to dominate his wife, but she had a determined will of her own and quietly resisted him. He later said that she "cured me of my stupidity in thinking I was born to rule over her, and in the end she became my teacher in nonviolence."[6] Thus the strength of his own guilt feelings seems very early to have given him a deep sense of the power of love to provoke guilt and the power of guilt to change the heart. It was upon these twin ideas that he later built his program of nonviolence.

Because he was the only boy in the family who finished school, it was decided that he should pursue his studies further. His father had died by then, and the family fortunes were low, but his brother found funds to send him to England. A trip across the ocean was still an unorthodox, even an irreligious venture for strict Hindus. His mother gave her consent only after he had taken a vow not to touch wine, women, or meat. The governing tribunal of the family's particular Bania caste remained opposed, however, and threatened to outcaste him if he made the trip. Despite this threat, though, he sailed for England in 1888 and studied law in London for three years.

Like many Indian students abroad, he had a lonely, difficult, awkward time. He had left his wife at home; he knew little English; and the meals served by his landladies consisted chiefly of meat. Fortunately, he found a vegetarian restaurant and a group of English people to whom vegetarianism had become a cult. Previously, he had refrained from eating meat only because of his oath to his mother. Now he gained his first concept of vegetarianism as a total discipline of body, mind, and spirit. It was at this time that he began the experiments in diet that were to become an important part of his later life.

It was in England also that he first became interested in religion. A devout Christian introduced him to the Bible, and "the New Testament . . . went straight to my heart."[7] British theosophists talked to him about his own Hindu scripture, the Bhagavad Gita, which he now read for the first time, in Sir Edwin Arnold's English version, *The Song Celestial*. He records that "the book struck me as one of priceless worth."[8]

When he went back to India after passing his law examinations, one section of his caste continued to treat him as an outcaste because of his overseas trip. Another section lifted the ban against him only after he had made a penitential pilgrimage. His work did not go well, and he had trouble finding clients. When one client came to him, it was only a $10 case, which he bungled badly: He became tongue-tied in court, could not collect his thoughts, and had to refund the $10 fee, which had been paid in advance.[9] His prospects were dim. However, through a family friend, he was offered a year's work in South Africa at a modest fee. It seemed the only escape from a hopeless situation.

It was in South Africa that Gandhi found his purpose in life, and with it the self-confidence he had previously lacked. The purpose came to him as a result of his first experience with racial discrimination. Because he was not white, he was ordered out of a first-class railway compartment for which he had a ticket, commanded to move into third-class instead, and forcibly removed to a station platform when he refused to move voluntarily. This and other experiences of discrimination shocked him profoundly. He was still more shocked when he discovered that other Indians in South Africa took such discriminations for granted.

Although he began organizing Indians in South Africa to fight discrimination as soon as he encountered it in 1896, he did not evolve his characteristic method of warfare, which he termed *satyagraha*, until ten years later. *Satya* means truth, which Gandhi regarded as the equivalent of love; *agraha* means firmness or force. He translated the term freely as "soul-force." His idea was that an opponent could be won over more surely by love, patience, and sympathy than by force—by conversion rather than by conquest. He believed that one could accomplish such a conversion only if one succeeded in banishing fear and hatred from one's own heart, ceased to think of the opponent as an enemy, and treated him courteously, patiently, and considerately even if he threatened not only one's liberty and possessions but also one's very life. Clearly, nonviolent noncooperation carried out in this spirit is the very antithesis of passive resistance. It is an active, determined attempt to change an opponent's attitude and beliefs through love and understanding.

Having evolved his concept of *satyagraha*, Gandhi continued throughout his life to try to develop increasingly the inner strength, selflessness, and self-discipline necessary to carry it out as perfectly as possible. As part of his struggle for self-mastery, he gave up sexual relations when he was thirty-seven, and remained abstinent until his death in 1948. He also gave up the many comforts and luxuries he had attained through the highly profitable legal practice he had developed earlier in Johannesburg. Gradually, he developed habits regarding diet, prayer, periodic silences, and occasional long and difficult fasts that were related to his central idea of *satyagraha*. Always a simple, unassuming man with a gay, kindly, mischievous sense of humor, he became increasingly a radiant, vital, compelling personality—and one of the towering figures in history.

In 1907, the South African Government passed an Asiatic Registration Act which required Indians to be registered and submit to fingerprinting. Gandhi refused to register, and was jailed. General Jan Smuts, then a cabinet member of the Union of South Africa, offered to repeal the Act if Gandhi would use his position of leadership to urge Indians to register voluntarily. He agreed, was released, and carried out his part of the bargain. Thousands of Indians registered, but the law was not repealed. Thereupon, he began organizing his followers for the consistent, methodical breaking of all discriminatory South African laws, including one imposing a special tax on Indian laborers and others restricting their movements. He taught his followers never to resist arrest and never to hit back when beaten.

In 1909, he organized a sort of "cooperative commonwealth"—which he called Tolstoy Farm—where the members of his movement could be trained for nonviolent resistance and the families of imprisoned resisters could be cared for. Life on Tolstoy Farm was simple and austere. Gandhi recognized no caste distinctions and himself performed many kinds of work which in India are customarily reserved only for the lowest castes.

Courting arrest, he led his followers in mass marches across provincial boundary lines in violation of immigration bans—serving several jail sentences for his activities. Finally, in 1914, General Smuts yielded to the pressure of *satyagraha* and secured the repeal of many of the obnoxious laws discriminating against Indians. Gandhi considered his mission in South Africa ended. After a brief trip to England, he returned to India in 1915.

His fame had preceded him, but he did not immediately take part in the independence campaign. As late as 1918, he even helped to recruit soldiers to fight in World War I. After the Amritsar Massacre, Gandhi reversed his position in favor of collaboration with the British and persuaded the convention of the Indian National Congress in 1920 to endorse noncooperation. For seven months, he toured the countryside on a tremendous propaganda journey, urging nonpayment of taxes and boycott of British courts and schools and foreign cloth. University students left their classes by the thousands. Clothing made of imported material was burned in dramatic bonfires. Prominent Congress leaders, including Motilal Nehru (the father of the present Prime Minister), gave up lucrative jobs or careers that had involved cooperating with the British. Some Indians warned that such a campaign could not fail to be inflammatory, leading to violence and a disrespect for law and order, and would be harmful in the long run. This was the conviction of the prominent Muslim Muhammad Ali Jinnah, later the founder of Pakistan. When Gandhi came into prominence, Jinnah left the Congress movement, and was never to return to it.

Civil disobedience led to violence in one small area in 1922. The difficult discipline of nonviolence had not yet been learned. Gandhi suspended the *satyagraha* campaign, and was promptly jailed by the British. There followed a lull in the independence movement. Gandhi seemed discredited. Many of his followers, including Nehru, had been greatly disturbed by his decision to halt a campaign of national significance because of a local incident. Not until 1930 did Gandhi initiate a new civil-disobedience campaign.

Between campaigns and when not in jail, Gandhi lived for the most part in the two *ashrams* (religious centers) he had founded: one at Sarbamati, in Gujarat, outside Ahmedabad; the other at Wardha, in central India, outside Nagpur. During these intervals, Gandhi created for Hinduism a new, modern form while holding fast to ancient principles and scriptures. He also worked out his views on a host of other matters: He stressed that the essence of India was her long-neglected villages and persuaded many of his followers to devote their lives to village uplift. He urged an economic program centering on the promotion of handloom and cottage industries. He developed novel ideas regarding education and urged that children be taught in their own mother tongues rather than English. He explained his convictions on prohibition and diet in relation to soul force. And he constantly argued for a better status for untouchables and for women.

In short, Gandhi was not only a political and religious leader. He was also a vigorous social reformer. Many Indians disagree with certain of his ideas. But much of modern India would be incomprehensible without reference to the profoundly exciting effect of his many-sided idealism. And the manner in which he used fasting and other techniques of nonviolent resistance continues to be emulated, usually successfully, by various leaders—in certain cases to achieve questionable purposes.

Toward Further Constitutional Reforms

In 1927, the British Government sent out to India the Simon Commission to consider further constitutional changes for India. The report of this Commission, finally released in 1929, recommended increased responsibility for the elected Indian legislatures in the provinces and eventual dominion status for India. It also suggested the holding of a roundtable conference to include Indians from both British India and the princely states.

Because the British Government had appointed no Indians to the Simon Commission, the Indian National Congress decided to boycott it. Feeling mounted. When it turned out that the Commission's report fell short of Congress demands, the Congress issued a declaration of independence and set January 26, 1930, as Independence Day. It was on the twentieth anniversary of this declaration that the Constitution of free India came into effect. The date is now celebrated annually as Republic Day, the Indian equivalent of the American Fourth of July.

Seeking a form of demonstration that would dramatize Indian discontent nonviolently, Gandhi announced that he would make salt on the seashore in defiance of the law specifying salt production as a government monopoly. With a band of followers that kept increasing along the way, he walked 241 miles in 24 days. The salt march was followed by a wide-scale and effective civil-disobedience movement. In less than a year, 60,000 persons were imprisoned.[10]

Following the recommendation of the Simon Commission, the British Government invited representative Indians to a Roundtable Conference. Held in London in November, 1930, it was boycotted by the Congress. Since it was useless to negotiate in the absence of any representative from the leading nationalist group, a compromise with Gandhi was finally made. The government withdrew its repressive ordinances and released political prisoners, while Gandhi agreed to go to a second session of the Roundtable Conference in 1931. When he returned to India, he found that repressive ordinances were still being enforced, and he resumed civil disobedience, as did tens of thousands of others. Disobedience on such a scale led increasing numbers of people in Great Britain to favor concessions to nationalist opinion.

The Government of India Act of 1935 gave complete autonomy to the provinces and provided ultimately for a federal structure at the Centre with dominion status for the country. Should the Congress continue noncooperation with anything British, including this new Act? Or should it contest the elections of 1937, held in accordance with the Act? The issue was controversial, but the Congress decided to contest the elections, and won majorities in seven out of the eleven provinces of British India, while Muslim ministries or coalition governments were formed in the others. The Indian ministries functioned efficiently, but they resigned at the outbreak of World War II. The two years of experience in full governmental responsibility gained thereby was a useful background for the larger problems that lay ahead after independence.

At the outbreak of the war, the Congress protested that the

British Government had no right to involve India in it without her consent, and refused to cooperate with the war effort unless granted self-government. The British Government offered to give Indians greater control over the central government of India immediately and promised a new constitution after the war; but it would not agree to a total transfer of power while the war lasted. In 1942, Gandhi persuaded the Congress to break off negotiations with the British and embark on a concerted "quit India" movement. Civil disobedience was widespread, and all the Congress leaders were jailed.

After the war, when the British Government tried to draw up the promised constitution for an independent India, it proved impossible to reconcile by agreement the conflicting demands of the Indian National Congress, the princes, and the Muslim League, which claimed to represent the entire Muslim minority.

Muslims formed one-fourth of the total population of the Indian subcontinent at that time. The antagonism between Hindus and Muslims was not the result merely of religious differences; educational differences and economic rivalries had led to a contest for political power. Hindu-Muslim antagonism has such continuing importance on the subcontinent of India, both as an internal problem and as a matter of international relations between India and Pakistan that it is worth reviewing its progressive development during the period of British rule.

Development of Hindu-Muslim Tensions

When the British occupied Bengal and subsequently other areas, most of the rulers thus displaced were Muslims. The Muslim aristocracy found themselves in a bad plight. As the recently defeated enemy, they were often excluded from government service. As members of a military or governmental elite, they were above most of the occupations now opened to them. Regarding instruction in the Koran as essential, they failed to take advantage of the new Western-type education, as had the upper classes of Hindus. While prosperous traders, businessmen, contractors, and others were emerging among the Hindus, the Muslim aristocracy remained aloof on whatever remaining land they might possess. In the villages, the poorer Muslims lived much the same type of life as did Hindu peasants or artisans, but usually their houses were in a separate area or hamlet. Although they had an accepted place in the organic economic life of the village, they were regarded as a separate community.

In the last quarter of the nineteenth century, British policy began to come to the aid of the Muslims. In 1875, with British help and backing, a Muslim leader, Sir Syed Ahmed Khan, founded a new type of school for upper-class Muslim boys at Aligarh, in what is now Uttar Pradesh. (This school later became a university.) Here Muslim boys not only were given the religious instruction regarded as essential, but were taught Western-type secular subjects as well. Aligarh became the center for a new, more dynamic Muslim approach to the world around them. But it was not easy for Indian Muslims, having taken to modern education so late, to catch up with the Hindus either in education or in business or government jobs. Because they lagged financially and educationally, they were all the more fearful of Hindu domination when the idea of representative government first was broached. Sir Syed Ahmed Khan specifically opposed constitutional changes in the direction of self-government.

In 1906, a group of Muslims of the Aligarh school, with British encouragement, drew up a petition which they presented to the Viceroy, asking for special consideration of their position as a minority group, for employment of a due proportion of Muslims in government service, and for the reservation of special seats for Muslims in the legislatures. The Viceroy, in reply, promised that Muslim interests would be safeguarded. In accordance with his promise, the Act of 1909 set up a system of separate electorates for Muslims by which Muslim voters could choose representatives to seats specially reserved for Muslim candidates—an arrangement strongly opposed by the Indian National Congress (except in 1916 and briefly thereafter) and regarded by many Indians today as the first significant step in a new British policy of "divide and rule."

This Aligarh emphasis on special and different treatment for Muslims became the basis of the Muslim League, which met for the first time in 1906. In contrast to this approach, there always remained some Muslim leaders who preferred to work within the

Indian National Congress, instead of within a political organization with a religious orientation.

In return for British support of its position, the Muslim League affirmed its loyalty to the British Crown—an affirmation that, of course, seemed to the Indian National Congress to betray the nationalist cause. In showing special favors to Muslims, did British officials seek deliberately to sow discord between them and the Hindus? There is evidence that at least some British officials explicitly believed in the policy of "divide and rule" as a way of perpetuating British control of India. They did not foresee, however, that it would lead to the partition of the subcontinent, since they believed that British rule would last indefinitely.

At the time of World War I, Muslims in India became temporarily less pro-British and more cooperative with Hindus. The reasons for this change stemmed from British policy toward Turkey. The Caliph at Constantinople was not only a temporal ruler, but he was also the religious head of much of Islam. Many Muslims in India therefore became strongly anti-British when Britain declared war against Turkey in 1914. By 1916, the Muslim League and the Indian National Congress had drawn closer together. In that year, they reached an agreement covering even the controversial reservation of seats in the legislature. Together, they asked that India be made a self-governing dominion. At the end of the war, when there were indications that Turkey would be still further dismembered, Muslim dismay increased. With Gandhi presiding, Muslims and Hindus joined in a large protest meeting in 1919, the Khilafat Conference.

But when the Caliph was deposed by the Young Turks in 1922, his cause collapsed. Tension between Hindus and Muslims in India reappeared, and riots broke out. Many Muslims swung back to their old reliance on British protection, especially after 1928, when the Indian National Congress explicitly repudiated its earlier support of separate electorates for Muslims. Yet, in the important elections of 1937—the first to be held under the 1935 Constitution, which granted self-government in the provinces—the Muslim League polled only a fraction of the seats even in the provinces where Muslims were in the majority. At that time, most Muslims still considered it wisest to work with the Indian National Congress, which had continued to grow in strength under the leadership of Gandhi.

The phenomenal growth of the Muslim League began immediately after these elections. Muhammad Ali Jinnah, head of the Muslim League, and later the first Governor-General of Pakistan, asked that at least some ministerial posts in the new provincial government be allocated to members of the Muslim League. The Indian National Congress, victorious in the elections, saw no reason to grant his request. Since its membership included people of all the religions of the subcontinent and since it had even had Muslim and Christian presidents, it regarded itself as a secular organization. It gave certain ministerial posts to Muslims, but only to Muslims who were members of the Congress movement. Jinnah then charged that the Congress was attempting deliberately to break the Muslim League and would never share power with any Muslim who was not subservient to Congress and to Hindu interests. He embarked on a large and successful campaign for increasing the membership of the League.

Jinnah was a brilliant, prosperous, Westernized barrister active in the Congress movement until the advent of Gandhi. Tense, inflexible, complex, cold in his personal relations, precise, formal, and aristocratic, he was clearly irritated by Gandhi's personality and methods. Through his monocle, he looked with distaste at the friendly, informal, middle-class little man in a loin cloth who mixed religion with politics and dangerously undermined orderly governmental processes by his emotion-based civil-disobedience campaigns. Before one Muslim audience after another, Jinnah kept repeating that Hindus and Muslims were two separate nations, that if the British should give up India, rule would pass to the Hindus, who would keep the Muslims forever in subjection. Eloquently, he preyed on Muslim fears. Not only religious freedom was at stake, but also jobs and opportunities of all kinds. However real his own apprehensions may have been, they seem to have been reinforced both by his dislike of Gandhi and by his personal ambition and drive to assert power.

By 1940, he had greatly enlarged the Muslim League and had persuaded it to adopt a resolution in favor of carving out of India a new nation, Pakistan ("Land of the Pure"). Just what territory the new nation should or would include was far from clear. Various Muslims worked out alternative plans. The general idea was to incorporate into it the areas where Muslims were in the majority. But since these areas were far apart—in the east and in the extreme northwest—some believed there should be two new Muslim nations. Others, including Jinnah, hoped to join the two Muslim areas by a corridor across north India. There were further complications. Taken as a whole, both the rich wheat-growing province of Punjab in the northwest and the rice- and jute-growing province of Bengal to the east contained Muslim majorities. But within each there were large areas where Hindus were in the majority. Should Pakistan claim these provinces as a whole, or only their Muslim-predominated portions? Jinnah aimed to get them in their entirety. But the Pakistan he finally secured—which he called "moth-eaten"—included far less territory than he had hoped.

Partition and Violence

At the end of World War II, the British Labour Party, which came into power in 1945, decided to fulfill the wartime promise to transfer power to a responsible Indian government. But what Indian government could it design that would be acceptable to both the Congress and the Muslim League? This was the question. At first, the British Government tried to avoid the partition of India. In 1946, it sent out a Cabinet Mission which designed a very loose three-tier federation, in an attempt to retain unity yet give the Muslim-majority areas sufficient autonomy to satisfy them.

The Viceroy, Lord Wavell, then attempted to form a joint Congress-League government at the Centre on the basis of this plan, but antagonism had risen to such a point that each party tried to block the other within the government. Charges and countercharges of bad faith between the Congress and the League multiplied. Tension mounted. The Muslim League selected August 16, 1945, as "direct-action day." Muslim parades, mass meetings, and speeches on that day led to bloodshed and violence between the two religious communities. Within five days, nearly

5,000 persons were killed in Calcutta alone.[11] Other serious outbreaks occurred in East Bengal, Bihar, and the Punjab. To appeal for a return to reason, Gandhi undertook a long walking trip through the difficult, waterlogged back-country regions of East Bengal. Where he went, he was effective in quieting communal tensions. But he could not go everywhere. In the Punjab, where he did not go, communal passions flamed. Bands of armed Hindus, Muslims, and Sikhs roamed the countryside.

As killings grew increasingly numerous, the British Government decided to hasten the slow march toward self-government. It sent a new Viceroy to Delhi in March, 1947, Lord Louis Mountbatten, with instructions to arrange the transfer of power to a single Indian government by June, 1948. The structure of that government was to be determined by agreement. Lord Mountbatten found the situation in India so explosive that within six weeks after his arrival, he advanced the date for independence to August, 1947. Because he could not secure agreement between the Muslim League and the Indian National Congress, he recommended partition and the creation of Pakistan. Under the complex self-determination formula that was part of his proposal, when partition did come, the important states of Bengal and Punjab themselves were partitioned between the two new nations.

Was the partition of India a mistake or was it necessary? Could it have been avoided if Mountbatten had not been so precipitous in the formulation of his plan? These are big questions which historians will doubtless argue for many years to come. Certainly the partition of the subcontinent was no small matter. It was to have lasting and troublesome implications for the defense of South Asia.

Strong opposition to partition was voiced both within Congress and by conservative Hindu groups, such as the Hindu Mahasabha, which believed that India must remain indivisible. Nehru, who had been made Prime Minister of the provisional government of India in 1946, reluctantly agreed to partition, believing it to be preferable to the civil war into which the country was rapidly drifting. On August 15, 1947, partitioned India attained its independence. Gandhi refused to attend the celebrations, saying: "Why all this rejoicing? I see only rivers of blood."[12]

The Punjab was in anarchy. Muslims slaughtered Hindus and Sikhs. Hindus and Sikhs slaughtered Muslims. Panic mounted. Frightened minorities on both sides of the new boundary that bisected the Punjab placed all their belongings in their bullock carts and started for the frontier. Hindus and Sikhs fled to India. Muslims fled to Pakistan. Soon the roads were clogged with bullock carts. Many people were massacred along the way. According to some estimates, at least half a million persons lost their lives. These terrible killings remain deep in the memory of every Indian; the possibility of their recurrence is a continuing fear.

Seeking to restore Hindu-Muslim harmony, Gandhi began still another fast unto death. As his frail and aged body began to fail under the strain, a hundred respected leaders of various religious groups promised in writing to do their best to restore harmony and "protect the life, property, and faith" of Muslims. Relying on these assurances, Gandhi ended his fast. But the religious passions that had been aroused were greater than these leaders could control. Many Hindus were incensed that Gandhi was tolerant of Muslims, that he read verses from the Koran at his prayer meetings, and that he had demanded that India pay over to the new nation of Pakistan a share of the assets of undivided India, as provided under the partition plan. Certain members of the militant extremist Hindu organization known as the Rashtriya Swayamasevak Sangh (RSS) began plotting to assassinate Gandhi. One of them hurled a homemade bomb at the Mahatma during his evening prayer meeting only a few days after his fast had ended. It fell short of the mark. Ten days later, on January 30, 1948, again at a prayer meeting, N. V. Godse, a fanatical high-caste Hindu from Maharashtra, bowed down before the Mahatma, then blocked his path to the prayer platform and fired three pistol shots straight into Gandhi's chest. Thus the man who had staunchly opposed violence for almost half a century died by violence. To millions, he was both the father of Indian independence and an actual incarnation of God.

The shock of Gandhi's martyred death brought some measure of peace between the two religious communities, but it did not halt the two-way migrations, which proved to be the largest in history. The greatest and most bloody migrations occurred in the Punjab immediately after partition. In later years, smaller migrations continued, especially from East Pakistan into eastern India and vice versa. Although exact figures are necessarily unreliable, an almost unbelievable 15 million Hindus, Sikhs, and Muslims are believed to have migrated by 1965. Of this total, India received close to 9 million refugees, while Pakistan received 6 million. Many of them lost all their possessions. Their gradual rehabilitation over the succeeding years has been one of the great achievements of the two new nations.

The Fate of the Autonomous Princes

With the approach of independence, the problem of the relation between the princely states and the rest of India (under direct British rule) seemed almost as insoluble as the problem of Hindu-Muslim antagonism. How could 562 large and small autocracies be joined with a democratic, self-governing India? Yet how could these states—many of them completely surrounded by democratic India—be separated from it? Having guaranteed many of the princes their sovereignties—subject only to British "paramountcy" or overlordship—how could the British Government with a clear conscience transfer its paramount rights to a new government in British India responsible to an Indian legislature? What hope was there of associating the princely states with British India voluntarily, even in a very loose federation where the princes would retain the right to govern as they chose within their own dominions? A federation of this kind had been provided for in the India Act of 1935, but the federal feature of this Act never came into effect because it depended on voluntary action by the princes. As independence neared, the rulers became increasingly fearful of being left at the mercy of the Indian National Congress.

The Mountbatten Plan of June 3, 1947, which laid down the terms for the transfer of power to independent India and Pakistan, stipulated that paramountcy would lapse rather than being transferred. The princes would be free to decide whether to join one of the two new dominions or to remain independent. Just before independence, however, most of the rulers were induced to sign an Instrument of Accession by which they agreed to "accede" to India or to Pakistan, whichever their territory adjoined. This "accession" was to bind them in three matters only—defense, foreign affairs, and communications—and would not in any way commit them in regard to the more difficult issues, such as their future internal form of government or their method of choosing representatives for the federal legislature.

The most important states that had not acceded before August 15, 1947, were the two largest—Hyderabad and Kashmir. Completely surrounded by Indian territory, Hyderabad had a predominantly Hindu population but a Muslim ruler, the Nizam. His attempt to remain independent was forcibly ended when the Indian Army invaded his territory in 1948.

Contiguous to both India and Pakistan, Kashmir had a Hindu Maharajah but a predominantly Muslim population. In the autumn of 1947, tribesmen from Pakistan territory invaded the state. Indians charge that they did so with the connivance of Pakistan. However that may be, the Pakistan Government did nothing to prevent them from passing into Kashmir territory. As they approached Kashmir's capital city, Srinagar, the Maharajah hastily fled and sent word to New Delhi that he would accede to India. Indian troops were flown in to defend Kashmir against both the tribesmen and the Pakistan Army, which had entered the state by the spring of 1948. India referred the Kashmir case to the Security Council of the United Nations, which has continued to hear the conflicting claims of India and Pakistan intermittently ever since. The two new dominions fought a war in Kashmir for over a year until a U.N. commission succeeded in arranging a cease-fire between them in January, 1949. Under the cease-fire agreement, India held about two-thirds of Kashmir, Pakistan the rest. (The later fighting in Kashmir will be discussed in Chapter 16.)

After the rulers of the various princely states had acceded to India on a limited basis, the Indian Government worked progressively for their closer integration into the nation. Although the princes' bargaining power had seemed strong before independence, it proved weak thereafter. The logic of geography, the mounting democratic demands of their subjects, and the veiled threat of economic or military coercion by India counted against them. The

Deputy Prime Minister, Sardar Patel, worked out individual agreements with each state whereby the princes surrendered all their ruling powers and agreed to the dissolution of their states in return for annual allowances or privy purses (usually a certain percentage of the annual revenue of the state in question). The states so taken over were either grouped together, joined with adjacent provinces of former British India, or kept intact as separate units in the federal Indian Union. Thus they were amalgamated into the rest of democratic India, and a problem that had seemed insoluble was worked out smoothly. But these arrangements—which terminated the pomp, pageantry, and political power of princely India—could not, of course, change overnight social conditions and attitudes within the princely states, which remain significantly different from those in the former British provinces.

After the integration of the princely states, the boundaries within the federal Indian Union remained in many places illogical or inconvenient. There were now twenty-seven states in federal India. Their boundaries followed lines that often had no more logic than the fact that British conquest had extended to a certain point and no farther. Partly for this reason, but especially because language considerations had become paramount in Indian politics, state boundaries were redrawn in 1956, largely on the basis of India's regional languages. The twenty-seven states were reduced to fourteen (later increased to sixteen). The large, proud state of Hyderabad was split into four pieces and distributed among its neighbors. This reorganization of the states gave geographical expression to a force, linguistic nationalism, which, if it should grow, could again divide this great land, which has lacked political unity more often than it has enjoyed it.

The Legacy of the Independence Movement

India's history since independence includes its experience with democracy under its Western-type Constitution and its attempts to raise the standard of living, to expand literacy, education, and greater equality of opportunity, to establish an independent position in world affairs, and to defend itself from Chinese incursions. These must be viewed against the background of the significant legacies of the independence movement.

Above all, the long protracted freedom struggle did for India what Bismarck had done in a different way for Germany and Cavour for Italy. It made the many regional differences among Indians seem of minor importance, at least while the struggle lasted, and it laid the basis for a new sense of nationhood. Men of all regions joined in the civil-disobedience movements and courted arrest side by side. Among the many who spent most of their mature lives continuously in and out of jail, there developed such a close emotional bond that India seemed, at least to them, truly one and indivisible. Even caste differences seemed to have lost some of their importance. The high-caste Brahmans of the Congress movement gladly accepted the leadership of the relatively low-caste Gandhi. Up to a point, also, religious differences could be said to have been partially bridged. Many Muslims worked beside Hindus within the Congress. Several leaders of the Congress were Muslims, including the highly respected Maulana Azad, President of the movement during 1946. That certain other Muslims held aloof or followed the quite different approach of Muhammad Ali Jinnah was an annoyance—but it seemed no more than that at first, as indicated by the extreme weakness of the Muslim League in the elections of 1937. The nationalist leaders who had served their prison terms looked forward to a day when all Indians regardless of region, caste, or creed would work together not just against a common enemy, but in the great task of building the single, indivisible new nation, the first united, independent India ever to occupy the subcontinent.

During the years between 1940 and 1947, while Muslim separatism was growing from small beginnings with cancerous speed, many Hindu leaders remained unable to believe that it really existed. They did not consider the terrible operation of partition to be necessary, not believing there to be a real malignancy. Although some Indians have since accepted Pakistan's existence with a degree of grace, others have not. Many still harbor the deep pain of the old surprise that Pakistan ever came into being. At the very moment when a free united India seemed at last almost attainable, a new country appeared out of nowhere to cheat not only Hindus but also the Muslims who had worked with the Congress of the legitimate goal that had been pursued for almost half a century. As the closest neighbor both to the west and to the east, this nation, whose very establishment seemed unnecessary to many Indians, serves as a constant tangible reminder of the divisive forces still existing within truncated India.

Besides contributing to the sense of Indian nationhood and profoundly affecting the Indian attitude toward the very existence of Pakistan, the independence movement greatly stimulated Indian idealism. Under the leadership of Gandhi, the fight for freedom was carried on in an intensely idealistic atmosphere. Prodigious self-discipline and self-sacrifice were required. In the exhilaration and excitement of the struggle, it came to seem possible and natural for Indians always to live like that, without regard to personal gain. Indians, it seemed, were inherently capable of greater selflessness and idealism than other peoples. Obviously, therefore, their nation when free would likewise behave idealistically and do what was intrinsically right, following domestic and foreign policies quite different from those of the older, more wicked nations. Perhaps such an attitude is not an uncommon characteristic of nations still too young to have discovered the realities connected with survival.

In any case, the independence movement at first gave to the very old land of India a certain measure of exuberant, confident new youth and of youthful willingness to experiment, to change, and to tackle seemingly impossible tasks. In the first decade of independence, the Indian Government committed itself to a wide range of economic and social changes: land reform, the abolition of discrimination against the lowest castes, drastic reform of the laws dealing with marriage and women's rights, industrialization and economic development along a wide front.

But by early 1965, it had become clear that economic progress could not be nearly so rapid as had been hoped. Food shortages, rising prices, labor unrest, scarcity of foreign exchange, an alarming population increase—these and other difficulties led to a new mood of discouragement. India no longer seemed young.

But that autumn, the war with Pakistan had the exhilarating effect of a shot in the arm. Observers noted a new sense of unity and national purpose. Quick changes of national mood, not uncommon elsewhere, seem especially pronounced in India.

7 • HINDUISM—THE RELIGION OF THE MAJORITY

POLITICAL OR ECONOMIC TRENDS in the West could easily be studied with scarcely any mention of religion. But this is hardly possible in studying the Indian scene. Religious considerations continue to play a major role in Indian politics, as well as in attitudes toward economic change and social reform. Underneath the surface events, the most significant single factor has been and continues to be the tug of war between the traditional and the modern elements of Indian culture. As the religion of the vast majority, Hinduism is of particular importance in this regard.

Probably no religion can be truly understood except by one of its believers—Hinduism perhaps least of all. Furthermore, the complexities and profundities of Hinduism, its contrasting guises and endless variations, its abundant mythology so full of ethical meaning to Hindus, so baffling to non-Hindus, certainly cannot be treated adequately in a brief chapter. Yet one cannot consider the India of today and tomorrow, the India torn between its own tradition and alien Western influences, without at least attempting to see the world through Hindu eyes. For the underlying suppositions and sets of values of Hinduism have a profound, often subtle, influence in shaping Indian attitudes toward current questions, and the nature of the changes taking place in India cannot be sensed without grasping something of the nature of the tradition with which modernism conflicts.

Quite contrary emotional reactions toward Hinduism are prevalent in the West. While some Westerners have hailed Hinduism as the most spiritual of all religions, others condemn it for its "irrational superstitions," such as the sacredness of the cow and "idol worship." Both types of reaction tend to stand in the way of an understanding of India. Like us, Indians live within a total culture, a total adaptation to life which is complex, many-sided, and constantly changing. To pass value judgments on one point or another—claiming superiority here, admitting inferiority there, blaming Indians for this "failure," praising them for that "success" —is to deflect attention from the essential question: What is the nature of their culture, of their total adaptation?

The Vast Variety of Hinduism

The first and most essential point that Westerners must understand is that Hinduism in no way fits into our concept of what a religion is. Most confusingly, it lacks the kinds of signposts which, by our definition, are the very essence of religion. If we ask what a Hindu must believe, the answer is that a very wide diversity of beliefs is not only tolerated, but regarded as natural and normal. According to their different backgrounds or levels of education or personal inclination, Hindus may hold any of a great variety of beliefs. They may believe in an all-pervading God so formless and omnipotent that he cannot be described. Or those who find such a God too difficult to conceive may believe in one or more personal gods with quite human attributes, who are regarded as manifestations of the absolute. For uneducated villagers, there are always the demons, spirits, and godlings of their particular locality who must be propitiated through various superstitious practices. But even these main differences do not begin to suggest the wide range and the contrasts within Hinduism. Over the centuries, many highly divergent forms of religious thought have evolved, and these continue to exist vigorously today despite what Westerners might regard as impossible contradictions among them. What then is Hinduism? The only possible answer is that it is a wide variety of beliefs held together by an attitude of mutual tolerance and by the characteristically Hindu conviction that all approaches to God are equally valid. There is no institution or authority, no equivalent of a church or a Pope, to decide matters of belief or to select and determine what religious writings should be included in a commonly accepted canon. Although there is a body of literature generally regarded as sacred, some persons give priority to certain writings, while others give priority to other writings which seem to teach quite different lessons. There is no common scripture corresponding to the Christian Bible or the Muslim Koran.

A man is a Hindu not because of any particular religious belief, but because he was born a Hindu, continues to live within the Hindu social framework, and regards himself as generally committed to a "Hindu way of life." Such a way of life is that laid down not only by one or another of the writings regarded as sacred, but perhaps more especially by the rules and customs of his particular caste or subcaste. If a Hindu departs too far from the Hindu way of life, as viewed by his caste, he may be outcasted —a punishment comparable to excommunication. But this punishment is used to enforce certain standards of behavior rather than of belief.

An important characteristic of Hinduism is that the ideas of "higher" and "lower" are deeply embedded within it. There are "higher" and "lower" beliefs, "higher" and "lower" castes, diets, occupations, marriage customs, and attitudes toward women. Hinduism has tended to grade into a hierarchy everything that it has touched.[1] For example, vegetarianism is regarded by many as "higher" than meat eating, early marriage as "higher" than late marriage, clerical work as "higher" than manual labor. A similar preference for a white-collar job is not, of course, unusual in other cultures; but the distaste for manual labor is particularly strong in India.

Thus, while the Hindu tolerance toward every possible form of belief is so broad that many have called Hinduism "undefined," "shapeless,"and "amorphous," it has not traditionally been the tolerance of equality. Those who follow the "higher" forms of Hinduism look upon the many "lower" forms of Hinduism as a father might look upon an underdeveloped child. This underlying assumption of inequality has been challenged by the Western doctrine of equality.

Early Hinduism (often called Brahmanism to distinguish it from later Hinduism) stemmed from the religion of the white Aryans who entered India about 1500 B.C. But it gradually incorporated various elements of the religion of the earlier Indus Valley civilization, such as phallic or fertility worship, worship of a mother god-

white ARYANS — 1500 B.C.

dess, and the sanctity of certain trees. The earliest Hindu sacred texts are the Vedas, the hymns and chants of the Aryans, composed in Sanskrit probably about 1500 B.C., but not reduced to writing until perhaps 2,000 years later, long after a script had been invented. Until the Buddhist protest in the sixth century B.C., Hinduism seems to have been the religion of the aristocracy only. It involved elaborate, costly sacrifice and ritual presided over by the Brahman priestly caste. When Buddhism rose to prominence, Hinduism went into partial eclipse for a number of centuries, although it probably continued to be practiced by many.

The new Hinduism that appeared in the fourth and fifth centuries A.D., after the long interval of Buddhist ascendancy, still placed emphasis on the Vedas but had accepted as legitimate more of the religion of the people than had Brahmanism. In so doing, it had developed its characteristic tolerance of widely different beliefs. It had accepted the cults of invaders subsequent to the Aryans, as well as ancient native cults which apparently had continued to be the religion of the masses despite the Aryan invasions.

But the Brahmans, while finding a place for these cults within their Hindu scheme of things, regarded much of the miscellaneous borrowings as "lower." Even as late as the nineteenth century, both the Vedas and other subsequent sacred writings were the special possession of the Brahmans, who were reluctant to make the study of Sanskrit or of the Vedas available to lower castes. Despite this exclusiveness, from the earliest times to the present day there has been a constant exchange and interaction between the "high" Aryan religion and the lower indigenous and non-Aryan cults, many of them local in nature—between what American anthropologists have called the "great tradition" and the "little traditions," more primitive and local in nature. The "higher" religion has been constantly accepting certain ideas, deities, and practices originating in the "lower" cults. Meanwhile, lower castes have tended to take over the religious and cultural ingredients of the "great tradition" whenever they learned what these were. They have imitated not only the ceremonies and ritual of the upper castes, but their social customs as well. This constant tendency toward imitation of the "higher" religion and of the "higher" castes has created a certain degree of unity within the heterogeneous mass of

Hinduism. Yet, because there is always a time lag in the process of imitation, it has paradoxically led to increasing attention to "high" Hinduism on the part of many lower- and middle-caste Hindus at the very time that the upper castes, whom they have sought to imitate, have come increasingly under the influence of the West.[2] Thus, in the last century, what might be called Hindu "orthodoxy" has been increasing rather than decreasing as more people have gained access to the Sanskrit texts in the original or in translation.

Village Cults

Only recently have we come to realize that village Hinduism—the Hinduism of close to 85 per cent of the Hindus—is quite different from the Hinduism stemming from the Sanskrit classics. The reason why village Hinduism has remained so largely unknown in the West is that the Hindus whom the British and other Westerners first came to know tended to be of high caste, hence familiar with the religion of the Sanskrit texts rather than the unrecorded practices of the village masses. Today, anthropologists are beginning to tell us what these practices are.

Most Indian villagers know something of the several personal gods who are worshiped by the more educated persons all over India, but their center of attention is still usually focused on a group of local spirits. These spirits—good, evil, or neutral—are not adored or worshiped, but feared. The various rites, ceremonies, and superstitious practices with which they are approached are attempts to control them and avert their wrath.[3]

The variety of local godlings can only be suggested. In a certain section of south India, a local cult concerns itself with an invisible watchman, Iyenar, who rides on horseback through the countryside at night to ward off evil. Along the roadside, one sees many little clusters of stone or clay horses donated to Iyenar by the villagers as extra mounts to speed him on his way.

Villagers all over India believe in a primitive mother goddess who has different names and requirements in different places. She usually has priests of all castes, requires animal sacrifices, and has crude shrines, often mere heaps of stones rather than temples. She often enters into people as an evil spirit. One of the more common forms of this goddess is that of Mariamma, the Goddess of Smallpox, who either inflicts or wards off this much-dreaded disease. In Mysore, for example, the villagers vigorously deny that smallpox comes through contagion. They believe on the contrary that it comes because the goddess has thrown her pearls about.[4]

None of us, of course, is separated from superstition, magic, witchcraft, and the like by as many generations as we would like to imagine. And even this degree of separation is due not to any inherent superiority but to the good fortune of education and of a safe margin separating us from starvation. Pressed hard by circumstances, Indian villagers must deal in the only way they know with the powerful and dangerous forces by which they feel themselves surrounded.

Sometimes the strongly held superstitions that such cults contain stand squarely in the way of reforms of agriculture and public health proposed under India's Five-Year Plans. All over India, government agents concerned with the application of science to India's problems constantly face the problem of persuading the villagers that the spirit world will not harm them if they abandon superstitious practices that stand in the way of improved agriculture or better health.

The Worship of Personal Gods

At a more developed level, Hindu worship centers around various personal gods who are viewed not as rivals but as alternative aspects of the Divine. In the big public temples, where elaborate sculptures remind the worshiper of the many legends connected with the gods, images of the gods are treated as though they were living persons. Priests clothe, feed, and bathe them, and even arrange their marriages. On special occasions, the god, treated as a king, is taken in a parade around the city. These are all symbolic acts. In India, as elsewhere, external ritual has its inner spiritual significance to the worshiper.

But despite these temples and their ceremonies, worship is essentially not congregational. Rather, it is an individual matter to be carried on privately, when and in whatever fashion the worshiper may choose. Every Hindu home has a spot set aside for worship—a puja place with a little ledge for images of the gods and for in-

Puja Place

cense burners, and usually with garlanded pictures of the gods hanging on the wall above.

Religious observance may take place not only at home but also in connection with work. Behind the great drill presses in a certain diesel-engine factory are little puja places created by the workers themselves. The Indian craftsman conceives of his art not as his own nor as the accumulated skill of the ages, but as originating in the divine skill of his god and revealed by him.[5] In many parts of India, craftsmen still worship their tools during an annual religious festival. The debut of a young professional dancer is essentially a religious ceremony—a consecration of the dancer to her art which itself is religious in its themes and motivation. Passing her palms over flaming camphor, then pressing them together, the young dancer touches her forehead to the ground before her teacher, who gives her the consecrated anklets of bells. (This is the form of the service as performed at the dance school Kalakshetra, in Madras.)

Since the period of Buddhist ascendancy, the two chief personal gods of Hinduism have been Vishnu, the preserver, and Shiva, the creator and destroyer. Vishnu is thought of as having appeared in a number of incarnations and as always being ready to come back to earth when there is a new need for a savior. In one of these incarnations, he was born as Krishna, the "divine cowherd" who lived in north India and performed marvelous exploits and miracles recounted in popular legends. His love for the lovely mortal Radha has inspired much music, painting, and poetry. To many Hindus, this love symbolizes the mystical union between the soul and the infinite spirit.

Rama, another of the incarnations of Vishnu, is the subject of one of the two great Hindu epics, the *Ramayana,* which tells of how Rama's wife, Sita, was kidnaped by a demon and carried off to Ceylon. It was only with great difficulty and the help of the monkey Hanuman that Rama finally recovered her. But during the long period when they were separated, she remained faithful to him; she is greatly revered for this as the perfect model of womanhood. Each year in north India, Rama's triumph over the demon Ravana, regarded as symbolic of the eternal triumph of good over evil, is celebrated in a festival lasting ten days and sometimes longer. The entire *Ramayana* is often acted out by local amateur

Vishnu – The preserver
Shiva – creator
Destroyer

groups. An American anthropologist has noted that in one particular year 321 towns in Uttar Pradesh alone gave such plays.[6] But it is difficult to say just how much of this rich drama of Hinduism should be regarded as religious and how much stems from an enjoyment of entertainment and color which in other societies would take secular forms.

Vishnu, whether worshiped in his own right or in one of his incarnations, is a kindly and consoling god, able to ease the human predicament. The other chief god, Shiva, is more remote, more awesome and terrible. Often depicted dancing surrounded by a circle of flames, he is the god of the eternal, inexorable rhythms of the universe—the dance of life, the ebb and flow, the destruction that makes way for new creation. In his temples, the central image is usually a phallic symbol in stone (lingam). There seems reason to believe that the origins of the worship of Shiva existed in India before the arrival of the Aryans and formed an essential part of the religion of the early Indus Valley civilization.

Not only Krishna and Rama, but also Vishnu and Shiva have wives, and these have many more names than need be noted. A significant number of educated Hindus worship a mother goddess, who seems to be a higher outgrowth of the less developed mother goddess of the Indian countryside—an embodiment of the sustaining primordial maternal principle. In certain areas, the goddess, worshiped under the name of Kali, requires blood sacrifices (for example, of goats). Kali is a dread creature, often represented in a horrifying form, with long fangs, wild hair, and a necklace of human skulls. Modern psychologists have made interesting speculations as to what the nature of Kali indicates about the repressed urges of her worshipers.[7]

"High" Hinduism

For philosophically minded Indians, all personal gods and goddesses are merely aspects or manifestations of the one nameless, indescribable reality that underlies everything. This eternal, universal essence is usually called Brahman (not to be confused with the priestly caste, also Brahman, or with Brahma, one of the personal gods of Hinduism). The supreme Brahman is neuter, impersonal, all-pervading, absolute. The souls of all living things, animal as well as human, are identical with it. It is only ignorance to regard the seeming separateness of objects in the external world as real. The only true reality is oneness in Brahman, and the only right and true purpose in human life is to realize this oneness. Man's essential duty is to transform his consciousness so that he can become one with Brahman.

Of all the contrasting aspects of Hinduism, it is this concept of Brahman that has had the widest influence outside India and has come to seem most characteristic of Hinduism. Within India also, it has had profound influence. Although uneducated Indians may not understand it and certain schools of Hindu philosophy do not subscribe to it, it forms the basis for many prevalent attitudes and unexamined assumptions.

Like many religious intuitions, the concept of Brahman raises questions that reason finds difficulty in answering. If everything is essentially part of Brahman, what then is matter? What is this hard earth on which we stand, this tree that we touch, this ego which urgently wants its own desires fulfilled? Some Hindu thinkers have answered that such things exist only in a relative sense, as emanations of Brahman; since Brahman alone exists, all that is merely relative is known as maya (illusion). Others tend to grant at least a partial reality to matter and to individual selves, arguing that Brahman can be present in such objects in various degrees.

Hence, between pure matter at one end of the cosmic scale and pure spirit at the other, there is a gradual ascent—from the inorganic to the organic, from mere life to consciousness, from consciousness to reason, and from reason to spiritual perfection and the Supreme Spirit. The great purpose in life should be to enhance spiritual values, to free the spirit from the drag of matter, to realize the spirit within one's self.

In order to do this, man should choose the god best suited to his understanding and subject himself to rigorous discipline. Three major types of discipline are recognized. Each is regarded as a yoga (a yoking); as a horse is under control when yoked, so a yoga is thought of as a way to bring body and mind under control so that the soul may be free to know itself. The three types are: the way of good works—karma yoga; the way of knowledge, meditation, and ascetism—jnana yoga; and the way of loving devotion—bhakti yoga.

Traditionally, the way of good works involved chiefly ceremony and ritual and often ignored the type of good deeds toward others on which Christianity places such stress. (But from Buddha to Gandhi, there have been religious leaders in India who have connected karma yoga with the concept of social service.) Nor is the path of knowledge precisely what a Westerner might expect. The knowledge to be sought is not rational or factual knowledge, but intuitive knowledge of reality in the absolute sense, to be attained through the suppression of desires. One technique, specifically known as the yoga system, employs certain bodily postures, control of breath, retraction of sense activities, fixation of the mind, and meditation in order to attain a mystic trance. Such an approach is common among Hindu holy men of all sects. The path of bhakti, or loving devotion to a personal god, has become of increasing importance in recent centuries and is now probably the form of discipline most frequently followed.

Though there are thus many different permissible conceptions of God and alternative ways of reaching union with the Divine, Hinduism contains certain generally accepted beliefs. One of these is reincarnation and the transmigration of souls—the continuity of the self through a series of lives, either here on earth or elsewhere, either as a human or as some other form of life. Closely allied to this is the doctrine of karma: What we are in any given life is the result of what we thought and did in our past lives. Not only a man's character but even his economic and social status are determined by the laws of karma. We forever suffer the results of our sins and reap the rewards of our good acts. To many Hindus, the Christian concept of forgiveness seems capricious and contrary to the orderly spiritual laws of the universe.

As one struggles through countless rebirths, the goal is moksha (spiritual release). If one leads good lives with purity, self-control, detachment, and truthfulness, if one fulfills in each life the special duties of one's caste, one will be reborn at higher and higher levels, both of caste and of spiritual purity, until one reaches a state where one can attain the truth. One's soul then recognizes its identity with Brahman, and rebirth ceases.

Since the Hindu view of the universe contemplates unimaginable aeons of time, the importance of this final release can easily be seen. A single day in the life of Brahma the Creator consists of 4,320,000,000 human years. On each such day, Brahma creates the world anew, then again dissolves it. For 36,000 such days of Brahma, this creation and dissolution continues.[8] Then Brahma returns to the Supreme Being. For the individual to carry his accumulated fate with him through all these trillions and quadrillions of years could clearly be a heavy burden. Hindus have come to look upon the process of rebirth with despair, regarding it as the "wheel of life," endlessly revolving through interminable aeons. Release is consequently highly desired, but regarded as rarely achieved.

Another important Hindu concept is that of dharma, the idea of a special duty to be observed in accordance with a man's station in life and especially according to his caste. Each caste theoretically has its own allotted function in the general division of labor. A man's dharma depends on his age also. Hinduism recognizes four stages of life, each with its appropriate duties: the student, the householder, the hermit or recluse, and finally the ascetic (sannyasi). A man is supposed to live a full marital life during the second stage. He should throw off the ties of family and society partially in the third stage and completely in the fourth, when he should renounce everything and devote himself entirely to meditation in solitude.*

Although Hinduism stresses moksha, it also grants a place to the more immediate purposes in which men are inevitably interested. Moksha is considered as only one of four goals to be sought by man; the other three are kama (the satisfaction of desires and natural instincts), artha (work and material prosperity), and dharma (the fulfillment of duty).

The Sacred Writings

As in the case of any religion, the Hindu sacred writings provide the outsider with the best clue to the ideals and values of Hinduism.

* An interesting example of this: An Indian woman friend of mine runs a large business selling earth-moving machinery—because her husband, the founder of the business, is now meditating in solitude.

Of the four Vedas (the earliest sacred texts), the *Rig Veda* is generally considered the most important, although many other Vedic verses are still used in ceremonies today. The Vedas begin with polytheism. The deities they celebrate are personifications of the great aspects of nature, such as Varuna the Heavens, Surya the Sun, Agni the Fire, and Indra the Thunder and Rain. Later passages in the Vedas move on to monotheism and then raise questions regarding the ultimate reality which antedated even the gods. They contain a conception of cosmic principles and of a fundamental system of law and order for the world.

The Upanishads, composed somewhat later than the Vedas, explore deeply the concept of the utter unity of the universe first touched on in the later sections of the *Rig Veda*. Their great message is the unity of the soul and the Divine:

> This soul of mine within the heart is smaller than a grain of rice or a barley corn or a mustard seed or a grain of millet or the kernel of a grain of millet.
>
> This soul of mine within the heart is greater than the earth, greater than the atmosphere, greater than the sky, greater than the world. . . . This soul of mine within the heart, this is Brahman.[9]

A beautiful Upanishad prayer provides an example of the breadth and simplicity of religious thought in these great works: "Lead me from the unreal to the real. Lead me from darkness to light. Lead me from death to immortality."[10]

The two great Hindu epics, the *Mahabharata* and the *Ramayana*, probably begun about the fourth century B.C. but gradually expanded over many centuries, contain stories and legends well known to every Hindu and even today provide the subject matter for plays and motion pictures. Embedded in the *Mahabharata* is the beautiful *Bhagavad Gita* (*Song of the Lord*), regarded by Gandhi and many other Hindus as the quintessence of Hinduism. Arjuna, one of the warriors engaged in the warfare that forms the subject of the *Mahabharata*, is on the battlefield on the eve of battle. The opponents include his own relatives. Deeply disturbed by the thought of killing his own people, he thinks seriously of allowing them to kill him instead. He confides his predicament to his charioteer, who turns out to be none other than the god

Krishna, incarnation of Vishnu. Krishna explains to him that the soul does not perish, and that he should not grieve over the possible death of relatives, who are essentially imperishable. Because Arjuna is a member of the warrior caste, Krishna advises him that it is his duty, his dharma, to fight. The essential moral point, Krishna explains, is not whether he should or should not fight but rather *how* he should fight. Whatever is done must be done not for oneself but as a duty, in a spirit of sacrifice to God, with detachment and without a feeling of personal stake in the results:

> Treating alike pleasure and pain, gain and loss, victory and defeat, then get ready for battle. Thus thou shalt not incur sin. . . .
>
> He who abandons all desires and acts free from longing without any sense of mineness or egotism—he attains the peace.[11]

This emphasis on personal detachment is a cardinal feature of Hinduism.

The poem tells of several routes by which the Divine can be approached and of the personal self-discipline required to follow these routes, then goes on to a great statement of the utter oneness of the universe. Identifying himself with the ultimate, all-embracing Brahman, Krishna says:

> I am the origin of all this world and its dissolution as well. . . .
>
> I am the taste in the waters, I am the light in the moon and the sun. . . . I am the sound in ether, and manhood in men.
>
> I am the pure fragrance in earth and brightness in fire, I am the life in all existences and the austerity in ascetics. . . .
>
> I am the intelligence of the intelligent, I am the splendor of the splendid.
>
> I am the strength of the strong, devoid of desire and passion. In beings am I the desire which is not contrary to law. . . .[12]

Composed in a quite different spirit is the Code of Manu, dating in its present form from about 200 B.C. Manu is considered the great law-giver of Hinduism. The Code is a collection of rules of life laying heavy stress on ceremonies and, above all, emphasizing the separateness of the four original castes, or orders of society.

During the first millennium of the Christian era, vast collections of old stories and legends were put together in the *Puranas*, which are perhaps the most important popularizations of Hinduism. It is largely through their narratives, often still transmitted orally in remote villages, that the religious ideals of Hinduism have been transmitted to the illiterate masses.

Between 1000 and 1700 A.D., a series of Hindu singers and writers added to the great body of devotional literature. Certain thinkers attempted to combine Muslim and Hindu thought. Often writing in the vernacular, rather than in the old Sanskrit, the medieval writers seem to have effected a profound change in the religious life of simple people.

Although the Vedas, the Upanishads, the epics, and especially the *Bhagavad Gita* continue to be recognized by most Hindus as the most important scriptures, writings regarded as sacred by some Hindus, but not by others, have been composed even as recently as the last few decades. To a Christian accustomed to a Bible whose contents are fixed and generally acknowledged, the indeterminate, elastic nature of the Hindu sacred writings is a confusing fact.

Hinduism and Daily Life

As noted, the superstitions of village cults have many significant practical implications. From the doctrines of higher Hinduism also stem several practices and tendencies that merit consideration.

In the West, it is often said that Hinduism leads to an attitude of passivity and resignation. This has perhaps been so for many, but it must not be forgotten that every religion contains an element of resignation (certainly prominent in early Christianity and still implicit in Christian theology, though stressed less today as a matter of practice). It is clear from the practical achievements of Hindu civilization in its periods of greatness that the Hindus of the time were far from passive. In any event, only the finest line divides resignation from the wise and mature acceptance of the inevitable—or of some limit to the possible—required for serene living at any economic level.

It is sometimes assumed that if only Indians were as dynamic, enterprising, and energetic as Americans consider themselves to be, their country would be as wealthy as the United States. But only a century and a half ago, Americans had a vast, virgin, almost uninhabited country to exploit, whereas India is a crowded land which for centuries has contained no semblance of an open frontier. Under these circumstances, a certain acceptance or resignation has been the strength of Indians and of Indian society.

A second important result flowing from Hindu thought is the sanctity of animals: If all created things are one, and if a person's soul was previously born in animal form and will be so born again, animals are clearly entitled to life fully as much as are human beings. This has led to strict vegetarianism on the part of some Hindus and to a general reluctance to kill animals. The origins of the cow's special sanctity are not entirely clear, but Hindus believe that cow worship stems from the fact that the cow was the source of milk, hence a symbol of motherhood. Because the monkey Hanuman played an important role in reclaiming Sita in the epic *Ramayana*, the killing of monkeys is also generally regarded as wrong. Of all Hindu customs, these two—the sanctity of the cow and the refusal to kill monkeys though they pilfer grain—have perhaps received the most impatient criticism in the West. We forget how deeply rooted in Hindu culture are such customs and also how peculiar to our own culture are the standards by which we judge them.

I. G. Patel, one of India's leading economists, recently made a thoughtful statement in defense of the sanctity of animals.[13] He explained that to him the moral attitude out of which this preservation stems seemed of greater value than any economic advantage to be derived from slaughtering animals that consume man's food. He argued that the Western assumption of the superiority of human beings to other creatures involves an ugly, dangerous arrogance—an attitude that is morally wrong. When a scholarly, Western-educated Indian thus challenges our Western assumptions, we gain a certain insight into the power of the preconceptions of both our culture and his.

A significant common practice of Hindus is the resort to astrologers. This practice does not stem specifically from the beliefs of Hinduism, for there are believers in astrology throughout the world who are not Hindus. But it seems significant that the vast majority of Hindus still do believe in astrology. Before a young couple marries, an astrologer must be consulted to ascertain whether their horoscopes match. Astrologers must also be consulted as to which times of the day or week or year are auspicious or inauspicious for any trip, business deal, or other undertaking. Many Hindus have criticized this tendency to resort to astrologers. Yet, even today, an educated Hindu who in one breath will assert, "I do not believe in astrology," may nevertheless go on to say, "Still, there may be something in it."

Stressing the role of astrology in Indian life, a prominent Indian journalist has written:

> Astrology is recognized as a subject of study in Banaras, Calcutta, and Patna Universities. A privately run astrological institute in Delhi which receives aid from the central and some state governments, has currently seven young men on its rolls preparing for doctorates. . . . The institution was founded by Mr. K. M. Munshi, one-time Governor of India's largest state, Uttar Pradesh, and now the driving force behind the conservative Swatantra Party. . . . Most of the members of Mr. Nehru's cabinet have their favorite astrologers who often travel across the continent to tender advice on state affairs. . . . Mr. Nehru has often expressed impatience with colleagues who consult astrologers . . . but . . . he has never made it a personal issue by proposing legislation against the practice.[14]

More important than the frequent resort to astrology is the pronounced tendency toward hero worship, which stems from the Hindu idea of the repeated incarnations of God in human form. If the Divine has appeared as Rama, as Krishna, as Buddha, as Jesus, as Gandhi, and as many other individuals, there is always the possibility of further incarnations—hence the expectation of encountering the Divine on earth. When reinforced by the form of religious discipline known as bhakti, this tendency acquires enormous strength. The loving, uncritical devotion given not only to Gandhi but also to Nehru by the masses suggests the possibly dangerous results of this Hindu concept of incarnation. Many thoughtful Indians are aware that it could lead to an acceptance of dictatorship.

This tendency is strengthened by the belief that intuition and spiritual insight are superior to logic—particularly the intuitions of the few great religious leaders, who are followed unquestioningly. Some observers warn that religious authoritarianism could easily prepare the way for secular authoritarianism, such as that of Communism. In the realm of ideas, perhaps the most crucial question facing India in the coming years is the relation between Western rational, scientific thought and the indigenous belief in intuition.

In regard to the problem of evil in the world, all religions encounter one kind of logical difficulty or another, depending on their view of ultimate reality. Christianity finds it hard to explain logically *why*, if God is both omnipotent and good, He permits evil to exist. Similarly, Hinduism has trouble explaining *how*, since God is in everything and everything is part of God, evil can possibly be real, not imaginary. Can some things be good and others bad? Or does the divinity of the world mean that the activities of even the pickpocket and the perjurer, for example, should be regarded as sacred and not to be interfered with? Sarvepalli Radhakrishnan, India's leading philosopher, who was elected President in 1962, raises this question in his fine book *The Hindu Way of Life*. His answer is that although there is nothing in which God does not glow, in some things or people the divine spark burns more dimly or more brightly than in others. The immanence of God admits of degrees. Hence, the pickpocket may be somewhat less sacred than the saint.[15]

But despite answers such as this, the question remains a stubborn one, and monism—the belief that ultimate reality is absolutely single—inevitably creates a moral climate quite different from that created by the dualism to which the West is more accustomed. Christianity, Judaism, and Islam all rest on the belief that although there is God, there is also Satan, and good and evil are at war. It is the duty of the individual to take active part in this war on the side of good. Thus the necessity for sharp moral choices between very real phenomena springs out of the very fabric of these three Near Eastern religions. In Hinduism, on the other hand, even if some things are more divine than others, evil does not have the hard, tough reality that it has in the religious beliefs of the West. To quote Radhakrishnan again, "The worst of the world cannot be dismissed as completely undivine."[16]

Perhaps more deeply than we realize, the thought patterns of even nonreligious persons tend to be molded by the underlying suppositions of the religion around them. A lay person who would never stop to ask himself whether he is a monist or a dualist will nevertheless behave quite differently depending on his unexamined assumptions regarding the nature of reality and the resulting relationship between good and evil. F. S. C. Northrop has argued that India's neutralism in foreign policy traces straight back to the Hindu concept of the singleness of ultimate reality.[17] Certainly, in many kinds of circumstances, Hindus are far less inclined to judge and condemn than are Westerners. An easy-going tolerance and an assumption that there is some good in everybody are characteristic Hindu attitudes.

Many observers have noted that Hindus value highly the process of mediation and conciliation, admire the successful mediator, and believe that all disputes can and should be settled by mutual agreement. This optimistic view of the possibilities of peaceful settlement seems likewise to trace back to the fundamental assumption of the underlying unity of reality.

In matters of domestic government policy, where the Western mind would consider outright choices inescapable, a Hindu is likely to be more inclined to hold that two apparently contradictory courses can be followed simultaneously, without detriment to either one or the other. Is private enterprise or socialization the better course? The current Indian answer is: "We will have both, and neither will suffer." Should there be decentralized democratic control over economic policy, or centralized state planning? Again, the Indian answer is: "Let us have both." The natural desire to avoid choices is apparently reinforced by the bias of Hindu philosophy. In believing that all beings and all phenomena are somehow one in Brahman, Hindus have become accustomed to the idea that reconciliation, even on a stupendous scale, is not only possible but indeed the natural order of reality.

A final significant implication of Hindu ideas is a built-in tendency toward evolution as opposed to revolution. Hinduism's vast tolerance includes a tolerance of the new, the strange, the different. Since there is no authority to lay down a dogma or fix in final fashion the meaning of the ancient scriptures, these scriptures can always be interpreted anew. Throughout its long past, Hinduism has continuously shown a flexibility, an adaptability, and a resilience which have undoubtedly been the key to its long survival. It gradually overcame the challenge of Buddhism.

It remained strong to face the challenge of Islam after 1000 A.D. It has reacted with similar flexibility to the challenge of both Western rationalism and Christianity.

The Reactions of Hinduism to the Impact of the West

By the early nineteenth century, Hinduism was at a low ebb. The great scriptures were barely known. Ceremony, ritual and dry formalism passed for religion. Idol worship had become far more literal than symbolic. Hindu holy men, often following extreme ascetic practices, concerned themselves only with the salvation of their own souls, not with the welfare of the society around them. Religion had become associated with a long list of social abuses, many of which were later attacked by Hindus themselves: infanticide, the marriage of very young girls, prohibition of the remarriage of widows, and extreme rigidity in the caste system. Perhaps the worst was the custom of suttee, whereby an upper-caste widow in north India was expected to burn herself on her husband's funeral pyre. Theoretically, widows made the suicide choice freely, but there are indications that coercion often took place.

Although a few Indians, especially in Bengal, had become interested in the customs of the West and wanted to know more about them, no institutions for the study of English and Western subjects existed until after 1819. The East India Company, more interested in practical matters than in reform, followed at first a policy of strict noninterference in native religions and social customs. Not until 1813 were Christian missionaries even allowed entrance into Company territory. The Company continued to permit suttee until 1829, after public attention had been focused on the abuse by the writings of Rammohun Roy, who vigorously called attention to the fact that the burning of widows was not sanctioned in the Hindu scriptures.

Rammohun Roy, one of the great intellectual figures of India of the last two centuries, was the first articulate Hindu leader to become profoundly troubled by the impact of Western ideas. He inaugurated what is usually spoken of as the Hindu Renaissance (or Reformation) of the nineteenth century. Born of an orthodox high-caste Brahman family, he was given not only the best available Hindu education, but also a Muslim education, necessary at the time to anyone who contemplated entering public service. Thus he had an opportunity at an early age to compare Hinduism and Islam. Besides knowing several Indian vernaculars, including his own language, Bengali, he knew Sanskrit (the language of the sacred Hindu scriptures), Arabic (the language of the Koran), and Persian (the language of the Mughuls, still used for governmental purposes). By the age of twelve, he had already reacted against much of the popular Hinduism around him. His unorthodox views led to a breach with his father—an occurrence far less common in India even today than it is in the West. Deciding to seek the truth for himself, he studied English in order to read the Bible, then Hebrew and Greek to read the Bible in the original. For several years, he worked in the service of the East India Company, which gave him additional contacts with Western ideas. He resigned at the age of forty, settled in Calcutta, and spent the rest of his life writing, stimulating reforms that reflected Western influence. Largely as a result of his urging, the East India Company passed a law in 1829 declaring suttee illegal and providing severe punishment for anyone associated in any way with the custom. Rammohun Roy also opposed polygamy, and advocated the remarriage of widows, trial by jury, and other innovations.

Rammohun Roy had close contacts with the Christian missionaries and greatly admired the teachings of Jesus; he "found the doctrines of Christ more conducive to moral principles and better adapted for the use of rational beings" than any other religion he knew.[18] But as with many other lesser Hindus later, admiration of Christian teachings or of other Western ideas were not sufficient to tear him loose from Hinduism. In his book *The Precepts of Jesus, The Guide to Peace and Happiness,* written in 1820, he endorsed Christian ethics, but criticized the Christian church and Christian theology. Despite its name, his book was a defense of Hinduism against the encroachments of Christian missionaries. He reaffirmed the theism of the old Hindu scriptures while condemning idolatry and other practices not sanctioned in them. His focus was on a rationalistic, universal religion and on social reform.

Believing that the upper-class Hindus should have increased opportunities to come in contact with Western learning, Rammohun Roy took part in founding the first college at which such subjects were taught. Originally known as the Hindu College, this later became the Presidency College, today one of the best colleges affiliated with the University of Calcutta. He also argued strongly that the East India Company should introduce in India the British system of education. In 1835, partly because of his influence, English was made the medium of instruction in colleges receiving financial aid from the Company. Western-type subjects rather than Oriental learning were placed at the center of the curriculum.

In 1829, Rammohun Roy began holding small weekly meetings of a religious nature at which passages from the sacred texts of Hinduism were read aloud. Significantly, the readings were not in Sanskrit but in vernacular Bengali translations. This in itself was a radical departure from ancient custom. Those who came to his meetings presently formed the Brahmo Samaj (Society of God), which sought to combine the best of Hinduism with the best of Christianity. Its members, known as Brahmos, took a vow to abstain from idolatry and to worship God by love and good deeds. Never a large organization, the Brahmo Samaj underwent successive splits after Rammohun Roy's death. From the outset, it had been faced by difficult questions. Should it incline more toward Hinduism or Christianity? Should it focus more on devotional worship or social reform? In the very act of trying to synthesize the best of the West and the East, it was itself torn by the conflicting forces it was trying to reconcile. After 1857, the offshoot of the original organization which was particularly concerned with social reform organized branches in many parts of India and actively promoted such novel and startling ideas as the education of women, the emancipation of women, and the remarriage of widows. The Brahmo Samaj was the seedbed of a movement that continued throughout the nineteenth century to press for reforms in harmony with social ideals learned from the West.

The impact of the West on Hindu thought produced not only the reform movement but also a quite opposite result. India also learned the lesson of nationalism, which tended in India, as in the West, to glorify the past and hence ignore defects or abuses rooted in the past. Accordingly, toward the end of the nineteenth century, there developed a current of Hindu revivalism and a strong, assertive reaffirmation of ancient Hindu traditions. Yet many of those who most strongly asserted the return to the ancient faith revealed in one way or another that they themselves had been influenced by the West.

One of the most important organizations embodying Hindu reaction was the Arya Samaj (Aryan Association), founded in 1875. It made its headquarters in the Punjab in northern India, where Aryan influence had always been strong. By its very name, this new samaj proclaimed to the foreign rulers, "We are Aryans like you."

The Arya Samaj was founded by a Brahman, Swami Dayanand Saraswati (1824–83), the son of a devout priest of Shiva. At an early age, the son became disturbed by doubts as to whether the image of Shiva was really God. Not satisfied with his father's orthodox answers to his questions, he ran away, entered an order of sannyasis (wandering holy men) and soon began to teach that Hinduism should be purified through the return to its original sources. His slogan was "Back to the Vedas." In his view, the Vedas contained all the truth and all the guidance that man needed. By his slogan, he brushed aside all the later scriptures, even the deeply philosophical Upanishads and the *Bhagavad Gita.* Influenced to some extent by the Brahmo Samaj, he preached that idolatry was irrational and degrading and that the sacrifice of animals and offerings of foods for the gods were mere superstitious rites. He argued that child marriage and even caste in its modern form were customs that should be reformed. Furthermore, he taught the practical value of Western science. Yet he urged the extirpation from India of all foreign religions and the reconversion to Hinduism of Muslims who had been Hindus. In 1882, he helped found the Cow Protection Association, for the elimination of cow slaughter under any circumstances. Since independence, members of the Arya Samaj have been active politically within the religious conservative parties, especially the growing Jana Sangh.

Another of the great religious leaders of the late nineteenth century was Ramakrishna Paramahansa (1836–88), who served most of his life as a priest of the temple of the goddess Kali on the banks of the Ganges just north of Calcutta. As a matter of routine, therefore, he sacrificed animals to the goddess, a practice that even Swami Dayanand Saraswati had condemned. Indeed, of all the nineteenth-century religious leaders, Ramakrishna was the most rooted in the Indian past. He was a mystic who believed he had actually seen the goddess Kali, as well as other divine beings, including Krishna and Jesus Christ. In reaction against the teachings of the Brahmo Samaj and Western-minded rationalism, which he regarded as cold and lifeless, he felt it was his mission to rouse religious feelings among Hindus and reaffirm the ancient truths. He urged on his disciples the supreme value of intuitive emotional contact with God, holding that such experience is the aim of human existence and should take precedence over good works or social reform.

It was Ramakrishna's chief disciple, Vivekananda (1863–1902), who brought modern Hinduism to America and laid the foundation for the Vedanta Society, which today teaches Hinduism in twelve American cities. In school in Calcutta, his English teacher, while speaking of the mysticism of Wordsworth, mentioned that a renowned mystic lived just four miles outside the city. Vivekananda went to see Ramakrishna and became his disciple. Leaving his comfortable middle-class home in Calcutta, he wandered on foot for five years throughout India, begging food from door to door in remote villages in the traditional fashion of Hindu holy men. In 1893, he went to the United States to attend a World Parliament of Religions in Chicago, where he made an impassioned defense of Hinduism, stressing its tolerance and the basic oneness of all religions. After touring the United States and England for three years, lecturing constantly, he received a hero's welcome on his return to India. The fact that he had so successfully preached Hinduism in the very lands from which the Christian missionaries came seemed to prove that political subjection need not involve religious subjection. Hindus could at least be proud of the essential truths of their religion. This reaffirmation of Hinduism served as an emotional counterbalance to the damage to Hindu self-respect caused by British political domination.

Vivekananda founded an organization called the Ramakrishna Mission to combine the Western concept of social service with the Hindu ideal of renunciation and spiritual salvation. The Hindu monks belonging to the Mission still operate excellent schools, colleges, hospitals, nursing homes, and other charitable institutions.

In discussing the Indian Independence Movement, we have

already touched on the religious revivalism of the nationalist leader B. G. Tilak. Tilak and his followers opposed the activities of the social reformers, holding that independence must come first. Although he was primarily a political revolutionary rather than a man of religion, he wrote a monumental commentary on the *Bhagavad Gita,* interpreting it so that it would accord with the activism he sought to inspire in the nationalist movement.

Reactionary nationalism was vigorously opposed by another and quite different Indian, Rabindranath Tagore (1861–1941). Primarily a poet in the Bengali language and a creative artist in many media, Tagore nevertheless concerned himself with the relation between Eastern and Western thought. A true successor of Rammohun Roy, he reasserted the importance of a new understanding between the spiritual tradition of India and the quite different spiritual tradition of the West. He vigorously opposed the idea (popular among Indians unsure of India's self-respect in relation to the West) that India had unique claims to spirituality while the West was purely materialistic. He advocated and actively promoted a new internationalism based on intercultural understanding.

Gandhi's Religion

The greatest religious leader in India in modern times, of course, was Mahatma Gandhi, who introduced still another new current into Hindu thought.

Although he had shown such interest in Christianity in his youth that his missionary friends hoped for his conversion, Gandhi remained a Hindu. He did not believe in conversion for he felt that a man is bound to the religion in which he is born by an indissoluble tie. He thought that "all religions are more or less true." He said it was up to a man "to arrive at perfection in his or her own faith."[19] Thus he opposed the efforts of the Arya Samaj to reconvert Muslims to Hinduism.

Gandhi did not claim to have originated any new principle or doctrine. He thought of himself as an orthodox Hindu because he believed in the Hindu scriptures, in cow worship, and in special duties for different castes—and because he did not disbelieve in idol worship. He interpreted all these points, however, in a new and broader fashion, in accordance with his own reason. He said, "I cannot let a scriptural text supersede my reason."[20] He defended idol worship as quite natural symbolism—an outgrowth of the universal yearning for a symbol, whether an image of the Virgin Mary or the child Krishna, a book or a cross.[21] He viewed the sanctity of the cow as a symbol of man's indissoluble relationship with the subhuman animal world. Although untouchability and caste discrimination were repugnant to him, he felt that one could not ignore the law of heredity, which bestows different qualities—hence duties and privileges—on different persons. Quite contrary to orthodox Hindus, he held that if a person who is born a Brahman does not act like a Brahman, he ceases to be one.[22] He deplored the restrictions on interdining and the "superstitions that are to be found masquerading as Hinduism."[23]

Instead of such inessentials, he placed emphasis on large problems such as self-purification, the search for truth, nonviolence, love, and service. For him, prayer and fasting took the place of traditional acts of ritual. He said:

> A genuine fast cleanses body and mind and soul. . . . A sincere prayer can work wonders. It is an intense longing of the soul for its even greater purity. . . .
>
> All fasting is an intense prayer or a preparation for it. . . .
>
> Prayer is the very core of man's life. . . . He who has experienced the magic of prayer may do without food for days together but not a single moment without prayer. For without prayer there is no inward peace . . . it is the passionate cry of a soul hungering for union with the Divine.[24]

Insisting on interpreting Hinduism in its broadest essentials, he selected the following as the most important single mantra (verse) in Hindu scriptures:

> God the ruler pervades all there is in this universe. Therefore renounce and dedicate all to Him, and then enjoy or use the portion that may fall to thy lot. Never covet anybody's possessions.[25]

Apart from his great concept of *satyagraha*, perhaps Gandhi's most striking contribution was the new social orientation he wove into traditional Hinduism. All too often, the concern of Hindu saints had been only their own souls, their own future incarnations, their own union with the Divine. Reinterpreting the ancient beliefs and practices, Gandhi focused on a new responsibility and concern for the welfare of others in the present incarnation. His compelling and revolutionary interest in social justice still haunts many Hindus for whom such a concept is both inconvenient and contrary to tradition.

Hinduism Today

Besides Rammohun Roy, Swami Dayanand Saraswati, Vivekananda, and Gandhi, many other influential religious or philosophical leaders could be mentioned, each of whom has reacted in different ways to the challenge of Western rationalism and Christianity.

One such was Sri Aurobindo (1872–1950). Before withdrawing from political activities to establish his religious retreat (ashram) in Pondicherry, Sri Aurobindo had been one of the leaders of the more violent wing of the nationalist movement in Bengal, and had served a term in prison. In his subsequent writings, he not only provided a comprehensive restatement of the outstanding school of Hindu philosophy, the Vedanta, but also vigorously opposed the negativism and illusionism often regarded as inherent in traditional Hindu philosophy. For example, he wrote, "If . . . we cast away or belittle the physical life which is our basis, or if we reject the mental and physical in our attraction to the spiritual, we do not fulfill God integrally, nor satisfy the conditions of his self-manifestation."[26] He warned against "a recoil of the life motive from life itself and a seeking after life elsewhere, flawless and eternal, or a will to annul life itself in an immobile reality or an original nonexistence."[27] His philosophy was designed to lay the basis for an affirmative and active way of life.

In a Western nation, a leading philosopher could scarcely hope to be elected President, but in India the election of Dr. Sarvepalli Radhakrishnan to this position in 1962 seemed quite natural, so great is the respect for this man who has devoted his life to working out a solid, systematic, reasonable intellectual basis for continued adherence to Hinduism. In a long succession of distinguished books, he has persuasively explained and defended the Hindu way of life, emphasizing similarities, parallels, or mutual influences between Eastern religion and Western thought.

Today, the drive to reassert the values of Hinduism in one form or another is strong. The Westernized intellectual may feel alienated from his gods and his temple, unable to realize himself in Brahman, and disinclined to devote his life to the attempt. But he forms part of a tiny minority. The majority of Hindus all over India continue their religious devotions and observances in their various traditional ways or in accordance with the teachings of one of the religious leaders of the nineteenth or twentieth century. There is still an abundance of ashrams where religious teachers gather their disciples into small but zealous religious communities, each with its own particular flavor and pattern of beliefs. Little puja places for personal worship are still everywhere. Even the destitute often contrive somehow to fix up such a place on an outer wall over the portion of sidewalk where they settle down to live. Except in a very few of the largest cities, cattle still wander at will, allowed to help themselves to supplies of grain. Merchants or other food vendors regard the resulting financial loss as unimportant compared to their religious duty toward these animals. More than half a million sadhus (holy men) still spend much of their time sitting cross-legged in deep meditation, living on whatever small coins or scraps of food may be given them by a populace that still believes in the validity of such a path toward God—the traditional "path of knowledge." The greatest wish of uncounted millions all over India is that they may die by the banks of the holy Ganges and that their ashes may be deposited in its waters. Film producers find that religious themes are the safest subjects for their films; one producer has stated that 80 per cent of the stories in Indian movies are based on traditional religious themes, though comedy, variety, and other features may be intermixed.[28] In the cities, hymn-singing groups called *bhajans* are common. Readings from the epics and the puranas attract hundreds of people to public halls. More than half of the public meetings announced in a busy modern city like Madras, for example, are devoted to such purposes.[29]

Thus Hinduism is still abundantly vigorous, many-sided, and of overriding importance to the vast majority of Hindus. Those Westerners who take their own religion for granted would totally misinterpret India if they were to imagine that any significant number of Indians approach religious matters with a similar casualness.

8 • THE RELIGIOUS MINORITY GROUPS

Although Hinduism is the religion of the vast majority of the population, it is a mistake to regard the words Indian and Hindu as interchangeable, as do some Westerners. This mistake quite naturally is distressing to the 15 per cent of the Indians who follow one or another of the six significant minority religions. For any nation, large religious minorities pose difficulties. For India, where religion matters much more to the average person than it does in most Western countries, the existence of substantial religious minorities presents special problems. The policy of the government—as it was of the Indian National Congress before independence—is religious neutrality. According to its Constitution, India is a secular state in which discrimination based on religious affiliation is unconstitutional. The Constitution also pledges special protection for religious minorities in cultural and educational matters and nondiscrimination among members of different religions in public employment. When the Indian Constituent Assembly—overwhelmingly Hindu in composition—adopted (in 1949) these provisions, it was no small step or one that could be taken for granted. Yet their adoption has not ended tensions or even violence between religious groups.

By and large, thoughtful members of the religious minorities credit Nehru with attempting to carry out in good faith the promise of a secular state, but they are not sure that his successors will necessarily follow his example in this respect. Militant Hindu political parties, highly critical of the principle of a secular state, have polled increasing percentages of the popular vote in the successive elections. Although the several religion-oriented parties together still have so small a following compared to the dominant Congress Party that they pose no immediate threat at the polls, the fact that they have grown rather than decreased in size leads the minorities to feel some concern.

One might imagine that Hinduism, which is so extremely and amazingly tolerant of every kind of belief within the fold of Hinduism itself, would have no difficulty extending the same tolerance to divergent beliefs outside Hinduism. Indeed, one characteristic that all Hindus claim for Hinduism is its all-embracing tolerance, its ability to encompass every faith, finding a niche for each in the vast scheme of things. From the point of view of certain of the minority religions, this is precisely the difficulty: Any religion that does not want to be encompassed, embraced, and indeed absorbed and perhaps ultimately transformed by Hinduism finds Hindu tolerance somewhat too demanding, since it is conditioned upon a basic acceptance of a Hindu view of life and of Hinduism's peculiar genius for absorption. The one thing that Hinduism finds it difficult to tolerate is the claim on the part of any faith that it alone is the one true faith. Hinduism says in effect: "You may believe anything you choose, worship in any way you see fit, have any code of ethics you like. But you must acknowledge that there are many paths toward God and that your way is merely yours." To the Muslims, Christians, Sikhs, and Parsis, such an approach goes against the grain. An acknowledgment that their faiths are not necessarily better than those of Hindu cults which they decry would seem to them like a betrayal of faith—tantamount to a conversion to Hinduism.

It is significant that the official tolerance of the minority religions that now prevails is based on the secular ideal imported from the West. Many orthodox, conservative Hindus vigorously criticize the secular ideal as an artificial concept. Since to them religion is the very essence of life, they feel that no attempt should be made to disassociate government from it. They want a specifically Hindu state. But how can such a state fail to alienate the 72 million Indians who are not Hindus? This problem is fully realized by India's more sophisticated and Western-minded leaders. But not every Hindu has the statesmanship to foresee the dangers inherent in further Hinduization of government and politics.

Muslims, Christians, and Sikhs

The Muslims form by far the largest religious minority. Before partition, about one-fourth of the population of undivided India were Muslims. Of the total, some 80 million were transferred to Pakistan in 1947, leaving almost half that number in the new India. Constituting 10 per cent of the population today, India's Muslims number 50 million. Except for Indonesia and Pakistan, India contains more Muslims than any other nation. The attitude of the more reactionary Hindus toward this minority remains an important factor in foreign relations and in politics. Liberals in the government always feared that if the government should be "soft" toward Pakistan, reactionary Hindus would turn violently against the Muslims in their midst, regarding them as a traitorous "fifth column"—thus perhaps leading to massacre on a scale that would dwarf even the carnage of 1947.

Westerners who think of Indians as essentially gentle and non-violent can scarcely imagine what a religious riot can mean in India. During the terrible days immediately after partition, when half a million people lost their lives, whole trainloads of refugees arrived at their destinations carrying only corpses, plus a few living persons who had been fortunate enough to be buried under corpses and thus to remain unseen by the murderous gangs of the opposing religion as they went through the train. Even in the comparatively minor religious riots in Calcutta during the preceding year, all the ordinary self-restraint of civilized life seemed suddenly cast aside as gangs descended upon neighborhoods occupied by members of the opposing religious group, looting shops and killing everyone they could find. It is as though all the despair arising out of Indian poverty, all the frustrations of life normally masked by Indian gentleness and self-restraint, are ready at any moment to burst beyond bounds—if released by intensification of religious rivalry.

No religious riots comparable to those in 1946 and 1947 have taken place since then, but smaller riots broke out in Bihar and West Bengal in 1964, when Hindu refugees from Pakistan brought back with them stories of maltreatment by Muslims, and others occurred elsewhere after the outbreak of the Indo-Pakistan war in 1965.

Feelings of rivalry based on religious differences are described as "communal" in India, since each religion is considered as a community. (Although "communal" has no unpleasant overtones in Western ears, to Indians the term brings back memories of the terrible violence of religious riots.) The resurgence of "communal passions," largely quiescent since Gandhi's death in 1948, was one of the most ominous features of the social and political scene in the early 1960's. Political parties based on religious loyalties showed mounting strength. In an attempt to block their growth, the more secular-minded government, under the leadership of Prime Minister Nehru, passed a law in 1961 to prohibit parties from contesting elections on the basis of religion, and established a National Integration Council to formulate plans for combating divisive forces, including those based on religious differences.

The 12 million Christians of India form the next largest minority. Although they constitute only a little more than 2 per cent of the population of India as a whole, they form 25 per cent of the population of Kerala, which is the area of their largest concentration. The Kerala Christian community is one of the oldest anywhere in the world. According to tradition, it was founded in the first century A.D. by the Apostle St. Thomas, who went east to India at the same time that St. Paul went west to Rome. But even if this is historically unfounded, it is certain that the Christian church in Kerala—calling itself Syrian—dates back at least to the sixth century A.D.

To the initial layer of early Syrian Christians were added the much later converts of Portuguese and French Catholic missionaries, who first arrived in the sixteenth century. British Anglican missionaries came after 1813, and missionaries of Protestant sects of all kinds came later in the nineteenth century.

Throughout the nineteenth century, schools and colleges run by Christian missionaries—and deriving considerable support from overseas—played a highly important role in the introduction of Western-type education into India. Furthermore, Christian concepts, as well as secular Western thought, stimulated the significant reform movement within Hinduism in the nineteenth century.

The Christian community of south India includes many highly

cultured and widely respected persons. In other parts of India, however, the converts have come almost exclusively from the lower levels of society, from among the so-called "untouchables" or from the aboriginal tribes in the jungles.

Since independence, the activities of missionaries have been under severe attack. Christianity has been identified with white Western influence, which in turn has been associated with the hated imperialism. Although some Hindus are willing to honor Christ and even regard him as an incarnation of the Divine, all have objected strenuously to the Christian stress on conversion and on the unique superiority of the Christian message. In April, 1954, a commission appointed by the state of Madhya Pradesh charged that missionaries had been forcibly converting the aborigines and were attempting to establish within India a separate Christian state. Despite repudiations of this charge by responsible Indian leaders, the Government of India has since placed severe restrictions on the entrance of new missionaries into India.

Indian Christians have Indianized their churches and tried to end their dependence on foreign missions. Complete independence may prove difficult, however, because so many of the Christians are not only poor but also completely out of contact with people who have money to give.

Kerala's large number of Christians and the strength there of church schools largely account for its exceptionally high educational level and rate of literacy. But tragically, education has outstripped economic opportunities, which are limited by the extreme density of population. Many of the educated (who are not necessarily Christians, even if educated in Christian schools) are unemployed. The Communist Party has taken full advantage of their frustration and discontent—thus creating the ironic and paradoxical situation in which the state with the most Christians also has the highest percentage of persons voting the Communist ticket. Elected to power in Kerala in 1957, the Communist Party quickly passed a law giving the state government a large measure of control over nongovernmental schools, including church schools. Christians were vigorous in their opposition to Communist rule and took an active part in the civil-disobedience movement of 1959 which unseated the Communists.

The third largest religious minority, the Sikhs, numbering 7.8 million, accounts for slightly less than 2 per cent of the population. Their history has an ironic twist. Starting as a contemplative, pacific religious sect, they became transformed into a tightly knit militant group as a defense against the Muslims, one of the two larger religious groups from which their religion originally stemmed. Since independence, they have been at odds with their other parent group, the Hindus.

The founder of Sikhism, Nanak (1469–1539), was born of Hindu parents in the Punjab in north India, then under Muslim rule. Just as certain Hindus in later generations, under British rule, felt impelled to reconcile their faith with that of their conquerors, so Nanak studied both Hinduism and Islam until he worked out a synthesis that satisfied him. The conflict had forced him to dig deep for essentials. Condemning the formalism of both Hinduism and Islam, he wrote:

> Religion consisteth not in mere words;
> He who looketh on all men as equal is religious,
> Religion consisteth not in wandering to tombs or places of cremation, or sitting in attitudes of contemplation.
> Religion consisteth not in wandering in foreign countries or in bathing at places of pilgrimage.
> Abide pure amidst the impurities of the world;
> Thus shalt thou find the way to religion.[1]

He preached that in the true worship of the high, formless, omnipresent God there was no room for distinctions as between Hindus and Muslims. His followers came to be known as Sikhs, from the Sanskrit word for disciple. They called Nanak their Guru (teacher).

After Guru Nanak's death, the leadership of the group passed in succession to nine other Gurus, who gradually transformed the loose group of disciples into a tightly knit community with its own language, literature, institutions, and social customs. The fifth Guru, Arjun, made a compilation of Nanak's writings, with certain excerpts from Hindu and Muslim texts. This became the Granth, the holy scripture of the Sikhs. In all Sikh temples today, it is the central object of worship. Executed in 1606 by the Mughul Em-

-2%

Granth

peror Jahangir, Guru Arjun thus became the first Sikh martyr. The next Guru built up a small private army, and the Sikhs became increasingly militant. After the ninth Guru had been decapitated in 1675, for refusing conversion to Islam on the command of the Mughul Emperor Aurangzeb, his son Govind established a new Sikh fraternity, the Khalsa (the pure). He made his followers drink out of the same bowl, required them to take Singh (lion) as their last name, and imposed upon them five symbolic distinctions, the "five K's": they must wear short drawers and a steel bracelet, they must carry a sword or dagger and a comb, and they must also keep their hair and beards unshorn. Today, the Sikhs still wear a distinctive turban over their uncut hair.

The tenth Guru built forts, formed a militia, and engaged in battle with the Mughul forces. His sons were killed, and he was later murdered. The line of Gurus ended.

As the Mughul Empire weakened, the Sikhs became increasingly independent, first taking cover in the foothills of the Himalayas, where central power could not easily reach them, then coming boldly down onto the plains of the Punjab. They formed a kingdom under the powerful and able Ranjit Singh. After his death in 1839, the British finally conquered the Sikhs in two hard-fought wars between 1845 and 1848. Under a skillful British administrator, they quickly became reconciled to British rule, and fought valiantly on the British side in the rebellion of 1857.

The largest concentration of Sikhs has always been in north India, especially the Punjab. Before partition, many of them lived in the part of the Punjab that is now West Pakistan. As the prepartition tension mounted, armed bands of Sikhs—as well as armed bands of Hindus and Muslims—roamed the countryside. With the mutual killings mounting, the Sikhs—and the Hindus—on the far side of the boundary line fled to India. Today, Sikhs form somewhat less than half of the population of the Indian section of the Punjab. Their leading political party, the Akali Dal, has been pivotal in Punjab politics.

Of sturdy build, the Sikhs are the leading wheat farmers in India. Enterprising, energetic, and often skillful with machinery, they are also the taxi drivers of Delhi, able somehow to make any ancient relic on four wheels chug onward. When they can afford even the simplest machinery, they often start small factories (to make such products as bicycle parts). Fighting men perhaps above all, they constitute 13 per cent of the Indian Army.

Although the Sikhs used to feel closer to the Hindus than to the Muslims, some Sikhs have begun to fear that Hinduism's tendency to absorb is beginning to threaten their cultural and religious identity. Since 1947, their political leaders have played on this fear. A symbol of their threatened condition has been the fact that Hindi rather than Punjabi (in which their holy scripture is written) is the official language of the Punjab. Although Punjabi differs only slightly from Hindi, and chiefly in its script, Sikh leaders have asked for a separate Punjabi-speaking state to be carved out of the Punjab. In 1961, the Sikh Master Tara Singh fasted for forty-seven days in the hope of forcing the Indian Government to divide the Punjab into two states. At the same time, two Hindu saints fasted on behalf of the continued unity of the Punjab. Nehru refused to divide the state, but assured the Sikhs that the central government would protect their cultural autonomy. In 1965, another Sikh leader, Sant Fateh Singh, was about to start a new fast in support of a separate state, but gave up the idea when the Indo-Pakistan war broke out.

Parsis, Jains, and Buddhists

The other minority religions of India have played a far less prominent role in Indian politics than have Islam, Christianity, and Sikhism.

The Jains, numbering over 2 million and concentrated chiefly on the west coast, are the ancient sect founded by Mahavira, a contemporary of the Buddha. In his autobiography, Gandhi recorded how strongly his mother had been influenced by the Jain doctrine of nonviolence and how this in turn had affected him. Many Jains are highly successful in business and trade, and they feel confident that their position and prosperity are assured. It is interesting that Hindus regard Jains as a sect within the Hindu fold. Although Jains consider their religion as separate, they have not emphasized their separateness as vigorously as have Muslims, Christians, and Sikhs. They seem to have had no great fear of Hindu dominance.

The Parsis, much less numerous, number only about 115,000 persons, of whom 60,000 live in Bombay. They were originally Persian Zoroastrians—fire-worshipers who followed the teachings of the Persian religious leader Zoroaster (Zarathustra), who is believed to have lived in the seventh or sixth century B.C. Their religion emphasizes the eternal struggle between the principles of good and evil, light and darkness, and the importance of aligning oneself with the good. In order not to defile the principal elements—earth, fire, and water—by contact with dead matter, they expose their dead to be eaten by vultures. When the Muslim invasion of Persia threatened them in the seventh and eighth centuries A.D., they fled to India, settling on the west coast. With no food prohibitions or caste distinctions, the Parsis early formed close contacts with the British in Bombay. Perhaps for this reason, they tend to be far more Western in outlook than the majority of Indians. Like the Jains, but perhaps even more markedly, they form one of the leading business communities in India. An outstanding Parsi family, the Tatas of Bombay, directs the largest single aggregation of private industry in India, with an annual output of goods valued in 1960 at close to $250 million.

The Buddhist community in India numbered about 4 million in 1961. Although it once enjoyed strong royal patronage (beginning with King Ashoka in the third century B.C.), had many influential monastic and educational centers, and probably attracted large numbers of adherents, it gradually gave way before the resurgence of Hinduism, and its vital centers were finally destroyed by the Muslim invaders. In recent years, it seemed likely for a while that the number of Buddhists would again increase, as Hindu untouchables sought an escape from their inferior status within Hinduism by conversion. In October, 1956, the great leader of the untouchables, Dr. B. R. Ambedkar, and 200,000 of his followers became Buddhists in a mass ceremony. Since then, the movement for the conversion of untouchables seems to have lost momentum. The Government of India now grants special privileges to untouchables such as scholarships, the reservation of seats for them in universities, and places for them in the civil service. But they lose these privileges if they are converted. Ironically, therefore, untouchability has come to seem, at least to some, an asset rather than a liability.

A noteworthy feature of all the minority religions in India is their separateness from one another and from Hinduism. Each is a community, a separate world in itself, with its own customs, food habits, and marital exclusiveness. In this respect, they resemble the separate castes within Hinduism itself. This was graphically illustrated to me recently, when an Indian student in New York, a personal friend, telephoned to tell me that the marriage he had planned with another Indian student in America had been vigorously and successfully blocked by both his family and hers because he is a Hindu and she a Jain. Yet both are members of India's tiny, most Westernized minority. Such is the strength and cohesiveness of the religious community in India.

The barriers between religious groups not only are religious and social in nature, but also affect economic opportunities. The tendency in India for jobs to go to persons of the same caste or religious community as the employer is great. It is perhaps in this respect that religious minorities suffer the greatest handicap, unless —as in the cases of the Jains and the Parsis—there are prosperous employers within their own community to whom they can turn.

To reduce the barriers—religious, social, and economic—between the various religions and to create a lasting secular state in a highly religious land is not an easy undertaking. The idealism characteristic of many Indians prompted the effort. Will it succeed? Will the practical, everyday tolerance of a sufficient number of individual Hindus measure up to the tolerance they attribute to Hinduism as a whole? Will the minority religious groups be reasonable in their demands and expectations? It is not easy to predict, but at least in the first eighteen years of independence the secular ideal has been followed with considerable, if not total, success.

9 • CASTE, FAMILY, AND SOCIAL CHANGE

However greatly India may differ from the West in its religious background, it differs perhaps even more sharply in the very framework of its society and the patterns of social behavior. The caste system, the large "joint family," arranged marriages—these and other traditional social institutions are quite unlike anything to which the West is accustomed. Are they right or wrong? This question, so often asked in the West, cannot really be answered. How can any of us be sufficiently free from the prejudices and preconceptions of our own particular culture to see another culture through impartial eyes? With a different location and geography, with a different history and religion, India might not have had a caste system. To say this is only to underline again the basic fact that all the various facets of a culture fit together organically, have deep roots in the past—and even a certain inevitability.

Today the caste system is changing. Its worst feature, untouchability, is on the decline. Among upper-class urban Hindus, intercaste contacts are now taken for granted, though even here intercaste marriages remain the exception. Industrialization and urbanization have tended to produce new classes which, to some extent, cut across caste lines. The hold of caste is certainly strongest in the vast rural areas, though here, too, the relationships between castes are changing. Because of the vast variety of India, it is difficult to make general statements as to the extent of change in any one place or area.

A prevalent conception in the West is that the caste system

may really be "on the way out." But this is certainly not the case. Whatever changes are occurring, the dynamics of the system as a whole continues to retain amazing resilience. To expect the situation to be otherwise would be to underestimate the tremendous momentum of the stream of life following its own channel in India as surely as it follows quite different channels in the West. Like other new Western borrowings, concepts of equality in some ways seem to float on the surface of Indian life like leaves on the surface of a river which has existed years before the leaves were even buds.

Four Social Orders and 3,000 Castes

Most societies have classes, but in few societies is the transition by an individual from one class to another so difficult as in India, and in none are there such pronounced and widely accepted restrictions on social relations between the various social groups.

Hindus often speak of their society as containing just the four castes referred to in the early Sanskrit writings: the Brahmans (priests and teachers), the Kshatriyas (rulers and warriors), the Vaishyas (merchants and traders), and the Shudras (workers and peasants). Outside this fourfold social order was a despised fifth group of still lower persons, often called "outcastes" or "untouchables."

The Western stereotype of the Hindu caste system quite naturally is based on this classic Indian description. The actual picture, however, is far more complex. Today a fourfold division exists only in theory. In the words of one prominent Indian publicist, "The fourfold caste is merely a theoretical division of society . . . it is a sociological fiction."[1] The effective units in Indian society today are some 3,000 separate castes and subcastes, the members of which do not normally intermarry or eat together except in the most Westernized circles. In other social contacts, also, caste is an important factor in how people deal with each other. Various strong taboos, prohibitions, and ideas of pollution maintain a wide social distance between certain castes. If a Western society were divided into 3,000 separate compartments, it would be fragmented indeed. In India, the traditional tolerance of every conceivable way of life tends to ease the situation. And whatever the differences between castes, they all share to a greater or lesser extent the bond of traditional Hindu culture.

Many Indians are reluctant to talk about caste, especially to foreigners. If they do, they usually suggest that the 3,000 castes of today are merely subdivisions of one or another of the more important four original castes, rather than significant divisions of society in their own right. But this view tends to obscure the nature of caste as an important present-day reality and to direct attention away from the real dynamics within contemporary society.

In the English language, the word "caste"—derived from the Portuguese—is commonly used to refer both to the four original groups and to the far more numerous groups of modern times. From the Sanskrit, however, Indians have two different words for the two distinct kinds of groupings: Varna refers to the original fourfold division, jati to today's more numerous groups. It may help to avoid confusion if one bears in mind this Indian distinction. The word "jati" used to be translated as subcaste. But since the jati is the effective social unit, the group within which all marriages normally take place, many sociologists today translate it as caste.

The varna system is clearly very old. It seems to have taken shape shortly after the Aryans entered India and may have had some beginnings even before that. The earliest Vedic hymns mention the first three orders of society, and later portions of the *Rig Veda* refer also to the fourth class—the Shudras, who were not permitted to follow the religious practices of the other groups.

All four groups mentioned in the *Rig Veda* were regarded as of divine origin, each having emerged from a portion of the Creator symbolically appropriate to its activities. The Brahmans were thought to have come from the mouth of God, the Kshatriyas from his arms, the Vaishyas from his thighs, and the Shudras from his feet. At the outset, the relationship between the four groups seems to have been somewhat fluid, although the Brahman was strongly entrenched at the top of the hierarchy. There was no prohibition of eating together, and intermarriage, though not favored, was not completely prohibited.

Some Indians hold that this fourfold grouping originated

merely with a broad division of labor. Others, however, tend to relate it also, at least in part, to racial distinctions. The early Vedas record the repugnance the Aryan invaders felt for the dark-skinned, snub-nosed natives whom they found in India. It is generally believed that they relegated these Dravidians to the laboring class, while the still earlier settlers or aborigines on whom the Dravidians in turn looked down, became the outcastes.

At an early date, the varna system became explicitly connected with religion. Each group had its own special duty (dharma), and it became important to do the duty appropriate to one's own group rather than that of another group. If a man lived a good life, he would be born into a higher order in the next incarnation. If a woman lived a good life, she might someday be reborn as a man. An immoral life led to rebirth as an animal or other subhuman creature. The Code of Manu, dating in its present form from about 200 B.C., systematized the fourfold division and laid down duties for the members of each order.

Did the more numerous groups, the jatis, develop by a subdivision of the varnas? Or did the jati system have a completely different origin? Again, there are various theories. The traditional Hindu explanation of the many separate castes of today is that the offspring of mixed marriages came to be treated as new groups. As the number of new groups increased, the possible kinds of mixed marriages increased, each producing a new caste. Modern scholars have been skeptical of this explanation. Some hold that the jati system arose out of the organization of society into hereditary monopolistic guilds. Others argue that a sufficient explanation is the almost continuous arrival over the centuries of new tribes. As we have seen, these were probably incorporated into Hindu society as new castes or were divided into groups, each of which became a new caste or subcaste assigned a place in the theoretical four original orders. One modern Indian scholar has argued persuasively that the jatis are essentially extended kinship groups. In any event, even jatis assigned to the same varna may differ from one another so radically in their customs that it is hard to believe that they could ever have been part of the same endogamous group (that within which marriage is permissible).[2]

The great unanswered question relates not to the large number of castes, but rather to the origin of the strong taboos and ideas of pollution which created the framework for the system of caste separatism and hierarchy. Perhaps the explanation lies in the fact that the fertile Indian peninsula not only attracted migrants, but also served as a dead end for those who came—a net that caught and held a variety of peoples unparalleled in any other place in the world. Because the differences among the many incoming groups were too great for all to be integrated into a single society, a mode of intergroup behavior was evolved which made it possible for them to live side by side without fusing and without mutual interference. Concepts of pollution, of ceremonial purity, and of the magic properties of food are common to all primitive peoples. In most societies, such concepts gradually disappear as civilization advances. The reason they have retained their vitality in India may lie in their usefulness in helping each group maintain its identity in the face of the appalling diversity around it. Certainly, the caste system proved to be a workable method of separate and parallel living—India's way of absorbing foreigners, of making complicated cultural adjustments possible.

Basic Features of the Caste System

More important than speculation on the origin of caste is the nature of the caste system as it has functioned generally in recent centuries, and as it still functions where Westernization and urbanization have not yet seriously affected it. Each of the 3,000 separate groups tends to have its own customs, rules, corporate life, community spirit, and sense of belonging—although some castes possess one or another of these characteristics to a greater degree than do others. Caste membership is determined by birth. So long as a member obeys the caste rules regarded as essential, no worldly success or failure ends his membership. Fewer rules are regarded as essential in this sense today than in the past.

Castes have elaborate restrictions on diet and on social intercourse. Some castes will eat meat such as mutton, goat, or chicken; others will eat fish but not meat. Some will not eat meat or fish, but will eat eggs; others will not even eat eggs. Each caste has its detailed rules as to who may cook the food its members eat and from whom they may receive water. The higher the caste, the more severe are the restrictions. A Brahman, for example, may not eat rice or grain cooked with water unless the cook is another Brahman. But he may eat vegetables cooked in clarified butter if prepared by those castes immediately below him.

Castes are thought to convey pollution in varying degrees. The most polluting castes are the untouchables; in most cases, it has been thought sufficient to avoid their touch. Until recently, in the state of Kerala, however, certain untouchable castes were virtually unseeable—that is, they were required to maintain great distances between themselves and members of upper castes.

There are regulations for a host of other matters. Each caste has its own particular way of washing, of brushing the teeth, of dressing, and of sitting or reclining; it has its own laws of inheritance and its own religious customs, obligations, and ceremonies; and, above all, it has its own restrictive rules as to marriage.

Besides prohibiting intercaste marriages, castes usually prohibit marriage within a particular lineage group of the caste and fix the degree of consanguinity (which varies greatly) permissible in marriage. Whereas marriage between cousins who are the children of two brothers is prohibited by virtually every caste, many castes in south India not only allow cross-cousin marriages—that is, the marriage of a boy to his mother's brother's daughter—but regard this type of marriage as preferable to all others. On the other hand, in the castes of north India, cross-cousin marriages are generally prohibited. Such differences between castes make it difficult to legislate on matters already governed by caste customs.

Other rules relate to ceremonial religious observances and to moral conduct. The conduct that is right for the members of one caste is often frowned upon by members of another caste. To the Rajputs of north India, it seems essential that they should be brave to the point of rashness, mettlesome, quick to perceive and resent an insult, proud, revengeful, skillful in stick fights. Rajputs may hunt game, eat meat, drink liquor and eat opium.[3] This ideal of conduct contrasts sharply with the moral code of various Brahman castes, which usually stress nonviolence and vegetarianism, long hours spent in contemplation or the performance of ritual observances and bathing, and nonattachment to worldly possessions or goals.

Many castes have traditional customs of their own which seem odd to a Westerner, but may have served a rational purpose in the past. Under modern conditions, some of these are changing. Among the caste of Nambudri Brahmans of Kerala, for example, only the eldest son has traditionally been permitted to marry. The younger sons were expected to continue living unmarried in the joint family home, tilling the undivided family holding of land—a custom that protected land holdings from fragmentation during successive generations. These younger sons traditionally formed liaisons outside the home with girls of the next lower caste—the Nairs—who for their part regarded such liaisons as legitimate marriages (though by no means all Nair women married in this way outside their caste). From the Nair point of view, a reason for the symbiotic relationship with the Nambudris was that the Nair men were traditionally warriors, often away from home serving as mercenaries in the many wars before the British imposed peace. Left alone, their women managed the family land and exercised a freedom unique among women in Hindu society. Unlike other Hindu castes, most of which are patriarchal and patrilinear, the Nairs followed a matrilinear system of inheritance. The joint family property legally passed down through the female line. If a man acquired property by his own efforts, it was inherited not by his children, but by his sister's children.

However well the special Nambudri-Nair relationship may have served the interests of both castes in an earlier period, it is now gradually breaking down and is increasingly resented by members of both castes. The Nair men resent the shortage of Nair women resulting from the marriages to Nambudris. The younger sons of the Nambudris resent the fact that tradition demands that they have no contact with their consorts except at night, and none whatever with their children, who are brought up as Nairs. One prominent younger son of a Nambudri family is Mr. E. M. S. Nambudripad, who served as Communist Chief Minister of Kerala from 1957 to 1959 and was chosen General Secretary of the Communist Party of India in 1962. In an interview I had with him in 1958, he claimed that his reason for becoming a Communist was his dislike of the traditional customs of his caste and his belief that the Communist Party is basically opposed to caste. He even defied caste custom and married a Nambudri girl.

Theoretically, at least, each caste in India has a hereditary occupation. There are castes of washermen, gardeners, goldsmiths, moneylenders, potters, oil-pressers, mat-makers, leatherworkers, water-bearers, carpenters, accountants, genealogists, barbers, tailors—the list is almost endless. Although there are also a number of large and important peasant castes, agriculture is an occupation supposedly open to all—as is service in the government or the army.

The hereditary caste occupation is not necessarily followed by all the members of the caste or even by the majority of the members. Various present-day forces tend to undermine the old caste occupational patterns. Even so, at least certain castes have a monopoly or a near-monopoly on their traditional occupations. The dhobis are still the washermen for everyone except those who are so poor that they must wash their own clothes. For most caste Hindus, Brahmans still perform the priestly functions, though a minority of Brahmans are priests.

Each caste normally exists within a limited geographical area, and its members usually share a common language. Thus their locus is within a single linguistic area, hence a single Indian state—though internal migrations may blur this picture. Within a single linguistic area, there is an average of 200–300 separate castes. Only some 20–30 castes will normally be represented in any one village, and some villages contain far fewer. Within the village, castes are closely interdependent economically, though they retain their social separateness.

Many castes have standing councils (panchayats), which decide questions of interest to the caste and undertake programs designed to enhance the general welfare of caste members. The word "panchayat," which literally means council of five, is also applied to village councils, which are quite different from caste councils and may contain representatives of a number of castes. Today neither caste councils nor village councils necessarily consist of only five persons.

The strength of caste councils varies greatly from caste to caste. Their functions often include the disciplining of caste members for the breach of caste rules, and the consideration of cases which in other countries would be brought before law courts. Such cases might involve, for example, the nonpayment of debts among caste members, refusal to carry out the marriage contract, petty assault, price-cutting. Indeed, before the coming of the British, kings recognized the judicial rights of caste councils and often exercised their own judicial powers only in disputes between castes. Punishments for wrongs done usually consist of fines and religious expiation. But in extreme cases, the panchayat may outcaste a member. Many of the Hindu social reformers of the nineteenth century had to undergo the stigma of this excommunication. And it will be recalled that Gandhi was outcasted as late as 1915 by the council of the Modh Banias for breach of their rule regarding overseas travel. Although outcasting did not stop Gandhi from going to England to study, and it did not check the fervor of certain other social reformers, such a punishment is severe in a society where the group, not the individual, is the effective unit. A man without a caste necessarily finds himself alone and unable to join other groups. Castes are thus small and complete worlds in themselves, with virtual governments possessing powerful sanctions for the enforcement of their decisions.

To Westerners who tend to be obsessed with inequality of status, probably the outstanding feature of the caste system is the concept of hierarchy. All the castes in any given area tend to be assigned to one or another of the four original Vedic orders and to be arranged in a rough scheme of ritual and social precedence—sometimes disputed and contested by castes that believe they are entitled to a higher rank than they are accorded by others.

From Brahmans to "Untouchables"

At the top of the ladder are the Brahmans, who today are divided into a large number of separate castes differing greatly from one another in their customs, food habits, rules, and social standing. A few of the prominent Brahman castes are the Nambudri Brahmans of Kerala, the Chitpavan Brahmans of Maharashtra, the Iyers and Iyengars of Madras, and the Kashmiri Brahmans of Kashmir. Prime Minister Nehru was a Kashmiri Brahman, but his family moved from Kashmir to the area now known as Uttar Pradesh seven generations before he was born.

Although their supremacy has often been disputed and has not always been effective everywhere in India, the long-continued high position of the Brahmans remains one of the most extraordinary features of Indian social history. This position seems to have been based largely, though not entirely, on their monopoly of "correct" religious practices and of education (closely allied with religion before the coming of the British). Particularly in certain parts of the country, Brahmans have also built up wealth as landowners. In view of their power, it is noteworthy that over the centuries Brahmans have seldom been kings or *de facto* rulers. Instead, they have usually contented themselves with advising kings who ranked below them in the social hierarchy. In classic Hindu thought, the king had the duty to rule justly in accordance with principles laid down in Sanskrit scriptures as interpreted by the Brahmans.

Brahmans constitute only about 6.4 per cent of the Hindu population and are unevenly distributed geographically—being proportionately most numerous in north India (especially in Uttar Pradesh and the Punjab), and least numerous in the Dravidian south.

When the British first came to India, their main contacts were with Brahmans, who, with a few other upper castes, were the first to profit by British education and to enter government service under the East India Company. Until the 1920's, Brahmans dominated the nationalist movement, and their hold on high government offices still remains greatly disproportionate to their percentage of the population. Of twenty-three Hindus in the Cabinet or Council of Ministers of the Indian Government in 1956, thirteen were Brahmans.[4] But the position of the Brahmans is becoming increasingly precarious. Anti-Brahman sentiment has been particularly strong in the states of Maharashtra and Madras. An anti-Brahman Justice Party played a prominent role in Madras as early as the 1920's. In Maharashtra, anti-Brahman feeling was greatly increased by the fact that Gandhi's assassin was a Brahman. After Gandhi's death, many Brahman homes were set on fire. Among the various complex, often ambiguous, or contradictory caste changes that are occurring in India today, the decrease in Brahman domination is the most clear-cut.

At the bottom of the social ladder is a group of castes officially known as the "scheduled castes." When India was under British rule, they were carried on a specific list, or "schedule," and were thereby entitled to special government protection and scholarship aid. Thus it is by this title that they are usually referred to in official documents of modern India. These lowest, most depressed castes are the "outcastes," or "untouchables." They have suffered from a number of civil and religious disabilities, which have now been prohibited by law but have not entirely vanished in practice. Traditionally, they were not allowed to enter temples, pass through certain streets, enter certain parts of the villages, or drink water from the common village well used by other Hindus. Often, they were required to live in special areas or hamlets outside the villages. In the south, the type of house they were permitted to build was prescribed. In various areas, they were forbidden to carry umbrellas, wear shoes, milk cows, keep domestic animals, or use ornaments. They were required to dress in specific ways in different parts of the country—the males often in mere loincloths. But today, in many places, the old restrictive customs are losing their force.

Except for the few who have received a good education and gained recognition as a result of their ability, the untouchables still do the dirty work of India, such as sweeping the roads and cleaning out the latrines; many collect the corpses of dead animals, skin these corpses, eat the carrion, and cure the hides. They also form the vast bulk of the landless agricultural laborers, unlikely to get more than brief, seasonal employment. Greatly "underemployed" and barely able to eke out livings, they exist on starvation diets in miserable hovels.

Untouchables used to receive (and sometimes still do, though probably to a lesser extent) abusive treatment. Examples of such treatment are numerous in the biography of B. R. Ambedkar, the brilliant, highly educated leader of the untouchables who rose to cabinet rank and served as chairman of the committee that drafted the Constitution of present-day India. Both Ambedkar's father and grandfather had served in the Indian Army, and the family was well-to-do and self-respecting, yet his teachers at school would not touch his notebooks. He was whipped and beaten for drinking at a public water fountain. When he first entered government service, the peons, or messengers—themselves of low caste, though not untouchables—flung office papers and files at him instead of handing them to him.[5]

Although the untouchables are sometimes called "outcastes," the term is misleading for there is no indication that these people or their ancestors were ever outcasted or that they had ever been caste Hindus within the recognized social hierarchy. Interestingly enough, however, they do have a caste hierarchy of their own. While their leaders demand the abolition of caste and social equality for all, the untouchables themselves are divided into more than 400 castes. All except the lowest of these tend to look down on other untouchables, whom they regard as their inferiors fully as much as do the caste Hindus. This fact suggests the extent to which the concept of hierarchy is embedded in Hindu thought.

According to the 1961 census, there were then about 60 million untouchable Indians, or 13.7 per cent of the population. Many authorities believe, however, that this census figure is low, perhaps because many untouchables prefer not to reveal their status to the census takers. It is generally thought that they actually constitute about 20 per cent of the population. The dividing line between untouchables and the more backward and underprivileged lower-caste Hindus is not easy to determine, however.

Present changes occurring in the status of the untouchables reflect not only the influence of Western concepts of equality but more especially the influence of Gandhi, who took an untouchable child into his home, did with his own hands work considered suitable only for untouchables, called the untouchables *harijans* (children of God), and persuaded the Indian National Congress to adopt a resolution pledging support of *harijan* uplift. For a number of years, Gandhi published a magazine called *Harijan*, devoted, among other things, to the welfare of the untouchables. In 1932, he undertook a fast until death on an issue involving their treatment as an integral part of Hindu and Indian society. It is interesting that his antagonist on this issue was the untouchable leader B. R. Ambedkar, who was seeking separate electorates for the scheduled castes—that is, they would vote in the regular elections, but separately from the rest of Indian society, and be permitted to choose untouchables for seats reserved for them in the legislatures. This would have given them the same special status in elections which the Muslims had received in 1909. Ambedkar gave in only when Gandhi's fast had brought him perilously close to death.

In a sweeping declaration, the Indian Constitution of 1950 abolished untouchability and forbade its practice in any form (Article 17). It also prohibited an inclusive list of specific discriminations: the denial of access to shops, public restaurants, hotels, and places of public entertainment; denial of the use of wells, roads, religious bathing places, and "other places of public resort" (Article 15). And it forbade the exclusion of untouchables from educational institutions maintained by the state or receiving state aid (Article 29). An Untouchability Offenses Act passed in 1955 provides penalties for discrimination.

Although untouchables are often too poor, too ignorant, or too frightened to assert their legal rights, discrimination is decreasing. The greatest protection for the untouchables lies in their new political importance. All adult untouchables are now enfranchised, and under the Constitution, untouchables have special representation in Parliament and in the state legislatures for twenty years. But they do not have separate electorates; everyone living within certain designated districts, whether an untouchable or not, must cast his vote for one or another untouchable. In the lower house of Parliament, 76 out of 506 seats have been reserved for them. Several untouchables have held cabinet rank in the central government. One untouchable, D. Sanjivayya, who served as the chief minister of a state government, was chosen President of the Congress Party in 1962. Perhaps it is fair to say that while feeling against untouchables remains very strong among the Hindus just above them on the social ladder, educated upper-caste Hindus now accord them opportunities and recognition. Increased funds have been set aside for scholarship grants to untouchables, and untouchable children who succeed in finishing the lower grades of school are virtually certain of securing scholarships for higher education. But the creation of a leadership group among the untouchables is hampered by their tendency to drop out of school before finishing their education.

Another section of the Indian population given special treatment is the "scheduled tribes"—the remnants of aboriginal tribes not assimilated into Hindu society. They are concentrated for the most part in the band of rough hills separating peninsular India from the northern plains, in the hills of Assam to the east, and in the Nilgiri Hills in Madras. Under the Constitution, their protection and privileges are much like those of the scheduled castes, but in varying degrees they resist assimilation and protection, cling to primitive customs, and ask only that the central government leave them alone. Members of the Naga tribe of Assam—head-hunters until recently—have fought a stubborn guerrilla war since the early 1950's for an independent Naga state to be carved out of Assam. Hoping to appease them, the Indian Government in 1963 set up for them a new state, Nagaland, but *within* the Indian Union. Not satisfied, Naga extremists continued their resistance. A cease-fire and peace talks in 1964–65 brought no solution.

Between the Brahmans and the untouchables lie the many castes generally assigned to the three lower orders of the old varna system. For example, the martial Rajput castes are regarded as Kshatriyas, the moneylending Banya castes as Vaishyas. The vast bulk of the peasants belong to the many separate castes lumped together as Shudras, and most of the artisan castes are likewise regarded as Shudras. In different regions, castes with the same occupation do not always hold the same rank.

Castes classified as Brahmans, Kshatriyas, or Vaishyas are spoken of as the "twice-born." Their boys, at the beginning of adolescence, go through a religious ceremony designed to initiate them into a second life, that of the spirit. As a symbol of this initiation, they wear a thread (the "sacred thread") diagonally across their upper bodies and over their left shoulders. The two most important cleavages in Hindu society today are those between the Shudras and the "twice-born" castes on the one hand, and between the Shudras and the untouchables on the other.

Although until recently individuals have not been able to rise or fall socially, castes as a whole may do so. Indeed, over long periods of time, the relative positions of all but the Brahmans at the top and the untouchables at the bottom seem constantly to have shifted. Especially during periods of prosperity and expanding trade, there seems to have been considerable caste mobility. As one modern authority has put it: "Trade and wealth . . . have always been explosive solvents of a hierarchical, theocratic, and materially poor society."[6] Especially when the skills of a particular caste were in short supply in relation to the demand, their chances of economic betterment, of course, tended to improve. Today, many castes are jockeying for a better position on the social ladder, and competition among them has become far more acute than in the past.

Economic betterment by itself does not bring a better social status. To stake out its claim to a higher social and ritual position, a caste must act like an upper caste. In some cases, this may involve imitating Westernized ways, but perhaps more often it involves copying the traditional cultural pattern of the local Brahmans: worshiping gods different from those of the lower caste, becoming vegetarians, giving up alcohol, adopting the Brahman system of marrying off daughters at an extremely young age, following the Brahman practice of treating the male head of the family almost as a deity. The members of the caste seeking to rise must also invent myths about its origin and ancestors, thus asserting a hereditary claim to membership in one of the higher varnas. Then they must wait for several generations until those who know the falsity of their claims have died. Finally, the status to which they aspire and which they have asserted may be generally accepted. Sometimes this change must also involve a shift in the kind of work they do, since work is also graded hierarchically—even to the extent of an order of precedence in the various forms of manual labor.

It is not unusual in any country that an attempt to rise in the social scale should involve the imitation of those at the top. But this common phenomenon has had interesting by-products in India. For one thing, it seems to have played a major role in creating a certain degree of cultural uniformity despite the many invasions and countless ethnic strands. Any lower caste that imitated the traditional culture of the Brahmans took over at least some parts of the great tradition of classic Hinduism—often mixing it with elements of their own tradition, but nevertheless establishing through the fact of imitation the beginning of a common denominator with other castes. This process—called Sanskritization—has brought at least portions of the great Sanskrit tradition to groups who know no Sanskrit and may be largely illiterate.

In all imitation, there tends to be a cultural time lag, and this is particularly significant in India today. While the lower castes have been imitating traditional Brahman customs, a considerable percentage of the Brahmans themselves have been imitating the customs of the West. Thus, "in the lower reaches of the hierarchy, castes are taking up customs which the Brahmans are busy discarding."[7] This time lag helps to explain the existence among the great bulk of the middle and lower castes of India of a traditionalism often greatly underestimated in the West.

The Caste System Challenged

Enough has been said to make it abundantly clear that caste is a social system radically different from the individualistic society we take for granted in the West. Although it contains certain opportunities for mobility, it is the group rather than the individual that moves. How much and in what ways is the system likely to change in the future, under the continued impact of Western ideas and technology? In considering this question, it is important to remember that this is by no means the first challenge caste has encountered. Over the centuries, long before the arrival of the British, new religions and reform movements within India also had repeatedly attacked the system.

The Buddha was the first to do so, in the sixth century B.C. Not recognizing caste among his own group of followers, he taught that a person's worth is determined by right conduct and right knowledge, not by caste position or the religious sacrifices and ritual for the observance of which lower castes had been dependent on the Brahmans. He stressed individual effort and responsibility. He even ate with untouchables; in fact, one account attributes his death to contaminated food he ate during one such meal.

It is not known how much effect Buddhism had on the caste system as a whole, but caste seems to have been very fluid in the first millennium A.D. However, this may have resulted not so much from the influence of the Buddha as from increased general prosperity brought about by the active commerce of the time.

The next major challenge to caste came with the Muslim invasions. The Muslims brought to India the explosive idea that people of high and low social status had equal dignity in the eyes of God—an idea so welcome to those in the lowest castes that many of them became converted in groups. Attempting to synthesize Hinduism and Islam, medieval teachers such as Ramanand, Ramanuja, Kabir, and Nanak (the founder of the Sikh religion) attacked caste explicitly and vigorously.

Yet, though these and other leaders were responsible for new anti-caste movements and sects, the caste system remained strong. Indeed, one of the ironies of the Indian social scene has been that again and again many of the new movements that started out as protests against caste gradually turned into new castes themselves. So pervasive is caste in India that even Indian Muslims are divided into caste-like groups. So, too, are the Indian Christians; in Kerala, for example, there are separate churches for high-caste and low-caste Christians. And caste is so entrenched today even among the Sikhs that a modern anthropologist reported finding not a single case of intercaste marriage in a Sikh village he studied.[8]

In one way, the first effect of British rule was to strengthen caste, for the British gave back special privileges to the Brahmans which the Muslim rulers had taken away. On the other hand, the British law courts disregarded the hierarchical principle that upper-caste persons should receive lighter punishments than those given for the same offense committed by lower-caste persons. In the cities that grew up during British rule, it became possible for untouchables or low-caste persons to "pass" as members of higher castes from some distant area. Intercaste contacts became difficult to avoid in buses and factories. Many more situations occurred in which caste considerations were not the determining factor. The new educated, Westernized, cosmopolitan elite in the cities began mingling socially with people of other castes but of their own financial position and class. Today, they decry caste and in many ways ignore it, but they still prefer to marry within their caste. Whereas a Westerner seeks to find an individual who will be a compatible mate, even educated Indians tend to take it for granted that compatibility of behavior and values can be found only within one's own caste.

It would be a mistake to assume that many Indians desire a casteless society. Even those who are opposed to the grosser forms of discrimination—and hence favor the abolition of untouchability—still cling to their own caste ties, which give them a precious sense of security and of belonging.

In certain ways, the caste system as a whole today seems stronger than ever. There has been a tendency toward the formation of larger, more inclusive, more active caste panchayats which interest themselves in taking action on behalf of caste members—setting up apartment houses to be rented only to caste members, hostels or dormitories for students of particular castes, colleges with endowments for the benefit of single castes.[9] Caste-consciousness has increased, and rivalries between castes have become more intense than ever. Nehru and other Indian leaders have repeatedly warned of the dangers of this new "casteism," which has been particularly vigorous in post-independence politics. Although the Indian Constitution recognizes the Western principle of social equality, the quite contrary hierarchical principle retains great resilience. Everything—every caste, every person, every occupation—continues to be appraised as higher or lower than something else. Is India more status-conscious than other societies? It is hard to make such comparisons. Certainly, many people in the West pay more attention to status than they may be prepared to admit, and it is easier to observe status-consciousness in others than in one's self.

There are three points about caste today that should be emphasized. First, India is officially trying to create social equality, while deep-seated habits of mind work against it. Second, competition for improved status seems to be on the increase. Although much of this competition takes on the form of intercaste rivalries, some possibility exists for the individual to rise above his caste, to move into a new class if he can secure a good job. For this, higher education is essential. Severe overcrowding of the universities and strains on the educational system have resulted from this competition. Third, the group—the caste—continues to play a unique role in India, persisting in a way that contrasts sharply with the situation in a more fluid society. In the United States, immigrant groups tend to dissolve after a few decades as a younger generation becomes Americanized and makes its way into the large society of "unhyphenated" Americans of many nationalities. In India, each caste has existed as such over countless generations, and castes show no signs of dissolving. Indeed, since the caste system has been the essential framework of Indian society, it cannot lightly be discarded.

Taking issue with the Western assumption that caste is on the way out, a leading Indian sociologist has argued that "the institution of caste has found new fields of activity," especially in politics. He adds that "caste is so tacitly and so completely accepted by all, including those who are most vocal in condemning it, that it is everywhere the unit of social action."[10]

Muslim Society

Space is too limited to cover the social organization of all the minority religious groups, but a few comments should be made about Muslim society in India, which is only somewhat more equalitarian than Hindu society. Upper-class Muslims, known as the *ashraf*, claim foreign ancestry either from Muhammad through his daughter Fatima, from some Arab tribe associated with Muhammad, or from Pathan or Mughul invaders. The lower-class Muslims, known as the *ajlaf* (commoners), make no such claims. As descendants of Hindu converts to Islam, many of them retain not only caste-like groupings, but other social customs that their ancestors followed before conversion. Marriages sometimes occur across the main dividing line between the upper class and the commoners. But the tendency is to marry within one's class.

The Importance of the Family

In India, as in much of Asia, the family and kinship ties have an importance far beyond that to which the West is accustomed. This is a fact of great relevance to many aspects of the Indian scene. It partially masks unemployment, and it profoundly affects personal attitudes toward authority and individual initiative. It leads to quite non-Western expectations as to what government officials, private business executives, or other persons with power or influence should be expected to do for family members. These are only some of the by-products of the Indian concept of the family.

In India, the individual is thought of always in a family setting.

Contacts are maintained with kin far beyond the immediate family, and some obligation is owed even to distant kin. The kinship group often has a closeness almost as great as that of the average Western family, while the family units within it have a closeness inconceivable in the West. Traditionally, the ideal family consists not just of a man and his wife and their children, but rather of a larger patriarchal "joint family" in which the sons bring their wives to the parental home and rear their children within it. Sometimes the joint family also includes married grandsons and their wives and children. Unmarried daughters and granddaughters remain in it only until marriage, when they become part of their husbands' joint families. When a joint family grows so large as to be unwieldy, and especially after the death of the head of the family, it tends to split apart, as brothers start new joint families of their own. The joint family has probably always gone through such cycles of formation and fission.

Whatever their size, the family groups used to live together under a single roof, sharing a common hearth. They held in common all the family property and often worked together at a common undertaking, whether agriculture, a craft or business. By the efforts of those who were able and energetic, the old and less able members of the family were supported. The group respected the authority of elders in general, but of the oldest male in particular, who was traditionally authoritarian. It was he who decided if any member of the family should be allotted money from the common family fund for a college education or other purposes, and he made many other decisions regarding their lives.

Only in the twentieth century did the concept of family solidarity begin to feel the challenge of the individualism inherent in Western thought. In 1900, the Madras Legislative Council, still largely composed of Englishmen, passed a Hindu Gains of Learning Bill to permit a man to retain, as his own income, the proceeds from a profession for which he had been specially trained. But the measure aroused so much opposition that the British Governor of Madras considered it necessary to veto it. Not until 1928 was a similar measure passed by the Central Legislature. Since independence, however, property laws have been revised to safeguard the interests of individuals and to permit inheritance by women.

A member of a joint family may now bring suit for the division of family property and receive his proportionate share.

The conditions of modern life have hastened the breakup of the joint families. The new forms of available employment have tended to undermine the family as a producing unit, with family members drifting in different directions in search of jobs. New land taxes and land-reform measures make it financially disadvantageous to keep the property in joint ownership. According to recent estimates, only about 17 percent of the households in India now consist of more than one couple and their children. But even when the joint-family property is broken up, and when couples go away to live separately, emotional ties remain strong, and family solidarity continues. Important decisions may still be made by the eldest male, and the extended family still has a specific geographic center—the old joint-family home, usually in a village. Countless couples living by themselves in some small room in a crowded city still look to that home as their true center.

A marriage is still regarded not so much as a union between two individuals as the establishment of a relationship between two families. It is arranged after long negotiations between the parents of the prospective bride and groom, the exchange of horoscopes, and agreement upon financial terms. A recent innovation has been to permit the prospective couple to have a brief glimpse of each other and allow them to veto the match if they desire. In most cases, however, the bride and groom still never see each other before the day of the wedding.

The search for a mate on the initiative of the young ones themselves is extremely rare. "Dating" does not exist except among the tiny minority of urban Indians who are extremely Westernized. Indian films have begun to portray tales of romance—of boys and girls falling in love and even flirting with each other—but they still do not show kissing or even the holding of hands. In one very popular Indian film of 1960, there came a moment when the boy reached down for the hand of the girl. As the two hands approached each other, the eye of the camera rose discreetly so that only the convergence of the forearms at the base of the picture suggested the forbidden touch below—an example of extreme Puritanism that provides an interesting contrast to the highly erotic sculptures of the medieval period and the explicit study of sexual techniques in the classic Hindu treatise, the *Kamasutra.*

Even so mild and decorous a romantic courtship as the one just described is more fantasy than a reflection of common practice. Most Indians still believe in arranged marriages, claim there is more chance of happiness under that system than under the Western one, and are highly critical of the frequency of divorce in the West.

Personality and interpersonal relations are inevitably affected by family structure. A child brought up in the warmth of a circle composed of many aunts as well as a mother, and many young cousins as well as brothers and sisters to play with, has an early experience in group living unknown to the child in a modern Western home. A daughter-in-law who must adjust herself to her mother-in-law's housekeeping fills a role totally unlike that of the free-wheeling young American wife. A married couple who come together as strangers and must get to know each other under the observing and critical eyes of parents establish relations quite different from those of a couple living alone. As the joint family changes, the entire background of personal life and character formation inevitably will change also. Joint families provided security, a rich sense of togetherness, and a comfortable knowledge that the man in charge would make the decisions. These are values to which Indians have become accustomed, as Americans in the pioneer days of the nineteenth century became accustomed to the contrasting value of self-reliance. When a young Indian leaves the security of family life in search of education or a job, he may well feel far more lonely and uprooted than would an American under similar circumstances.

The Position of Women—Yesterday and Today

The position of women in India deserves special comment because it is one of the factors that continue to buttress the traditionalism of Indian society as a whole. In ancient India, the position of women seems to have been high, but it deteriorated in the Middle Ages. The Muslims brought in the custom of purdah—the rigorous seclusion of women and the covering of their faces and clothes in the company of all except their immediate family.

Although the working women of the villages probably never observed complete purdah, most Hindu women tended to imitate the practice in varying degrees. Village women still often keep out of sight when men are present, or at the very least modestly pull the ends of their saris over their heads.

By the time the British arrived, the legal and social position of women was extremely low. Polygamy and child marriage were customary. The custom of suttee was practiced in north India, though not by all castes (it was unknown in the south). Some castes prohibited the remarriage of widows, even those who had lost their husbands during childhood or adolescence. Lacking not only emotional outlets, but also education and any means of self-support, their condition was not a happy one.

Throughout the nineteenth century, both missionaries and Indian social reformers fought to improve the status of women. Under the influence of the Brahmo Samaj, a Widow Remarriage Act was passed in 1872. But to pass a law is not necessarily to effect a reform. In reviewing the struggle that followed, one catches a glimpse of the tremendous social pressures that can lie behind the customs of a society. Families of widows sometimes resorted to violence to prevent a widow from remarrying. Men who married widows were shunned or even persecuted by their castes. Only slowly, and with much personal sacrifice on the part of the reformers, did widow remarriage gain some measure of acceptance. The education of women also moved slowly in the face of strong prejudice in many parts of the country. But a few women graduates began emerging from the universities at about the turn of the century, and women gradually took a more active part in public life.

The first modern organization of women was started in 1917 under the inspiration of two British women who had been active in the Irish home-rule agitation, Mrs. Margaret Cousins and Mrs. Annie Besant. In 1927, this organization was enlarged to become the All-India Women's Conference. It first concentrated on women's education and social welfare, but later moved into the fields of social legislation, the legal status of women, and economic opportunities for women. Today, it has vigorous branches in many cities.

The greatest change in prevailing attitudes toward the role of women occurred under Gandhi's leadership, when they took an active part in his various civil-disobedience campaigns. Women picketed shops that sold foreign cloth, prepared and distributed nationalist literature and news sheets prohibited by law, carried messages verbally back and forth between nationalist leaders when other means of contact were prevented by the police, and even served as underground leaders. As a result of their participation in Gandhi's salt march in 1930, 17,000 women were imprisoned.[11]

The first steps toward women's suffrage in India were taken in the early 1920's when the legislatures of certain provinces granted them the vote subject to property qualifications. Since women had only a limited right to hold property, very few could vote until the new Constitution of 1950 granted the suffrage to all men and women over twenty-one years of age, without property-holding restriction.

A very great change in the legal status of women has occurred since independence. In matters of religion, marriage, succession, inheritance, maintenance, and family relations, the British rulers had permitted the personal laws of the various religious groups and castes in India to prevail. On all these matters, there were great variations in different parts of the country and among different castes, but on the whole, except in Kerala, women held an inferior position. Polygamy was still permitted, though not frequently practiced. Divorce, though not uncommon in lower castes, was not allowed among higher castes. A woman could not adopt children, and female children could not be legally adopted by anyone. Worst of all, Hindu women could not inherit property—although, since 1937, a widow has had the right to enjoy her husband's share in the joint-family property during her lifetime.

Shortly after independence, Prime Minister Nehru sponsored a Hindu Code Bill to codify Hindu personal law and at the same time introduce drastic changes that reflected the influence of Western thought. The Bill encountered vigorous opposition at first. Orthodox Hindus could not admit the right of a legislative body to deal with such matters since they were covered by caste rules and customs. The Western features of the Bill seemed alien and strange to them.

After years of struggle, various parts of the original Bill were separately adopted by the Indian Parliament between 1954 and 1956. Together, they are known as the Hindu Code. The Special Marriages Act of 1954 permits persons of different faiths to marry without being required to renounce their faiths. The Hindu Marriage Act of 1955 prohibits polygamy and provides for both judicial separation and divorce in cases involving desertion, cruelty, leprosy, venereal disease, mental unsoundness, adultery, or renunciation of the world (an interesting and significant reminder of a religious practice that continues in the twentieth century). The Act sets the minimum age of marriage at fifteen for the girl and eighteen for the boy, thus confirming the age provided for in an act passed in 1929. The Adoption and Maintenance Act of 1956 gives women the right to adopt children and makes it legally permissible for female children to be adopted.

The most revolutionary of the new Acts is the Hindu Succession Act of 1956, which gives women the right to inherit property by will and gives daughters, widows, and mothers the right to share equally with sons in the self-earned property of the man who dies without a will. But, as in the case of many of modern India's reforms, there have been unexpected and undesirable consequences of this Westernizing attempt to give women a more assured status. Since the land holdings must now be divided among both the daughters and the sons, there has been increasing fragmentation of these holdings. And since women, particularly in north India, marry outside their own village, this sharing has created a new class of absentee landladies.

Special laws relate to Muslim, Christian, and Parsi marriage and inheritance rights. Muslims are still permitted to have four wives in accordance with Muslim religious law, but Muslim women enjoy rights of inheritance to property as full and absolute as those of men.

Although her legal position has been greatly improved, the Hindu woman, except in Westernized circles, is still bound by ancient traditions of behavior that emphasize her submission, obedience, devotion, and absolute dedication to her husband and his every wish. Her husband is almost a god, and the home is her life and her career. This is not to say that Indian women never work outside the home. Many do, especially among the poor, who cannot afford to be idle. Women plant, weed, harvest, and thresh. They work in the coal and manganese mines, and in the factories of all the big cities. For middle-class women, new careers are opening up, especially in medicine.

Among the tiny emancipated Westernized minority, there are many outstanding and forceful women prominent in public life. One such is the late Nehru's sister, Madam Vijayalakshmi Pandit, who served as the Indian Ambassador to Moscow, Ambassador to Washington, and then President of the United Nations General Assembly in 1953–54 (the only woman ever elected to this office). Several universities have women as Vice-Chancellors, and many colleges have women principals. The late Nehru's daughter, Mrs. Indira Gandhi, has taken an active and capable role in politics, serving as President of the Congress Party in 1959–60. She was even mentioned by many as a possible successor to her father as Prime Minister of India.

But such women are the exceptions. The vast majority are far less educated than the Indian men. In 1961, the rate of literacy among women was less than half that among men. Because women still generally follow tradition, successive generations of Indian children—even those of Westernized fathers—learn the old values and modes of thought from the womenfolk who bring them up. This is another reason for the tenacious hold of many old customs and for the continued coexistence of the new and the old.

The Pace of Change

Changes of social customs, attitudes, and values are occurring unevenly in different parts of India and among different groups—only slightly among the poor, particularly in the rural districts, and more rapidly in the cities, especially among the more privileged classes.

In this brief treatment, it would be hard to suggest the variety of ways in which change is occurring or the many ways in which the old tends to persist side by side with the new. Many Indians seem to live simultaneously in two worlds: the traditional, static, religion-oriented, caste-bound, family-centered world; and the new Westernized, rationalistic world of dynamic individualism and social progress. In daily life, they may repeatedly move back and forth from the one world to the other. A man may wear a Western business suit to his office, but change to an Indian dhoti at home in the evening. At one moment, he may seem as rationalistic and modern-minded as any Westerner; at the next, he may argue earnestly that the men who composed the Vedas 3,500 years ago knew about the airplane and the atom bomb, or he may cancel an important engagement because his astrologer has warned him that the time is not auspicious. Although his job may be part of the national effort to raise the standard of living, he may speak of economic progress as "mere materialism."

How do so many Indians manage to live in the two worlds with such apparent ease? Underneath the surface, are they not perhaps troubled, even tortured, by the profound contradictions involved? Or does Hinduism give them the faith that even these contradictions in their own lives are, in fact, reconciled in the all-embracing Brahman? It is impossible to answer such questions from the outside, and the answer doubtless would vary greatly from individual to individual.

But not every Indian handles the inner conflicts of today with such ease. The quite visible unrest occurring among one small sector of the population, the university students, illustrates the difficulties of social transition. The young have traditionally been expected to conform, to obey authority, to submit to rigid discipline, to adapt themselves to the customs and mode of living of the group to which they belong. Today, students are beginning to think of themselves as individuals rather than as members of a group. A new concern with ambition, initiative, self-development, and social justice is challenging the old respect for established order. Students reject the concepts of reincarnation and of inherited prescribed roles for certain castes. They want new opportunities, but they also still want old securities. As one thoughtful Indian has put it, "Our society is now like a two-headed [*sic*] Janus —not able to make up its mind. This dilemma is reflected in practically every phase of our life."[12] Disparity between the new dreams of romantic love and the actual opportunities for mixing with girls produces further unrest among the students.

The political democracy and economic development to which

India is committed require a nation of dynamic individuals, not of static groups. Such dynamism is emerging among India's student population, but explosively. Many are confused and subject to irrational, emotional storms that burst out repeatedly in student defiance of school, college, or university authorities. Students have frequently gone on strikes, attempted to intimidate professors, and indulged in acts of vandalism. In 1965, a state-wide student strike in Madras over the government's language policy was so violent and so destructive of government property that the army had to be called on to suppress it and Madras University was closed for several weeks.

At its outset, this strike was no doubt a spontaneous result of Madrasi distrust of the central government, which many Madrasis believe to be unfair to the south. In its later stages, it may well have been manipulated and prolonged by Communist agitators. But the strikes of students cannot be explained solely by possible Communist activity on the one hand or by the validity of some student grievances on the other. Part of the trouble clearly lies in the unrest and personal anxiety felt by the students themselves. Most students are extremely concerned about the problem of finding employment when their education is over. But the greatest difficulty seems to lie in the tensions caused by rapid changes in social values. It is significant that these student outbreaks are referred to as "student indiscipline"—underlining the transitional approach to the question of discipline. Should the student still bow to authority? Or should he learn how to create a dynamic life for himself? If so, what must he do? Young people are confused by these questions.

The unrest among the student population suggests the far greater social upheaval that may well develop when larger numbers of underprivileged people become familiar with disturbing Western concepts, so alien to the old Hindu social order. With its genius for synthesis, can Hinduism again incorporate the new ideas and still retain something of its own? Will it exercise a stabilizing effect? Or will a social revolution occur which even Hinduism cannot keep in bounds? The answer is far from clear.

10 • LANGUAGE BARRIERS AND CULTURAL LINKS

One of the most baffling problems that modern India faces is that of language. India is a veritable "tower of Babel," and the multilingual nature of the land affects every aspect of Indian life. It creates social cleavages in addition to those created by religion and caste. It greatly complicates the already difficult problem of education. It gives linguistic foundation to regional, as opposed to national, loyalties. It cuts across interregional communications of all kinds. Local political leaders often have difficulty communicating even with the national leaders of their own party. National conferences—whether of trade unions, women's organizations, or any other group—inevitably must grapple with language barriers.

The central government is acutely aware that language barriers, particularly if they are not offset by the progressive development of a strong sense of nationhood, pose a potential threat to national unity. It is actively fostering a number of programs to help people in the various regions to develop an awareness of the rich variety of India's cultural heritage and a pride in their nation.

Besides these government programs, various other unifying forces exist, not the least of which is the common Hindu culture: the many myths and legends accepted all over India; nationwide recognition (among the Hindus) of the all-embracing Brahman and of Shiva, Vishnu, and other personal gods; the nationwide acceptance of the ideas of reincarnation, karma, dharma, and moksha; and religious shrines and centers that attract pilgrims, rich and poor alike, from all over the country, giving them a chance to see many other regions besides their own. Yet, whatever the underlying feeling of oneness stemming from the Hindu religion, language remains one of India's most difficult problems.

The Problem of a National Language: Hindi vs. English

The governing elite of India all speak English—some extremely fluently, others less well. English serves as the common language for upper-class Indians in various parts of the country. Unfortunately, it is usually the *only* common means of communication between people of different regions. Yet English is spoken by only 1–2 per cent of the population. To be a successful democracy, clearly India needs an official language spoken by more than such a tiny fraction. Yet she also needs a "link language," for inter-regional communication. This is the dilemma—perhaps an insoluble one.

Hindi, the Indian language spoken by the largest number of Indians, is distinctly a regional language—of the north. In one form or another, it is the language of almost all of the great Indo-Gangetic plains. Although Hindi is spoken or understood by 32 per cent of India's population,[1] many people in other parts of the nation are resentful of the language and fearful of the domination of the Hindi-speaking north. If English is dropped, then people whose mother tongue is not Hindi will be at a disadvantage in securing the much-coveted jobs with the central government. They will suffer other economic disadvantages as well.

In 1949, the Indian Constitutional Assembly decided that Hindi should be the official language of the Indian Union—that is, of the central government. Each state was to decide for itself what language or languages to adopt for its own official purposes. Those in favor of Hindi as the language for the Indian Union won by the narrow margin of a single vote. But while voting for Hindi, the Constitutional Assembly decided that the change-over from English should not take place until 1965. It was thought that the intervening years would give people in the non-Hindi areas time to learn Hindi. Furthermore, it was hoped that by 1965 Hindi would become better suited for use as an official language. For Hindi is a relatively new language. It had no literature before the nineteenth century. Before then, it existed merely as a dialect in what is now the eastern part of Uttar Pradesh. At that time, other dialects, similar in structure, were spoken in other areas of the north. (At least two of them, Urdu and Punjabi, had been used for literary purposes before Hindi.)

Critics of Hindi say that it has not yet achieved standardization,

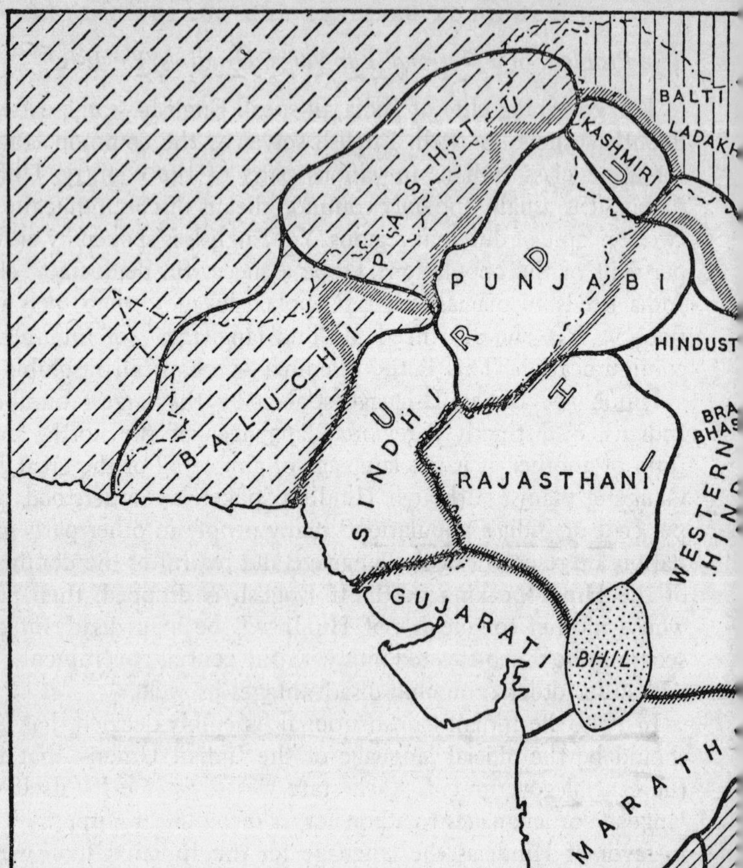

SOURCE: Hugh Tinker, *India and Pakistan: A Political Analysis* (New York: Frederick A. Praeger, 1962; London: Pall Mall Press, 1962); reproduced by courtesy of Professor Tinker.

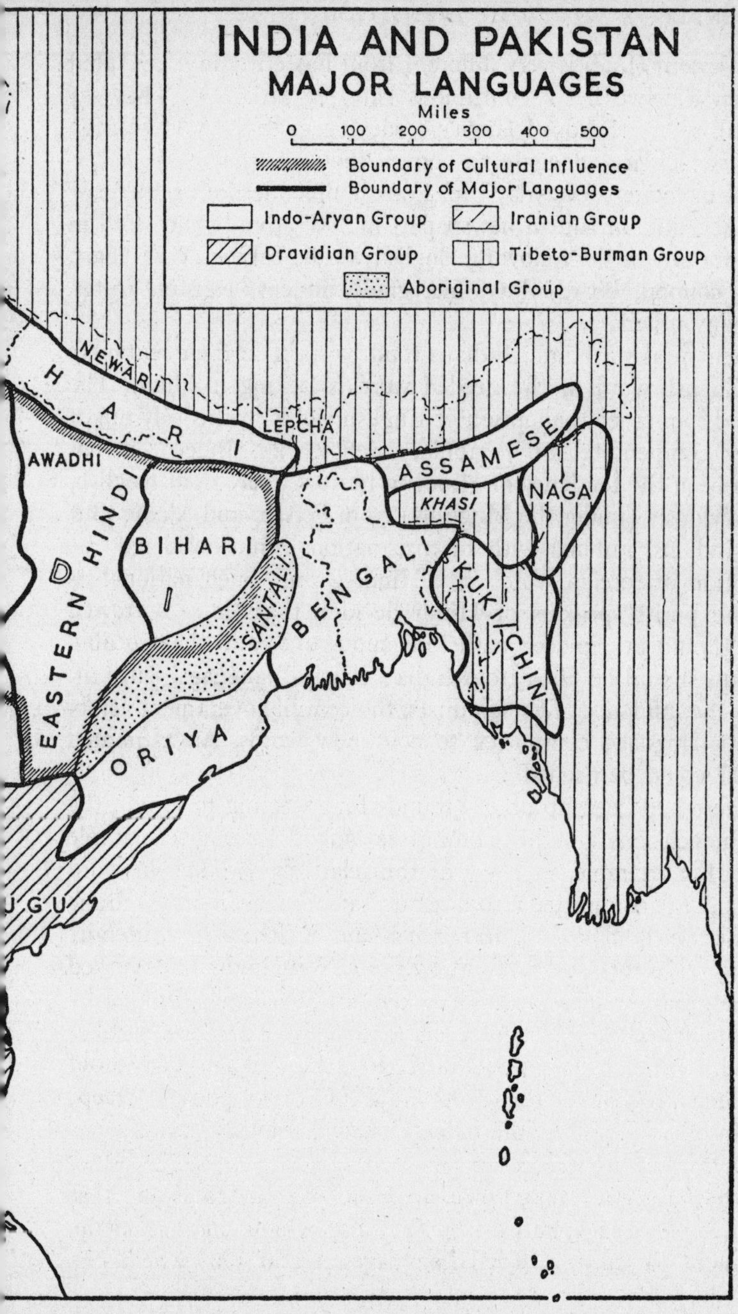
INDIA AND PAKISTAN
MAJOR LANGUAGES
Miles
0 100 200 300 400 500
Boundary of Cultural Influence
Boundary of Major Languages
Indo-Aryan Group
Iranian Group
Dravidian Group
Tibeto-Burman Group
Aboriginal Group
NEWARI
H A R I
LEPCHA
AWADHI
EASTERN HINDI
BIHARI
SANTALI
BENGALI
ASSAMESE
KHASI
NAGA
KUKI-CHIN
ORIYA
UGU

that Western Hindi is very different from Eastern Hindi, and that between the two lies a continuous band of variations. They say it is still an undeveloped language, lacking grammatical precision and a vocabulary adequate to convey thoughts that must be expressed in modern everyday life. For example, according to newspaper accounts in Indian newspapers in 1965, there is no word in Hindi for any of the following English words: cabinet, cart, chart, check, coupon, board, duty, file, grade, indent, register, roster, and many others.

When speaking Hindi, Indians tend to sprinkle their sentences with English words if the needed word is lacking in Hindi. The free and spontaneous adoption of English words in this way might quickly compensate for vocabulary deficiencies. Indeed, it has always been the tendency of Hindi to borrow freely from English, and previously (under the Mughuls) from Persian and Arabic. But some Indians, imbued with intense nationalism, considered the absorption of foreign words into Hindi wrong. Such nationalists and the purist speakers of Hindi decided that these borrowed words should be replaced with indigenous ones and that vocabulary gaps should be filled from India's classical language, Sanskrit. Under the influence of these purists, the central government established a language committee to coin new words. An estimated 300,000 would be needed!

If there had been no other grounds for objecting to Hindi, the recommendations of this committee might have given ample reason. For example, in place of the relatively well-known word "station," the committee recommended an absurdly long, synthetic Sanskrit word, *agnirathyantraviramsthan*, which means literally "resting place for a chariot run by fire." Non-Hindi India rocked with laughter over this and other complex archaisms proposed by the committee. Yet many Indians felt more indignant than amused. Why should the committee imagine that language could be created in a committee room? How could they possibly accept such an abomination as the official language of their central government?

In the late 1950's, opposition to Hindi became so strong that Nehru found it necessary to compromise. Under his leadership, Parliament passed an Official Languages Act in 1963 which permitted the continued use of English as an official language for an indefinite period after 1965, the year originally set for the change-over. Nehru made a still greater concession: He promised, orally, that English would continue to be used until the non-Hindi areas themselves felt ready to accept Hindi.

But Nehru cautioned that Hindi would have to be used sooner or later, and he urged everyone to learn it. With this objective in mind, a "three-language formula" for education was worked out. Under this formula, the first years of schooling everywhere would be taught in the child's mother tongue. Then, in the non-Hindi areas, English and Hindi would be taught as second and third languages. In the Hindi areas, the children's third language would be "another Indian language." It was apparently intended that this other Indian language would be that of another region, perhaps one of the proud southern languages. But not infrequently, the classical language, Sanskrit, was taught instead.

Despite this formula, very slight progress was made in teaching Hindi to non-Hindi children. As the 1961 census revealed, only 1.8 per cent of the people whose mother tongue was not Hindi had learned Hindi; few northerners had learned a southern language.

By 1965, Nehru was dead. Certain of the members of his successor's cabinet were not content to be patient until the whole country had learned Hindi in school. Some of them did not regard Nehru's oral promise about Hindi as binding upon them. The crucial date was January 26, 1965, India's Republic Day, the fifteenth anniversary of the day on which the Constitution first came into operation. Several cabinet members issued directives making it clear that after that date they intended that communications from their ministries to the various states should be issued in English. The south, where there is the greatest opposition to Hindi, went wild. Students went on strike, not just leaving their university classes, but derailing trains, cutting telegraph and telephone lines, destroying telegraph stations and any other available property of the central government. The disorder and violence continued for over a month, fifty-two persons were killed, and Army detachments had to be called in to protect public property. And Prime Minister Shastri found it necessary to repeat Nehru's promise that Hindi would not be "imposed" against the will of the states. Pointing out that nothing less than the unity of the nation was at stake, he pleaded for calm and sanity.

The 1965 crisis left the country in a condition of more or less permanent bilingualism. English would be retained for those who wanted it, but all state papers would have to be issued in Hindi as well as in English. This duplication involved considerable additional expense which India could not easily afford.

Worse than that, the 1965 language crisis stirred up the chauvinism of other language groups who had asserted themselves only to a lesser degree so long as the place of English was undisputed. A total of fourteen regional languages are listed in the Constitution—for what purpose it is not quite clear. In 1965, some began to argue that if Hindi was to be official, then all thirteen other languages should be official also. Few were ready to consider realistically to what expense the central government would be put if all official documents had to be translated into so many tongues.

Fortunately for the government, the national fervor stirred up in 1965 by the war against Pakistan enabled it to appeal for an end to language agitation, at least temporarily. Pleading for the utmost national unity, it postponed indefinitely a vote on proposed amendments to the Official Languages Act.

The Major Languages and Language Groups

The languages of India fall into three main groups: (1) the tribal languages spoken by the aborigines, who have not yet been absorbed into Indian life; (2) the Dravidian languages of the south; and (3) the Indo-Aryan languages of the north, which stem from Sanskrit. The southern Dravidian group includes four important languages: Tamil, the chief language of the state of Madras; Telugu, that of Andhra; Malayalam, the language of Kerala; and Kannada, that of Mysore. Although all four have borrowed words from Sanskrit, their basic pattern is utterly different from the northern Indo-Aryan languages.

The most important of the northern Indo-Aryan languages is Hindi, but a number of its neighbors and close relatives cannot be easily dismissed. Of all these, Urdu has probably the most distinguished literature. Having originated as the local dialect in the area around Delhi, the Mughul capital, it absorbed more words from the language of the Mughul overlords than did the other northern languages or dialects. Unlike the other northern languages, which are written in scripts reading from left to right (as is Sanskrit), it is written in Arabic script reading from right to left. But at least in its oral form, it is easily understood by those who speak Hindi. In their oral forms, indeed, Hindi and Urdu are merely two faces of one and the same language, differing only in the proportion of Arabic as opposed to Sanskrit words in their vocabularies.

During the nineteenth century, British educators stressed the common denominator between these two languages, helping to foster a language halfway between them, which the British called Hindustani. At the time of independence, this term was dropped. Urdu became the official language of West Pakistan, while Hindi was adopted as the future official language of India. The two languages are still quite similar, but there are increasing attempts within Pakistan to drop out words derived from Sanskrit, and within India to drop out words derived from the Arabic. Meanwhile, Urdu remains the language of the Muslim minority in north India. Many Hindus also are more at home in it than they are in the less developed Hindi. Urdu was Nehru's mother tongue. Many still regret that a combination of nationalism and religious feelings should have led to its eclipse.

A third important and controversial language of north India is Punjabi. In its spoken form, it closely resembles Hindi, but it uses a different script, Gurmukhi, in which the Sikh holy book was written. Punjabi is essentially the language of the Sikh religious minority.

Other important Indo-Aryan languages include: Assamese, the language of Assam; Bengali, the language spoken in the area around Calcutta; Oriya, spoken south of Calcutta in the eastern coastal state of Orissa; Gujarati, spoken in the western state of Gujarat; Marathi, the chief language of the multilingual city of Bombay and of the state of Maharashtra; and Kashmiri, spoken in Kashmir.

The four Dravidian languages and the nine Indo-Aryan languages mentioned above have been given recognition in the Indian

Constitution and are generally regarded as the "regional" languages. The Constitution also gives separate mention to Sanskrit, which has only a few hundred contemporary speakers.

Each language tends to be concentrated within a particular region, although there is much overlapping, especially near the borders of each linguistic area, and migrants have made the big cities multilingual.

Linguistic States and the Three-Way Tug of War

At present, a complex three-way tug of war is going on between advocates of English, advocates of Hindi, and advocates of the regional languages.

The stress laid on the regional languages since independence stems in large part from the influence of Gandhi, who argued that the use of English was creating a growing intellectual and cultural gulf between the educated and the uneducated—between men and women, as well as between the elite and the masses. He also held that it was intellectually crippling to force young Indian students to master a language as different from any Indian language as is English, and that only by using their mother tongues could young students learn to think freely and creatively.[2]

Even as early as 1920, the Indian National Congress organized itself along linguistic lines. Its provincial divisions followed the boundaries of the regional languages. Shortly after independence, there was strong political pressure for India's inner state boundaries to be redrawn on the basis of language differences. Prime Minister Nehru withstood this pressure until 1953, maintaining that the new nation faced other problems of greater importance and that in any event national loyalty rather than linguistic regional loyalties should be paramount. In 1952, agitation became acute, especially among the Telugu-speaking people, most of whom were still incorporated in the state of Madras, which was dominated by speakers of Tamil. One respected Telugu leader, Potti Sriramulu, used the Gandhian technique of a fast until death to enforce his demand for the formation of a separate state composed of those areas where speakers of Telugu were in the majority. He died as a result of his fast, and his death brought popular clamor to such a pitch that Nehru yielded to the demand for the formation of this one linguistic state. It was named Andhra Pradesh, a name recalling the glories of an ancient local kingdom which had flourished from about 250 B.C. to 250 A.D.

Once the central government had yielded to the demand of the Telugus, increasing demands arose in other parts of the country for states organized similarly on a linguistic basis. To examine these demands and to recommend new state boundaries, a States Reorganization Commission was appointed, and it submitted its report in November, 1955. A year later, the state boundaries were redrawn largely on the basis of this report. In the main, language boundaries were followed. The twenty-seven states that had previously existed were reduced to fourteen. All but two of these were relatively homogeneous from the linguistic point of view, though there tended to be sizable linguistic minorities in the large cities and near the state boundaries. Because of the overlapping of linguistic groups, no line could be drawn in such a way as to avoid these.

In two of the new states, there remained large, vocal, and politically active linguistic minorities. One, the new state of Bombay, had to be divided into the two states of Maharashtra and Gujarat in 1960 because of continued linguistic dissatisfaction. In the other bilingual state, the Punjab, the Sikhs, who speak Punjabi, occupy an area that could be separated from the remaining Hindi-speaking part of the state. Agitation for such a separation has been carried on vigorously by a portion of the Sikhs, but has been resisted by the central government. Since Hindi and Punjabi are closely related, it is argued by many that the demand for a separate Punjabi-speaking state is a demand based on religious rather than linguistic grounds.

The formation of linguistic states provided a geographical foundation for alarming new subnationalisms—reminding one that India had always been politically fragmented before the British came. Indeed, the great period to which any one group looks back with pride was almost inevitably achieved at the expense of its neighbors. Will India split into pieces again? Are there forces for unity sufficient to preserve the union?

Many Hindus answer that the great body of Sanskritic culture is a sufficiently powerful force for unity. They say that although India had never been politically united before the coming of the British, Hinduism had long given it a basic cultural unity of which the new political unity was a logical and natural expression. Others argue that the common interest of all of India in the economic development of the country and the basic reliance of the regions on the greater financial resources of the central government will prove to be the pivotal factors that will hold the country together.

It is hard for an outsider to judge the strength of the centrifugal, as contrasted with the centripetal, forces in India. But the chief opposition party in the Tamil-speaking state of Madras openly favored the secession of the south from the Union—until advocacy of secession was banned by law. And the Nagas, although granted a separate state within the Indian Union in 1963, fought a vigorous guerrilla war for complete independence not only before Nagaland was created for them, but also afterward. One reason why the Indian Government has refused to hold the plebiscite in the state of Kashmir that it promised in 1947 (to determine whether Kashmiris prefer to be part of India or Pakistan) has been the knowledge that if self-determination were granted in one instance, people in other states might likewise demand plebiscites and perhaps opt to leave the Union. Foreigners who believe that India has been unreasonable—indeed, irrational—in its tenacious hold of disputed Kashmir tend to forget that what is at stake for India is much more than the mere possession of territory.

Indians say to Americans: "You fought a war to prevent secession from your Union. We would too." The Indian Army is perhaps the most secure guarantee of continued unity. But it is by no means certain that a major military showdown will prove necessary in order to hold the Indian Union together.

The Cultural Renaissance

The vigorous renaissance of music, dance, painting, and the arts in general that has taken place since independence has a bearing on national integration, for it has begun to create new interregional links, at least for the elite.

Until twenty or thirty years ago, musicians and dancers had long been regarded as of low social status, virtually members of the servant classes. Serious interest in the arts had almost died out. Classical Indian music and dance forms had been forgotten. Indians were almost completely out of touch with the best of their own cultural heritage. In the second quarter of the twentieth century, as the nationalist movement increased in strength, educated Indians developed a new conviction that India, in her periods of greatness, had by no means been inferior to the West in the arts or in any other form of endeavor. Pioneering upper-class men and women pored over long-forgotten writings dealing with classical dance and music and then created classical forms on the basis of the old texts. Rukmini Devi, with her dance school at Kalakshetra, was one of the first of these. At his educational center at Santiniketan, the many-sided Bengali genius Rabindranath Tagore —poet, novelist, dramatist, essayist, writer of songs, painter, and prophet—spoke unceasingly and vigorously about the importance of a cultural revival for India as a whole, and practiced what he preached by his prodigious creativity in so many art fields.

The renaissance of culture caught the interest of educated Indians. In many of the leading cities, but especially in New Delhi, well-attended concerts and dance recitals by distinguished artists have become frequent. Increased public interest in painting and sculpture has brought into being many new art galleries, which exhibit and sell the works of a growing number of contemporary Indian artists. On an amateur level also, new music societies and new drama groups have been multiplying.

Although vigorous in its own right, this renaissance has had substantial government support which has greatly stimulated interregional cultural exchanges. In 1953–54, the government established three national academies to promote art and culture. The Lalit Kala Akademi—concerned with painting, sculpture and other graphic arts—holds a national exhibition every year at New Delhi, and this exhibit is also sent on a tour of state capitals. The Akademi makes substantial financial awards to outstanding artists and has published a number of books on the paintings and art works of various periods and regions. The Sangeet Natak Akademi organizes dance, drama, and music festivals, awards prizes, and promotes cultural exchange among the regions in these three art forms. Affiliated with it are a number of regional academies. Together with the parent body, these are surveying the music, dance, and drama of different parts of the country. The Sahitya Akademi is perhaps the most important of the three from the point of view of the promotion of national unity. Dealing with literature, it has published a national bibliography of all books of literary merit published in the twentieth century in the major regional languages, and a comprehensive "who's who" of Indian writers. It has also had translated a number of Indian and foreign classics into the various Indian languages. Its publication of these has created a new and highly important channel for the exchange of ideas and interests among educated people of the various linguistic regions. (To take charge of the interchange of exhibits and cultural missions with foreign countries, the Government of India has also established the Council for Cultural Affairs, which has a fine new building in New Delhi and an active program.)

The spontaneous new cultural effervescence in all the arts, as well as the government-sponsored activities, has transformed the city of New Delhi into a major cultural capital. A new dance troupe does not feel it has truly tested itself until it has performed in New Delhi. The same is true of painters and musicians. A patron of any of the arts must watch New Delhi, where he can see work that is representative of the country as a whole and gain a national perspective on Indian culture.

This emergence of New Delhi in the cultural field is a new development since independence—and one of great potential significance. If France succeeded in becoming a nation rather than a collection of regions, each pulling in different directions, it may well have been due in part to the fact that Paris emerged (perhaps especially from the time of Louis XIV) as the accepted cultural capital for all. It is too soon to assert that New Delhi can play as unifying a role as Paris, or that the cultural links being forged among the educated minority can eliminate regionalism from politics. But it must be remembered that some regionalism exists in the politics of every country. It becomes a matter of degree. The very fact that unifying factors are at work is certainly significant for the future of India as a nation.

11 • EDUCATION: PROBLEMS AND PROGRESS

To Westerners, the high proportion of illiteracy in India (76 per cent of the population in 1964) may suggest that India's chief educational need is quantitative expansion. How can a democracy continue to exist unless a far larger number of its citizens can be taught to read? How can economic progress take place when the printed page is meaningless to so many?

Serious though these questions are, many Indian authorities are even more concerned with the problem of quality in Indian education. It is a many-faceted problem—and the various facets are interconnected. First, there is what might be called the technical aspect. On the whole, although there are notable exceptions, the teaching is not good, and the textbooks and educational materials are inadequate in quality as well as quantity. Educational standards are not only lower than those in the West, but also lower than one might expect in a country that has had for so long a highly educated elite. Then, too, Indian education is far too bookish. In too many cases, it fails to prepare students for practical life, either by training them in some specific skill or by teaching them to think for themselves and use their minds analytically, imaginatively, or even systematically.

A limiting factor, affecting both the quantity and the quality of education has always been and continues to be the poverty of the country. Neither private nor public funds have ever been available for education on anything approaching the scale taken for granted in the West. But the problem of quality is also connected with the fact that the educational system and the content of teaching are foreign in their origin. Even today, almost twenty years after independence, the subject matter taught is too often unrelated to the Indian scene. In some of the Indian states, history courses still give undue attention to English or European history as opposed to Indian history. The literature studied is often the literature of the West. Even in the social sciences, the same Westward look tends to prevail. A sociology course may deal with Western sociology rather than with the Indian caste system. Courses in economics and political science may be modeled on Western patterns and fail to deal with the rich and intricate fabric of life close to home.

Until recently, few Indians had challenged this situation. If Oxford taught economics in Western terms, why should an Indian with an Oxford degree strike out on a different path on his return to India? In any case, poverty made it difficult to do so. Few Indian scholars have had the time or the financial backing to conduct the original research that alone could provide Indian content for courses in the social sciences. Furthermore, a tradition of individual scholarly research, comparable to that in the West, is still in its early stages in India.

As for courses in the humanities, Western content often seemed necessary in order to convey the best of Western tradition—which, after all, by the end of the nineteenth century, had come to be regarded by educated Indians as part of the Indian tradition also. Western literature at least exposes the student to the rationalistic, secular, liberal thought of the West—to the whole world of ideas and values so different from those in the Hindu myths, legends, and religious teachings. Western values can, of course, be learned more easily through Western than through Indian subject matter.

Since independence, there has been a growing conviction that education should also teach Indian values. One of India's leading experts on education, Dr. Humayun Kabir, long Minister of Science and Cultural Relations of the central government, has warned:

> The divorce of modern education from the Indian context is still a fact which threatens danger to the country's life . . . danger in . . . the weaning away of the literate classes from the culture of the country. . . . The new literates no longer derive their strength from the age-long traditions of the land. Their outlook is Western or

more frequently pseudo-Western. Cut off from their moorings, they are unstable, loud, and factional.[1]

According to modern Indian thinking, the best of the Western tradition should somehow be joined with the best of Indian tradition. Indian educators are working toward the creation of such a synthesis. But it is not easy. The educational problem is linked with the far larger problem of cultural conflict and assimilation, which the country as a whole has not yet solved.

From the point of view of national policy, other questions can be asked. What should be the objectives of the educational process? What kinds of trained manpower will India require to accomplish the purposes decided upon by the Indian Parliament or by the Planning Commission? How many doctors, scientists, engineering graduates, electrical engineers, chemists, and other professionals will India need? How should Indian boys be trained if they are to become factory managers, businessmen, economic planners—citizens of a viable democracy? The successive Five-Year Plans have laid down educational targets in quantitative terms, but the qualitative problem remains to be dealt with.

In the last decade and a half, as thoughtful Indians have become more and more concerned with this problem of quality, the educational system has had to deal with a tremendous influx of new students from the lower classes with no educational background. This has put a heavy new strain on the existing facilities, teachers, and administrators, and has created an entirely new set of problems. As the West has discovered also, the teaching of children of uneducated parents is far more difficult than the teaching of children with backgrounds of education. Subject matter suited to the one group may be totally unintelligible to the other.

These general observations apply differently to the various levels —the primary school, the secondary school, and the college or university. Since the educational system varies from state to state, the break-off point between these levels is not identical everywhere. In most states, the primary level includes grades 1 through 5, and the secondary level grades 6 through 10 or 11. But sometimes grades 9, 10, and 11 are referred to as the high-school level and the preceding three years as the middle-school level. In most universities, higher education leading to a B.A. or B.S. degree involves only three years.

Background of the Educational Problem

Before the coming of the British, Indian education was almost entirely religious. The Muslims had schools, in conjunction with their mosques, and the chief stress in the colleges (madrasahs) was on subjects connected with religion—the Arabic language, theology, and law. Upper-caste Hindu boys usually studied under an individual teacher, a guru, who taught only a few students. Often the students lived with the guru for as long as twelve years. It was their duty to work for him and to absorb everything he could teach, whether of a practical or a religious nature. A close emotional relationship existed between the guru and the student, the latter regarding the former with almost religious adoration. The masses had no education whatever except religious teachings passed on from one generation to the next in the form of stories, myths, legends, songs, and plays performed annually.

With the arrival of the British, there was no quick change in education. Bent on profit, the East India Company tried to avoid establishing schools except for the children of its own employees. At first, it severely restricted missionary activities within its territories. However, in 1813, under pressure from evangelical reformers in England, the British Parliament required that the Company lift its restrictions on missionaries. Mission schools and colleges began to be established. Some of the finest educational institutions in India were founded by missionaries. In 1813, also, Parliament required the Company to set aside a sum of money each year for educational purposes. The great issue became whether this money should be spent to stimulate indigenous education in Sanskrit, Arabic, Persian, and other classical Oriental languages, or used to promote a Western-type education, with English as the medium of instruction. There were sharp differences of opinion among both Englishmen and Indians. The Indian reformer Rammohun Roy was among the strongest advocates of the English type of education. Another alternative, not given equal attention in the early years, was that of teaching in the various Indian vernaculars, the students' mother tongues. Upper-class Indians of the early nineteenth century still looked down on the vernaculars much as European intellectuals in the Middle Ages had looked down on the vernaculars that later became modern French, Spanish, and Italian, clinging instead to Latin.

In 1835, the English essayist Lord Macaulay, then a member of the Governor-General's executive council, submitted a memorandum favoring English education. Dismissing with incredible arrogance the profound speculation and beautiful language of the Sanskrit classics, he said, "I doubt whether the Sanskrit literature be as valuable as that of our Saxon and Norman progenitors."[2]

Following Macaulay's recommendation, the Governor-General, Lord Bentinck, adopted the policy of giving financial support only to colleges teaching Western-type subjects in the English language. The emphasis was placed entirely on higher education as opposed to primary or secondary education. No attempt was made to reach more than a small upper-class elite. It was believed that from this elite Western knowledge would filter down to the masses. The policy was frankly one of Westernizing India. Lord Macaulay himself said, "We must do our best to form a class who may be interpreters between us and the millions whom we govern; a class of persons Indian in blood and colour, but English in taste, in opinions, in morals, and in intellect."[3] Although the government later gave aid also to institutions teaching non-Western subjects, English education became increasingly popular after 1844 when the Governor-General, Lord Hardinge, ruled that Indians educated in English-type colleges would be given priority in government employment. A degree thus became essential for worldly success. It scarcely mattered what one learned. This attitude has continued to prevail to the present day.

Within twenty years, it became clear that Western knowledge was not, in fact, "filtering down" to the masses. The Brahmans had been the first to profit by the new education. The barriers between them and the castes below were great enough to block almost completely the filtration that had been expected.

Sir Charles Wood, chairman of a commission to investigate education, was the first to stress primary education, in 1854, when he urged an integrated plan for the development of primary, secondary, and high schools, as well as colleges and universities.

He also recommended that government grants be given to private schools if they submitted themselves to government inspection; stressed secular education and religious neutrality—a blow to the missionaries; and recommended that three universities be established.

His emphasis on primary education—repeated at intervals by subsequent education commissions—led to little progress, especially in the rural areas. The peasants had no desire to have their children educated. Village children were needed to tend cattle and do other work in the fields. If they spent a year or two in school, they later forgot what they had learned because they had no occasion to use it. By the end of the century, three out of four villages were still without schools, and only one-fifth of the boys and a still smaller percentage of the girls of primary-school age were in school.[4]

Sir Charles Wood's other recommendation was implemented in 1857 when a university was established in each of the three "Presidency" cities—Bombay, Madras, and Calcutta. Modeled on the University of London as it existed then, the universities were of the "affiliating" type only. They were given the responsibility for coordinating the various colleges that already existed. They controlled the courses of study and the syllabuses to be followed, set the examinations, gave the degrees, but furnished no teaching themselves and had no residence halls.

Because of the policy of government inspection and grants to private educational institutions, India had a state-dominated system of education far earlier than did countries in the West. In the last eighteen years of the nineteenth century, an attempt to reduce the extent of centralized government control led to a drop in standards, and there followed renewed government control in 1904. Under Lord Curzon, Viceroy of India during 1899–1905, the universities were given teaching powers. Beginning in 1917, stress was laid on their development as unitary residential universities. Some of the existing universities were reformed in accordance with these ideas, and new universities were established. But control over the material to be taught still did not pass into the hands of professors. The syllabuses drawn up by the universities continued to be the determining factor. Anything resembling Western campus life remained almost nonexistent.

Before the end of British rule, a series of education committees or commissions under British chairmen had pointed to defects in the educational system that continued to plague India: Primary education was neglected. Even to the extent to which it existed, much of it was wasted because children did not stay in school the four years necessary to become literate. Secondary education was still dominated by the ideal of preparation for the university matriculation examinations. University education was too much dominated by concern with the final examination. Teachers at all levels were inadequately trained. The curriculum was not suited to the rural environment. More technical education was needed.

While the schools and colleges officially recognized by the British Government of India continued to struggle with these and other problems, the nationalist movement in the twentieth century led to other developments. Gandhi's concept of noncooperation involved nonattendance at government-recognized schools. New institutions were established which did not seek government recognition or aid. In the intervals between his more active political campaigns, Gandhi evolved a system of primary education that he called "basic education." The teaching was to be based on crafts and occupations that could later be useful to the children. He believed that many schools could finance themselves by selling the products that the children had made. Above all, he stressed that the teaching should be in the child's mother tongue.

In 1921, when the Montagu-Chelmsford Reforms—by which the British gave new powers to the provincial legislatures—came into effect, control over education passed from the central government and the British hierarchy of administrators to the provincial legislatures. Education today is still a "state subject." But after independence, and especially with the beginning of the Five-Year Plans in 1951, the central government again began playing a more active coordinating role in education, using central finances as leverage. On the other hand, in the late 1950's, as new stress came to be laid on political decentralization, several states placed control over village primary education, at least nominally, in the hands of indirectly elected bodies, Samitis, representing groups of about a hundred villages. It is too soon to judge what these Samitis—usually composed of the leading peasants of the area—will do. But it must be remembered that because education in India is almost entirely government-controlled, political pressures operate upon it at one level or another.

The Clamor for University Education

After independence, university and college education was the first level to receive careful consideration. In 1948, a University Education Commission was appointed to suggest improvements in higher education. Its Chairman was the distinguished philosopher and educationist Dr. S. Radhakrishnan, who later became the President of India. The Commission made a long series of thoughtful recommendations. Among them are the following:

The salaries of university teachers should be raised and their hours of actual teaching limited. The total number of pre-university years of schooling should be increased to twelve. (The normal number until then had been only ten, or eleven in some states, as opposed to twelve in the United States. Thus boys and girls had been entering universities at a younger age than in the West.) As a further step toward improving the quality of the students entering universities, the Commission recommended that secondary education should be completely re-examined and reformed. The standards of admission to the universities should be raised and the number of admissions limited. The Commission also suggested that steps should be taken to divert students at the end of their secondary education to new occupational institutes, as an alternative to academic higher education. It urged that more stress be laid on professional and vocational education, such as agriculture, commerce, engineering, technology, law, and medicine. As another step to reduce the rush into the universities of young persons not really suited for higher education, it suggested that a university degree should no longer be required for entrance into the administrative services of the government. Noting that village boys who succeeded in getting a higher education seldom went back to live in their villages once they had a degree, the Commission urged that special rural universities be set up to teach subjects important in village life, such as water-control engineering, scientific agriculture, and rural sociology. Above all, the Commission recommended that a University Grants Commission be established to allocate central-government funds for higher education and thus to help set standards.

It would be impossible to discuss briefly the implementation of these significant and valuable proposals—all directed, it should be noted, toward improving the quality of higher education. Although only a few of them have been fully adopted, they continue to serve as guideposts. As recommended, a University Grants Commission was established by law in 1956. An effort has been made to reform secondary education. Fourteen rural universities have been established. Far more stress has been put on professional education, though perhaps still not enough. In 1948, India produced only 900 graduates in engineering and 300 in technology;[5] by 1963–64, the number of such graduates had increased tenfold.[6] But 7 out of 10 students are still enrolled in courses in the humanities, despite the urgent need for young leaders with more practical training. The continued shortage of scientific, engineering, and technological courses is only one reason for this. The students themselves are partly to blame. Thousands of students want a college degree for the sake of the degree itself and without regard to the type of training involved. Fearing that they may fail a science course, those with inadequate intellectual background tend to choose the "softer" option of the humanities. The shift to courses directly related to careers and jobs also runs counter to the conviction deeply rooted in tradition that spiritual values should prevail over material values and the mere earning of a living.[7]

The recommendation in the Radhakrishnan report that the number of years of pre-university schooling be increased has not generally been adopted, although some states have added one year to the school course, while shortening the university course by a year. So far, the states have not been able to afford to do more than this. Contrary to the Commission's suggestion also, a degree is still required for entry into all but the lowest and most menial levels of government service.

Probably the most important recommendation of the Radhakrishnan Commission that has *not* been implemented is that the standards of admission to the universities be raised and the number of admissions strictly limited. The general expansion of education since independence has been most marked at the college and university level. In 1947, there were 200,000 students enrolled for higher education; by 1965, the number had soared to a million and a half—a sevenfold increase in eighteen years. Today, college and university students constitute about 1.8 per cent of the young men and women of their age group.[8] This is not a high percentage by Western standards, but it may be higher than the Indian economy can afford. It certainly includes many students totally unable to keep up with their studies. Of those who enter, 50 per cent fail their intermediate examination, which screens the student body after two years of study. Of the remaining 50 per cent, another 40 per cent fail the final examination leading to a B.A. or B.S. degree. The economic waste involved in offering education to so many students who cannot absorb it is a matter of real concern to India's leaders.

The sensible solution, of course, would be to follow the recommendations of the Radhakrishnan report regarding entrance standards and a firm limit on the total number of students admitted. But since every adult now has a vote, regardless of his caste, class, or educational background, any drastic limitation of educational opportunity would be politically impossible.

As a result, facilities for higher education have been swamped by the influx of new students. In Calcutta, for example, many college buildings are used in three shifts, with scarcely time between the shifts for the most superficial cleaning to be done. Almost all college teachers have so many hours of actual teaching that adequate preparation seems out of the question.

To meet the mounting demand for higher education, many new colleges have been established in recent years, most of them by private enterprise with very inadequate financial resources. Because science and engineering courses require expensive equipment, these new and inadequately financed colleges have perpetuated the old evil of too many courses in the arts or humanities.

As the colleges have increased in number, so have the universities. (All recognized colleges still must be affiliated with one or another university.) By 1965, there were sixty-one universities in India—about three times the number in undivided India before partition. Although most of the universities today teach at least some students directly, the chief responsibility of many of them is still to try to maintain—or to raise—the standards of the heterogeneous colleges affiliated with them. These colleges are often located many miles from one another and from the parent body. The great majority are "private" institutions, but some are run by state governments. Others trace back to missionary origins, although today a substantial percentage of their faculty and a still higher percentage of their student bodies are usually non-Christians.

Despite the fact that too many colleges are of poor quality, certain of the colleges maintain very high standards indeed and offer their students an education that would be regarded as excellent in any country.

Although the universities still prepare and grade the examinations for the students in the college, political pressures make it hard for them to hold the poorer colleges up to the high standards they regard as desirable. Except for four national universities that are supported directly by the central government, the universities are controlled by the state governments. In most cases, the state governments choose the vice-chancellors (the equivalent of university presidents in the United States), and they grant aid both to the universities and to their affiliated colleges. A university vice-chancellor can scarcely be severe toward a college of poor quality without receiving strong protests from influential state politicians interested in the survival of that college. In any case, if a university sets examinations that are truly stiff, it is likely to provoke an outbreak of student strikes and unruly violence which may threaten the very continuance of classes.

The existing system of examinations has been under challenge from educators as well as students. The student's mark depends only on his performance in his examination; nothing else counts. Based on fixed syllabuses and corrected by someone unkown to the student, the examination stresses facts and requires great feats of memory rather than of understanding and reasoning. In cramming for such examinations, students tend to turn away from books to predigested handbooks. The teacher knows that if a low proportion of his students pass, his reputation will suffer. So he discourages discussion lest students be distracted from memorizing.

It is generally agreed that the examination system must be changed. The Indian Ministry of Education has called in American experts to help formulate a long-term plan for the better evaluation of students' work.

In the somewhat discouraging picture of Indian higher education—which suffers from too many students, too little money, equipment, and facilities, and too much pressure from state politicians—a hopeful and positive factor has been the role of the University Grants Commission. With funds of the central government to spend on higher education where it feels that such money can do the most good, this Commission has helped to provide more nearly adequate buildings, equipment, laboratories, libraries, hostels, and staff quarters. Above all, it has helped to raise teachers' salaries. Not only because of the increase of students, but also because of low pay, teachers in some of the big cities had been teaching in more than one college and bearing teaching loads of as many as 36 classroom hours a week. In 1959, the University Grants Commission fixed 24 hours a week as the maximum load (still high in comparison to Western loads), promulgated a pay scale, and offered to pay four-fifths of the salary increases of any university complying with the scale. These measures brought a marked improvement, but even so, the salary of lecturers, who constitute the vast majority of the university teachers, ranges from $50 to only $100 a month, and the top salary fixed for a senior professor is no more than $250 per month.[9] Such salaries make it impossible for the teaching profession to compete with government service or business in securing the ablest men. Because of the pressure of work and the fixed nature of the syllabuses to be followed, an academic life in India offers fewer compensations for low pay than it does in the West—and less time for creative thought.

In the eyes of society and of their students, the status of college teachers is low. This lack of student respect for their teachers—and lack of contact between teachers and students in the large lecture-type classes—is part of the background of student indiscipline already mentioned. By any standards, and especially when contrasted with the traditional guru system, modern Indian higher educational is cold and impersonal.

Dr. Margaret Cormack, an American scholar who has spent

many years in India, has summarized the present situation in a succinct criticism, with which many Indians would sadly agree:

> Higher education is . . . largely foreign in its origin and nonfunctional in its current application. It has not undergone the changes seen in English higher education, is not based on a corps of instructors steeped in sound academic tradition, and has discarded the tutorial system inherent in both the English and the ancient Hindu systems.[10]

There is a notable absence of vocational counseling or guidance, although there are ample signs that students are deeply troubled by problems of all kinds that lie ahead of them, from earning a living to deciding where they stand in the puzzling conflict between Western and traditional values. Even today, only 15 per cent of the students enrolled for higher education live in hostels or dormitories.[11] Many students spend their student years in such appalling poverty, living in such cramped quarters, that one can only marvel that they can study at all. A recent survey of the living conditions of students at the University of Calcutta revealed that 33 per cent of them lived in dwellings where their average share of the total floor space was no more than 24 square feet altogether (the area that a single bed in the West would occupy)—representing not only their sleeping area, but their share of the living, dining, cooking, and washing space as well.

The tragedy is that students will endure anything to secure a university degree. It is not that they want education, but that they must have a degree to get a good job. Perhaps they will not get a good job even with a degree, but without it they regard themselves as lost. The desperation of India's poverty is thus an integral part of the educational problem of the country.

As if all this were not enough, higher education also is burdened with the language problem. Formerly, English was the actual medium of instruction in many or most secondary schools, as well as in all colleges and universities. This meant that the child had developed in secondary school sufficient mastery of English to learn through it all the subjects of the curriculum. Today, in secondary schools, the trend is toward the use of the regional languages as the medium of instruction, with English as a separate subject. Although some schools still continue to teach in the English medium and to maintain rigorous standards, they are a progressively smaller proportion of the total. More and more young people who seek to enter colleges and universities are only meagerly equipped for the use of English in higher education. Lectured to in English in large, crowded lecture halls, they feel lost and hopeless—another element in the prevailing dissatisfaction of students.

Although most of the universities still use English as the medium of instruction, seventeen of the sixty-one universities have recently made arrangements for teaching at least some classes in Hindi or a regional language.[12] The political pressures for a shift away from English are great. Because of financial aid from the state governments, the universities find these pressures difficult to resist.* But there are almost no textbooks in the Indian languages. And technical terms, especially in the sciences, are in English. Thus good higher education in a regional language is an impossibility. Then, too, a student educated in a regional language normally cannot find employment in any other region. If the regionalization of higher education should continue, India would find herself soon quite literally without national leaders capable of communicating with even the leaders at the regional level.

The language problem has presented the universities with a dilemma not easily solved. How can they teach in English when students are barely able to understand the language of the textbooks and the lecturers? How can they yield to the pressure to shift to the regional languages when so few textbooks exist in those languages and India so clearly needs an elite with a mastery of English? In opposition to state political pressures, the University Grants Commission has taken a strong position against the precipitate abandonment of English.

Whatever the present deficiencies in higher education, the ferment of thought regarding it—and the determination to improve it—will certainly produce changes. A significant undertaking of the University Grants Commission—not yet completed—is a re-

* An interesting decision by the Indian Supreme Court in 1962 ruled that a university has no right to compel its constituent colleges to change their own medium of instruction.

consideration of the entire content and method of higher education. Why is a particular subject taught? Are the facts to be conveyed and the method of conveying them up to date? How can more intellectual curiosity be stimulated? Such are the big questions it is asking. In short, although Indian higher education is beset by problems, these problems are being tackled with vitality and initiative.

Changing Patterns at the Secondary Level

As had been recommended by the University Education Commission, a Secondary Education Commission in 1953 made a thorough study of the problems of schools at this level. It pointed out that secondary education in India is of particular importance because not even one out of ten secondary students goes on to a university. For the remaining nine, secondary education is terminal. But it found that, despite this fact, the course of studies at the secondary level was completely dominated by the university matriculation examinations. It recommended diversification in the curriculum and the establishment of trade schools and junior technical schools. It held that education at the secondary level should stress preparation for life rather than for university entrance.

Since this report, 2,000 "multipurpose" high schools have been established which theoretically offer courses in agriculture, technology, home economics, business administration, commerce, crafts, and technical training, as well as the arts and humanities. These still form, however, a small proportion of the total number of secondary schools in the country—75,000 in 1962. They have faced difficulties in finding teachers adequately trained for the new courses, and have not yet moved far from the old academic pattern. But increasing sums are to be devoted to their development under the Fourth Five-Year Plan (1966–71).

Only slightly less than the universities, the secondary schools have been burdened with a heavy increase of students. The number has grown seven times since independence, from 3 million in 1947 to more than 20 million in 1962.[13] As part of its Constitution, India has theoretically adopted the principle that education should be free and compulsory for all children up to the age of fourteen, thus including the first three years of secondary education as well as primary education. Actually, no one has yet seriously considered how compulsory schooling in India could be enforced or how a sufficient number of schools could be provided. As yet, only 22.8 per cent of the children between eleven and fourteen are in school, and only 11.5 per cent of the high-school age group.[14]

As in the case of colleges, some schools are state-operated, some are Christian missionary schools in origin, some are private institutions. But again, virtually all schools are dependent on the state governments for financial aid. Only a fraction of the secondary-school teachers have yet received any teacher training. Indeed, only half of them have even completed secondary education themselves.[15] Textbooks and equipment are inadequate, but a Central Institute of Education has been actively studying the textbook problem, preparing model textbooks and teachers' handbooks which it hopes the various states will adapt for their own needs and translate into their own regional languages.

The general feeling that the university entrance examination should not be the only available test of the student's schoolwork has resulted in a movement to establish independent boards to conduct secondary-school–leaving examinations. These have been set up in all but three states.[16] Unfortunately, half of the students fail their school-leaving examination—another example of educational wastage.[17]

Primary Schools for All

Although free, universal, and compulsory education for children between eleven and fourteen is still a distant goal not really taken seriously, determined efforts have been made to bring all the children of primary level into schools. Many villages have new one- or two-room schoolhouses. By 1966, it is planned that there should be such a school, if not in every village, at least in enough villages so that no child will have much more than a mile to walk to school. The total number of primary schools in the country as a whole has doubled since independence. There are now 34.3 million children in primary grades, half again as many as the number of children of the corresponding age group enrolled in school in the United States[18]—a heavy load for any nation. It is hard to find teachers and still harder to raise the money to pay them a living wage, and it is difficult to equip them with textbooks and even the simplest supplies.

Theoretically, Gandhi's plan of "basic education," involving stress on the teaching of crafts in schools, has been accepted as the model. But it has not proved practical. To teach along the lines suggested by Gandhi requires more ability than do the older methods. However, Gandhi's ideas have resulted in the introduction of some simple crafts and manual activities into ordinary schools, thus bringing at least some of them more in line with the modern teaching methods of the West. In other schools, though, the children still sit in sedate rows, poring over printed pages with hardly a picture to help them understand the words that they laboriously learn to read.

Although the lack of interest on the part of rural parents in education for their children is perhaps diminishing, it is still not at all uncommon for parents to withdraw their children from school after one or two years. Out of every 100 pupils who enter the first class, only 35 reach the fifth class.[19] It is at the primary level that stagnation and wastage in the educational process are especially marked.

Western countries did not achieve mass education at primary or secondary levels all at once. Such education grew gradually. The problems in India seem staggering perhaps only because India is trying so desperately to do so much in such a short time.

Female and Adult Education—A Special Need

At every school level, the attendance of girls is disproportionately low. Even as late as 1958–59, there were only 40 girls enrolled in school for every 100 boys. The ratio was far lower than this for the middle-school level (30) and the higher secondary level (22).[20] A reason for the very large gap between the proportion of boys and girls attending school is the shortage of women teachers and their unwillingness to serve in rural areas. Conservative families do not consider it proper for girls to be taught by men. Under India's Third Five-Year Plan, various incentives have been proposed to increase the supply of women teachers—the provision of quarters for them, and of special allowances, scholarships, and stipends for women-teacher trainees. New abbreviated courses for women in the rural areas are being given in the hope of preparing them to teach in their own localities.

In addition to these special courses, efforts are being made to stimulate adult education in general, partly in an attempt to cut through the peasants' indifference to the education of their children. Fifty thousand adult classes or study centers have been started, with an enrollment of more than 8 million adults. (There are 200 million adult illiterates, of whom about two-thirds are women.[21]) Known as "social education classes," these are designed to teach not only reading and writing, but more especially citizenship, health, certain skills, and the rudiments of science as applied to everyday life. What they actually teach depends on the knowledge and outlook of the teachers. In the social education classes I have visited, the teachers have prided themselves on having taught their women students how to sew—an art often unknown because of the custom of using unsewn yardages as clothes—how to embroider or do basketry or other handicrafts, or how to preserve fruit in jars. These classes are at least a beginning.

An Over-all Review of Educational Problems

In 1964, a new education commission, headed by Dr. D. S. Kothari of the University Grants Commission, was appointed to re-examine all aspects of Indian education and to make recommendations in 1966 as to how all the various levels and branches of education should be developed and improved. This was the first time since independence that a commission had been directed to approach the many problems from an integral point of view.

Consultants from the United States, the United Kingdom, Japan, France, and the Soviet Union were invited to work with the Commission. UNESCO also volunteered to lend help. Like the recommendations of earlier commissions, the recommendations of this commission are not binding on the central government—least of all on the state governments, which jealously insist that, under the Constitution, theirs should be the final say in all educational matters. But it is at least hoped that this new unified approach to educational problems will lead to a new and widespread understanding of the need for improvement of the quality of education.

New Research Institutes

One cannot convey a balanced view of the level of learning in India without at least some mention of the achievements in research. The Government of India has developed a chain of National Laboratories—twenty-five in the last ten years—to conduct high-level research in applied science in a wide variety of fields, from nuclear physics and solar energy to the building of cheap durable roads. A food-research institute in Mysore is concerned with such matters as methods of canning food under Indian conditions, ways to extract protein from vegetables to provide a more balanced diet for vegetarians, and experiments with new food products such as macaroni made out of tapioca, corn flakes out of mangoes, cheese out of peanuts. Another important research institute is working on techniques for using India's low-grade coal for coking purposes. Other laboratories are concerned with research in leather, chemicals, glass and ceramics, electrical technology, and the development of drugs best suited to Indian needs, diseases, and sources of supply.

India has three atomic reactors, the first of which went into operation outside Bombay in 1956. India is also building several nuclear electric generating stations. Because atomic materials are available locally, it is expected that these power stations will be economically profitable. India's atomic scientists have also found many constructive uses for atomic isotopes in agriculture.

Nehru was hopeful that these research laboratories would find ways of breaking through some of the economic problems that seemed well-nigh insoluble before. In any event, their existence is a vivid reminder that India is by no means a land of illiterates only. In 1930, a distinguished Indian, Dr. C. V. Raman, received the Nobel Prize for studies in light refraction. Many other Indian scientists have won world-wide honor and fame. Thus both extremes must be borne in mind. If there are illiterates, there are also brilliant intellectual leaders. If bullock power and human power are still the chief forms of energy for many purposes, the most modern technology is also understood and utilized.

12 • NEHRU AND INDIA'S WESTERN-TYPE GOVERNMENT

Nehru's Background and Early Life

ANY STUDY OF THE POLITICS of modern India since independence must start with a discussion of the towering figure of Nehru—that brilliant, complex, introspective, hard-working, idealistic, sometimes indecisive man who dominated the Indian political scene for eighteen years.

Unlike Gandhi, Nehru was an aristocrat by birth. He was born into a wealthy, Westernized Brahman family who then lived at Allahabad on the Ganges, but had ancestral roots in Kashmir. When Nehru was ten, his father, Motilal Nehru, an exceptionally prosperous lawyer, bought a palatial home in an exclusive residential area occupied chiefly by Europeans. The house had two swimming pools and was staffed by an army of servants. Nehru's father imported the first motorcar into India, and a British tutor for his son. Except for his tutors, the boy was very much alone, read avidly, and developed a taste for English literature.

At fifteen, he was sent to England for the best English education, first at Harrow, then at Cambridge, where he specialized in chemistry, geology, and botany. This early training in science doubtless stimulated the rationalism and modernism that became prominent features of his intellectual approach and that always contrasted sharply with the more tradition-bound attitudes of the majority of his fellow countrymen.

After Cambridge, he read law in London, was admitted to the bar, and then returned to India in 1912, when he was twenty-two. Back in his father's mansion in Allahabad, he entered without zest or interest into the practice of law for eight years. In the pages of his autobiography, he depicted the Nehru of that time as a spoiled, dreamy, comfort-loving, condescending, even arrogant rich man's son, with no ambition or purpose in life beyond pleasure.

Then came three developments that jarred him into an awakening. The first was the Amritsar massacre of 1919, when a crowd of unarmed Indians were shot down by order of a British general.

A second pivotal experience was his first sight of village life a year later, when he spent three days in the countryside far from railroads or regular roads. Of this experience, he later wrote that it filled him with

> . . . shame at my own easygoing and comfortable life, and our petty politics of the city which ignored this vast multitude of seminaked sons and daughters of India. . . . A new picture of India seemed to rise before me, naked, starving, crushed, and utterly miserable. And their faith in us casual visitors from the distant city embarrassed me and filled me with a new responsibility that frightened me.[1]

Then, in 1921, came Gandhi's first campaign of nonviolent civil disobedience, perhaps the most important of all the formative influences in Nehru's life. In this campaign, Nehru found an outlet for his indignation over Amritsar and a way of redeeming his self-respect. He gave up the practice of the law and devoted all his energies thereafter to the nationalist movement. Like others, he was jailed repeatedly by the British for his participation in the civil-disobedience campaigns. Altogether, he served nine prison sentences totaling nine years. In prison, he worked out a routine of self-discipline carefully designed to keep up his health, his spirits, and his intellectual activities. He devoted certain hours of the day to physical exercises, and others to reading and to writing. He wrote three books in jail that were of such quality as to make him the outstanding writer of nonfiction in modern India.

One of these was *Glimpses of World History*, written in the form of letters to his daughter—the first coherent study of world history as seen through Asian eyes. The second was his autobiography, *Toward Freedom*, written in 1934—not only a frank and self-searching examination of the inner springs of a remarkable man, but also an important document of Indian nationalism. It was the first book to draw the sympathies of many Westerners to the Indian struggle for independence and to publicize widely the Indian, rather than the British, side of the case. In 1944, in his last and longest prison stay, he wrote perhaps his finest book, *The Discovery of India*—the first vivid study of Indian history from a non-British point of view.

Between his trips to jail and during lulls in the independence campaign, Nehru traveled widely in Europe and later in Asia. In 1927, he attended the Communist-sponsored Congress of Oppressed Nationalities, in Brussels. The interest of the Communists in the cause of nationalism attracted him. He paid his first visit to Moscow the following November and was impressed by their programs and goals, although he recorded as early as 1934 that "the Communists often irritated me by their dictatorial ways, their aggressive and rather vulgar methods, and their habit of denouncing everybody who did not agree with them."[2]

He went to Spain in 1938 for a firsthand view of the Civil War, then to Czechoslovakia and later to Italy. Deeply troubled by the rise and spread of fascism, he seems to have leaned toward Communism in those early days, chiefly because he thought there might be no middle road in the impending struggle between Communism and fascism, which he regarded as the greater evil. He read much Communist literature between 1929 and 1938, but whatever sympathy he had for Communism was dispelled by the cynicism of Stalin's pact with Hitler in 1939.

Through all the long years of the independence struggle, from the time he joined it in 1921 until its culmination in 1947, Nehru worked closely with Gandhi and was Gandhi's explicit choice as his successor. But there were profound differences in thinking between the two men. Whereas Gandhi believed in nonviolence as a fundamental principle of life, Nehru believed in it only as a means sometimes applicable to particular circumstances. He often disagreed with Gandhi as to the wisdom of starting a particular nonviolent campaign, and he disagreed still more strongly when Gandhi, having launched such an effort, called it off for what seemed to Nehru inadequate and even capricious reasons. With his scientific and secular mind, Nehru objected also to Gandhi's method of mixing religion and politics. Whereas Gandhi wrapped his message in the symbols of traditional Hinduism, Nehru spoke out in modern and Western terms. Above all, there was a marked difference between the two men regarding economic policy. Nehru did not share Gandhi's distrust of mechanization or his interest in spinning and cottage industries. He believed in the industrialization of India and in the building of major hydroelectric dams. In many ways, Gandhi was a conservative, while Nehru was a radical. Nehru believed in the state ownership or control of key industries, in steeply graduated income and inheritance taxes, in far-reaching land reforms. Gandhi's reliance on renunciation and on the voluntary use of wealth as a trust for the less fortunate seemed to Nehru too idealistic and too impractical. He wanted the Indian National Congress to adopt a program of radical social reform as an essential part of its platform. With the help of other young socialists within the organization, he hoped to convert the Congress as a whole to socialist beliefs. While Gandhi lived, he did not succeed in this.

At a time when other nationalists were content to ask for self-government within the British Commonwealth, Nehru was one of the first to urge complete independence. In 1946, however, he agreed that India should remain a member of the Commonwealth, but as an independent republic. He staunchly defended Commonwealth membership for the rest of his life.

The Years of Leadership

In view of Nehru's differences with Gandhi, many were surprised when the latter supported Nehru for election to his first term as President of the Indian National Congress in 1929. In doing so, Gandhi said that although Nehru was rash and impetuous, he was also prudent and practical. He added: "He is pure as crystal. He is truthful beyond suspicion. . . . He is a knight *sans peur et sans reproche*. The nation is safe in his hands."[3]

Later, in 1942, Gandhi more specifically designated Nehru as his political heir, stating, "When I am gone, he will speak my language."[4] This prophecy proved incorrect. Nehru continued to hold views in many ways diametrically opposed to those of Gandhi.

Nehru stepped into power within the independence movement not only because of Gandhi's support, but also because his father, Motilal Nehru, had been a prominent nationalist leader for many years. When Nehru took over the Congress Presidency for the first time in 1929, his father was the outgoing President. It was not until eight years later that he won widespread popular support in his own right. Before the elections of 1937, he campaigned with prodigious energy on behalf of various Congress candidates, traveling 50,000 miles in less than five months and addressing more than 10 million people.[5] The campaign revealed to him his enormous power to reach the Indian masses. For the first time, he became a major political figure.

The President of the Congress Party is elected annually. Nehru held the position on four separate occasions before independence. It was the fact that he happened to be party President in 1946 that led to his elevation as Prime Minister in the provisional cabinet formed that year by the Viceroy, Lord Wavell. By 1964, he had served as Prime Minister for eighteen consecutive years. He worked an average of seventeen hours a day, with barely a vacation, until he was taken ill in January, 1964. He died that May.

When tired and stale from long hours of desk work, interviews, parliamentary wrangles, and other such routine, Nehru found relaxation not in personal relations, as other men might, but in contact with large masses of people. From trips around India, crowded with speaking engagements, he returned to Delhi refreshed and invigorated by a renewed sense of communication with his people. He was probably the easiest speaker in the world. Whether standing in Parliament to answer the questions of the educated legislators who faced him or addressing mass meetings of hundreds of thousands of illiterate peasants, he was never tense or at a loss for words. Few of his speeches were prepared in advance. He spoke simply and informally—often rambling, repeating himself, or being inconsistent, as though he was thinking out loud. But he reached his audience by his obvious sincerity and earnestness and by his ability to reduce his subject matter to the simplest terms.

The masses thronged to hear him. His power over them gave him an important leverage in facing the various factions within his party and in dealing with the strong opposing currents in Indian politics. The fact that he was the indispensable vote-getter at election time often made it possible for him to impose policies otherwise unacceptable to large groups within his party.

From 1947 to 1950, the wing of the Congress Party that most vigorously opposed Nehru's policies was still strongly entrenched. Many were not reconciled to partition and urged retaliation against Pakistan; many also opposed Nehru's ideas on socialism, economic planning, world affairs, and especially a secular state. The Hindu Code Bill had aroused a storm of opposition.

Nehru decided in 1950 that a showdown was necessary. He resigned from the Working Committee of the Congress Party, which then found it necessary to give way. In 1951, the Congress elected Nehru as its President for the fifth time. His triumph was clear-cut.[6] Yet the party machinery remained in the hands of politicians, many of whom were unenthusiastic about much of his program. With remarkable skill, he conciliated divergent points of view and did not always insist on having his way—although his hold over the masses was such that he might have become a dictator if he had so chosen.

Modernization—Western, rational, and scientific in character—was the keynote of his program. Following is a brief survey of his major points of emphasis (to be considered in more detail in subsequent pages):

1) He constantly exhorted Indians to work for the unity of India as against the many divisive forces of language, regional interests, and caste—a goal not only important in itself but also fundamental to economic progress.

2) He was a vigorous spokesman for a "secular state" in which religious differences would no longer be of political significance and the religious passions which had bathed India in blood would gradually die down.

3) Economic planning was always one of his chief interests. It was he who, in 1937, urged the Indian National Congress, then an independence movement rather than a political party, to set up a planning commission, and it was largely as a result of his interest that influential Indians had become convinced of the wisdom of planning even before independence was attained.

4) He believed in socialism, and he persuaded the Congress Party in 1955 to pass a resolution endorsing a "socialist pattern of society." He was most emphatically not a Communist, however. He repeatedly criticized Communist methods, and did not hesi-

tate to imprison without trial large numbers of Indian Communists during a period of Communist insurrection. In 1950–51, it was said that there were more Communists in jail in India than in any country outside the Soviet Union—an ironic jest that may well have been true. Indeed, Nehru's socialism was of a pragmatic and liberal variety which he tried to adapt in a balanced way to the needs of India. Since private capital is scarce in India, he thought the state should take the initiative in many areas, but he did not believe that all enterprises should be nationalized. So he urged a "mixed" economy, with private enterprise operating alongside enterprises undertaken by the government. His socialism stressed economic and social equality—a classless, casteless society, with large-scale economic planning by the government.

5) However much of a socialist Nehru was, he was essentially a democrat, committed deeply to the idea that the will of the people must be consulted. His commitment to a democracy was all the more impressive in view of the adulation he received and the opportunities he therefore had to become a dictator.

6) Another basic principle of Nehru's was "nonalignment" in foreign affairs. It should be recalled that long before independence, Nehru had traveled more widely than any other leader of the Indian nationalist movement. He frequently presented resolutions on international questions for adoption by the Indian National Congress and was regarded by the members of that organization as their leading authority on international relations. The international prestige he seemed to have won for himself after independence was a source of great gratification to Indians.

Nehru repeatedly urged that international decisions should be considered on a high moral plane rather than on a level of national self-interest or expediency. To many foreign observers, this tendency to "preach" was often irritating. From their point of view, certain of his own policies in international affairs had not been above reproach, particularly in regard to Kashmir and the seizure of the Portuguese enclave of Goa in 1961. It must be remembered, however, that both these questions look quite different within India than they do from abroad. Like statesmen in other countries, Nehru could not escape the pressures of internal politics and national interest. To many, his "preaching" was an irritating aberration. His concept of the potential role of idealism in international relations was perhaps an illusion. His defense of his own policies sometimes seemed to foreigners tortuous self-righteousness. But the personal idiosyncrasies of any statesman are of less significance than his role in his country's affairs. When the foreign policies for which Nehru was widely criticized in the West are examined (in a subsequent chapter), it may become clear that they had far deeper roots than Westerners generally realize.

Both as a person and as a leader, Nehru was a complex, many-sided, often self-contradictory figure. As one Indian journalist has written, he was a "Hindu aristocrat by birth, an Englishman by education, a revolutionary by training, and a politician only by force of circumstances."[7] He had radiant personal charm, was warm, simple, and friendly, yet often impatient, irritable, and intolerant—an introspective intellectual who devoted the best part of his life to ceaseless activity in the full glare of publicity.

As a leader, his breadth of vision, his sincerity of purpose, his dedication, and his idealism were unquestioned. But he did not know how to delegate authority or place adequate responsibility in the hands of subordinates. Because of his towering stature, he was able to prevent the development in India of the chaos that seemed so likely in 1947. While Pakistan, India's twin, floundered politically for twelve years, India under Nehru recovered quickly from anarchy and embarked on a coherent and positive program. Yet, precisely because India so long enjoyed the leadership of such an unusual man, many real problems remained hidden during his lifetime, "swept under the rug." Deep conflicts that his political skill enabled him to bridge or avoid facing remained at his death unresolved.

Then, too, Indians had become so accustomed to the inspiration derived from his contagious sense of purpose and mission that they could not easily fill the gap when he was gone. At his death, there seemed to die with him his vision of the great new India of the future—an India that would become increasingly unified, that would develop rapidly on the economic front, and that would increasingly provide equality and social justice. Without him, Indians felt an acute loss of national self-confidence.

Yet many Indians had come to realize that great as Nehru was, he was by no means perfect. An evaluation of him by a prominent Indian editor in the autumn of 1964 expressed what seems to this author to be a viewpoint widely held in India: "The blaze of glory in which Jawaharlal Nehru lived and died was a triumph of personality." But the editor added that no one was more painfully aware of the dark shadow that fell between his promise and his performance than Nehru; that he knew that after sixteen years of secularism, communal and casteist elements were more strongly entrenched in political life than before, and that the rapid growth of bureaucracy had led to an enormous increase in abuse of power and corruption.[8]

In another article in the same magazine, an opponent of Nehru, the Communist leader E. M. S. Nambudripad, prophesied that Nehru would be remembered above all as the first Indian leader to adopt a thoroughly modern and scientific approach to every aspect of national life—social, cultural, political, and economic. Pointing out that Tilak and Gandhi, the two chief leaders who had preceded Nehru, were revivalistic in their approach, he conceded that Nehru's modernism was indeed an important contribution.

After Nehru, what have been the political trends? Before considering this question, it will be useful to examine the governmental and political context in which he moved with such consummate ease.

Why the Constitution Is Western

The Indian Constitution is so Western in type that one might be tempted to imagine India to be a democracy in precisely the Western sense. This is not the case. But before examining the non-Western nature of Indian politics, it will be useful to note the main features of this Constitution.

Its roots go back to the successive acts of the British Parliament—in 1909, 1919, and 1935—gradually increasing self-government in India. In its main outlines, the Constitution follows the Act of 1935, which created a framework of government for all of India. Some of its provisions, however, are borrowed from the constitutions of the United States, Canada, and Ireland. Only occasionally does some faint suggestion of a traditional Indian idea peep through the Western constitutional phrases and terms. More than any other single person, it was Nehru who was responsible for the general nature of the Constitution. It was he who rose in the Constituent Assembly in 1946 to introduce an "Objectives Resolution" outlining the Western features to be adopted in it.

There were many in India who would have preferred a far more Hindu type of government, perhaps under a monarch advised by Brahmans, who would have been careful to carry out the precepts of Hinduism, or perhaps based somehow on village councils, or panchayats. In Gandhian thought, the village was the essential unit of politics and economics. In support of idealization of the village, the famous statement by Metcalfe about village republics* was repeatedly referred to in the Constituent Assembly. But the advocates of a specifically Hindu or traditional form of government were not numerically strong in the Constituent Assembly, which had been elected under a limited franchise in 1946. And none of them came forward with a blueprint sufficiently clear, precise, or complete to persuade the constitution-makers to abandon the British model.

Next to Nehru himself, probably the most vigorous supporter of a Western-type constitution was the untouchable leader B. R. Ambedkar, who was Chairman of the Drafting Committee of the Constituent Assembly. Not only trained in law, but also a man of wide erudition who had studied the constitutions of all the Western nations, he was especially vigorous in his opposition to a government based on village panchayats. To those who quoted Metcalfe, he retorted, "These village republics have been the ruination of India. . . . What is the village but a sink of localism, a den of ignorance, narrow-mindedness, and communalism?"[9]

Although the advocates of a Western-type constitution were not effectively challenged in the Constituent Assembly, discontent with their work was great. Many deplored the Constitution "as a betrayal of Gandhian ideals and of the ancient spirit of India."[10] One prominent leader, who later became the Chief Minister of Uttar Pradesh, went so far as to say: "Our Constitution is a miserable failure. The spirit of Indian culture has not

* Quoted above, p. 40.

breathed on it. The Gandhism by which we swear so vehemently at home and abroad does not inspire it. It is just a piece of legislation like, say, the Motor Vehicles Act."[11]

Finished and adopted in the autumn of 1949, the Constitution went into effect on January 26, 1950—the twentieth anniversary of the date proclaimed as Independence Day by Gandhi as he prepared for the new civil-disobedience movement of 1930. The Constitution gives the vote to all people, both male and female, over twenty-one years of age and of sound mind, except those who may be disqualified by their state legislatures for crime and corruption. Under the 1935 Act, only 14 per cent of the population had the vote, and under the preceding acts still smaller proportions.[12] This new, total enfranchisement is one of the daring, perhaps foolhardy, certainly idealistic undertakings of modern India. It is one of the most significant illustrations of the impact of the idea of democracy upon Indian minds. Universal adult suffrage was not adopted lightheartedly. The members of the Constituent Assembly knew it was a serious decision, but they believed that in a country where such a large proportion of the people were illiterate and owned no property the introduction of any educational or property qualifications whatever would mean rule by a small minority, and hence a negation of democracy. Orderly general elections have been held under the Constitution at five-year intervals—in 1952, 1957, and 1962.

Cabinet Government and Federalism

The form of government provided for in the Constitution is a federal union of states with parliamentary government both at the state level and at the Centre.* The executive is thus not separate from the legislature as in the United States. It consists of persons who are members of the legislature—a cabinet form of government, like that in Great Britain. The Prime Minister is the parliamentary leader of the party or coalition of parties commanding the support of the majority of members of Parliament.

* The federal government of India is referred to as the Centre. Besides its sixteen states, India includes a number of Union territories, centrally administered: Delhi, the Andaman and Nicobar Islands, the Laccadive Islands, Himachal Pradesh, Manipur, Tripura, Nagaland, the Northeast Frontier Agency, Pondicherry, and the former Portuguese territories (Goa, Daman, Diu, Dadra, and Nagar Haveli).

The actual wording of the Constitution is somewhat ambiguous on this point, for it gives full executive power to the President of India, elected for a five-year term by the members of Parliament and of the state legislatures jointly. The members of the Constituent Assembly, however, informally agreed that the Prime Minister should normally act for the President and that the latter should have the purely titular position of the British sovereign. This informal understanding has been carried out in practice up to the present time. But if cabinet government should become unstable, the President would be constitutionally entitled to play a far stronger role than he has to date. If the majority of Parliament should not support the Prime Minister and his cabinet, the President would have the responsibility of making the important choice between dismissing the Prime Minister or dissolving the Parliament. Moreover, he would be legally empowered to take over the functions now exercised by the Prime Minister. Thus the President has sufficient constitutional powers so that he could play a truly decisive role if there were no strong Prime Minister.

The central Parliament consists of two houses. Most of the members of the upper house—the Rajya Sabha, or Council of States—are chosen by the state legislatures. A few are appointed by the President. They serve for six-year terms, one-third of them retiring every two years. This upper house is less powerful than the lower house—the Lok Sabha, or House of the People—whose members are elected directly by the people for five-year terms. The upper house has only advisory power regarding money bills, and if the two houses disagree on any other bill, the final decision is reached by a joint sitting of both houses. Since the lower house has twice the membership of the upper house (roughly 500 members as against 250) it can outvote the latter in such cases of disagreement.

Increasingly, in recent years, the Indian Parliament has served as a real forum for debate. Sharp questions are asked of the ministers, and the ministers are required to answer. But while Parliament is a useful instrument through which public opinion can be brought to bear upon the executive branch of the government, it is by no means as self-assertive a legislative body as is the U.S. Congress or the British Parliament. This is partly because one party, Nehru's Congress Party, has held an overwhelming majority within it (about 70 per cent) ever since it was formed. It may also be due partly to the relative newness of representative institutions in India and to the Indian tendency to accept authority—in this case the authority of Nehru.

The Supreme Court of India has the power to interpret the Constitution, as in the United States. But since the process of amending the Constitution is relatively easy, the Supreme Court is unlikely to play the formative role in the evolution of the Indian Government that it has played in the United States. Amendments require the vote of two-thirds of the members of each house present and voting, and the approval of the majority of the total membership of each house. But certain important types of amendments do not have to be ratified thereafter by the legislatures of the states.

Whenever the Supreme Court hands down a decision that has the effect of blocking some program favored by the Prime Minister or Parliament, Parliament can quickly adopt a constitutional amendment to prevent the Supreme Court from interfering in such a question in the future. During the first years of independence, it did so on several occasions. For example, in 1955, after the Court had upheld the claims of former landholders that their property had been taken from them without just compensation, the government pushed through the Fourth Amendment, providing that the question of the reasonableness of the compensation should no longer be a matter for the courts to decide. Thus the Prime Minister, through Parliament, rescued the land-reform program and at the same time demonstrated clearly that under the Indian Constitution the Prime Minister and Parliament are above the Supreme Court.

Although the Government of India is theoretically a federation, the Centre is far more powerful in relation to the states than is the U.S. Federal Government—so powerful, in fact, that some political scientists do not consider the Indian Government a true federation at all. Within the Indian context, this may be fortunate. If a true federation is to work successfully, there must be enough agreement among the important political parties so that no breakdown or civil war will occur if one or more states should pass into the control of a party not in office nationally. But the degree of underlying agreement which both Democrats and Republicans in the United States take for granted does not exist among the various political parties in India.

The whip hand of the central government over the states is very great. It can create new states, change their boundaries at will, or even abolish them. It did, in fact, abolish a number of states in 1956, merging them with their neighbors. And it split one great state, Hyderabad, into four parts, giving each part to a neighbor. Even the form of government in the states is laid down within the Union Constitution. By its emergency powers, the Centre can take over all the powers of the state governments under certain circumstances. The Centre has a monopoly of the forms of taxation that tap the largest sources of revenue, including income, inheritance, corporation, and sales taxes, and customs. This leaves to the states, as their chief sources of revenue, the land taxes and taxes on agricultural income, which are far less productive of income. The states are, therefore, heavily dependent on the Centre for grants and financial aid. Under the Second Five-Year Plan (1956–62), 60 per cent of the financial requirements of the states came from the central government.[13] Through its power of the purse, the Centre can dictate to the states even on matters theoretically within state jurisdiction, and it has progressively trespassed on state powers in this way.

Although the original distribution of powers as laid down in the Constitution is thus not an entirely reliable guide to the actual balance today, it may be useful to record here how the various powers were allocated in the Constitution. To the Centre was given jurisdiction not only over matters of obvious national concern such as defense, foreign affairs, interstate trade, and currency control, but also over a number of other matters where federal jurisdiction might seem less necessary, such as the control of highways, the regulation of mines and mineral developments, and the incorporation of banks, insurance companies, and businesses. To the states, the Constitution left control over public order, the police, local government, public health, education, agriculture, and irrigation (except for interstate rivers). Besides the "Union List" and the "State List," the Constitution also includes a "Concurrent List" on which both the Centre and the states may legislate. This list includes price control, control over professions, and the treatment of refugees. Any residual powers not covered in one or another of these long lists are granted to the Centre rather than the states.

The states have the same British form of cabinet government as does the Centre. Their chief ministers—who correspond to the Prime Minister—are responsible to the state legislative assemblies. But they also have governors appointed by the President of India, and these have real and important powers. It is the duty of the Governor to decide which leader commands the greatest legislative support and to select him to be chief minister of the state. Especially when no single party wins a clear majority in the state legislature, this power is pivotal. For it involves deciding what kind of coalition has the greatest chance of functioning harmoniously with the multiparty legislative assembly. Furthermore, the Governor can dismiss a ministry if he believes it is engaged in activities contrary to the national interest. He can also dissolve the state legislative assembly—whose members are normally elected for five-year terms—and call for new elections. He can refuse to give assent to a bill passed by the legislature and send it back for reconsideration, or he can reserve a bill so passed for the approval of the President of India.

Emergency Powers of the Central Government

An outstanding feature of the Indian Constitution is the very strong emergency powers it gives to the President of India—powers actually used so far by the Prime Minister. If the President is satisfied that a grave emergency exists on a national scale because of war, financial breakdown, or other circumstances, he may take over both the legislative and the executive powers, in the Union as well as in the states. He must, however, lay his proclamation of emergency before Parliament, and it will expire after two months unless Parliament approves it. In the case of an emergency in a particular state, the President may take over all the functions of the state and declare that the powers of the state legislature shall be exercised by the central Parliament. Again, the proclamation lasts for only two months unless approved by Parliament, which has the right to revoke it or to continue it for six-month periods up to three years. During an emergency of this kind, the centrally appointed Governor becomes, in effect, the chief executive of the state. Fundamental rights are suspended.

A national emergency was declared for the first time in October, 1962, when the mountain warfare between India and China began to grow acute. On several occasions, furthermore, emergencies have been declared in connection with particular states, which have been placed under "President's Rule." In most of these cases, the declaration of emergency came after there had been clear indication of political instability within a particular state. India has a very large number of political parties. When no single party has emerged with a clear majority in a state legislature, a coalition ministry has often been necessary in that state. Such coalitions have had the instability so often found in multiparty democracies, as, for example, in France before the rule of De Gaulle. Several times, when state ministries have fallen, the taking over of the state government by the Centre has created a breathing spell in which state political leaders could review the situation, consolidate their forces, or find new ways to form a more solid coalition.

On one occasion, law and order broke down completely within a state—in Kerala, in 1959. The Communists had emerged from the 1957 general elections as the strongest single party, and were able to form a ministry and take control of the state government. Worried lest the Communists use their power in such a way as to entrench themselves and make it impossible ever to unseat them through the ballot, the Congress Party in 1959 determined upon a vigorous nonviolent attack on Communist rule. The techniques of noncooperation and civil disobedience that had been evolved under Gandhi's direction were used. Non-Communists went to jail until the jails could hold no more. Non-Communists lay down in the streets of the capital city of Trivandrum in such numbers that the Communist ministers could not get to their offices by car. In July, 1959, the Governor reported the crisis to the President, and the Union Government invoked the emergency powers. The Communists went out of office, and the Governor took charge of the administration of the state on behalf of the central government. New elections, held in February, 1960, resulted in a victory of the Congress Party by a narrow margin, although the Communists actually polled more votes than they had in the preceding election. A coalition non-Communist ministry came into office.

However grateful non-Communists may be for the fact that Communist rule in Kerala was thus supplanted at least temporarily, it is well to remember how different this sequence of events would have seemed if the shoe had been on the other foot—if the Communists had been in control of the central government and had used both the emergency powers of the President and the mighty weapon of nonviolent civil disobedience to force out of power the Congress Party democratically elected in the state.

Fundamental Rights and Directive Principles

Following the example of the Bill of Rights of the U.S. Constitution and other subsequent constitutions, the Indian Constitution contains a section on fundamental rights—the most elaborate and comprehensive such list yet framed. Many of the rights guaranteed cannot be as easily taken for granted in India as they might be in many Western countries. The constitutional guarantee of equality directly contradicts the hierarchical principle still embedded in the caste system. The sweeping prohibition of discrimination of any kind on the ground of religion, race, caste, sex, or place of birth is a radical provision in a land where such discriminations have abounded. The Constitution also declares that untouchability is abolished and its practice is prohibited. Such a sweeping change is as impossible to achieve by legislation alone as is the abolition of discrimination in the United States.

The fundamental rights include not only freedom of religion in general, but also special protection for religious minorities in cultural and educational matters, and nondiscrimination among members of different religions in public employment. Other rights are freedom of speech and association, and guarantee against arbitrary arrest and detention.

But the Constitution explicitly permits the passage of preventive-detention laws, under which persons who have not yet committed a crime may be imprisoned for one they are expected to commit. India is one of the few countries in the world which have specifically authorized such laws. The first Preventive-Detention Act was passed by Parliament in 1950 and used vigorously against the Communists, then in an active state of insurrection. In the first year of operation of the Act, more than 10,000 persons were imprisoned without trial. The Preventive-Detention Act has repeatedly been renewed, but the number of arrests under it declined sharply until in 1960 there were fewer than 200.[14] This was in large part due to a change of tactics on the part of the Communists—from insurrection and violence to participation in national politics as an ostensibly peaceful opposition party. (The number of preventive arrests sharply increased again after the Chinese invasion of 1962.)

The most outstanding single case of preventive detention has been that of the popular Kashmiri leader Sheikh Abdullah. Once a supporter of Nehru and of Kashmir's accession to India rather than Pakistan, Sheikh Abdullah later urged more autonomy or perhaps independence for his state. He was arrested in 1953, detained without trial until 1958, then released, but again arrested three months later, released in 1964, and again arrested in May, 1965, after he had made contact with Chou En-lai.

As long as the Act remains on the statute books, the Indian Government has a tremendous weapon for the preservation of law and order and for the suppression of agitation and civil strife of all kinds—religious as well as political. But such an Act could, of course, be a useful implement of dictatorship. Ironically, the Indians took the idea of preventive detention from British practice in India. Preventive detention had been used repeatedly against nationalist agitators in the independence movement.

A unique feature of the Constitution is a group of "directive principles of state policy" which are specifically declared not to be enforceable in any court of law. The Constituent Assembly envisioned them rather as ideals, moral precepts, or purposes to be kept in mind in subsequent legislation.

One of the directive principles (Section 48 of the Constitution) reveals with starting clarity the conflict of cultures in India. For it combines in a single sentence the directive that animal husbandry should be organized on modern scientific lines with the contrary directive that the slaughter of cattle should be prohibited by law. Other directive principles include goals to which Gandhi gave high priority, such as the promotion of cottage industry, the organization of village councils and rural cooperatives, and the prohibition of intoxicating drinks. Still others embody expensive Western ideas of social welfare not easy to implement in a country with as limited resources as India. For example, the state is directed to provide free and compulsory education for all children under fourteen, to give public assistance in case of unemployment and old age, to protect the health and strength of workers, and to raise the level of nutrition.

The directive principles also stress equality of economic opportunity. This Western concept, so alien to the hierarchical principle at the root of the caste system, came to be embodied in the thinking of Indian leaders partly because of the idealism of Gandhi and others, and partly because the Congress Party had to make promises to the masses if it was to secure mass support during the independence movement. Once the promise of equality of opportunity had been made, it was politically difficult to go back on it. Accordingly, the Constitution directs the government to secure the welfare of all citizens, to prevent the concentration of wealth, to make sure that the workers be given equal pay for equal work, to prevent exploitation, to ensure a decent standard of life for all, and to protect the backward classes of society.

At the outset, many observers expected that the directive principles would have little effect. In practice, however, they have been followed with a seriousness hardly anticipated. In certain cases, the directive principles have prevailed even when in conflict with enforcible fundamental rights. To follow out the directive principle that the education of the backward classes should be promoted, the government of the state of Madras passed a law reserving for these classes certain places in government colleges. This law, which in effect discriminated against the upper-caste Brahmans, was successfully challenged in the courts as a contravention of the fundamental right of equality. Parliament then passed in 1951 the First Amendment to the Constitution, which provides that the right of equality shall not be construed as preventing states from making special provisions for the advancement of any social or educationally backward classes.

To follow the directive principle regarding equality of economic opportunity, various state governments have passed land-reform measures. In 1952, a landowner challenged one of these in court on the ground that it violated the fundamental right to hold property. In this case, the Supreme Court held that the land-reform act was constitutional since its purpose was to further a directive principle. The First, Second, and Fourth Constitutional Amendments, adopted by Parliament with no need for state ratification, were all designed to implement by law the directive principles, which had originated as social ideals rather than constitutional provisions. The principle that the interests of society come before the interest of the individual has thus been strongly affirmed.

The Strong Administrative Framework

A significant part of the government of India not spelled out in the Constitution is the administrative hierarchy, one of the best administrative machines in the world, but not originally designed to work within the framework of a democrary.

In the West, one thinks of a government employee as one totally removed from the sphere of policy-making, one who is essentially the servant of a legislative body. The older generation of civil servants in India, on the other hand, were trained to be policy-makers as well as administrators, each in his own sphere. They remember the days when no legislature guided or checked them, and when they had to answer only to the all-powerful Viceroy above. Even today, permanent civil servants still make many policy decisions which in the United States would be the responsibility of Congress. Undoubtedly, cabinet ministers in every nation rely heavily on the permanent staff below them, and also, under the parliamentary-cabinet form of government, parliament usually rubber-stamps—after more or less argument—the proposals of cabinet ministers. But in India, far more than in most Western countries, what has often been called the "steel-frame" of the administration *is* the government. Over the past decade, the habit of vigorous discussion has steadily increased in Parliament. But the administration has continued to carry on its activities with remarkably little modification since independence.

Thus it is important to understand the British design of the Indian governmental administration. In the old days, the Viceroy was the apex of the British administrative pyramid. From him, the chain of command was unbroken almost down to the local level. Below him, the administration fanned out through the various central ministries and through the provinces (the equivalent of the Indian states of today), down to the most important subdivisions of the provinces, the districts. Each district was the realm of the district officer, so absolute within his jurisdiction that he was regarded as the *ma-bap* (the mother and father) by the million or more people whom he ruled.

From the district level on up, the chief administrative posts were in the hands of the highly trained Indian Civil Service, composed at first entirely of Britishers. Only in the twentieth century did Indians succeed in entering it in any numbers. At independence, the ICS numbered about 1,150, of whom half were British. Working below this elite corps at various levels, the clerks and other employees of lower rank were normally Indians. (Separate from the ICS were various other, more specialized services such as the Indian Police Service, the Postal Service, the Railway Service, and the Forestry Service.)

The districts—of which there are 313 in present-day India, exclusive of Kashmir—were further divided into taluks and tehsils, presided over by Indian members of the administrative services. These, too, were part of the administrative command running down from the Viceroy. Below the heavy pyramid of this administration, little scope was left for local self-government, except in the cities where municipal councils had been organized. Although some of the members of such councils were still appointed by British officials until independence, gradually the proportion of elected members increased in the early years of the twentieth century. In the villages, most of the village councils, or panchayats—believed to have existed before the coming of the British—had gradually died out. To the extent that the villages still managed their own affairs, this was done by hereditary village headmen or acknowledged high-caste village leaders.

After independence, Indian administrators who had helped the British run the country found themselves serving under Indian ministries (at the state and national levels) composed of nationalist leaders whom they had helped imprison as agitators. This fact as well as the shift to democratic control produced an uneasy relationship between professional civil servants and the politicians above them which continues to the present time.

After the ICS lost its British members and also those Muslims who chose to become Pakistanis, there remained in the service only 451 Indian ICS officers. Of these, only a little more than 200 are still on active duty today. India has taken steps to train a new administrative corps called the Indian Administrative Service to augment their members and replace them as they retire. The quality of the IAS is generally admitted to be somewhat lower than the old ICS. Yet the "steel-frame" of permanent, professional, trained government servants is one of modern India's great assets. Here the problem is not quality, but quantity. India has not yet trained *enough* civil servants to man the very large programs under way. The total membership of the Indian Administrative Service as of May 1, 1960, was only 1,971, including the remaining ICS officers.[15]

The first major change in the network of administrative authority throughout the country since independence occurred in connection with the establishment of the Community Development Programme in 1952. For it, new administrative subdivisions consisting of approximately 100 villages each (or a population of 60,000 to 70,000) were created. Each of these development "blocks" was placed in the charge of a block officer, assisted by a number of technical officers such as advisers on agriculture, public health, animal husbandry, rural industries, cooperatives, and the like. This officer and his technical advisers then supervised the "village-level workers," each of whom had the responsibility of stimulating development in five to ten villages. The village-level workers were expected to profit by many forms of technical advice available through the specialists at the block level and to hand on this advice to the villagers.

A New Trend Toward Decentralization?

In 1957, an official committee headed by Balvantray G. Mehta reported that the Community Development Programme was not proceeding satisfactorily. Because it seemed to the villagers like a program imposed from above, it did not enlist their cooperation. The committee recommended that new emphasis be placed on local self-government, and it outlined a plan for a three-tier system of government within the districts called Panchayati Raj. At the base would be the village panchayat, elected by all the citizens of that village. A higher Panchayat Samiti at the block level would then be elected by the various panchayats within the development block. A still higher Zila Parishad—to lay down policy at the district level—would then be elected by the Panchayat Samitis within the district.[16]

Since 1959, all but three of the state legislatures have passed laws authorizing the establishment of this system, defining the responsibilities of the panchayats for local self-government, and granting to the indirectly elected Samitis and Zila Parishads certain powers formerly exercised by officers appointed from above. In the laws of the various states, the powers and relative importance of the three tiers vary.

It is too soon to judge how this new development will work out. The appointed professional civil servants at the district and block levels remain at their posts. Theoretically, their duty now is no longer to make decisions, but to implement the decisions of the Zila Parishads and the Panchayat Samitis, and to tender advice to these bodies. But with greater education than the members of the indirectly elected groups they advise, they doubtless can find ways of continuing to run matters their own way if they so choose. Here then, at new levels, arises the question of the cooperation between administrative officers and politicians—a question that already is troublesome at the state and national levels.

The responsibilities contemplated for the Panchayat Samitis are very great. All the money for economic development at the block level is to be placed in their hands. Theirs is to be the decision as to how this money should be spent. Their job supposedly is no less than "decentralized planning"—a term that to an outsider seems self-contradictory. They will still be able to call on the staff of specialist technical assistants at the block level. But it seems—at least to this observer—fanciful to expect representatives of the villagers to endorse enthusiastically the relatively modern and Western orientation of these technicians. To the extent that the Panchayat Samitis do, in fact, make the decisions that are theoretically theirs to make, their "decentralized planning" is apt to be quite different from what the planners in New Delhi expect of them. But then it may be that officials in that busy, forward-thinking capital city have underestimated the difficulties of modernizing a nation of more than 490 million people with emotional, religious, and cultural roots so deep in the past.

One result of the new system of Panchayati Raj has already become clear. Panchayat elections have aggravated factional tendencies within many of the villages and friction between castes, as each faction or caste seeks to gain control over the panchayat, so valuable as a vantage point for improving their economic status. Some observers have found that the economically stronger interests in the village usually succeed in dominating the panchayat.[17] If such is the case, panchayat elections will only increase the gap between the rich and the poor. On the other hand, other observers have described particular villages in which the larger, less privileged castes have gained control of the panchayats and used their new position for their own economic advantage.[18] On balance, it is not yet clear which group of castes or which economic level of society will profit most by the new system.

In the past decade, it has been argued by some political leaders that direct elections should be held at the village level only and that even the state and federal legislatures should be included in the system of Panchayati Raj. The proposal is that the Zila Parishads—at the top of the present three-tier system—should elect the members of the state legislatures, and that the state legislatures in turn should elect the members of the central parliament. Thus there would be a five-tier system of representative government in which each of the four top tiers would be selected by the tier below. The leading exponent of this idea is Jayaprakash Narayan, a highly popular leader.

A Western political scientist familiar with the disadvantages of indirect elections may see the danger that such a many-leveled pyramid might be awkward, uncontrollable, inefficient, and unsuited for the carrying out of a concerted attempt at economic development. The advocates of the Panchayati Raj, on the other hand, often advance it as the cure for all the many political problems besetting India—the only way of stimulating initiative, creating a democracy in a land of illiterates, ensuring that government is truly responsive to the will of the people. In short, it has all the attractions of a panacea.

13 • THE INDIAN NATURE OF INDIAN POLITICS

THE POLITICAL FORCES that operate through India's Western-type Constitution are so completely non-Western that such familiar terms as "Communist" or "socialist"—or even "political parties"—lose much of their Western meaning and overtones. As we should know, but so easily forget, Indian politics derive directly from Indian conditions. They reflect the history, the religious attitudes, the peculiarly Indian relations between man and man—in short, the Indian people's whole way of living. The high rate of illiteracy, the poverty, the lack of communications (taken for granted in the West) would naturally make a great difference by themselves. But they are only part of the picture. Caste and religion play significant roles in politics. Personal leadership counts far more than do party platforms. Regional and local interests overshadow national, let alone international, considerations. Finally, these and other factors tend to lead to the multiplication of political parties. Those of us who take the two-party system for granted can scarcely imagine what a difference this makes.

Radios, Newspapers, and Public Opinion

1 : 245 Radio-

There is no television in India, except for an experimental operation in New Delhi. Of the existing forms of mass communication, radio is the most influential. But there are only some 2 million radios throughout the nation—an average of one for every 245 people. About 56,000 of these are community sets attached to loudspeakers so that groups of people can listen to them. Through such sets, between 12 and 14 per cent of the Indian villagers have some contact with the outside world.[1] In remote towns, I have seen many little groups of men wrapped in their flowing dhotis stopping for a moment near the squawking community radio, listening with wondering faces, then going on their way as though they had just heard a voice from Mars.

Radio broadcasting is a government monopoly. The government-owned All-India Radio broadcasts music, dramas, news bulletins, speeches, and discussions from twenty-eight stations in the various regional languages. Between elections, it has brought the voices of Nehru and other government leaders to out-of-the-way places where the villagers might otherwise have failed to realize that the British rulers had departed. Attempting to be politically impartial, the All-India Radio has not permitted pre-election political broadcasts because of the inability of the various political parties to agree on a formula for the allotment of radio time. But this "impartiality" in itself has tended to benefit the party in power.

In 1962, there were 481 daily newspapers in India, with a combined circulation of 5.7 million. The 49 English-language papers together had a larger circulation (29.3 per cent of the total) than did the papers in any single Indian language. The combined circulation of the newspapers in Indian languages was only a little over 4 million—for about 118 million Indians who are literate in an Indian language but know no English.[2]

However, it should be pointed out that a single copy of an Indian newspaper is passed on from reader to reader. Although no estimate of newspaper readership can be more than a guess, the Indian newspaper-reading public may easily be four times the circulation figure. A survey has indicated that a fifth of all the villages are reached by at least one newspaper.[3] Sometimes, in a remote village, a single copy of a newspaper—which may have reached the village as the wrapping around a parcel brought home from the nearest market town—may be read by every literate villager. Carefully pressed flat, it is shared by all. Many eyes strain at it, many forefingers follow its lines. Those who are literate read aloud to those who are not. Heads nod. It makes no difference if the paper is several weeks old. What is printed must surely be true, for why else should such an extraordinary thing as print be used!

Although in India, as in other countries where freedom of the press exists, there are some irresponsible and sensational newspapers and periodicals, the leading newspapers are of good quality considering their very real financial limitations. The reporting of the speeches of public figures is accurate and full. In the English-language newspapers, at least, the proportion of space devoted to foreign news is high. The British, who founded many of these papers, were quite naturally interested in events in the West. The stress on foreign coverage which they initiated has been continued.

The great weakness of Indian journalism is in its coverage of Indian news other than speeches or official press releases. If an opposition member of Parliament makes a speech attacking some government project, both the attack and the government's answer will very likely be printed in full. But the reader may search in vain for fresh and independent journalistic material shedding light on the issue. Rarely will a journalist visit the project in question to give an eyewitness report or pry into the matter from other angles. A reason usually given for this is the poverty of the newspapers—a reflection, of course, of the poverty of their readers and of the country as a whole. The newspapers do not have the money to send reporters off in search of firsthand material. Even within the city where he works, the reporter may have to rely on his own bicycle as transportation, or go long distances on foot if he leaves the routes served by public conveyances. There is no direct censorship of the press, but government control over the limited supply of newsprint acts indirectly as a further deterrent to the kind of vigorous journalistic investigation carried on by the leading Western newspapers.

The scarcity of journalistic investigation has unfortunate results. What the limited reading public knows about developments within India is based either on the official version or on the vitriolic criticism of the opposition press, which too often lacks signs of any factual support for its points. Unable to check the assertions it reads, the public believes whatever the mood dictates. It may be overoptimistic at one moment, and destructively cynical the next. In short, the lack of independent journalistic investigation does not contribute to the stability of national morale.

Under autocratic rule since time immemorial, the Indian public is far from accustomed to the thought that it has the right—let alone the duty—to control the government. It must be remembered that unrestricted adult suffrage dates back only to 1952. For countless generations, the people looked to the government as their *Ma-baap* (mother and father). As Maurice Zinkin, a perceptive former member of the Indian Civil Service, has noted: "There is none of the feeling one finds in America that one must be perpetually finding out what government is doing so that it can be told to stop it. The reason for this dependence is that, badly though governments have behaved in India, they have also performed certain functions essential to the public welfare, notably irrigation and famine relief, in a way they did not do in Europe."[4]

But the attitude toward government is beginning to change. Increasingly, the educated people, the elite, are concerning themselves with the policies and actions of the government, criticizing them where there seems to be ground for criticism and expressing their views in vigorous letters to the newspapers. In a very real sense, public opinion is beginning to exist as a force in politics, although the public in question is a small minority of the total population. And a degree of cynicism is developing, particularly among the intellectuals who are poor.

The Nature of Elections

An Indian election is a stirring and colorful event. The campaigning that precedes it is vigorous. In the cities and larger towns, the candidates make frequent speeches, many of them outdoors. Glad as always of any break in the monotony of daily life, Indians throng to hear them. Party jeeps with loudspeakers blare forth music to attract attention. Jeeps or bullock carts also carry the party message from village to village. The names and slogans of the candidates are painted on walls along with the symbols that have been adopted to help identify them to the illiterate voters. Each party has its own symbol to be used by its candidates; among the symbols used are a pair of bullocks, a lighted lamp, an elephant, a peasant's hut, a ladder, a bicycle.

The polling stations are sufficiently numerous—225,000 in the 1962 elections—so that few voters have to go more than a mile in order to cast their ballots. In each general election, about half

Ma-baap = gov't
mother-father

the eligible voters have cast their ballots—and as many as 54 per cent in 1962.[5] Although these percentages fall short of the record election turnout in the United States—64 per cent of the eligible voters in 1960—they compare favorably with many Western elections.

On election day, people of all ages crowd the polls early. As near the voting station as is permitted by law, each of the various parties sets up its temporary headquarters, which may be just a table or, more ambitiously, a tent decorated with gaily fluttering party flags. Often the parties rival each other in creating a carnival atmosphere, offering various attractions, such as rides in camel carts or trucks, to the children of the voters. Few cases of inter-party disorders or violence have been reported. On the whole, the elections are orderly, peaceful, and festive. They illustrate the eagerness with which Indians can create joyful celebrations out of even the most meager materials.

In many areas, the women come to the polls dressed in their best saris (perhaps even their wedding saris, taken out of their storage chests). While waiting to vote, women and men usually form separate lines, the women carrying their babies on their hips, while children just able to walk tag along at their skirts.

Inside the voting station, representatives of the various parties sit beside the voting officials to check the procedure. As each voter comes forward, his name is verified on the list, and a mark of indelible ink is placed on his finger as a further precaution against his voting more than once. The voting booths are simple—often formed by tacking a piece of burlap across the corner of the voting room—but they enable the voters to mark and fold their ballots in secret.

In the first two general elections, each polling station contained a separate ballot box for each candidate, marked with the candidate's name and symbol. All the boxes were hidden behind a screen. The voter placed his unmarked ballot in the box of the candidate of his choice.

This system was changed in the 1962 elections, and a less cumbersome system was substituted. Voters were given two ballots, a white one to elect a representative to the central Parliament, a pink one to elect a representative to the state assembly. Each ballot contained the names and symbols of all the candidates for the office in question. The voter was required to place a mark opposite the candidate of his choice and then deposit his folded ballot in the single box provided for all ballots.

Particularly in the first two general elections, many illiterates failed to understand that the symbols were only *symbols* and that, in choosing among them, they were making a choice among human candidates rather than the animals or inanimate objects represented.

> Many inexperienced voters in the rural areas were confused when they arrived inside the voting booths, because they had expected to offer their ballot to a living animal, or place it in an actual "lamp" or "boat" or "cart," or whatever the symbol they had chosen. . . . Some voters brought grass to the polls to feed the "bullocks" . . . some women voters, finding no bullocks within the booth, kept their ballots and placed them on the backs of the first cow or bullock they met on their return home. A man whose intention was to vote for "tree," climbed a tree beside his polling station and placed his ballot on the topmost branch.[6]

Even in 1962, there was still evidence of confusion as to the very nature of the process of voting. In a village on the outskirts of Delhi, I saw a voter try to take his ballot with him out of the voting station because the presiding officer of the station would not promise that it would be handed directly to Pandit Nehru in person. He therefore decided that he himself would send it to Nehru.

Many Indian observers and editorial commentators have expressed misgivings as to whether universal adult suffrage is suitable for a land with such a high rate of illiteracy. Others claim that the majority, even of the illiterates, make real choices among candidates, that on the whole voters choose well, and that direct elections have "brought the Indian people a stronger sense of nationhood than they ever had before."[7]

As in the West, the voter's choice may be based on any of a number of rational or irrational factors: personal intuition as to the quality of the candidate, the appeal of a slogan, more or less explicit feelings of satisfaction or dissatisfaction, and, especially, the advice or directives of some respected local leader. The more educated and intelligent local members of a caste tend to evaluate the effect that the elections may have on their caste and pass the word along. Thus, paradoxically, the caste system, which in certain respects is a major obstacle to the leveling process of democracy, also acts as a mechanism through which democratic elections can serve the interest of the voter. Like the caste leaders, the leaders of minority religious communities are looked to by the voters for guidance in voting; thus, in a sense, they fill the role of political bosses.

Caste and Politics

Although Nehru and other leaders have exhorted the nation to pay less attention to caste differences and have denounced what they call "casteism," the role of caste in politics has tended to increase rather than decrease. Just as parties in the United States may appeal to the Polish-American vote or the Italian-American vote in particular areas, so parties in India seek to capture the vote of the strongest local castes. Often two rival parties will choose members of such castes as their candidates. But there are always many other castes to be courted; hence there is always a temptation for minor parties and independent candidates to enter the race, hoping—often in vain—for votes from enough small castes to win.

In almost every state, caste rivalries play the dominant role in state politics. The way this occurs varies, of course, from state to state. But it must be remembered that while national leaders in Delhi may discuss Western-type issues (such as the proper balance between the federal and state governments, or between public and private enterprise in the industrial field) politicians at the grass roots are preoccupied primarily with matters related to the old jockeying for status among the various castes—a kind of concern not at all in accord with the fundamental principles of the Constitution.

Then, too, the very complexion of each political party (particularly at the local and state level) is largely determined by the interests of the caste or castes from which it draws its chief local or state support. While national leaders of the various parties talk in terms of ideological principles, caste interests (rather than ideology) determine what a party actually stands for in the states.

Universal adult suffrage has shifted the center of political power downward from the upper-caste Brahmans, who provided most of the leadership in the nationalist movement and have dominated Indian society through countless centuries. Today the larger castes at the center of the caste hierarchy—the peasant castes, for example—have greatly increased their influence.

This shift of power has important politico-cultural implications. Brahmans have always been the intellectual and educated elite within Hindu society. When the new Western-type education became available to the few in the nineteenth century, it was primarily they who profited by it. They became far more Western, cosmopolitan, and modern in their outlook than any other caste. This is not to say that they gave up basic Hindu beliefs. Some of them did, but many followed the lead of Rammohun Roy in attempting to synthesize those beliefs with lessons learned from the West.

As the political parties court increasingly the vote of the larger, less educated middle castes, the intellectual level of the representatives elected—and hence of the central and state cabinets—will almost inevitably decline. A leading American authority on Indian politics has noted: "In all probability the new generation of leaders will be less well educated and much less oriented toward the West."[8] The tone of government and of political life will certainly become more expressive of indigenous and traditional Indian preoccupations, among which religion still remains pivotal.

Religion and Politics

At least five political parties take their point of departure from a specific religious, rather than a political, interest. One of these parties, the Jana Sangh, showed a marked increase in strength in the 1962 elections, emerging as the chief opposition in the two largest states, Uttar Pradesh and Madhya Pradesh.

But the effect of religion on politics must not be judged only by such an obvious measuring rod as the number of votes polled. The outbursts of violence between Muslims and Hindus that accompanied partition have already been discussed. Lesser outbreaks of violence have continued to occur and the possibility of more riots remains a factor in all political thinking.

At the opposite end of the moral spectrum, religious ideals and the concept of saintliness affect the very tone of Indian politics also. The saintly man who has renounced personal gain has a far greater political appeal than a politician who lets his ambitions show. Many Indians have little confidence in the legislators they elect, just because these legislators campaigned openly for themselves. Personal renunciation and dedication account in large part for the hold of both Gandhi and Nehru over the Indian masses. To leaders who have the necessary moral qualities, those masses offer worship that is truly religious in mood. Indeed, they virtually require a leader whom they can find it possible to worship.

Because of the religious orientation of Indian thought, the most effective political techniques are often ones that seem to a Westerner not at all political. Gandhi's methods were a case in point. The prolonged and difficult fasts he endured to accomplish so many of his purposes have been imitated since independence by various leaders to achieve political goals. Potti Sriramulu, the Telugu leader who fasted until his death in 1952 to champion the formation of a separate Telugu-speaking state, was only one of many who have used this technique. Almost equally noteworthy were the fasts of the Sikh leader, Master Tara Singh, and of the two Hindu saints who fasted over the issue of a divided Punjab.

But religious leaders are not the only ones who use fasts as a political weapon. In June, 1961, A. K. Gopalan, a Communist leader in Kerala, fasted to oppose the eviction of squatters from a particular area of forest land to make room for a hydroelectric project. His action was clearly a direct appeal for the squatters' votes, rather than the expression of a religious conviction.

Nehru strongly opposed fasts as an unfair means of coercion. They tend to generate great excitement among the followers of the fasting leader, galvanizing them into active and militant support of his position.

Gandhi's religion-based nonviolent civil disobedience, used successfully against the Communists in Kerala in 1959, is a factor of immeasurable potential importance. The technique is available of course to other groups for other, perhaps less laudable purposes. No government can rule in the face of large-scale, organized, persistent civil disobedience. If pushed to an extreme, *satyagraha* could cause the total destruction of government and result in anarchy.

Politics in the Princely States

The political atmosphere in the 562 former princely states differs even more sharply from that in the West than it does in the larger portion of India which was formerly under direct British rule. In British India, at least a small minority were given the opportunity to learn certain rudiments of the democratic process and to participate in representative institutions in the last years before independence. With few exceptions, the princely states provided no such experience. Particularly in the smaller princely states, Western or modern influences of any kind were minimal. Society and social attitudes remained feudal. Concepts of democracy and of party organization gained no real foothold before independence. Even eighteen years after independence, unquestioning loyalty to the ruling princes tended to persist. Almost all the ex-rulers or their relatives who chose to run for Parliament were overwhelmingly elected.

A story that well illustrates the veneration accorded members of the princely families was told to me in 1958 by Her Highness the Maharani of Gwalior, the widow of one of the major ex-princes of India (a descendant of the Maratha chief Sindhia, who controlled the Mughul Emperor at the time the British captured Delhi). In the election of 1957, Her Highness ran for Parliament on the ticket of Nehru's Congress Party, whose symbol was a pair of yoked bullocks. Her chief opponent ran on the ticket of the Hindu Mahasabha, a right-wing, orthodox Hindu party opposed to Nehru's secular state and dedicated to the transformation of India into a Hindu religious state.

Knowing that he had little chance of being elected if he openly opposed Her Highness, the Hindu Mahasabha candidate went from village to village in Gwalior with a speech that ran roughly as follows:

"I hear that a mistaken rumor has been spread among you—that if you want to choose Her Highness in the coming election, you must put a piece of paper in a box bearing the picture of a pair of bullocks. What a shocking thought! Have you so quickly forgotten that Her Highness is royal and descended from royalty? How, then, could you imagine that mere bullocks would be her symbol? No! Her Highness' box will be the one bearing the picture of the man on horseback. Do you not know that His Highness has the finest horses in the land? Have you not heard that he takes joy in riding? Quite naturally, Her Highness has chosen as her symbol the picture of her husband on a noble horse."

In her palace in the capital city of Gwalior, Her Highness heard about her opponent's campaign and decided that she must make a personal appearance to undo his subtle mischief. Bumping in a jeep over back-country roads and roadless fields, she traveled from village to village carefully explaining that the bullocks were indeed her symbol.

However, her wily opponent followed her, going again from village to village. This time, he wrung his hands and said: "Oh, I feel so badly that I was mistaken about Her Highness' symbol when I was here before. How fortunate that in her great kindness she has deigned to come to our humble villages and enlighten us on this point so that there can no longer be any confusion. Now that we clearly understand this, we shall, of course, place our offerings in the box with the bullocks. But I have been considering what our offerings should be. Some have said they should be pieces of paper. But surely such a high personage deserves some offering better than paper. Our royal family is favored by the gods. They are almost gods themselves. Should we not, therefore, give her offerings such as those we make to the gods—offerings of coins or of flowers? As for the pieces of paper that will be handed to you as you go toward the boxes, you can, of course, put those worthless little scraps into the box of the man on horseback."

The Hindu Mahasabha candidate made his second round too late for Her Highness to retrace her steps and set matters right again before the election. Although her ballot boxes did contain sufficient paper for her to win the election, they also contained flower petals and coins.

Voters as gullible as this, as devoutly loyal to feudal rulers, form only one part of the political spectrum of India. Between the wide extremes—of education and illiteracy, of wealth and poverty, of urbanization and rural isolation, of Westernization and orthodox traditionalism, of feudal loyalty and sharp class cleavages—lie endless variations. To such a varied electorate must the political parties of India direct their attention.

The Large Number of Parties

Perhaps the most important single feature of Indian politics is the large number of rival parties and of independent candidates running for office. This political fragmentation is an expression of the many kinds of differences among people in India—differences not only in political ideology or economic interest, but more especially in religion, caste, and regional loyalties. Within the Indian context, the two-party system, which is taken for granted in Great Britain and the United States, seems fully as impossible and incredible as does the fabulous wealth of the West.

In the elections of 1962, for example, sixteen parties were given official recognition by the Election Commission, and several additional smaller parties succeeded in electing one or more candidates to the Lok Sabha or to a state assembly. (Even more parties had contested the previous general elections.)

In addition to the many contesting parties, a large number of independent candidates run for office. In the 1962 elections, out of an average of four candidates for every seat contested, at least one or more were generally independents. It is significant that in the 1962 elections, independent candidates polled 12.36 per cent of the total popular vote—far less of course than the winning Congress Party, but more than any single opposition party.

The large number of independent candidates is partly accounted for by the ever-present opportunity for a candidate to seek the support of some caste not yet courted by an existing party. However, independent candidates may also be prominent leaders formerly associated with the nationalist movement or the Congress Party who have not been allocated seats on the Congress ticket. Or they may be former princes so sure of the support of their erstwhile subjects that they see no need for a party affiliation.

The Congress Party

As already noted, Nehru's Congress Party has continuously held control of the central Parliament since independence. On several occasions, it has had to form state coalitions with other parties in order to retain control of the state governments. And there was a period of two years when the Communist Party assumed control in the state of Kerala. But with these few brief exceptions, the Congress Party has held the reins over the entire nation since 1947, providing eighteen years of political stability—an unusual phenomenon for a newly independent country.

The Congress Party is the heir and successor of the Indian National Congress, by far the most active and outstanding nationalist organization during the independence movement. During the long years of struggle against the British, this movement gradually acquired characteristics that remain important today. Under Gandhi's leadership, it became a mass organization with a network of units at the local level directed by committees at the district level which, in turn, took orders from provincial committees. At the top of the pyramid was a large All-India Congress Committee with power to make decisions between the still larger annual conferences of the Congress as a whole. A small Working Committee served as the effective executive. The Congress Party of today has inherited this extensive and valuable organizational framework, which no other party has yet been able to duplicate. By 1939, the Indian National Congress claimed to have 3 million dues-paying members and thus to be the largest political organization in the world at the time.[9] To appeal to the masses, it was necessary to make at least general promises of equality of opportunity, quite foreign to the traditional views of many of the high-caste leaders of the organization.

Aside from the overriding goal of independence, however, no single, clear-cut, unequivocal ideological line was ever adopted. Many issues were left unresolved. Because of the all-engrossing nature of the nationalist struggle, people of every conceivable viewpoint joined, and every income bracket and occupation—peasants and trade-union members on the one hand, large landholders and industrialists on the other—were represented. Hence, there always were—and still are—widely divergent factions and even organized groups within the movement.

Many of the parties of today originated at the time of independence, when a number of such groups and factions split off to form new parties. They left behind them people within the Congress who shared their points of view but preferred to stay on in the large and powerful party which now controlled the government. Thus every shade of political thought that can be found among the opposition parties can still be found in the Congress, too. These include extreme right-wing conservatives, moderate socialists, left-wing socialists, near-Communists (and even Communists), orthodox Hindus opposed to Westernization, former members of the Muslim League, representatives of big business and private enterprise, large landowners, the landless laborers.

Throughout the first seventeen years of independence, because of Nehru's leadership, the Westernizing, modernizing approach was dominant within the Congress leadership at the Centre. (Certain state leaders have been less Western in their orientation.) Perhaps the chief goal of the central leadership was the creation of a secular—as opposed to a Hindu—state. A second main objective was, and continues to be, the raising of the standard of living through industrialization and a series of Five-Year Plans. Much of the Congress Party election manifesto of 1962—the equivalent of a party platform in the United States—reads like a summary of the three Five-Year Plans adopted by the government since independence.

In 1955, the party went on record as favoring a "socialist pattern of society," the exact nature of which has never been defined. The personal view of Prime Minister Nehru tended to shape its broad outlines. There were perhaps three main strands to Nehru's socialism: One dated back to his early interest in Marxist socialism and was reinforced by his admiration for the success of the Soviet Union's Five-Year Plans. Another was related to his deep belief in political freedom and his affinity with the British Labour Party's approach to socialism. And the third strand seemed simply to equate socialism with greater equality of opportunity—an ideal to which Nehru had been deeply dedicated ever since his first, early contact with Indian village life. What the resulting socialism looks like in practice will become clearer when we examine the Indian economic scene. It must be remembered, however, that there remain within the Congress Party conservatives who would prefer that private enterprise be allowed as large a role in the economy as it is capable of filling, and who try to prevent such equalizing measures as land reform from interfering with their vested interests.

The Congress Party under Nehru's leadership was responsible for the passage of the Hindu Code Bills already mentioned—Westernizing measures obnoxious to the more traditional, conservative, Hindu-minded members of the party.

Finally, and most important, the central leadership of the party attempts to stand for national unity against the divisive forces of regionalism, religion, language, and caste. Yet, in many states, these very forces, so deeply embedded in Indian society, form the basis of the divisive factions within the party itself.

That the Congress remained unified in spite of its variegated membership was largely due to the political skill of Prime Minister Nehru. In the 1960's, as he began to show his increasing age, his hold over the miscellaneous factions decreased, and party discipline began to give way in many states to bitter factional disputes. Everywhere, bosses of factions began "defying ministries, ignoring the party mandate of the chief ministers, obliquely circumventing the instructions even of Prime Minister Nehru."[10]

Eighteen years in office bring new problems to any party. In the 1950's, the crusading fervor of the independence movement disappeared. Whereas, before independence, membership in the party often meant jail sentences or other sacrifice, now it can mean material advantage, the spoils of office, patronage, and power. Charges of corruption have multiplied. It would be impossible to judge whether there is, in fact, more corruption in India than in other countries or whether the growing disillusionment with Congress rule results from expectations of honesty in government greater than human nature can maintain.

In any case, the conception of national as opposed to family or group interest is still in its infancy. "Wrong-doing in the form of lying, stealing, or bribing—*if done for kin*—is minor compared to the *right-doing* of helping family. . . . It has been family against the world."[11]

Significantly, Congress is the only party with a truly national organization. The strength of other parties is confined to certain areas or, in a number of cases, to single states. In the first general elections, in 1952, the Congress won 44.4 per cent of the popular vote. In the second general elections, in 1957, it gained strength, winning 47.78 per cent.[12] In the third elections, in 1962, it fell back slightly, winning 45 per cent of the popular vote.[13] Although all these percentages are short of a clear majority, no other single party in any election has polled more than 11 per cent of the popular vote.

In terms of candidates elected to the Central Lok Sabha, the Congress has consistently fared still better. Out of 494 elective Lok Sabha seats, Congress candidates won 353 in 1962, while the largest opposition bloc—at that time, the Communists—won only 27 seats.[14] In each election, the Congress has captured more than 70 per cent of the seats. This great difference between the percentage of votes polled and the percentage of seats won is a result of the fragmentation of the opposition.

Before Nehru's death, there had been some apprehension that the Party (and the nation) would not succeed in effecting an orderly transition to a new government when the "irreplaceable man" died. This fear proved to be groundless. At the time of Nehru's death, the President of the Congress Party was Kamaraj Nadar, a politician of skill and determination. Deciding that it was of the utmost importance that the new Prime Minister be chosen unanimously, he persuaded the Congress Party members in Parliament (who under parliamentary practice were the ones to choose their new leader) to authorize him to find out which candidate commanded the largest support. Having privately canvassed the Congress members, he decided that the best candidate would be Lal Bahadur Shastri. Kamaraj then persuaded (some say forced) the other candidates to withdraw. Shastri was chosen without a dissenting vote.

The reason for his selection was that he was a middle-of-the-road man in his economic policies—and Congress was not prepared to make a clear-cut choice between its right and left wings. Also, Shastri, though a northerner from Uttar Pradesh, was acceptable to the chief southern leaders. Then, too, he was regarded as a man of the people—never rich, not Westernized, thoroughly Hindu. (When Gandhi had advised the boycott of British schools, he had attended a Hindu school, and had swum the Ganges each day to reach it.)

Comparing him with Nehru, Indians found him short, thin, frail, unprepossessing, uninspiring. He perhaps lacked the necessary firmness to keep affairs of state under steady control. Early in 1965, many Indians asserted, "It is either Shastri or chaos." This statement reflected an awareness of the deep divisions in the Congress Party and the fact that anyone stronger or more assertive than Shastri might be completely unacceptable to one or another wing of the party.

In his first year in office, Shastri met an avalanche of problems: acute food shortages, soaring prices, labor unrest, an alarming decline of reserves of foreign exchange, increasingly critical clashes with Pakistan (culminating in war), and extremely serious language riots. He vacillated. Many thought him weak. Meanwhile, the Congress Party in almost every state was sharply split into irreconcilable factions. Until the outbreak of the war with Pakistan, it seemed probable that one or more of the national leaders aspiring to take Shastri's place would try to seize control of the party machines in the states, thus giving factionalism a dangerous national dimension. But Shastri's firmness against Pakistan in the autumn of 1965 brought him great popularity, made him seem strong, and enhanced the Congress Party's chances of continued success in the next general elections, in 1967.

The Praja Socialist Party

In 1934, a number of socialist-minded members of the Indian National Congress formed the Congress Socialist Party (CSP) for the purpose of influencing Congress policy from within, especially in favor of agrarian and labor reform. In 1948, shortly after Gandhi's death, the CSP seceded from Congress to become the Socialist Party. Though a Socialist himself, Nehru did not join the secession. In 1952, the Socialist Party merged with another small party, which had recently been formed by a prominent Gandhian, Acharya Kripalani. After the merger, the combined parties took the name of the Praja Socialist Party, or People's Socialist Party (PSP). These two newly united groups had together polled the largest vote of any party other than the Congress in 1952. The PSP seemed likely to emerge in subsequent elections as the chief opposition party. One of its leaders was the popular Jayaprakash Narayan. In 1954, Jayaprakash withdrew from party work to devote himself to Bhoodan, the land-gift movement of Vinoba Bhave. His withdrawal, and the division of the PSP into divergent factions decreased the party's strength—though not Jayaprakash's popularity, which remained very great until he urged a compromise with Pakistan over Kashmir. Until he took this unpopular stand, he was often mentioned as a possible successor to Nehru.

The party has lost ground rapidly. In the 1962 elections, it polled only 6.88 per cent of the popular vote—as against 10.41 per cent in the elections of 1957—electing a total of only 149 members to the various state legislatures and 12 to the Lok Sabha.[15]

The decrease of the PSP's popularity is due in part to the adoption by the Congress Party in 1955 of the principle of a "socialist pattern of society." This made it hard for the PSP to establish in the public mind a clear concept of its difference from the Congress. Yet a difference does exist. The PSP criticized Nehru for leaning too much toward the Communist countries in his foreign policy and of being insufficiently neutral. A section of the PSP has tended to stress a kind of socialism quite different from Nehru's socialism of large dams, government-owned steel plants, and the like. Instead, it has emphasized the religion-based Gandhian socialism, or *Sarvodaya* (meaning the "service of all" or "a cooperative commonwealth"). Some characteristics of this socialism are the stress on decentralization, village self-sufficiency and self-government, cottage and small-scale industries, land reform through Bhoodan, and "a new humanism based on absolute devotion to nonacquisitiveness, nonviolence, and truth."[16] Although the PSP passed a resolution in 1952 supporting the *Sarvodaya* ideal, other factions within the party believe in Marxian socialism or in the democratic socialism of the British Labour Party.

The Communist Party of India

The Communist Party of India (CPI) is the chief single opposition party, although it cannot by any means compare in strength to the Congress Party and has been under vigorous attack since the first Chinese invasion in 1959 and especially since the more serious invasion of October, 1962.

The CPI polled 8.92 per cent of the popular vote in the 1957 elections and 10.4 per cent in 1962. In 1957, it won control of the Kerala state legislature, which it held until the special election of

1960. It also became the chief opposition party in 1957 in four additional state legislatures—Andhra Pradesh, Madras, Punjab, and West Bengal. In 1962, despite its increase of votes polled, it emerged as the chief opposition party in only three states—Andhra Pradesh, Kerala, and West Bengal—losing ground in both Madras and the Punjab.[17]

To view the Party's problems and prospects in perspective, it may be useful to examine briefly its history. Communist groups were organized on a small scale in northern India in the early 1920's, chiefly through the driving force of one Indian, M. N. Roy, in close contact with Russia and a prominent figure in the Comintern. Under Lenin's direction, the first official policy of the Communists in India was to gain influence in the Indian National Congress. Just when this policy seemed to be on the verge of success—and after Nehru had made a trip to Moscow in 1927—it was reversed. In 1928, the Comintern declared that even the left wing of the Indian National Congress should be regarded as part of the bourgeoisie, with whom there could be no cooperation.[18] (The reason for the reversal lay in the disillusionment of the Soviet leaders with the bourgeois Chiang Kai-shek, who had turned against the Communists in China in 1927.) Since then, similar reversals, dictated by outside events, have occurred at intervals.

The arrest and trial of thirty-one Indian Communist leaders by British authorities in India in 1929 in the famous Meerut conspiracy case made martyrs of the Communists in the eyes of many Indian nationalists, and for the first time placed Communism on a sure footing in India. Socialist and Communist ideas became fashionable among India's educated elite. In 1934, the British authorities declared the Party illegal. Those members who were not jailed began working underground and within the Congress Socialist Party, through which they also gained access to the main body of the Congress movement itself. By 1939, there were twenty Communists on the All-India Congress Committee, which, next to the smaller Working Committee of the Congress, was the most important policy-making body of the nationalist movement.

At the outbreak of World War II, the Communists in India branded the war as "imperialist." But in June, 1941, when Germany attacked Russia, the CPI suddenly discovered that the war was a "people's war" and urged cooperation with the British. The British authorities in India then lifted the ban on the Party and released the Communists who had been in jail. Because of their wartime collaboration with the British, the Indian Communists were expelled from the Indian National Congress.

While the most influential nationalist leaders spent the war in jail, the Communists busily infiltrated various mass organizations such as the All-India Trade Union Conference (AITUC), the All-India Students Federation, and the leading group of peasants. The support they received from the British authorities during the war led to a tremendous spurt in the Communists' strength. Between 1942 and 1945, Party membership increased more than sixfold.[19] The CPI's record of wartime collaboration with the British is still a handicap to it, however.

During and immediately after the war, the CPI adopted a policy aimed at dividing India. The Party not only supported the formation of Pakistan, but also listed, in 1942, seventeen Indian "nationalities" entitled to similar self-determination. These nationalities were, of course, the linguistic groupings which remain a possible threat to the survival of Indian unity. Although the CPI later modified somewhat its stand regarding these "nationalities," the issue remains one that it can again use in the future.

After its conference in Calcutta in 1948, the CPI soon embarked on an active campaign of subversion and violence. Looting, the destruction of factory equipment, the murder of police and of rival labor organizers became frequent. In the eastern section of the princely state of Hyderabad, which now forms part of Andhra Pradesh, local Communist groups seized the land and drove out landlords and local government officials.

The Nehru government treated this Communist insurrection firmly: It banned the Party in a number of states and jailed thousands of Communist leaders under the Preventive-Detention Act. The Indian Army marched into Hyderabad and restored order. Full peace did not return to this troubled region, however, until 1951, when Vinoba Bhave walked through it on foot as he began his movement for voluntary gifts of land for the landless.

In 1951, as the first Indian general elections approached, the CPI declared that it would confine itself to legal action as an opposition party. Many Communists were then released from jail and contested the election. Throughout the 1950's the CPI's overt policy remained one of moderation and limited criticism of Nehru, much of whose foreign policy it supported. This moderation and restraint from insurrection may well have been on orders from Moscow since it clearly furthered the Russian purpose of seeking at least the benevolent neutrality of the Nehru government. The appearance of Communist political respectability was probably responsible for the great increase in the Communist vote in the 1957 elections.

Two years later, the first Chinese invasion of Indian territory posed for the Party the always latent dilemma as to how Indian Communism may be reconciled with Indian nationalism. One faction of the Party favored following the lead of Russia, another the lead of China. The factionalism within the party became increasingly acute until it resulted in an outright split in 1964 between the pro-Russian (or right) wing and the pro-Chinese (or left) wing, each of which then organized itself separately. The former Communist Chief Minister of Kerala, E. M. S. Nambudripad, became the leading spokesman for the left wing, which indicated impatience with gradualist methods and endorsed more militant tactics. Charging that the left wing had formed a conspiracy to take over the government, the Home Minister, G. L. Nanda, imprisoned several of its leaders in 1964.

In both factions, the leaders are predominantly college graduates and members of the intelligentsia—doubtless because the less educated people have neither the inclination, ability, nor opportunity to grasp the complex ideology of Marxist materialism, so alien to their ingrained religious traditions. The fact that many Communists are Brahmans has counted against the Party in areas such as Madras and Maharashtra, where anti-Brahman feeling is strong. So far, the Party has made no serious appeal to the truly disinherited Indians, the untouchables and the proletariat.

The membership of the Communist Party is not large. In May, 1962, it was estimated at about 178,000.[20] It appeared to have declined by about 40,000 since the beginning of the Chinese invasion in 1959, and has probably declined further since the intensification of warfare in late 1962. The disciplined, hard core of the Party—the actual Party members—accounted for less than 2 per cent of the votes polled by the CPI in the 1962 elections. In some states, Communist strength at the polls seems to have been due not at all to ideology, but to preoccupation with caste and caste rivalries. In certain cases, the Party has seemed a good vantage point from which certain local castes could attack or undermine the position of rival castes firmly entrenched in particular branches of the dominant Congress Party.

Then, too, until the disillusionment of 1962, vaguely formulated ideas of a Communist nature had considerable appeal in India. Communist ideals had seemed similar to the socialism which is the dominant political philosophy of the nation. For this reason, some voters apparently cast their ballots for Communist candidates simply in protest against the corruption which they believed existed in the Congress Party, and without intentionally indicating a preference for a different ideology.

It may be useful to glance at the three states where the chief strength of the CPI lies.

In Andhra Pradesh, the Party has had strong support in the Kamma caste. One of the two prosperous and largest peasant castes in the state, the Kammas have always been rivals of the Reddis, the caste on which the Congress Party's strength in Andhra Pradesh is largely based. Many consider this intercaste rivalry responsible for Communist strength in the state. In 1962, the CPI won 51 seats in the Andhra Pradesh state assembly out of a total of 300, while the Congress won 176.[21]

West Bengal contains the largest city in India, Calcutta, which has such complex problems of housing, transportation, public sanitation, and water supply that the cost of solving or even appreciably lessening them would be staggering. West Bengal as a whole has suffered a series of misfortunes in recent years. In 1943, it was devasted by floods and a famine in which countless thousands died and countless others left their land in the vain hope of finding food in the great city. In 1947, the boundary established between India and Pakistan cut off West Bengal from the rich agricultural land of East Bengal, which became East Pakistan. Calcutta had relied on East Bengal for the raw jute for its chief industry, jute manufacturing. Since 1950, a long stream of Hindu refugees from East Pakistan has poured into West Bengal. Numbering more than 3 million, the refugees have added greatly to the already insoluble problems of Calcutta.

These misfortunes befell a people—the Bengalis—whose leading families had had long and full exposure to Western thought, had produced several of the great figures of the Hindu renaissance of the nineteenth century, were proud of their culture and intellectual traditions, and had early absorbed the intellectual content of Marxism. During the independence movement, Bengalis tended to be scornful of Gandhian nonviolence. Terrorist methods were more to their taste. Bengalis tend to be explosive in temperament, thus quick to break out in strikes, riots, and vandalism. Because of labor unrest, Calcutta has gradually been losing its commercial and industrial pre-eminence. New businesses have tended to prefer Bombay or one of the other growing industrial cities. This, of course, has added to the vicious circle of poverty and despair.

In the 1962 elections, Communists won 50 of the 252 seats of the West Bengal state legislature, as against 157 won by the Congress Party.[22]

Kerala has the highest population density in the world, the highest rate of literacy in India (about 50 per cent), and the highest rate of unemployment (and many of the unemployed are well educated and articulate). Its untouchables still occupy the most degraded position. Moreover, Kerala has received a disappointing, perhaps disproportionately low allocation of financial aid from the central government for industrialization or planning. Caste rivalries also play a role in the unrest. The state leader of the Communist Party, Mr. Nambudripad, is a Brahman, and the rank and file of the Party includes many Ezhavas, the largest low-caste group in Kerala. (The Ezhavas used to be ranked as untouchables, but have more recently had some success in making good their claim that they are not.) Both the Nambudri Brahmans and the Ezhavas are rivals of the Nairs, who have been strong in the Kerala Congress Party.

The twenty-six months during which the Communists held control of Kerala after the election of 1957 provided India with an instructive glimpse of Communist methods. The electoral rolls of the state were padded, and an education bill was adopted to require even private schools to choose their teachers from lists prepared by the state. The bill increased state control over textbooks and gave the government the right to take over even the property of private schools. Measures such as these convinced the opposition that it would be impossible ever to vote the Communists out of office and that it was, therefore, necessary to launch quickly a civil-disobedience campaign. After the Governor of the state had recommended that the President of India take over Kerala under his emergency powers in the Constitution, new state elections were held in 1960. The Communists garnered an even larger percentage of the popular vote—43 per cent (as against 39.65 per cent in the preceding election)—and more than any other party.[23] But the coalition of opposing parties—the Congress Party, the Praja Socialist Party, and the Muslim League—won a majority of the seats in the legislature and formed a government. Only in this sense did the CPI lose the election.

In 1965, when the next state elections took place in Kerala, the total Communist strength declined to 27 per cent of the votes cast. The left wing, headed by Nambudripad, ran far ahead of the right wing, winning 19.5 per cent of the vote and forty seats in the state legislature. The total Congress vote rose to 44.9 per cent, but it was divided between two rival factions. Therefore, the forty left-wing Communist legislators formed the largest single group in the newly elected legislature. Of these, twenty-nine had been arrested the previous December and were still in jail without having been brought to trial. Nambudripad claimed (perhaps incorrectly) that if the twenty-nine were released, his group, plus certain non-Communists willing to cooperate with it, would be able to command a majority in the legislature, and should, therefore, be entitled to form a government. Instead, the central government proclaimed a new period of President's Rule for Kerala. The newly elected legislature was not even convened. The imprisoned legislators remained in prison. Nambudripad indignantly asked how the party in power at the Centre could rightly detain members of other parties on grounds which it would not bring before a court of law and thus deny them the right to function within a democratic framework.[24] Even among non-Communists, there was criticism of the government's handling of the matter.

Many thoughtful Indians wondered what would happen after future elections if the voters in additional states should elect to their state assemblies majorities (or large pluralities) of representatives of opposition parties. Would the Congress Party again use President's Rule to keep all opposition parties out of power in the states so long as Congress maintained a majority at the Centre?

Whatever the answer to this question, India as a whole is not likely soon to go Communist by popular vote.

The Swatantra (Freedom) Party

One of the chief features of the 1962 elections was the emergence for the first time at the polls of a new party with a conservative economic program. The Swatantra (Freedom) Party opposed the increasing trend of the Congress toward socialism and especially toward agricultural "cooperatives" under official control (which seemed to many to be dangerously similar to Communist-type collectives). It opposed the increasing governmental regulation of private industry, the "totalitarian," "Soviet-type" economic planning, and the "obsession with gigantism that dominates current governmental thinking." It criticized the increasing number of government enterprises, stressing the "incompetence of the government to run business and industrial undertakings," the "wasteful use of resources . . . red tape, a disregard of costs and rigidity of action." It urged an end to deficit financing, the control of inflation, the abolition of the Planning Commission, and the "employment of the bulk of available resources in agriculture and light industries."[25]

The Swatantra Party polled 8.5 per cent of the popular vote in 1962—slightly less than the percentage polled by the Communist Party, but more than that of any other single opposition party. The Swatantra emerged as the largest single opposition party in three states: Bihar, Gujarat, and Rajasthan. It later gained the status of chief opposition party in still another state, Orissa, through a post-election merger with a strong local party, the Ganatantra Parishad. Altogether, it elected a larger number of candidates (161) to state assemblies than did the CPI (149) or any other party besides the Congress (1,768).[26]

After the split of the Communist Party, the Swatantra became the chief opposition party in the central Parliament. In 1965, one of the leaders of the party, Minoo Masani, made a strong plea for outright alignment with the West in foreign policy. The party suffers, however, from inner contradictions. Its founder was one of the grand old men of the freedom movement, the influential Chakravarti Rajagopalachari (affectionately known as Rajaji), who had served as Governor-General of India after the retirement of Lord Mountbatten. To build up his party, Rajaji enlisted the support of a number of dissimilar political leaders, each with his own following, many of them in areas that had been under princely rule until independence and where princes still command loyal allegiance. The views of the Swatantra leaders are widely different, and the party's complexion varies greatly from place to place. In southern Bihar, for example, the Swatantra's success in 1962 was due largely to the efforts of one feudal prince, the Rajah of Ramgarh, who campaigned in a Russian helicopter.

Before Nehru's death, many had expected that the Swatantra would pose a serious threat to Congress in the 1967 general elections in an increased number of states. But Shastri's shift toward a slightly more conservative policy than Nehru's, with more emphasis on consumer goods than on heavy industry, may have stolen part of the Swatantra's appeal to the voters.

Hindu Communal Parties

The religious conservatives showed a growth of strength in the 1957 and 1962 general elections. The several groups that constitute the religious right wing are called "communal" groups because their purpose is identified with that of a particular religious community, the Hindu community. Before independence, these groups concentrated chiefly on opposition to another communal group, the Muslim League. Since independence, they have vigorously opposed the Westernized Indian community and the strong influence of Western thought in the central government.

The Western notions that orthodox Hindus oppose include the idea that Parliament has a right to legislate on matters such as marriage, which was previously regulated by Hindu customs. In general, they tend to look with disfavor on modern science, since all truth and all science, they believe, appeared in the ancient Vedas. When money is appropriated for medical schools, they urge that it should go to train practitioners of ancient Ayurvedic medicine, which is based on the concept that all ailments are traceable to a lack of balance among the three "humors" of the body: wind, bile, and phlegm. They feel uneasy living within the framework of a Western-type constitution, which many of them would like to remodel in one way or another. They are disturbed by the erection of large dams, factories, and other projects requiring the concentrated application of Western technology. But instead of attacking such projects directly, they may press for decentralization and the revival of cottage industries. They remain unreconciled to the 1947 partition of India, and urge the reunification of India and Pakistan and the rule of India by Hindus. A slogan of one of their chief leaders, V. D. Savarkar, was "Hinduize politics and militarize Hindudom."

The earliest of these Hindu communal groups to be formed was the Hindu Mahasabha, organized in 1915 to promote the celebration of Hindu festivals, the popularization of Hindi as the national language, and the reconversion of Hindus who had been converted to Islam, and to represent the communal interest of Hindus in all political controversies. Thus the Mahasabha was engaged in both religio-cultural and political activities. Many of the early Mahasabha leaders were active in the Congress movement also, but in the 1930's they became increasingly skeptical of the Congress because they believed that Gandhi had appeased Muslims.

One of the influential communal groups is the Rashtriya Swayamasevak Sangh (RSS), which is not itself a political party. A semimilitary organization of Hindu youth, it is divided into local units that are strictly disciplined and require attendance at daily meetings and occasionally in their training camps; activities at such meetings include physical exercises, drills, calisthenics, games, Sanskrit prayers, and weekly discussions and lectures. Its primary aim is to establish within its own group a model of a revitalized Hindu society and eventually to secure the adoption of this cultural form in the whole country.[27] During their initial period of membership, the members may not marry.

At the time of partition, when the membership of the RSS numbered approximately half a million, more than 100,000 of its members, organized in unofficial armed bands, roamed the troubled area of the newly divided Punjab. They helped Hindu refugees fleeing from Pakistan, and also apparently killed many Muslim refugees headed in the opposite direction. After Gandhi's assassination in January, 1948 (by a Maharashtrian Brahman who had been connected with the RSS), the organization was banned for over a year.

Youths trained in this organization are now among the active leaders in the largest and most rapidly growing Hindu communal party, the Jana Sangh, formed in 1951 under the leadership of a former president of the Hindu Mahasabha. Intense, devoted, dedicated middle-class persons—steeped in the world of Hinduism—the leaders of the Jana Sangh contrast sharply with the princes and the cosmopolitan, Western-minded leaders of the other leading conservative party, the Swatantra. Like the Swatantra, though, the Jana Sangh opposes cooperative farming, tax increases made necessary by large planning, and the growing inflation caused by deficit financing. But its emphasis is not on economic considerations, but rather on matters related to a national cultural resurgence along Hindu lines. Its election manifesto of 1961 (written before the Indian invasion of Goa) urged "the complete integration of Kashmir," "opposition to soft-pedaling of disputes with Pakistan," and "the use of force to put an end to Portuguese colonial rule on our soil."[28] In an election year, such a pronouncement by an opposition party would tend to affect the policy of the party in power in any country.

The Jana Sangh has stressed national defense and national unity, and proposed to amend the constitution to declare India a unitary rather than a federal state. Yet it also endorsed the village panchayats. The manifesto said that in "proper and quick industrialization, instead of copying Western patterns, we should develop our own technique . . . [and] make small-scale and cottage industries the basis of [India's] program of industrialization." It emphasized Indian self-sufficiency and urged greater independence of foreign capital and foreign aid.[29] Above all, the Jana Sangh has been militantly anti-Pakistan.

This party emerged from the 1962 elections as the chief opposition in the two great states of Madhya Pradesh and Uttar Pradesh, electing 41 and 48 legislators to their respective assemblies, as opposed to 142 and 248 elected by the Congress. Polling 6.38 per cent of the total popular vote, it became the fifth largest party nationally (after the Congress, the Swatantra, the CPI, and the PSP).[30] Its future potential is hard to judge because it places less reliance on a few outstanding leaders than do other parties, but it has a better organizational network in its areas of strength (largely the north) than does any party except the Congress. Will these characteristics cause it to grow faster than other opposition parties? Or do Indians still require outstanding leaders to revere? The answer is not clear.

The Jana Sangh has always protested that it is not "communal" since it will admit non-Hindus as members. But the Hindu bias of its outlook is so strong that non-Hindus are unlikely to join it in substantial numbers.

The growth in strength of the Jana Sangh shown in the past two elections is a significant indication of the resurgence of traditional Hindu thought, whose proponents stress its relevance to legislative and governmental policies, as well as to personal life, where its influence at no time has declined. As the nation settles more surely into its independence, the Western idea of a secular state may progressively lose the appeal that Nehru's leadership long gave it. The trend toward the reassertion of Hindu values is linked to the fact that increasing numbers of non-Westernized persons are receiving some education and becoming articulate. It is also linked to the mobility of castes and the tendency of castes to become more Sanskritized as they seek to rise in the social scale.

When the Congress Party in the autumn of 1965 adopted a militant anti-Pakistan policy, it may have undercut the position of the Jana Sangh, since the latter's uncompromising militancy was its biggest attraction for many voters.

Minor Parties

Mention must be made of certain minor parties, which are not organized on a national basis, but play noteworthy roles in the politics of particular states.

One of these is the Muslim League, which was the second largest political party in undivided India. Now it exists only in the south, where relations between Hindus and Muslims have usually been less strained than in the north, where the Muslim minority is far larger. In Kerala, the Muslim League polls between 3 and 5 per cent of the popular vote in each election—enough to give it the balance of power in a close contest between the Communist Party and the Congress. The 1960 electoral understanding between the Congress Party, the Praja Socialist Party, and the Muslim League and their subsequent coalition government were strongly criticized by Hindus in northern India. They argued that the Kerala Congress Party, by coming to terms with a "communal" party whose basis of existence was religious affiliation, had betrayed the ideal of a secular state. Subsequently, when new disturbances broke out between Hindus and Muslims in central and northern India in 1961, there were many who blamed the resurgence of Hindu communalism on the Congress Party's tolerance of Muslim communalism in Kerala. In the midst of mounting unpleasantness, the Muslim League retired from the Kerala coalition government, decreasing that coalition's already narrow margin over the Communists in the state assembly.

Another communal party, which exists only in the Punjab, is the Akali Dal, the Sikh party led by Master Tara Singh. Followers of the Sikh religion constitute less than half the population of the Punjab, but are concentrated in certain areas. The goal of the Akali Dal is the creation of a separate state in those areas. Although the Akali Dal does not command the votes of all the Sikhs—indeed, the Congress Chief Minister of the Punjab is a Sikh—it is the strongest single opposition party in the Punjab. It secured 19 out of the 154 seats of the state legislature in 1962, as against the Congress Party's 90.[31]

The chief opposition party in the state of Madras is the DMK (Society for Dravidian Uplift). It openly urged the secession of the Dravidian south from India—until such advocacy of secession was officially prohibited in 1963. Its leaders regard the Indo-Aryan north as utterly different racially and culturally from the south. They complain that southern India has received less than its rightful share of the sums allocated for development purposes and has been dominated and exploited by the north. They strongly oppose the adoption of Hindi as the official national language, regarding this as an imposition upon them of northern culture.

The DMK did not obtain support for its demand for secession in any southern state except Madras, where it captured 53 of the 206 seats in the state legislature in 1962.[32] When the party leader, C. N. Annadurai, expressed in Parliament in May, 1962, his demand for secession, Prime Minister Nehru answered that the demand was "so outrageous I can't conceive of it," and added that any attempt at secession would be "resisted with all our force." Such divisions, he added, would break India into "thousands of bits."[33] With the DMK in mind, the government drew up a sixteenth amendment to the Constitution, to permit restrictions on freedom of speech and assembly in the interest of the "integrity and sovereignty of India." Under this amendment, candidates advocating secession were prohibited from contesting the elections.

Three other parties deserve brief mention. The Jharkhand Party of tribal aborigines in south Bihar—led by Jaipal Singh, a tribal member who was educated at Oxford—demands that a separate state be carved out of south Bihar. In Orissa, a number of former princes and landowners, banded together in the Ganatantra Parishad, are solidly backed by their former subjects and tenants, largely tribal aborigines. The chief opposition party in the state of Orissa, the Ganatantra Parishad has reached an understanding with the conservative Swatantra Party. In Assam, the largest opposition party, the Hill Leaders' Conference, is also composed of tribal people.

This by no means exhausts the list of parties—for instance, there is also a Republican Party whose symbol is an elephant! (Unlike its U.S. counterpart, though, its members are untouchables.) But it may suggest the basis of party formation.

It is worth stressing again how strong the over-all position of the Congress Party is in relation to the various smaller parties, whose strength is limited to certain areas or, in some cases, to only one state. But in a number of states as well as nationally, the Congress is badly split into factions. In the states, these factions are based largely on caste or religious divisions rather than ideology. At the Centre, they tend to be based on ideology and also to reflect differences of opinion as to the persons best suited for national leadership.

After Nehru's Death

In India, as in the United Kingdom and other countries with a parliamentary system of government, if any party has a clear majority in both houses of parliament, the choice of a Prime Minister lies with the members of that party in parliament. Under the Indian Constitution, the President of India has the right to appoint the Prime Minister, but, following the modern practice of the King or Queen of England, in each case so far he has endorsed the choice of the majority party's members in Parliament.

In Nehru's last years many Indians and most foreigners speculated that after his death there would be a sharp contest for the position of Prime Minister. How could it be otherwise? Some of the members of Congress were known to be confirmed socialists, far more radical and leftist in their views than other, more conservative members who favored the private-enterprise approach to economic questions. The relative strength of these two groups is debatable, but they were generally believed to be roughly equal.

Of the left wing, the leaders were Nehru's daughter, Mrs. Indira Gandhi, V. K. Krishna Menon, and K. V. Malaviya, who, as Minister of Oil, had done what he could to place as large a sector of the nation's oil industry as possible in the hands of the government. Of the conservative group, the leaders were S. K. Patil, former Food Minister, and Morarji Desai, former Finance Minister, both openly pro-Western and opposed to a further expansion of socialist-style projects.

Aside from the differences in its members' economic views, the Congress Party was also divided by regional jealousies. For these reasons, a contest for the succession to Nehru was expected. But as already mentioned, no contest occurred, thanks largely to the force and determination of the strong Congress President, Kamaraj Nadar, who pressed hard for the unanimous selection of small, colorless, selfless, dedicated, middle-of-the-road Gandhian

Lal Bahadur Shastri. Shastri's economic policies seemed a compromise between those of the left and right wings of the Congress.

Even more important was the fact that Shastri, though a Hindi-speaking northerner, was acceptable to the leaders of the southern states. For the influence of the south within the Party had been increasing. In the 1957 elections, representatives elected from non-Hindi-speaking areas accounted for only about 35 per cent of the total number of Congress Party members of Parliament. In the 1962 elections, this figure had jumped to over 45 per cent.

Having never been outside of India until several months after his elevation to the position of Prime Minister, Shastri was far less Western in his approach than Nehru had been. Above all, he lacked Nehru's self-assertive quality of leadership. Political power, which had previously been concentrated in the hands of one man, now passed to a coalition of leaders from various regions and representing various shades of thought on every urgent question that arose: whether India should produce an atomic bomb, the relative importance to India of the U.S.S.R. and the United States, the official language policy, fiscal policy and economic planning, and how to handle the acute food shortage which soon developed—and which Shastri, in his first speech as Prime Minister wisely recognized as the chief problem faced by the nation.

Over the diverse coalition supporting him, Shastri presided calmly, but in a vacillating manner. When political pressures built up in opposition to policies he had already announced, he changed those policies—a dangerous invitation to more pressures for change.

In his first year in office, the opposition introduced motions of "no confidence" into Parliament on two occasions. Under the parliamentary system, if such a motion is carried, the Prime Minister must resign. Both these motions were defeated, but, significantly, many members of Shastri's own party vigorously criticized him from the floor of Parliament—notably the late Nehru's sister, Madame Pandit, who said that the nation needed "a spark which our leadership has not given us. . . . What one misses is a soul lifting and inspiring address from the Prime Minister."[34]

A third no-confidence motion was introduced in August, 1965, over India's relations with Pakistan. This resolution charged Shastri in effect with being too soft toward Pakistan. Before a vote was taken, Shastri ordered the Indian Army to seize several army posts on the Pakistan side of the Kashmir cease-fire line. Pakistan, quite naturally, retaliated sharply. The no-confidence motion was defeated—but at the cost of a war, and potentially of a war with two neighbors at once. Perhaps a stronger man would have found a way of calming the hotheads in Parliament who demanded such a dangerous course as a tough policy toward Pakistan while China threatened in the north. (India's relations with Pakistan and China will be discussed more fully in Chapter 16.)

At an important meeting of the All-India Congress Committee in July, 1965, Morarji Desai, who had been one of the main contenders for the position of Prime Minister after Nehru's death, openly criticized Shastri's leadership and even challenged him vigorously by opposing the re-election of Kamaraj Nadar, a strong supporter of Shastri, to the Presidency of the Congress Party. But the Committee adopted, with only slight modifications, the resolution that Shastri had asked for, making it possible for the Congress President to have a second two-year term. Shastri appeared to have won a significant victory within his own party, but the dissident factions remained strong, and until the outbreak of the Indo-Pakistan war, it seemed probable that either a right-wing leader (such as Morarji Desai) or a left-wing leader (such as Krishna Menon) might try to organize nationwide opposition to him within the Congress, in a bid to replace him after the 1967 general elections.

In the summer of 1965, the continued political stability of India seemed to depend on the ability of this small, frail man somehow to prevent his party from breaking apart and thus causing a multiparty situation in which no one party would command a majority either at the Centre or in the states. The surge of nationalistic feelings generated by the Indo-Pakistan war strengthened his position immensely. But it remained to be seen whether the nation could remain united behind a personage admittedly of lesser stature than Nehru after the flush of military fervor subsided.

14 • VILLAGES AND CITIES

THE VERY ESSENCE of India is her 550,000 villages, where 82.7 per cent of the population live. The great majority of these villages contain no more than 500 people (a village of 2,000 people is considered large), yet they have often been described as little worlds in themselves, so self-sufficient have they seemed in the past. In reality, even before the new developments of the 1950's brought them into somewhat closer contact with urban thought, the villages were probably not as isolated at least from one another as some have believed. Villagers always seem to have maintained contact with relatives as much as 100 miles away, and in some parts of the country they tend to marry their daughters into villages far from home. This has meant visits back and forth, particularly when a wedding occurred. Then, too, villagers left home from time to time on religious pilgrimages or to take a trip to a market town or city. Thus they probably always had some realization of the land around them. It would be more accurate to think of the villages not as worlds in themselves, but as cells in the larger organism of Indian society.

As we turn to an examination of the economic aspects of India as a whole, it seems best to start with a consideration of the social and economic life of village India.

The Village Standard of Living

Even flying over the Indian countryside after dusk, one can sense the poverty of the village masses. Virtually no lights are to be seen for mile after mile except where the rare city or market town passes below. In the many tiny villages dotted between these, millions of people who have just finished their day's work spend their evening in darkness. Increasing numbers of villagers now own kerosene lanterns with chimneys, in place of the tiny chimneyless homemade lamps of the past. But they use lanterns sparingly because they can afford little kerosene. In a very few rural areas, electricity is available and may be used to pump water for irrigation, but electric lines seldom run into the villages themselves.* The use of electricity for domestic purposes in the villages is still a distant target. Indeed, even in cities, only a fraction of the population can afford to take advantage of electric services.

Another illustration of the low standard of living is the lack of medical care, available only rarely in the villages. Most of India's 81,000 Western-trained doctors—many of them up to the highest Western standards—practice in the large cities. State governments, with developmental aid from the central government, have begun establishing what are called "primary health units," small medical centers in some of the larger rural towns or district headquarters. By 1965, there were 7,000 such governmental units.[1] A few similar medical missions are run by social-welfare organizations.

A governmental primary health unit consists typically of a nurse and a medical practitioner who may not be a fully trained doctor. It may have a one- or two-room hospital or clinic, and a medical van that tours the adjacent countryside, stopping briefly at certain villages. At each stop, villagers come forward with their ailments, are given quick diagnoses, and perhaps some medicine from one of the several big bottles which the medical van carries. Each such unit is expected to serve an entire Development Block (an average of 66,000 persons in a zone of 150 to 170 square miles). Time, staff, and facilities are not adequate to treat more than a fraction of those needing treatment, or to do, even for those few, more than a fraction of what a well-staffed, well-equipped modern hospital could do. The vast majority of mortal illnesses in the countryside go undiagnosed. The chief single cause of death in India is listed simply as "fevers"—with no breakdown as to the type of fever in question or the cause thereof. For such routine matters as childbirth, village women still use local midwives—many of whom are untouchables, because contact with childbirth is regarded as polluting.

* Only 6 per cent of the villages had access to electricity in 1963.

However low the average per capita income of the Indian population may be (it was estimated at about $69 per person in 1961, a sum that might be equivalent in purchasing power to $300 in the United States), the income of the villagers is certainly still lower. (At best, rural-income figures are only estimates, since much of the income in the rural areas still consists of what the peasants raise for their own consumption or acquire by barter without reference to the market or prices.)

Indian economists believe that the food the villagers eat constitutes 66 per cent of their total income. Even so, close to a third of the villagers are normally undernourished, especially in regard to protective foods containing vitamins, minerals, and proteins.[2] Perhaps 10 per cent of the average income goes for clothing—meaning, in practice, about two lengths of cheap cotton cloth each year to wind around the body as saris for the women or as dhotis, lungis, or loincloths for the men. Another 5–7 per cent is spent on traditional ceremonies, especially on the expensive hospitality required by social custom whenever a wedding occurs. Only about a fifth of the earnings remains for all the other necessities of life, including housing, kerosene, and payments to the moneylender or credit cooperatives, to whom the peasant is chronically in debt. Although the use of shoes is increasing, many go barefoot.

The possessions of a village household tend to be limited to a few bare essentials: copper and earthenware pots for cooking, carrying water, and storing grain; a few cotton quilts or other bedding; a small tin box in which to keep the few clothes or other valuables; some religious pictures or figures of the gods; and one or more of the inevitable charpoys (cots of woven string), which are used not only as beds but also as tables on which grain may be dried in the sun, as well as for many other purposes.

Today, a few men in each village may own a bicycle—a new luxury to be used by adult males only. The increased number of bicycles is one of the more visible reflections of the increased per capita income in the last ten years. It is estimated that some 4 million bicycles are now in use in India, as against only 304,000 private cars.[3] The chief means of transportation in the countryside, however, remains the two-wheeled carts (there are 9.5 million of them) pulled by slow-moving pairs of bullocks.

How a Village Looks

In different regions, the villages are laid out differently and use different building materials. In the south, houses are usually set apart from one another, with coconut palms or other fruit trees between. The walls, as well as the thatched roofs, are often made of vegetable fibers. In the north, the traditional fear of invasion led to the clustering of the houses of each village in a compact group forming almost a solid mass. Most of the houses are unsubstantial mud huts, easily eroded in the rains. In both the north and the south, a village may also contain a few pukka brick buildings, homes of the wealthier peasants, plus perhaps a new two-room schoolhouse serving also as a community center, library, and temporary clinic on the rare days when a medical van passes by. But most village homes have only one room, or two at most. The cattle are often brought indoors at night to protect them from robbers. Most homes are dark, and often have no windows at all; this lack is sometimes attributed to the fear of robbery—a window would mean one more aperture to lock (and the heavy iron locks required for the doors cost more than enough by themselves). The floors are of mud, carefully swept and coated with a thin paste made of cow dung and water, which when dry leaves a cement-like surface. Most of the homes contain literally nothing but the few essentials already mentioned. The home of the village headman frequently contains one object not found in the other homes, and normally tucked away in the rafters above—a battered wooden chair to be brought down and dusted off whenever a government agent, official, or other distinguished visitor comes to the village.

Close to the village is a pond, or "tank" of stagnant water, from which the cattle drink and in which the washing is done. The fields and pasturelands lie outside the village, not within it. They form a patchwork quilt of small irregular plots separated from one another by low earth banks (bunds). Around the edge of the village, cow-dung cakes are usually stacked in piles as reserves of household fuel against the rainy season, when dung will not dry. There may be a few trees for shade or fruit, but none for fuel. In most parts of India, wood is too valuable to be burned.

The typical village has neither a post office nor a shop, though the village moneylender may keep in his home a small stock of cloth, matches, kerosene, salt, combs, soap, flashlights, and other small articles for sale. The villagers buy and sell mostly at a market town, if there is one nearby, or at some spot on a roadside toward which the bullock carts of a number of villages converge once a week, thereby creating a market center.

Although a few richer families may have wells of their own, especially where the water level is near the surface, village life usually centers around one or two common wells, from which the women carry home the water for cooking, drinking, and washing in large jars on their heads. There is a great difference between a good new well and an old one. Old wells tend to be mere holes in the ground, their shafts faced with stones only roughly fitted together. Into them, surface water can easily flow back, polluting their contents, and birds can find good places for their nests on the stones of their shafts. A good new well, on the other hand, has a smooth-faced concrete shaft where birds cannot perch. A concrete platform raises the mouth of the well above ground level, and a waist-high wall around the opening gives further protection against surface water. New wells may also have pulleys to ease the labor of pulling up the buckets of water. A safer water supply through the building of improved wells of this kind has been one of the objectives of the Community Development Programme.

In north India especially, all except the poorest village homes have a tiny courtyard in which much of the family living takes place. In a corner of the courtyard, a pair of bricks or stones or two little ridges of dried mud support between them a cooking pot under which the fire of cow-dung cakes is built. Chimneys are still rare, although they are recommended by Community Development officials to prevent eye inflammation resulting from smoke. The more self-respecting village homes may keep another corner of the courtyard reserved for washing purposes, but latrines are still virtually nonexistent.

Although the interiors of village homes are generally kept reasonably clean and sometimes spotless, a similar tidiness for the village as a whole has not been traditional, and it is one of the objectives toward which the Community Development Programme has been working. The dumping of refuse in the narrow lanes between the tightly-packed rows of village homes is probably decreasing. Some villages are even beginning to pave their lanes with bricks so that they will no longer turn into mires of mud in the rainy season.

Village Castes and the Division of Labor

Most of the families in a typical village belong to some peasant caste, but the village also contains one or more families from each of a number of castes whose specialty is other than agriculture, though they may do some field work, too. These include Brahmans, astrologers and soothsayers, barbers, goldsmiths, shepherds, oil pressers, potters, weavers, carpenters, and other artisans. Unlike Western farmers, who usually do many kinds of work beside tilling their fields and who may pride themselves on their versatility, the Indian peasant relies on the specialized services of these other castes. Although the castes remain separate socially, they are closely knit together economically.

Traditionally, each peasant family had a permanent hereditary relationship with some family in each nonpeasant caste in the village. In return for an annual share in the harvest of grain, these other families would undertake to supply the peasant family year after year with all its annual needs in specified kinds of goods or services. Barbers would give unlimited shaves, and potters would make as many pottery vessels as were required.

In the exchange of goods and services, each village caste was both a patron and a client of every other village caste. They were bound together in a permanent and relatively stable, unequal relationship, in which those who were the richest and most powerful were in a position to secure the better bargain in the exchange.

There was a certain security in this arrangement, known as the jajmani system. Though the peasant might have a bad harvest, his responsibility toward the artisans who served him continued. They would eat less well if he had ill-fortune, but so did he. These old relationships are changing with the progressive introduction of a monetary economy, which was stimulated by British rule and has increased rapidly in recent years, but is not yet complete.

The government estimates that today only 43 per cent of payments in rural areas are made in goods and services, as against 57 per cent in cash. This progressive shift to a monetary economy is necessary if the new Indian industries are to find a mass market. But the transition has made deep inroads in the old mutual loyalties between peasants and artisans, masters and servants. It entails difficulties and real hardship for many. The peasants, hard pressed by the dwindling of their acreage as population increases, can less easily afford to support permanent retainers and are more inclined to give temporary employment instead. Where new roads have been built, members of artisan castes from one village can more easily offer their services in competition with their fellow caste members in neighboring villages.

The decrease of the patron-client relationship has brought special hardship to the lower section of the rural population, the landless agricultural laborers, of whom it is estimated that fully 20 million are underemployed (that is, they cannot secure employment for enough days during the year to make a decent living even by Indian rural standards). Between them and the villagers who own land or hold it as tenants, the financial gap has apparently greatly increased.

Community Development and the New Panchayats

First launched on Gandhi's birthday in 1952, the Community Development Programme was originally conceived as an intensive, many-sided attempt to make a drastic change in village life in a very few selected areas, or "blocks." It was hoped that three to five years of intensive outside aid would develop new attitudes and concepts in the villagers so that they would continue thereafter to re-create their villages with the help only of sustaining government grants for a few additional years. It proved politically impossible, however, to restrict the program to a small number of areas. By 1962, it had been extended to more than two-thirds of the nation—with a consequent reduction in the quality of the effort.

To each Community Development Block, there were assigned experts in each of a number of subjects relevant to village betterment: agriculture, irrigation, animal husbandry, health, cooperatives, soil reclamation and rural engineering, social education,

C.D.P. 1952

and rural industries. Young men known as village-level workers were employed to take to the villagers the essential information from all these fields. Although they were given special training for a year or more, their task was truly difficult. They had to face not only traditional conservatism, but also complex feuds and rivalries within the villages. For real success in generating new attitudes, they needed to have exceptional talent not only as teachers but also as diplomats and leaders.Most of them found it impossible to generate any permanent change and pressed instead for more tangible statistical achievements: a certain number of compost heaps started, a new well dug, so many feet of village lanes paved, etc. As long as government funds were available to pay the costs of such improvements, the villagers accepted them docilely, but for the most part new attitudes of self-help did not spring up.

In 1958, a government committee, known as the Balvantray Mehta Committee, called attention to the fact that the Community Development Programme had become purely an administrative program focusing on numerical targets of a uniform kind and had failed to promote self-reliance and cooperative action on the part of the people. "Decentralized planning," or Panchayati Raj, seemed to be the answer. Where that system has been put into effect, the decisions as to how Community Development funds are to be spent are made—actually or theoretically—by councils representing the villagers, instead of by appointed officials, who are now supposed to serve in an advisory capacity only.

Will the councils endorse the introduction of new techniques in agriculture, rural industries, and other matters of rural concern? Or will they use the funds over which they now have control for purposes not at all in line with the kind of development the central government contemplates? Can "decentralized planning" prove to be other than a contradiction of terms? What effect will the councils have on the disparities of wealth and social status within the villages? These are some of the questions that remain to be answered.

The Extent of Change in the Villages

Officials of the Indian Government tend to agree that *planned* changes in the villages have so far been far more superficial than had been hoped. Perhaps no society can be transformed so rapidly or so closely according to preconceived plans as the Government of India expected in 1952. Yet changes are occurring and will doubtless continue to occur at an accelerating pace. Forces beyond government control are at work, such as the increasing monetization of the rural economy, the growth of the population, and the resulting progressive decrease in the size of land holdings. These and the many forms of government action—government expenditure on village development, continued presence in the villages of extension workers, the new panchayats, land reforms, and, above all, road-building programs—cannot fail to transform the villages in the long run, though not always in the directions hoped for.

Because of the endless variety within India, it is hard to make valid generalizations as to the extent and nature of the changes up to now. Quite naturally, change is greatest where contact with the cities or large towns is the closest. In spite of road-building programs, probably the majority of the Indian villages still are approached only by wavering footpaths over which jeeps can pass only in good weather. The distance from the nearest road and then the distance along that road to the nearest town or city, and the existence or nonexistence of bus service—these are pivotal factors. A nearby city means a market for village produce, city jobs for a few people who often commute by bicycle, and the modernizing impact of new urban ideas, especially among the younger generation, who have begun to challenge the traditional values of the elders. But while some villages struggle to digest modern or Western ideas, others are not yet aware that British rule has ended.

Mrs. Kusum Nair, one of the few Indian journalists who has made an extensive tour of Indian villages in recent years, reports that in many (but not all) villages, she found the peasants "inert and indifferent," "still rooted in or identified with religious belief," and "paralyzed by limited aspirations."[4] But if the villagers have "limited aspirations," they also have a marked ability to make the most of the simple pleasures available to them—an ability associated with the traditional acceptance of fate. The Western stereotype of the Indian village as a place of unrelieved misery and unhappiness takes no account of the gay mood of holiday times or of market day, the quite visible pride of the peasant in a good stand of golden grain, or the equally visible joy of both men and women in the sight of small children awkwardly learning the first rudiments of living and thus carrying forward the rich continuity of the generations.

It is generally agreed that what has been called "the revolution of rising expectations" is only just beginning in rural India, and it is often argued that if the villagers are to improve their lot, their "felt needs" should be increased. In other words, they must be made more dissatisfied so that they will be less inert and more enterprising in adopting modern techniques.

But what if the old religious attitudes of resignation and detachment from desires should be given up sooner than the Indian economy as a whole can provide the villagers with a significantly higher standard of living? What if "felt needs" should race ahead of any possibility of their satisfaction? What if the villagers, when they have learned to be dissatisfied, should turn in anger against their government, which cannot give them all the good things they then may want? Questions such as these have created the sense of urgency with which the Indian Government faces the problem of developing industry and the economy as a whole. The government's attitude has been that if a great catastrophe is to be avoided, the rise in the standard of living must be quick.

Rapid Urban Growth

Although cities and towns of over 5,000 people still account for only 17 per cent of the population of India, many of them have grown rapidly in recent decades as migrants from the overcrowded land poured in, whether or not there were jobs awaiting them. The 1961 census showed a smaller increase in the over-all urban population during the last decade than had been expected, but certain cities experienced fantastic rates of growth. The twin cities of old Delhi and New Delhi together increased by 70 per cent in ten years, Bombay by 46 per cent, the steel city of Jamshedpur by 52 per cent, the newly developed eastern port city of Visakhapatam by 67 per cent. The largest increase of all was registered by Bhopal, which more than doubled. The capital of the state of Madhya Pradesh, Bhopal had been chosen as the location for the new publicly financed heavy-electrical-equipment industry.

In the 1961 census, five Indian cities had populations of more than a million each: Calcutta, with 2,920,000 within the city limits, but 5,500,000 in the greater metropolitan area; Bombay, with 4,146,000; Delhi, with 2,340,000; Madras, with 1,725,000; and Hyderabad, with 1,252,000. About a hundred more cities have populations of over 100,000 each. Although India is still primarily a land of villages, her cities are most certainly a significant and troublesome part of the picture.

The many Indian cities which were used in the British period either as cantonments for troops or as provincial capitals contain two sharply contrasting parts—the Indian section and the former British section, now occupied by well-to-do Indians or those whose positions in the government or the army carry with them the right to a house. The former British section is spacious, and its streets are broad and well laid out. It contains a shopping district with large stores displaying Western-type goods. For the most part, the houses are one- or two-story "bungalows" (a word of Indian origin) set well back from the tree-lined avenues in the middle of large "compounds" consisting of gardens and lawns well planted with trees and shrubs. Here and there among the gracious compounds, new streamlined stucco apartment houses are now springing up, designed in one or another version of the Western twentieth-century international style. Whether in apartments or bungalows, the living rooms of middle and upper-class Indians are often pleasantly and tastefully decorated, though from a Western point of view their overstuffed chairs are often forbiddingly bulky. Particularly since independence, fashion has dictated the use of lovely, colorful Indian handloom fabrics for the window draperies and the hangings at the doors. And handicraft objects in brass or copper (trays, bowls, jars, and such) remind one of the vigorous new interest in old Indian skills and crafts. One note that most Westerners find strange is that the most conspicuous place in the dining room is often occupied by a shiny, white refrigerator. The explanation is simple. Refrigerators are a recent innovation which only a few can afford—and in which food is not yet customarily stored. The old tradition of buying and cooking each day only enough for that one day is still followed. The refrigerator is useful chiefly for the cooling of soft drinks—and for some people perhaps also as a status symbol.

In the Indian section of the cities, there is none of the spaciousness of the former British section. Buildings cover every inch of the land, except the narrow twisting streets and still narrower alleys, not built for wheeled vehicles. The streets are lined with tiny shops with open fronts instead of windows. Competing merchants, dealing in particular commodities, cluster together on particular streets or sections of streets. Grain merchants have their own area or bazaar, as do dealers in cloth, brassware, jewelry, and other items. Traffic is a tangled mass. Honking violently, the rare automobile must plow its way slowly through dense crowds of pedestrians, bicycles, bullock carts, pushcarts, and pullcarts. Tragically, it is cheaper in many cities to pay two or three men to pull a five- or six-ton load in a hand cart than to have the same load pulled by a truck or by bullocks.

Behind and above the rows of tiny shops live not only the very poor, but also, in some cases, persons who may be moderately well-to-do or even rich (merchants, bankers, or moneylenders, for example). More traditional in their outlook than those of comparable wealth living in the former British section, they prefer not to associate themselves with Western ways, and do not want to live in an area where it is thought correct to have refrigerators and overstuffed chairs. By choice, they may either have wooden cane-bottomed chairs or sit on the floor or on a very low divan or pad covered with a neat white sheet. Feeling no need for the spaciousness of a bungalow, entire joint families may live in only a few rooms.

The poor in the Indian section live in incredibly crowded conditions. In certain areas of old Delhi, the population density in 1951 was almost half a million per square mile.[5]

The old pre-British Indian cities and the Indian sections of British cities grew up without planning. They became crowded because it was profitable to be as near as possible to the center. The narrow roads and poor transportation discouraged dispersion.

Some of the larger cities have now spread out over many square miles beyond the theoretical city limits. As far as they extend, they tend to be packed tight. Most city dwellers must walk to work, although increasing numbers now have bicycles or can afford to take a bus.

The Misery of the Slums

Urban growth has been so rapid, the new migrants have been so poor, and the financial resources of the city so limited that neither private enterprise nor public authorities have been able to provide even housing for more than a fraction of the newcomers. In the poorer sections of the cities, water supplies, drainage, and sewage systems, are totally inadequate. In many such areas, public sanitation of any kind is most startlingly nonexistent. Garbage and rubbish are dumped on the sidewalk or in open drains which thereby become clogged, then overflow and fill the streets with filthy lakes.

In Bombay a characteristic slum building is four or five stories high, with windows on its outside walls but none to light its large, dark center. Lines of small, tightly packed cubicles receive their air only through their single doors which open on narrow verandas around small air shafts. Each cubicle holds at least one family, often more, so that sleeping must be done in shifts for lack of floor space. One-fifth of Bombay's population live in tiny rooms shared by more than six people.[6] For the twenty or thirty families whose lives center around a single air shaft, there may be one or two latrines and a few taps of cold running water. Cooking is done on a brazier on the floor of the cubicle, often without benefit of chimney.

In many cities, the slums consist of tiny shelters improvised by the homeless themselves out of any old scrap of cloth, sacking, matting, or discarded metal or thatch that they have been able to find. These shelters are clustered together in colonies of poverty inconceivable to Western minds. Thousands more have no homes but the sidewalk. The 1961 census estimated that pavement dwellers in Calcutta alone numbered 19,000. All experts agree, however, that even this figure is far below the actual number of people sleeping on the streets—which may be as high as half a million. Sometimes people sleep on the street because it is more comfortable than their own miserable, overcrowded quarters. Street sleeping is also a symptom of transportation difficulties. If a man cannot afford a bicycle or bus fare, it may take him so long to get home from work that he may find it more restful not to try.

Americans are inclined to turn away from the very thought of Indian slums. The desire not to know of such misery is both deep and understandable. Imagine, then, how painful it must be to Indians who have experienced a better life to be constantly reminded of the condition of the masses who are their fellow countrymen. Perhaps a reason for the attitude of aloof, disdainful superiority on the part of some upper-class Indians may be their deep emotional need to disassociate themselves from such appalling misery. More certain is the fact that thousands of educated Indians overcome any such urge and work with devotion and dedication for the welfare of the masses, both in government service and in social work.

Attempts at Urban Improvement

When India embarked on its ambitious and much-publicized Community Development Programme, no corresponding sums were set aside for the urgent and growing problems of the cities. There is a powerful anti-city sentiment in Indian politics. This stems perhaps from the fact that the larger cities were regarded in British days as the centers of colonial expansion. The feeling was increased by the Gandhian emphasis on the villages as the salvation of India, and by the sheer weight of numbers of the rural vote. Then, too, the problems of the cities are so great that any real improvement would involve sums of money staggering within the Indian context—as well as the use of cement and other construction materials far beyond India's capacity to produce.

Furthermore, it is generally recognized that substantial improvement in the cities—even if this were financially, physically, and politically possible—would certainly increase the flow of migrants from the country districts unless these also were improved. The various Five-Year Plans have included sums for housing and urban renewal. The Second Five-Year Plan (1956–61) allocated $500 million for the purpose. Even so, the shortage of houses in urban areas was twice as great in 1961 as it had been ten years before. The Third Five-Year Plan has allocated a slightly smaller amount than the preceding one for the purpose and makes quite clear the fact that the shortage of housing, estimated in 1961 at 5 million dwellings, will increase rather than decrease. In the attempt to stretch housing funds as far as possible, housing of very low quality has been erected in some cases, sometimes mere "skeletal houses" (with only roofs on pillars) to be finished by the occupants, or the provision of land alone—"open developed plots"—where the poverty-stricken people themselves can put up minimal houses on space that at least has drainage.[7]

Indian leaders are only just beginning to think in terms of urban planning, to prevent cities from growing even worse than they are now, as more migrants arrive. Town-planning concepts borrowed from the West clearly do not fit the Indian situation. A new school of town planning has been erected in Delhi, and Indians are beginning to evolve principles of planning that they believe will fit the Indian context.

In 1960, the Ford Foundation made a grant of $1.4 million to help the Calcutta Metropolitan Planning Organization make a master plan for the city and decide on the division of funds among such services as water, drainage and sewage, public housing, transportation, possible subways, and education. The needs of the city are so great that any one of these services, if adequately supplied, could use up all available funds. To illustrate only one facet of Calcutta's many problems, most of the water supply of the city is now taken directly out of the Hugli River, near the city. It is filthy and unfiltered. A filtered water supply also exists, but it is inadequate, available only at certain parts of the city, and not truly safe. A few safe deep "tube wells" exist, privately owned. A program under contemplation calls for the building of some 350 additional tube wells and the piping of their water overhead to distribution points from which people could carry it home in jars.

At most, the problems of India's major cities can probably be alleviated only slightly. And this can be done only if new industries are located in other and smaller cities and if there is a simultaneous improvement in the rural districts—hence in the entire economy.

15 • TOWARD ECONOMIC DEVELOPMENT

One of the poorest nations in the world, India decided in the early 1950's to try to industrialize herself and raise the standard of living with the aid of a series of Five-Year Plans.

Although she borrowed the idea of economic planning from Russia, India insists that planning can be carried out without the use of totalitarian methods. Is she right? Can democratic planning succeed? Can poor nations afford democracy? For the answers to these questions, many watch the Indian experiment. One thing is clear: Starving people want food more than they want freedom.

Unfortunately for India, the Sino-Indian border conflict of 1962 —when India was invaded briefly and defeated by China—and the 1965 war with Pakistan made it necessary to divert to defense large sums that might otherwise have been used for development.

Inevitably, Indian economic development has been, and will continue to be, compared to that of China. Both countries started from about the same economic level in the early 1950's. Since then, both have made every effort to increase agricultural and also industrial production. The significant difference is that China has used compulsion, which India has determined not to use.

Five years from now, how will the output of the Chinese peasant, forced to join a commune against his will, compare with the output of the Indian peasant still on his little plot of land, using new techniques only to the extent that he has been persuaded to use them of his own free will? In the construction of needed public works of all kinds, can India push forward as fast with her hired labor as China with its forced-labor battalions? By 1965, India was still far short of her economic targets. Nor had hunger and want by any means disappeared from China; perhaps, indeed, they had not even decreased since the Communist takeover of the country. The Great Leap Forward, heralded in the 1950's, was no longer mentioned. Was this merely the result of several successive years of weather unfavorable for crops? Or was it an indication of the bitter fruits of compulsion? Whatever the answers to these questions may be—and one might well question the validity of Chinese statistics—the future of the free world could hang on the outcome of the economic race between India and China.

The Difficulties of Democratic Planning

If it is hard to get the best work out of men through the use of totalitarian methods—and it doubtless is—it is also hard to direct, coordinate, and plan the economic life of a country with a population of 490 million free people, all of whose interests do not run in the same direction, and who can use the machinery of democracy to put conflicting political pressures on those leaders in the central government who must try to iron out such disagreements and concoct a plan finally acceptable to parliament.

The making of an Indian Five-Year Plan is a long, slow process of study, consultation, negotiation, and compromise. First, detailed studies are made by staff members of the various ministries of the central and state governments, aided by panels of economists, scientists, and experts on many subjects (land reform, health, housing, agriculture, education, and industry). The result is a mass of opinions based on whatever data are available, which may or may not be adequate.

On the basis of all these preliminary studies, the staff of the Planning Commission of the central government draws up a draft outline for the forthcoming plan, which is then discussed throughout the country. Then people of every conceivable interest group submit comments and the state governments draw up their own proposed plans. The fact that under the Constitution of India the states have jurisdiction over at least three important subjects with which planning concerns itself—agriculture, education, and health—is an obstacle to coordinated planning. The powerful persuasion of central-government subsidies is the chief instrument for keeping the state governments at least somewhat in line with the thinking of the planners.

When the staff of the Planning Commission has digested all the suggestions made by private groups and by the state governments, it begins consultations and negotiations with state officials at staff level. After these have been completed, consultations at the ministerial level begin. (As elected officers, the state and national cabinet ministers, of course, cannot fail to reflect political pressures.) After still more give and take, a draft Five-Year Plan for the nation as a whole is finally published. It is then considered by the National Development Council, which includes the chief ministers of the states and certain cabinet ministers of the central government. Here again, it may be attacked from any and every angle. After more compromise, a final version is published and submitted to Parliament, where it is again debated before a vote is taken. Needless to say, a plan that must run such an obstacle race cannot be as crisp and decisive as one that is imposed.

The general philosophy of Indian planning is that all available resources should be mobilized and allocated to specific purposes. By and large, this has been done, though the allocations have sometimes been changed during the period of the plan, by the decision of the National Development Council alone. Each plan contains a number of numerical targets which the planners believe can be achieved on the basis of the allocations made. For example, the Third Five-Year Plan (1961–66) stated that national income was to be increased by 30 per cent, the number of students enrolled in schools at all levels by 47 per cent, agricultural production by 30 per cent, over-all industrial production by 70 per cent. Targets were set also for the increased production of each type of commodity falling within the major headings.[1]

Besides specific targets, each Plan also sets out a number of ambitious objectives, toward which progress can less easily be measured. The Third Plan, for example, proposed to "combat the curse of poverty," increase productivity and national income, create more job opportunities, "build a technologically progressive economy," reduce "disparities of income," provide various welfare services, "promote a socialist pattern of society," combat the "tendency toward the concentration of economic power," and provide "sound foundations for sustained economic growth."[2]

Some of these aims seem incompatible with one another. While a clear priority of goals would certainly make for surer progress, that could scarcely be expected under democratic planning. And all the grand objectives of the plans seems so desirable that Indians tend to minimize the possible conflicts between them. There probably comes into play the Hindu tendency to believe that black-and-white choices are not necessary and that the reconciliation of conflicts is always possible.

Having so many purposes, the plans have concerned themselves with many aspects of Indian society and economy. Besides allocating specific sums for agriculture, community development, heavy industry, and transport, they deal with animal husbandry, the establishment of cooperatives, land reform, small-scale and cottage industries, the development of mineral and other natural resources, electric power, irrigation, public health, housing, social welfare, education, and family planning.

The Successive Plans

Each successive plan has been much bigger than its predecessor and has reflected somewhat different ideas as to priorities. The First Five-Year Plan (1951–56) was modest in scale—about $7 billion of investment for the entire period. It did little more than carry out in more unified fashion a number of projects that had already been begun under separate ministries of the government. Its goals were achieved for the most part.

The Second Five-Year Plan (1956–61) was twice the size of the first and involved a shift of emphasis away from agriculture, community development, and irrigation and toward large-scale industry. (Three new steel plants figured prominently.) India encountered serious foreign-exchange problems beginning in 1957, was forced to negotiate for the largest possible foreign loans, and also had to cut or postpone certain Second Five-Year Plan projects. The foreign-exchange shortage greatly hurt industry by making it impossible to import machines, spare parts, and raw materials in the quantities needed. Even so, some success was achieved under the Second Plan. National income rose by 20 per cent, keeping well ahead of the population increase. Agricultural production rose by 13 per cent, against 18 per cent planned. In spite of the lack of needed imports, industrial output increased by 39 per cent.

The necessity for a greater and faster rise in the standard of living seemed so urgent in 1961 that the government adopted a still larger plan involving an investment of $21 billion in the following five years, retaining the emphasis on new government industries. In 1964 it proposed to double even this very large plan during the five years from 1966 to 1971, but with considerable shift of emphasis back to agriculture.

The relative sizes of total investment (public and private) under the four plans can be seen in Table I. It is significant that each plan concerned itself not only with investment to be undertaken by the government itself, but also with that of private enterprise.

TABLE I

Investment Under the Five-Year Plans
(in millions of dollars)

	Public sector	*Private sector*	*Total invest.*
First Plan (1951–56)	$ 3,276	$ 3,780	$ 7,056
Second Plan (1956–61)	$ 7,665	$ 6,510	$14,175
Third Plan (1961–66)	$13,230	$ 8,610	$21,840
Fourth Plan (1961–66) (projected)	$27,000	$14,650	$42,000

SOURCE: Government of India, *Third Five-Year Plan* (New Delhi, 1961); and *Eastern Economist* (New Delhi), December 25, 1964, p. 1341. (Rupees converted at the rate of 21 cents per rupee.) In the following months, the size of the Fourth Plan was hotly debated. As this book goes to press, the figure for the total investment has provisionally been set at $43 billion, but some government leaders are known to favor drastic reduction of this figure.

In 1965, because of strained relations with Pakistan and China, many Indians urged a sharp increase in defense budgets. Such an increase would mean smaller annual appropriations for Plan projects. Except for agricultural incomes, most sources of taxation had already been tapped to the limit, and, with a general election due in 1967, the government hesitated to touch rural taxation.

The Population Problem and Family Planning

Basic to many of India's problems is her population. With every succeeding generation, the overcrowding of the land increases. Not only is India's population large in relation to its area, but it is also growing at an increasingly rapid rate. The modern problem of "population explosion" is not, of course, confined to India, but it has particular significance there because the land was so crowded to begin with.

The people of India constitute 15 per cent of the world's total population, although the nation itself occupies only 2 per cent of the world's land area. The 1961 census, which revealed that the population had risen to 439 million, came as a particular shock, for it indicated a growth of 21.49 per cent in ten years (against an expected growth of 17.45 per cent). India had acquired 77 million more inhabitants in one decade—more than the total population of many countries and almost half the population of the United States. Until 1950, her rate of population growth had not differed greatly from that in the United States. The birth rate was higher, but so, too, was the death rate, leaving the net increase in the decade from 1941 to 1950 a mere 13 per cent, as compared to 14.5 per cent in the United States over the corresponding period. The rise in the rate of growth in India since 1951 has resulted from successful public-health measures, control over large epidemics, and especially the decrease of infant mortality from 13 to 9.2 per thousand.[3]

"Overpopulation" is, of course, a relative matter. The important factor is how the people in question are making (or trying to make) a living. In general, industrialized areas can support a far larger population than agricultural areas. The Ganges Valley, still predominantly agricultural, now has a density of population comparable to that in many Western industrialized areas (for instance, in Germany, Great Britain, Massachusetts, Rhode Island, and Connecticut).

The tremendous growth of population makes the problem of economic development all the harder. For it increases the amount of everything that must be produced even to maintain the present low standard of living—let alone to raise it. Every year, the load of young, nonearning dependents increases, and large numbers of young persons enter the labor market searching for jobs that do not exist. Above all, the higher the proportion of dependent persons, the harder it becomes to save money and form capital, basic to economic development.

Studies have shown that the majority of Indians do not express opposition to family planning. There is no religious prejudice against birth control. There is, however, a universal desire to have sons, and fertility worship apparently has been part of the religion of the common people since the earliest Indus Valley civilization. The technical problem of family planning is not easy to solve in a country such as India because of the vast numbers of people who must be reached, their inaccessibility in remote rural areas, and their low level of education. Furthermore, until 1964, when a new intra-uterine device, the "Lippes loop", was proved 98 per cent successful, the price of any safe contraceptive was prohibitively expensive for the rural masses.

Now the Indian Government has greatly intensified its efforts in the field of family planning. It is manufacturing the new loop at the rate of 4 million a year, and hopes that its family-planning clinics (and rural health units) will be able to fit 40 million women with the device within ten years. Some of the health units also sterilize males (paying bonuses or allowances for work days lost).

If in the course of ten years 40 million loops are in fact distributed, if 3 million of the more conventional type of contraceptive are also distributed, and if 3 million sterilization operations are performed, it is estimated that India's annual rate of population growth would be halved from 2.4 per cent in 1964 to 1.2 per cent in 1974. But this will require skillful, well-organized mass education in family planning.

The Agricultural Base

Agriculture is still the chief industry in India, accounting for almost half the national income and serving as the means of livelihood for more than 70 per cent of the working population. Seven out of every eight village families are wholly or partially dependent on agriculture for a living. The eighth village family supports itself by trade, by a craft, or by supplying services to the other villagers.

There are practically no modern tractors, harvesters, or other machinery, except on a few large-scale government farms and reclamation projects. Not only would they cost too much for the peasants, but they would be of limited usefulness in their tiny plots. Even the steel plow, taken for granted in the West, is still a rarity in India. The ordinary plow is a wooden stick (sometimes tipped with a half-inch of steel) pulled by a pair of bullocks. For many, the only other agricultural implement is a heavy, short-handled hoe used both for hoeing and digging.

Many of the old techniques involve tremendous amounts of manpower at certain times of the year. Whole fields of rice are planted by setting out individual rice plants, one by one. The work is usually done by women bent double in ankle-deep mud from dawn to dusk. In the dry months, men, boys, bullocks, and camels labor incessantly to bring up water from field wells to the parched earth. Men do this by treading a walking beam. Or they may attach their bullocks to a rope that goes over a pulley and into a well; to raise the bucket at the end of the rope, they drive the bullocks away from the well, and to lower it, they back up the bullocks again. Or a man may drive his pair of bullocks or his camel around and around a central pivot connected by a set of rusty gears with a "Persian wheel," which brings up the water in a long chain of tiny buckets. These are techniques that have scarcely changed in 2,000 years.

At harvest, men and women cut the grain by handfuls with crude sickles, and the threshing is commonly done by hitching several pairs of bullocks together and driving them around the threshing floor on which the grain has been laid, so that the action of their hoofs separates the kernels from the stalk.

Over three-quarters of the land under cultivation in India is sowed to food grains. Cotton, groundnuts, sugar cane, mustard, oil seeds, and tobacco are other important crops. Large plantations at altitudes of 3,000–9,000 feet produce the chief export crop, tea, which alone accounts for about 20 per cent of India's earnings of foreign exchange.

Despite the large acreage sowed to food grains, India has not been self-sufficient in these, has used up valuable foreign exchange to purchase grain abroad, and has received from the United States loans of food worth $2,911.5 million. The soil, worked for centuries while the dung served as fuel, needs food. The factory output of fertilizers is constantly being increased. But even including imports, the total supply (distributed largely through government channels) is still by no means sufficient even to replace the nitrogen annually lost from the soil, let alone to improve or restore it.

Only the richest peasants can buy fertilizers, equipment, or even a new pair of bullocks except on credit. The village moneylender has habitually charged high interest rates. Rural indebtedness is heavy. To provide more credit at lower rates and promote the greater use of fertilizers, the government is establishing a subsidized network of credit and marketing cooperatives.

In many areas, deeper plowing with steel mold-board plows would be more productive, but the old light wooden plows are all that the peasants have. The Third Five-Year Plan put new emphasis on the supply of a few simple but improved basic tools. New, improved strains of seed should also increase crop yields. Supplies of such seeds are gradually becoming available. But here again, the peasant needs both credit to buy them and a convincing demonstration that they are not merely an unreliable newfangled idea. Occasional mistakes have been made. In the early years of planning, a new strain of wheat was promoted by the Ministry of Agriculture, but its stalks proved too weak to hold upright its heavy heads of more abundant grain. A still newer strain was then promoted. It stood upright in spite of its abundant grain, but its stalks were too tough for the cattle to chew, so it was no longer a crop with the old dual purpose.[4] When any one such agricultural innovation proves unsuited to local conditions, the results can be disastrous to the peasants and their families. Small wonder that they cling to the old ways, rather than gamble on the new in the hope of some larger harvest that may never be reaped. In India, the conservatism not uncommon among farmers the world over is reinforced by lack of capital, lack of credit, lack of knowledge, lack of any reserve on which to fall back in case of emergency.

Greater yields could be expected if peasants could be taught new techniques of sowing, cultivating, composting, protecting the land from soil erosion, protecting plants from blight, pests, rats, and animals, and preventing the great waste of soil erosion. Although 30,000 village-level workers have tried, it is not easy to teach more than 75 million peasant families matters of this kind.

Though yields are still low, agricultural production has risen, as the following figures[5] indicate:

Year	*Food grains* (*million tons*)	*Cotton* (*million bales*)	*Sugar cane* (*million tons*)
1950–51	50.0	2.9	5.6
1960–61	79.2	5.3	8.5

When one considers every aspect of the Indian economy, the real achievements already made must be balanced against the sometimes stupendous problems that lie ahead. An agricultural production team sponsored by the Ford Foundation and cooperating with the Indian Government, reported in April, 1959, that yields could be at least doubled if all methods of increasing production were used together: better seeds, better tools, better cultivation methods, more credit, protection of the crops from animals, pests, and diseases, more fertilizers, better drainage and soil conservation, and increased irrigation.[6] To demonstrate the possibility of this, certain areas were then chosen—15 out of the 313 districts of India—and in each of these selected districts, such "package programs" were begun with Ford Foundation aid.

In three years, most districts increased output by 50 per cent or more; one district, indeed, almost doubled output. This was an encouraging indication of the possibility of far greater crop yields all over India if the needed agricultural "inputs" were available. But the supplies of fertilizers and other needed inputs are by no means adequate for the country as a whole, and they cannot easily be increased sufficiently. Also it will require time to train enough skilled extension workers so that they can reach the peasants. It took the United States a quarter of a century to build up its agricultural extension services and through them to accustom farmers to modern scientific agriculture. Given favorable weather, though, perhaps India can achieve a 4–5 per cent annual increase in output in the next five years.

Irrigation—Big Dams and Deep Wells

In a country like India, where two crops a year can be raised in most areas if water is available during the dry season, irrigation is clearly of the utmost importance. From very early days, Hindu kings developed irrigation systems that were strikingly large and bold for their time. Seen from the air, south India is still dotted with innumerable silver triangles where earth embankments were long ago thrown across the beds of small or large streams to impound their floodwaters during the rainy season and save them for later use. Various Muslim rulers diverted the waters of certain northern rivers into canals, and the British Government of India developed a wide network of irrigation canals (also in north India), using the waters of the Ganges and of the tributaries of the Indus. By independence, India had 50 million acres of land under irrigation—more than any nation in the world.

Independent India has pushed forward certain irrigation projects that were on the drawing boards before 1947, and she has also gone ahead vigorously with many new ones. The Indian Government's yearbook, *India, 1964*, listed seventy-seven "principal irrigation projects," stating in a footnote that the list was a selective one. Following the multipurpose pattern of the Tennessee Valley development in the United States, many of India's new projects are designed for three purposes in varying combinations: irrigation, hydroelectric power, and flood control.

Probably the most spectacular of the river-valley developments is the Bhakra Nangal project in the Punjab, with a 740-foot-high dam—one of the highest in the world—and 652 miles of canals designed to irrigate 3.5–6 million acres and result in an increase of over 800,000 tons of wheat annually. An exciting part of this project is the Rajasthan Canal, designed to carry water 425 miles from the Sutlej River to the arid desert of western India. Another major project is that in the Damodar Valley in Bihar and Bengal. It includes four storage dams and several hydroelectric powerhouses, plus three thermal power stations. It is of particular importance because it lies in the heart of India's chief industrial area, where power is especially needed. The flood-control aspect of this development is significant because in the past, the

Damodar River has repeatedly flooded large sections of the agricultural land through which it passed. Also important are the Hirakud project in Orissa and the Tungabhadra project in Andhra and Mysore.

In 1950–51, 51.5 million acres were under irrigation in India. By 1960–61, the total had been increased to 70 million acres. A further increase to 90 million acres was contemplated under the Third Five-Year Plan.[7] These figures include minor irrigation projects consisting largely of the improvement of field wells. A deep shaft well, or "tube well," going down 200 feet or more and using a gasoline or diesel engine, can irrigate fully 100 times as large an area as can a Persian wheel. With the help of the U.S. Technical Cooperation Mission, some 3,000 such wells have gone into operation in recent years.

Until 1965, irrigation had not yet increased agricultural output as much as had been hoped. Many peasants were reluctant to take water from the canals fed by the large new dams, at first because there was a water rate to be paid. Then, when the government offered the water free for an initial period in some places, many remained reluctant for other reasons: They would have to build small canals of their own to link their land with the main supply; they would have to level their fields and build new bunds to contain the water; on irrigated land, it would be necessary to plow and sow differently, perhaps even raise new kinds of crops to which they were not accustomed. All this meant not only extra work, but more especially change and uncertainty. To many, it seemed best to cling to the old pattern of agriculture which they knew so well.

To overcome peasant indifference to big new dams (and other major projects), Nehru suggested that they be treated as the pilgrimage centers of modern India. He felt that peasants should be inspired to hang pictures of such dams in their huts alongside their pictures of the gods—and to garland them with flowers in traditional religious fashion. It may be that an emotional sign language of this kind is necessary to convey to the peasants the wonder of what is springing up in their midst, and thus to stimulate them to relate to it. But a bridge between the peasants and the new projects, between traditionalism and technology, is hard to build, and no major attempt has been made to follow Nehru's suggestion. Meanwhile, the use of the new irrigation facilities is increasing, but with a wasteful gradualness that is frustrating to India's leaders.

Land Reform and Land Gifts

At independence, much of the agricultural land of India was held by a small number of absentee landlords, large landholders, zamindars, or "intermediaries." These were hereditary tax gatherers who had long squeezed the peasants. Below the intermediaries were several layers of tenants and subtenants, and even sub-subtenants. The sub-subtenants, particularly, worked under oppressive conditions, paid high rents, and had uncertain tenures. At the very base of the pyramid were the landless agricultural laborers, with not even a patch of rented land to till. India's leaders believed that the system of landholding had smothered initiative and the peasant's desire to improve the land he tilled.

For this reason and because of the ideal of social justice promoted by Nehru, a land-reform program was undertaken in the early 1950's. Land-reform laws have varied from state to state. In general, the large landholders and intermediaries have been allowed to retain only their home farms. They have been compensated—though not to the full value—for the land or the rights taken from them. Land-reform legislation in many states has also attempted to bring about a reduction in land rents, give tenants security of tenure, and make it possible for them to acquire ownership of the lands they till on payment of moderate compensation spread over a period of time. To reduce the size of large home farms, certain states have imposed ceilings on present or future agricultural holdings. The purpose is to distribute land expropriated under the land-ceiling legislation to landless agricultural laborers. But the amount of land acquired by state governments under these laws has been small compared to the vast amount needed if this purpose is to be achieved.

Quite naturally, land-reform legislation has raised a storm of opposition, both because of the expropriation involved and also because it tends to penalize efficient and enterprising farms. It is hard to assess the over-all impact of the measures adopted. In most areas, big estates have certainly been broken up. This apparently has benefited the chief tenants—the more prosperous peasants—but not their subtenants or any but a fraction of the landless agricultural laborers.

Mrs. Nair observes in her book on village life: "Though since 1947 India has enacted perhaps more land-reform legislation than any other country in the world, it has not succeeded in changing in any essentials the power pattern, the deep economic disparities, nor the traditional hierarchical nature of intergroup relations."[8] One significant but unplanned consequence of land reform has been the breaking up of large joint families, which have tended to divide their joint land holdings among the family members to escape the full impact of land-ceiling legislation.

As holdings are broken up, new problems arise. An increase in the number of holdings and a decrease in their size does not make for efficiency or increased output. How can the many small farms be organized together to regain the economic advantage of working large units of land? The Government of India seeks to solve this problem through the organization of cooperatives.

Apart from the governmental land-reform program, a nongovernmental, typically Indian attack on the land problem has been under way. Called Bhoodan ("land gift" movement), it was initiated on a modest scale in April, 1951, by Vinoba Bhave, one of Gandhi's leading disciples. At that time, Bhave was walking through the state of Hyderabad, where order had only recently been restored by the Indian Army following a peasant insurrection under Communist leadership. In one village, a landlord offered Bhave some of his land for the landless—and this gave him his idea. Thereafter Bhave walked many thousands of miles up and down the length of India, averaging 15 miles a day. Behind him lumbered a covered bullock cart containing the records of the land-gift mission. His goal was to collect 50 million acres, one-sixth of the cultivable area of India. By 1962, he had collected about 5 million acres, five times the amount collected by the state governments through the application of the land-ceiling laws.

However, much of the land given was of poor quality, and the legal title to it was unclear in some cases. Also it proved to be more difficult to distribute land than to collect it. These were probably some of the reasons why Bhave's movement had begun to lose much of its earlier momentum by 1962. Which of the many landless should receive this land? How could Bhave's movement provide them with capital with which to buy implements and bullocks? Partly to answer these questions, a number of other *dan* ("gift") movements have become associated with Bhoodan. Their various names signify the gift of work, the gift of wealth, and the gift of one's entire life. One of these movements is Gramdan—the gift of entire villages, which are then turned back to the villagers to be managed cooperatively.

However, land reform or even social reform was not Bhave's chief target. He considered his movement an attempt to lead India to a deep change of heart, a mass conversion to the religious spirit of giving and sharing. Indians respond to such a call for selflessness and dedication far more readily than many people would.

Cooperatives—or Collectives?

Believing that cooperatives are the answer to the problems posed by the fragmentation of landholdings, the Government of India has actively promoted their formation and linkage in a nationwide chain. Those so far established (over 200,000 by 1965) are largely so-called "service-type" cooperatives to supply credit, fertilizers, marketing assistance, and other facilities to peasants. Since the initiative comes not from the members themselves, but from the government, they are not cooperatives in the Western sense. Heavily subsidized, they are, in effect, even administered by officials paid by the government. At the end of the Third Five-Year Plan, it was widely recognized that the management and leadership of the cooperatives badly needed improvement.

Although no adequate study of the operation of these cooperatives is yet available, there are indications that the brighter, better-educated, more prosperous, resourceful villagers tend to use them to gain control of the credit provided by the government—thus increasing their prosperity in relation to the more underprivileged members of the village. (At every step in its many-sided attempt to increase equality of opportunity, the government is bedeviled by the fact that its efforts seem to produce results other than those intended.)

In January, 1959, the Congress Party adopted a resolution favoring cooperative farming—quite different from mere service cooperatives. Under this proposal, as embodied in the Third Five-Year Plan, private holdings would be pooled for joint cultivation. The pooling would be entirely "voluntary," but withdrawal from the pool would be permitted only under exceptional circumstances. The plan proposed to use about $12 million to stimulate the formation of cooperative farms.

It does not seem likely that the Indian peasants, with their deep traditional love of their own little plots of land, would voluntarily join such cooperatives. But they need credit. If the government pursues the plan to form cooperative farms, it has only to make credit available to these farms more readily than to peasants who prefer not to pool their land. They would then have no choice but to join "voluntarily."

Would there be any real distinction between such cooperatives and the collectives or peasant communes of the Communist type? Indian conservatives think not. Opposition to cooperative farms, which served as the starting point for the formation of the new conservative Swatantra Party, has discouraged any substantial implementation of the cooperative-farming policy so far.

Industries—Large and Small

India's raw-material situation is highly favorable for industrial development. She has the largest known deposits of high-grade iron ore in the world, as well as an almost limitless supply of coal. Much of this coal is not fit for coking and metallurgical use except through a special process, but progress has been made in preparing to utilize it. India also has the world's second largest reserves of bauxite for aluminum, and ample atomic materials like thorium. With Brazil and the Malagasy Republic, India supplies most of the free world's manganese, essential to the making of steel. She supplies four-fifths of the free world's mica, essential for the electrical industry. And she also has great hydroelectric potential.

The only major gap in the industrial-resources picture has been petroleum, but even here important reserves have been discovered in recent years—in Assam in the extreme east and in Gujarat in western India. Geological studies have indicated that there may be a number of other important oil-bearing areas.

The first small beginnings of India's industrialization date back to the 1850's, with the development of coal mines in Bengal, cotton-textile mills in Bombay, and jute mills in Bengal. The Tata family, enterprising Parsis with a wide variety of industrial interests, started an iron and steel industry in 1906. After 1921, when India first had the benefits of tariff protection, there was rapid industrial expansion. The number of factory workers—900,000 in 1914—had doubled by 1939. Many new light industries—making such products as cement, rubber, leather, glass, paper, and soap—were started. During World War II, still more new industries sprang up: in chemicals, sewing machines, bicycles, electric motors, transformers, diesel engines, machine tools. An aircraft plant began assembly operations, and shipbuilding was undertaken. By 1947, India was probably the fourth or fifth leading industrial nation in the world, although industrial expansion had not been great in relation to national income and the large size of the population.

Since the war, there has been a tremendous expansion of production in existing industries and further development of a host of new industries. Automobiles, locomotives, railway coaches, telephone equipment, cables, industrial chemicals, antibiotics, electronic equipment, fans, radios, light bulbs, ball bearings, rayon, razor blades, linoleum, air conditioners, fertilizers, and many new kinds of machines and machine tools are among the products that were formerly imported but are now being made in India. Contrary to a widespread impression in the West, most of this burgeoning new industrial activity is in the hands of private enterprise. On the other hand, the government itself has gone into those types of heavy industry which require larger concentration of capital than seemed available to private entrepreneurs.

Under the Second Five-Year Plan, a major objective was to increase steel capacity from 1.4 million tons to 3.5 million tons per year. The largest existing private steel concern, the Tata Iron & Steel Works, was encouraged to double its production. The government itself undertook three new steel plants. One, at Rourkela in Orissa, was erected with the help of a West German firm, Krupp-Demag. A second, in Durgapur, West Bengal, received the assistance of a group of British firms. The third, in Bhilai, in Madhya Pradesh, was built with financial and technical assistance from the U.S.S.R.

The steel plants—with their great chimneys and sheds, blast furnaces and rolling mills, miles of railroad tracks, and freight trains snaking their way in and out among the various structures —are strange islands in the midst of the surrounding agricultural land. Their screeching whistles, marking the end of each shift, penetrate to fields where peasants whose work shift never ends cannot even grasp the nature of what has sprung up nearby. Low-caste persons from the neighboring villages find jobs in the plants as coolies. Bringing home wages that are low by Western standards, but still high for their social status in the villages, they seem to the higher-caste villagers no longer to "know their place." Even landholding peasant families may lose one or another of their sons to the new, smoky monsters—perhaps to be trained to tend a furnace. Returning to the family mud huts to sleep, the boys, with their new talk and new ideas, are like strangers in the family circle. The old folks shake their heads. The ripples of social change widen.

The new steel plants began to operate by 1961, and, according to some authorities, India is now producing steel more cheaply than any other country in the world. The new supplies of steel have stimulated the expansion of the many industries using steel, especially those producing machine tools and machinery.

However, the steel plants did not achieve *full* production as soon as had been planned—partly because of the shortage of coking coal, railroad cars, and transportation in general. Although India has the best railroad network in Asia—35,000 miles of rail routes—the equipment is not adequate in quantity or quality for industrial expansion. Under the plans, efforts have been made to improve the railways, but the old, small freight cars, pulled in many cases by antiquated engines, still move slowly over old, bumpy, lightweight rails.

Bottlenecks—whether of transportation, power, or other essentials—have continually hampered progress. Perhaps they are not an unusual feature in any centralized planning. How can mere mortals be sufficiently wise and omniscient to plan for the growth of an entire subcontinent? How can they fail to overlook some factor essential to the operation of the entire plan? The Indian planners answer that they can only do their best, but that planning is essential despite their mistakes. Since time is of the essence, the best coordination and direction that are humanly possible in a democracy are needed to speed the process.

The Fourth Plan called for one or two additional new steel plants, and for the further expansion of the existing ones. Among the many other industrial targets was a fivefold increase in nitrogenous fertilizer, essential to agriculture. Sadly, though, much of the capacity of the new fertilizer factories may have to be used to produce explosives for defense. (In October, 1965, it was announced that all Fourth Plan projects and targets would have to be reconsidered in the light of new defense needs.)

Altogether, India has made rapid strides toward industrialization in recent years, and a real basis has been laid for further industrial expansion. Even so, it should be remembered that India remains predominantly agricultural. Mining, manufacturing, and small enterprises together accounted for only 18.6 per cent of the national income in 1960–61.[9] However, this was a higher percentage than that of any other developing country. The total number of factory workers in India in 1959 was about 3.6 million, or somewhat under 3 per cent of the total working force.[10] In ten years, there had been no marked shift in the percentage of people engaged in agriculture and industry.

By making steel available at low cost, the large new steel plants have greatly stimulated the development of small industry. In recent years many little enterprises (completely in private hands) have sprung up. Employing fewer than fifty workers—and often only a dozen or so—they make such articles as bicycle parts, cardboard boxes, matches, shoes, carpets, umbrella ribs, aluminum utensils, shoe polish, and preserved foods. Using simple machinery, they need little capital per man employed. For this reason, the government has actively aided them, giving them electric power, floor space in factories, and other facilities at nominal cost in over a hundred locations called "industrial estates."

In contrast to the small industries (which employ power, machines, and modern technology), there are the cottage industries —handloom, hand spinning, and handicrafts—carried on wholly or primarily by members of a family, often in their own homes and using ancient techniques. More people—about 20 million—

are engaged in cottage industries than in any other occupation except agriculture. Fearing unemployment, the government gives them substantial aid and markets their products. Without this aid, they probably could not survive. But, as one economist has noted, "India's basic problem is the inefficient use of manpower; it is no solution to protect inefficiency."[11] The promotion of the small-scale but mechanized industries mentioned above seems a better solution. The government realizes this, and the present trend is toward the greatest possible stimulation of these.

Labor Organizations and Labor Policy

Perhaps about half of the factory workers in India are unionized, though it is impossible to give exact figures on dues-paying members. Indian trade unions and organizations of trade unions are dominated by politicians and have close affiliations with one or another political party. The largest of these organizations—the Indian National Trade Union Congress (INTUC), with a membership of about a million—is dominated by the Congress Party. The next—the All-India Trade Union Congress (AITUC), with over half a million members—is an arm of the Communist Party. The role of unions in protecting the interests of their members is greatly restricted by the Industrial Disputes Act, passed by the government in 1947, which not only set up machinery for the conciliation of labor disputes, but also gave the government the power to refer disputes where conciliation did not prove successful to industrial courts for adjudication. After such a reference, a strike in connection with a dispute is illegal. The award of the industrial court is binding on both parties, and there are penalties for illegal strikes and lockouts.[12] Minimum wages for various kinds of work have been set in most of the important large-scale industries, and employers are required to pay their employees additional "dearness allowances," which increase as prices rise.

The Dimensions of Unemployment

Despite all the new industries—big, medium, and small, public and private—three times as many persons were unemployed in 1961 (9 million) as in 1951 (3 million).[13] In relation to the 1961 population of 439 million, this was not a large number. Even in the

United States, with a population of about 180 million, 4 or 5 million unemployed is not unusual. In India, however, an additional 15–18 million were "underemployed." Unable to find gainful employment for a large enough portion of the year or at high enough wages to support themselves, these would probably be included among the unemployed in other countries. India's unemployment and underemployment would be nationally unbearable if it were not for the way families tend to take care of their jobless relatives.

By 1965, the government estimated that the number of totally unemployed had climbed to 15 million.[14] Counting "underemployment," Ford Foundation experts estimated 55 to 60 million "man years" of unemployment per year. In short, almost a third of the total time of the total work force (estimated at 192 million in 1965) may have been wasted in unemployment.[15]

The most tragic are the "educated unemployed," who have had high-school and sometimes even college educations, but cannot find jobs. Why can't these young men and women at least be sent out into the country districts to serve as teachers and thus spread literacy? The answer seems to lie in the fact that they are untrained as teachers, that Indians tend to be reluctant to go back to the villages once they have had an education, and that, in any case, there is not enough money to pay many more teachers even a sub-minimum wage.

The Ideal of Socialism in Theory and Practice

In India, "socialism" (seldom defined with any precision) is a good word, much as "capitalism" and "private enterprise" are good words in the West. Almost every political party advocates socialism, some of them in very general terms. In practice, India is somewhat less socialist than most Westerners might therefore imagine. Indeed, some Indians argue that it is even less socialist than the United States, since private enterprise contributes about 90 per cent of the national income in India, as against only 80 per cent in the United States. But this comparison is misleading since agricultural income (almost wholly private in both countries) is included and constitutes a far larger proportion of the total in India. Thus the statistics disguise the fact that a relatively large part of Indian industrial development is in the hands of the government. In the last few years, the rate of growth (measured in terms of invested capital) has been much greater in the public sector than in the private sector. The government has gone almost entirely into industries requiring large concentrations of capital.

Besides starting new industries, the government has nationalized a few existing ones. It now owns not only the railways and the telephone and telegraph services (publicly owned before independence), but also all the airlines of the country, the entire life-insurance business, and the largest bank (with many branches throughout the country). Each of these cases of nationalization arose out of special circumstances within the industry in question, and Nehru has repeatedly stressed that further nationalization of existing private concerns is not contemplated. The official position is that India should have a "mixed economy" in which private enterprise and government enterprise will exist side by side.

Two policy resolutions, one in 1949 and the second in 1956, have set the dividing line between these two sectors and broadly outlined the spheres within which each presumably will operate. The resolution of 1956, stating the policy in effect today, declares: "The state will progressively assume a predominant and direct responsibility for setting up new industrial undertakings and for developing transport facilities. It will also undertake state trading on an increasing scale." It divided all types of industries into three categories. As to the first, it declared that the state would take the exclusive responsibility for future development. Industries in this category included heavy industry, mining, the processing of minerals, heavy machinery and equipment, shipbuilding, the manufacture of telephones and electrical equipment, the production of defense equipment, aircraft, and the operation of airlines and airways. The second category—in which "the state will generally take the initiative in establishing new undertakings, but in which private enterprise will also be expected to supplement the efforts of the state"—includes the chemical industry, road and sea transport, and most of the industries making machinery and equipment not included in the first category. In the third category are the textile and cement industries, papermaking, and the production of other consumer goods—all to remain generally in the private sector.[16]

Government spokesmen contend that if heavy industries were to be established at all, government initiative was essential because the available capital in the private sector was totally insufficient for projects of such size. Possibly the Tata combine—already established in the steel industry—and one or two of the other leading business families of India could have undertaken more than this argument suggests. But the government has also wanted to prevent the monopolistic growth of a few large companies. Social policy, as well as economic necessity, has been the basis for the government's very considerable entry into the industrial field.

Except in one or two cases, the leading Indian industrial families have created an unfavorable image in the public mind, as did the American "robber barons" of the late nineteenth century. A reason for this is the fact that—like tycoons in the early phase of the Industrial Revolution elsewhere—they have usually looked for large, quick, short-term gains rather than long, steady growth with more modest profits.

The Indian Government would like to achieve industrialization without increasing the gap between rich and poor. For this reason and because capital and foreign exchange are scarce, Indian private industry is under government regulation. Through a system resembling compulsory arbitration, the government can fix wage rates and fringe benefits. It can prescribe prices, methods and volume of production, and channels of distribution. Private industries must turn to government for permission to float capital issues, to import or buy scarce materials, to produce new articles, or to change their location. (However, the government does not control private enterprise as thoroughly in actuality as it does in theory. An indication of this is the fact that the private sector grew far more rapidly in the period of the second plan than the government had proposed to allow it to grow!)

The established industrialists who have succeeded in getting the necessary permits do not strongly object to the existing regulations, although they do involve red tape and delay. Indeed, some of them are frank to admit that the controls have increased their profits by decreasing competition. Those less fortunately placed, who have not yet become known or established, take a different view. They charge that permits are secured only by personal favoritism and the corruption of government officials. It would be impossible for an outsider to judge how much graft exists. Certainly, the opportunities for it are many, as they would be in any country where the government tries to control the entire economy.

A recent indication of the trend of government policy regarding socialism was the announcement in the draft Fourth Five-Year Plan that 64 per cent of the total new investment during the plan period would be in public enterprise, with only 36 per cent in private enterprise. Indian businessmen have vigorously protested the emphasis on the public sector, but have been unable to command sufficient political support to check it.

Paying for the Plans

Involving an average annual investment (public and private) of a little over $8 billion, the Fourth Five-Year Plan may seem small by Western standards. But it is very large in relation to the Indian economy. Any investment—whether in new equipment, machinery, or other improvements—essentially requires savings out of Indian income or the use of Indian reserves (which have been rapidly dwindling), unless there is an injection of foreign resources, either in the form of government loans or grants or of private foreign investments.

But it is hard to save out of meager incomes, and savings have not increased greatly. In 1951, they were about 6 per cent of India's national income—the same level as in the United States. By 1961, they had increased only to 8.5 per cent (against the level of 11 per cent envisioned ten years earlier).[17] Of course, taxation is a way of forcing savings, but India's tax rates—among the highest in the world—have reached the point where there is danger that further tax increases might not only hamper economic development, but even produce smaller yields.

In any case, besides raising money internally in rupees, India needs foreign exchange with which to buy industrial raw materials and machines for development from abroad, and also for imported food grains in times of emergency. Even if the Indian Government could mobilize far greater resources within India than it has been able to do, it would still need foreign aid to supply the foreign currencies essential for these purposes.

Plans are under way to promote exports to earn more foreign exchange through trade. Stress has been placed also on private foreign investments, as opposed to governmental aid. In the last few years, an increasing number of large American corporations have made investments in India in joint ventures with Indian companies. This is a pattern encouraged by the government in many instances. At present, private foreign investments in India total about $1.29 billion, more than half of which has been invested in the last ten years. British capital accounts for about 80 per cent, and the American share is 13.4 per cent.[18]

But exports and private foreign investments together can cover only a small part of what India anticipates as her need for foreign exchange (which amounted to about a fifth of the total financial requirements of the Third Five-Year Plan). Loans and grants from foreign governments are by far the most important source of foreign exchange. Between 1951 and 1965, the United States provided the largest single outside contribution to Indian development—$5.9 billion either transferred or committed up to February, 1965 (including the very large so-called "wheat loan" agreements involving the shipment to India of such surplus American agricultural products as wheat and flour, rice, cotton, other food grains, tobacco, dried milk, fats, and oils). The agreements have provided for the repayment of these loans in rupees, which has greatly helped the Indian foreign-exchange position. A high percentage of the repayment has been either lent or granted back to India by the U.S. Government. By February 8, 1965, the value of the wheat loans (including the 1951 emergency loan) had reached $2.91 billion, accounting for almost two-thirds of all American aid to India.[19] Since 1957, when the U.S. Development Loan Fund was established, and when India experienced her severe foreign-exchange crisis, the rate of aid has been greatly stepped up.

Next to the United States, the World Bank and its two affiliates (the International Finance Corporation and the International

Development Fund) have been India's greatest source of foreign loans. Up to 1963, these agencies had lent India over $1 billion, much of it for the rehabilitation of railways and the improvement of transport, communications, and power supplies.[20]

After the World Bank, the largest contributor of foreign exchange to India has been the U.S.S.R. Between 1954 and December, 1962, the Soviet Union agreed to lend India rubles equivalent to about $800 million. Carrying interest at 2.5 per cent, these loans are repayable in twelve years. West Germany, the United Kingdom, Japan, Canada, and France have also made loans to India in varying amounts, as have the International Bank and the International Development Fund. Small credits have come from East European countries and Switzerland.

As India entered the period of the Third Five-Year Plan in 1961, she had at her disposal the promise of the equivalent of $4.2 billion in foreign exchange, as against an anticipated need of $5.4 billion for the five-year period. (Table II provides a breakdown of this aid promised when the Third Five-Year Plan was written in 1961.) India hoped for the continuation of foreign aid under the Fourth Plan in at least this quantity, and preferably more.

TABLE II

Foreign Aid Pledged to India for Third Five-Year Plan
(*in millions of dollars*)

United States	$1,045
West Germany	425
United Kingdom	250
Japan	80
Canada	56
France	30
International Bank and International Development Association	400
Agreement for new "wheat loan" from U.S. (May, 1960)	1,300
U.S.S.R. (Rs. 238 crores)	500
Loans from other countries (Rs. 67 crores)	140
Total	$4,226
Expected external assistance needed for five years (Rs. 2600 crores)	$5,460

SOURCE: *Third Five-Year Plan*, pp. 114–15.

India's leaders do not believe that foreign aid can or should continue indefinitely, but they point out that loans from abroad have been essential to many countries (including the United States) in the early stages of industrialization. Until the Chinese invasion of 1962, the Indian Government had hoped to make its economy "self-generating" by 1970—able to grow on its own momentum and produce itself the machines and equipment previously bought from abroad in foreign currency. Perhaps this hope was not realistic. The Third Five-Year Plan had fallen behind schedule even before the invasion, and it fell further behind thereafter, as increasingly large funds were channeled into defense. (Such an interference with India's development may well have been part of the Chinese intent.)

Few of the targets of the Third Plan were reached. In the important matter of food grains, there was no progress whatever for the first three years of the plan. Fertilizer production, essential to agricultural improvement, was only half of the target amount. Other "short-falls" occurred in the additional acreage brought under irrigation, in electric power installation, in steel production, in machine tools, in the yardage of cloth manufactured—indeed, in almost every item covered by the plan. National income increased by only a little more than 3 per cent a year, scarcely more than enough to keep up with population increase.

Yet, as much money had been spent on the plan as had been called for. But this money had accomplished far less than anticipated—partly because of inflation which forced upward the cost of every development project, perhaps also because of corruption or poor administration of certain parts of the plan.

As India prepared to launch her Fourth Plan in 1966, the "take-off point," at which she would no longer need foreign aid, seemed further away than it had five years earlier. For one thing, India's total borrowings from foreign governments had gradually grown so big that the servicing of foreign loans had come to be a major problem in itself. For the year 1965, India owed a total of $240 million for the servicing of her external debt—$80 million of interest payments and $160 million of repayments on principal—or approximately a fifth of the new borrowings of the year. During the Fourth Plan period, debt servicing was expected to eat up as much as two-fifths of new foreign aid, assuming that aid remained at the same level as under the Third Plan. Unless India could persuade her creditors to postpone the dates for repayment of principal, she faced a most discouraging prospect.

Progress and Problems

The fact that few of the overambitious targets of the Third Plan were reached should not obscure the degree of progress that India did make during the first fifteen years of planning. By 1965, food-grain production had increased by 35 per cent and industrial production by 135 per cent. The amount of fertilizers used had risen tenfold. Facilities for technical education had more than doubled. Even per capita income had risen by 20 per cent—despite the increase in population. Everywhere, new factories, new dams, new roads, new power plants, new schools, new hospitals gave the visual impression of a country that had undergone incredible change in a decade and a half.

But the Indo-Pakistan war, which began in the summer of 1965, threatened to undo all progress and seriously undermine the economy. Even before the war broke out, it was clear that colossal problems lay ahead.

By 1965, one of the most pressing problems had come to be inflation, caused chiefly by deficit financing of the increasingly large plans. In the first four years of the 1960's, wholesale prices had risen by 26 per cent. Especially in 1963 and 1964, food prices rose even more sharply. The rate of increase varied in different parts of the country, but in the important state of Uttar Pradesh, for example, food prices were 65 per cent higher in December, 1964, than they had been only four years earlier.

The Communists charged that the rise in food prices was due to speculative hoarding of grain, and demanded that the government take over the trade in food grains. Unwilling to go this far, the government nevertheless set up a Food Trading Corporation to try to stabilize the prices of food grains by marginal buying and selling at fixed prices. To stimulate production, it announced minimum prices higher than those which had previously prevailed. In the hope of building up reserves of food grains, it introduced rationing in seven of the largest cities.

Speaking for the private sector, the Federation of Indian Chambers of Commerce pointed to many danger signals in the economy. Taxation, said its report of February, 1965, had risen to such a point that savings had dried up. The financing of new investments in the private sector had become virtually impossible. The stock market was in a slump. When the government announced that the Fourth Plan would be twice the size of the Third, the Federation protested vigorously. How, it asked, could the government succeed with such a plan when the Third Plan, half that size, had not succeeded fully and had proved too heavy a burden?

In effect, the government's answer was that if per capita incomes were to be raised at all noticeably (say, 3 to 4 per cent per year), the plan adopted would have to be large enough to produce an increase of 7.5 per cent in total national income per year. The government argued that no plan smaller than the one proposed would achieve this result, so necessary from the political point of view.

As for the disappointing rate of progress in the Third Plan, government spokesmen held that it had been due to bad weather for crops and to an unforeseen time lag between investment in new enterprises and their full production. They argued that sound foundations had been laid and urged patience. Real improvement, they suggested, was just around the corner.

The output of food grains in 1964–65, 87 million tons, did indeed set a new record, and, in that year, industrial production also rose encouragingly. John P. Lewis, the American economist then serving as head of the U.S. AID mission in India, estimated that in the future a 5 per cent increase per year in agricultural yield seemed to him quite possible, and that he expected a 6.5 per cent increase in total national income.[21]

But patience was something that much of the public was beginning to lack. Promises made in the past had been too high. There had been too many disappointments. What has been called "the revolution of rising expectations" was well under way.

16 • FOREIGN POLICY AND THE CHINESE THREAT

UNTIL THE INVASION OF India by the Chinese Communists, foreign policy was not a major concern even of most educated Indians. It has never been a prominent issue in election campaigns. Indians quite naturally are preoccupied with the vast and intricate web of exclusively Indian activities and problems. Their land is wide and large, stretching out in continental proportions. Except on rare occasions, foreign countries seem incredibly distant and unreal.

During the first ten or twelve years of independence, Indians were content to leave foreign policy in Nehru's hands. Not only Prime Minister but Minister of External Affairs as well, Nehru worked out his own conception of India's world role. Having traveled widely in his youth and been deeply concerned with world politics since the 1920's, he had his own fully developed philosophy regarding foreign policy. Until the 1960's, this policy was never seriously challenged in the Indian Parliament. Although it was in a sense Nehru's personal creation, it clearly reflected also the outlook of the vast majority of Indians.

Almost immediately after independence, India emerged as a leading nation on the world scene—an astonishing development, particularly in view of the many critical internal problems India was facing at the same time. Nehru's clear view of the role he hoped his country could fill as a nonaligned nation was a major reason for the prominence in world affairs that India so quickly attained. Other reasons were the sheer size of India, her great cultural traditions, and the high level of education on the part of the Indian leadership group—all of which commanded respect in many other nations of Asia and Africa. Relations between India and these nations were by no means totally harmonious. But a group of nations generally followed Nehru on important world issues, particularly anticolonialism, championship of Communist China, and what the West regarded as "neutralism" in the Cold War. (India's international prestige declined sharply after the Chinese invasion, and she eventually lost her position of leadership.)

Nehru again and again indignantly denied that he was neutral, protesting that he regarded neutrality as out of the question where right and wrong were involved. He held that his policy was merely that of reserving his freedom to judge each case on its merits. Rather than using the distasteful term "neutralism," he insisted that the Indian attitude toward the Cold War should be called "nonalignment." By this policy, Nehru hoped to remain in a position where he could mediate between two opposing blocs, and thus prevent the existing tension from leading to outright war. This seemed to him a constructive policy quite different from the negativism of neutrality.

However, to some Westerners, India's relations with the Soviet Union and China seemed so cordial until 1962 that they did not see how India could rightly be called either nonaligned or neutral. But India was always closer to the West than to the Soviet Union in basic outlook, she was and is a member of the British Commonwealth, and Nehru criticized Soviet Cold War moves from time to time, as he did those of the West.

Colonialism—The Great Evil

One of the many reasons for India's position in regard to the Cold War was her strong feeling on the subject of colonialism—a feeling never thoroughly understood in the West. Americans were once under alien rule, but so long ago that the memories of revolution have become purely historical. However, for the present generation of Indians, alien rule was a vivid, humiliating, personal experience, as it was for the first citizens of the United States. Indians want all subject peoples to be free and have vigorously supported the claims of nationalist movements in many countries, from Indonesia to Algeria. The United States and Great

Britain, faced with world-wide commitments and the complex problem of leadership in the non-Communist world, have not always agreed with India on specific colonial issues in the United Nations. Certain that they are right about colonialism, Indians have not understood what has seemed to them the continuance of imperialist tendencies on the part of the NATO countries. Throughout the 1950's, many Indians were too critical of those Western countries which still held colonies to have any desire to side with the West.

The issue of Goa brought out clearly the difference in perspective between India and the West. When India attained its independence from England in 1947, there remained on the subcontinent a few small pockets, or enclaves, belonging to France and Portugal. To Indians, it seemed axiomatic that independence would not be complete until these enclaves were also incorporated into India. In 1954, France voluntarily transferred to India the administration of the French enclave of Pondicherry, on the southeast coast below Madras. Portugal was less accommodating. The chief Portuguese enclave was Goa, on the west coast south of Bombay—an area of 1,537 square miles, with a fine port, a population of 638,000, and significant resources of iron ore. From the first, Nehru insisted that Goa must become part of India, but until 1961 he emphasized that this must be accomplished without the use of force. His restraint regarding Goa was repeatedly attacked by opposition parties.

In August, 1954, and again the following August—on the anniversary of Indian independence—groups of unarmed Indians, *satyagrahis* following the Gandhian principle of nonviolent but active resistance, tried to enter Goa. Portuguese police and troops fired on them, killing a score or more in 1955. The expeditions were organized by a Goa Liberation Committee sponsored largely by Communists and members of the Praja Socialist Party. Neither expedition had the backing of the Congress Party, but the attempt at peaceful invasion commanded widespread support throughout the country, and large anti-Portuguese demonstrations were held in many Indian cities. Meeting in September, 1955, the Congress Party decided to oppose not only military action, but also further peaceful marches on Goa. Thereafter, the government stopped the *satyagrahis* at the border. This action, not an indication of a lack of interest in Goa, stemmed from a growing realization that civil disobedience—however nonviolent and whatever its objectives—is a threat to civil authority. To those responsible for law and order, *satyagraha* campaigns inevitably look quite different from the way they look to parties or persons out of power.

However, Nehru did continue to press for a change in the status of Goa by diplomacy. He compared the Indian position in regard to Portugal in Goa with the situation faced by the United States at the time of the Monroe Doctrine in 1823. He stated, "I place my case quite clearly—the Portuguese retention of Goa is a continuing interference with the political system established in India today."[1] He said there could be only one outcome, the merger of Goa with the Indian Union. He would discuss with Portugal only its timing.

A new dimension was added to the problem when Khrushchev, who was visiting India in December, 1955, made a speech attacking the Portuguese position regarding Goa. Two days later, the American Secretary of State, John Foster Dulles, and the Portuguese Foreign Minister, Cunha, issued a joint statement criticizing Khrushchev's remarks on the "Portuguese provinces in the Far East."[2] The Indian press was enraged by this phrase, and the United States quickly issued a statement that it was neutral on the Goa issue and was merely concerned with Soviet action in stirring up trouble.

As it became apparent that the Goa dispute would not be resolved by peaceful means, more and more Indians demanded that the enclave be taken by force. In 1961, Communists and members of the Jana Sangh—the two political extremes—became vocal. It was a pre-election year. In August, 1961, Nehru, for the first time and perhaps reluctantly, said that he did not rule out the use of force. In October, 1961, several huge rallies in various Indian cities demanded Goa's liberation. Finally, on December 16, 1961, the Indian Army overran the little enclave. The West became indignant at how "peace-loving" Nehru could stoop to such aggression. But to Indians it did not seem like aggression. In India in 1962, almost every educated Indian answered the charge of aggression by saying, "It was not aggression; Goa belonged to us anyhow," or "Portuguese control over Goa was an unprincipled and indefensible relic of former imperialism."

Why did Nehru follow a different policy in 1961 from the peaceful policy he had strongly advocated in 1954–55? Partly because it was a pre-election year, partly because diplomacy had not gained Goa for India, partly because of the increased number of newly liberated nations, now gaining increasing strength in the U.N. In September, 1961, Nehru attended a conference of neutral nations at Belgrade, where it is reliably reported that he found himself for the first time a relative conservative among the representatives of the newer states. To maintain a leading position in the neutralist world, perhaps he needed to take more positive action against Portugal, disliked by the African nations because of its hold over Angola. In this sense, India's occupation of Goa reflected the shifting balance of world forces.

Nonalignment and Relations with the Soviet Union

During Stalin's rule, relations between the Soviet Union and India gave no hint of the cordiality that was to develop later. Perhaps hoping to put obstacles in the way of the many profitable enterprises in India still directed by Britishers and financed by British capital, Soviet leaders repeatedly referred to India as a "stooge" of the imperialists and capitalists. Since the Indians were not yet sufficiently accustomed to independence to dismiss this as an obvious untruth, such references rankled.

But soon after Stalin's death, Khrushchev decided that India was worth courting. Even before his own personal domination was fully established in the Soviet Union, he and Bulganin (with whom he then seemed to share power) took a trip to India in December, 1955. Khrushchev made many ingratiating speeches and enthusiastically declared himself on India's side on the two controversial questions most important to Indians at the time—Goa and Kashmir. Such a courtship could not fail to be effective. Any nation is likely to welcome strong diplomatic support of its position. Moreover, Indians had no positive reason to resist the courtship. As an American and an Indian who made a joint study of Indo-American relations observed: "Indians missed the entire personal experience of frustration and menace that Western leaders underwent at the hands of the Russians during the war and subsequent to the German and Japanese surrenders."[3]

The imperialism of the Soviet Union—its success in extending its control beyond its own borders—is understood only by an insignificant number of Indians. In the very years when Soviet designs became frighteningly evident to the West—the years immediately following World War II—Indians were far too preoccupied with the great upheaval preceding and following Indian independence to watch the developments in Eastern Europe which revealed so clearly to the West the imperialism of the Soviet Union.

The Soviet Union's cynical disregard of the agreements reached at Yalta and Potsdam, its use of Soviet troops to prevent democratic elections in Poland, Rumania, and elsewhere, its clear indication of an intention to impose its will on all of Eastern Europe, its support of Communist guerrillas in Greece, its closing of the access routes to Berlin in 1948—this entire pattern emerged during India's time of troubles and was never viewed in India in the same perspective in which it appeared in the West.

By the middle of 1949—when India had begun to be confident that she could at least survive as an independent nation—the West had already taken firm steps to meet the Soviet menace. The Berlin airlift had proved a success. The positive policy of economic and military support to Greece and Turkey (adopted in March, 1947), the European Recovery Program (adopted in March, 1948), and the North Atlantic Treaty (April, 1949) had laid the foundations of a firm policy of containment. Soviet expansion, which had been so rapid between 1945 and 1947, was halted for the time being. Thus what Indians saw when they looked outward at the world was a Soviet Union talking about its peaceful intentions, and a coalition of Western powers "talking tough"—not yet sure that they had said enough to make clear their will to resist further extensions of Soviet domination. Was the West dominated by war-mongers, as the Soviet Union declared it to be? Some Indians thought that perhaps it was.

Curiously, the new imperialism of the Soviet Union did not seem to Indians like colonialism. They had not experienced it personally, as they had British imperialism. What happened in

Lithuania and Estonia was too distant to matter. It certainly did not touch the old raw wounds left by British rule, as did the overseas colonialism of the Western powers. The Russians had never given Indians a feeling of inferiority, as the British had. Indeed, the fact that the Soviet Union had long had to endure the hostility of the West created an emotional bond. And because the Soviet Union had pulled itself up by the bootstraps in a series of five-year plans, there was a real feeling of identification.

When Khrushchev's diplomatic support on Goa and Kashmir was followed by substantial economic aid, including a Russian-built steel plant and three oil refineries, gratitude was added to all the other reasons for close ties.

Besides the emotional reasons for nonalignment, rooted in India's history under British rule, there were practical reasons as well—related to geography, economic pressures, and other considerations of national self-interest.

Although no Indian territory actually borders on the U.S.S.R., the southern extremity of the Soviet Union is separated from the northwestern section of Kashmir only by a strip of Afghanistan and West Pakistan territory. All across the rest of India's northern border lies China—in some places fronting directly on Indian territory, in other places separated from India by Nepal, Bhutan, and Sikkim. This close presence of the two great giants of the Communist world gave India a quite different perspective on the so-called Cold War from that of the United States. A policy of peace and friendship with these giants at any cost might provide an alternative to heavy defense expenditures.

Peace was advantageous to India also for the sake of her own internal consolidation and development. In this respect, her need for noninvolvement was similar to the need that led the United States, during its first century and a half of existence, to cling to a policy of neutrality. Throughout the 1950's, when Westerners argued that India should side with the West since the preservation of freedom is the concern of everyone, a cogent Indian answer was that freedom means little to those who are hungry, that the first Indian responsibility was to eliminate the poverty of the Indian masses, and that so far as India was concerned, Communism could best be combated by an intensive program at home.

Then too, in one way or another, all the military pacts created by the West to contain the Soviet Union adversely affected India's national interests. For this reason alone, it would have been difficult for India to align herself with the West. Two of the pacts included—and apparently thereby strengthened—Pakistan, which India regarded as her chief adversary. Pakistan is a member of the SEATO Pact of 1954 because of the proximity of East Pakistan to Southeast Asia, and she belongs to the Baghdad Pact of 1955 because of West Pakistan's proximity to the Middle East. Even NATO, distant though it appeared to be, affected India by making the Western nations reluctant to press their ally Portugal to yield to India on the Goa issue. To make matters worse from the Indian point of view, the United States began giving Pakistan direct military aid in 1954. (Nehru turned down the simultaneous offer of military aid to India, fearing the strings that might be attached and the resulting encroachment on the independence of his nation.[4])

A final practical reason for nonalignment was that it offered (so Indians believed) some slight chance of decreasing the likelihood of a war between the major powers. Any war between the West and the East, even a nonnuclear one (if there could be such a war), would be contrary to India's interests. For it would absorb resources (on both sides) otherwise available to India as foreign aid. India's growth depended on peace.

The practical considerations that led to a policy of noninvolvement were buttressed by the assumption—inherent in Hindu philosophy—that there is some good in all things. In clashes such as that between the East and the West, India considered that neither side was all black or all white, and she believed that there was no issue on which agreement could not be reached by negotiations.

After the Chinese invasion, paradoxically, a policy of nonalignment seemed even more necessary than before, for India needed to appeal for military aid from both sides if she was to build up her defenses, especially her air force, sufficiently. Apparently because of Pakistan's fears and protests, fast, modern American fighter planes were not available to India. But the Soviet Union not only supplied Russian MIGs, but also offered to help build a group of factories in India where MIGs could eventually be produced. Clearly, India could not afford to antagonize the Soviet Union.

When the United States, in 1963, offered India a powerful American radio transmitter, provided it could be used by the Voice of America at certain hours when Air India was not using it, the arrangement was vigorously criticized in Parliament. Speaker after speaker pointed out that this would mean that anti-Soviet propaganda would be transmitted from Indian territory. The government had to turn down the offer. A number of other such incidents could be cited to illustrate the care India has taken not to offend the Soviet Union.

In short, the majority of Indians continue to regard nonalignment as highly suited to India's total circumstances. If events prove that India misjudged her own self-interests, she will not be the first nation to have done so.

Relations with the Afro-Asian Bloc

Although Nehru repeatedly denied any aspirations to the leadership of the nonaligned world, he made every effort to stimulate cooperation and a common front among Asian and African nations. In March, 1947, before India attained independence, he used a private organization (the Indian Council of World Affairs) to convene an Inter-Asian Relations Conference in Delhi to promote mutual understanding. Two years later, he convened another conference, again at New Delhi and this time on the official level. Attended by representatives of nineteen Asian governments, the conference protested Dutch military action against the Indonesian nationalists and asked the U.N. Security Council to order the complete independence of Indonesia within a year. Six years later, Nehru was one of the sponsors of the most ambitious attempt yet to bring harmony to the Asian nations—the Bandung Conference of April, 1955, attended by representatives of twenty-nine nations, including Communist China, which had not been represented at the previous conferences, held before the Communists had completed their conquest of the Chinese mainland.

At Bandung, it became clear that there was far less possibility of Afro-Asian unity than Nehru had hoped. The nations represented had many quite contradictory ideas as to what the conference should sponsor. In Asia and Africa, as in the rest of the world, the real national interests of neighboring nations do not, by any means, necessarily coincide.

With a number of these nations, India has special problems arising from the existence of sizable Indian minorities within them. Overseas Indians include, on the one hand, prosperous bankers and merchants (often resented by the citizens of the country where they live because of their wealth and alleged sharp practices), and on the other, unskilled coolie labor brought in to work on plantations at very low wages (hence resented because they depress local wages and take jobs away from local workers).

The country with the largest Indian minority is Ceylon, whose government actively promoted the recruitment of Indian plantation workers—Tamils of south India—until Ceylon's independence in 1948. After receiving her freedom, Ceylon tried in every way possible to rid herself of her Indians, who number about 1 million out of her population of 9 million. Predominantly Buddhist, the people of Ceylon—the Sinhalese—resent the presence of Hindus for religious reasons as well as economic rivalries. Riots between Tamils and Sinhalese have been frequent.[5] Ceylon refused to grant citizenship to people of Indian descent, except under conditions that would preclude the vast majority of them. They were thus left stateless, since they did not have citizenship rights under the Indian Constitution either. After repeated conferences between the governments of Ceylon and India, an agreement was finally reached in 1964 whereby about a half-million Indians would be transferred to India, 300,000 would be retained on the tea estates of Ceylon, and the future of the remainder would be considered later.

India has additional problems with Burma, where there were 500,000 Indians until the early 1960's. Burma expropriated the large landholdings of rich Indians living there and later passed a law nationalizing trading concerns, which was enforced in such a way as to discriminate against Indians. Indians were not asked to leave Burma, but conditions there were made unbearable. Large numbers of them have now migrated back to India.

India's relations with Indonesia—cordial in the early 1950's because of India's vigorous championship of Indonesian independence—cooled gradually as time went on. With a nation of 85 million people behind him, President Sukarno apparently was not content to follow the leadership of Nehru and developed leadership ambitions of his own.

Like the Burmese, the leaders of the newly emergent African countries have felt far from cordial toward the rich and comparatively well-educated Indians living in their midst. This, too, has colored international relations. After the Chinese invasion of 1962, India found to her dismay that the Afro-Asian nations did not rally behind her, as she had hoped they would. Instead, they applied to this conflict the old Indian policy of nonalignment and urged negotiations between India and China. Six of these nations (Burma, Cambodia, Ceylon, Ghana, Indonesia, and the United Arab Republic) jointly pressed India to negotiate. Thus the bloc India had led deserted her in her emergency.

The Kashmir Problem and Tension with Pakistan

The neighbor with which India has had the most difficulty, of course, is Pakistan. With partition, an acute internal rivalry based on a mixture of religious, political, and economic considerations was suddenly transformed into an international rivalry. Intense passions were aroused by the appalling death toll in the riots and mass migrations that ensued and by stories told by refugees fleeing from Pakistan and by those fleeing from India as well—horror stories of atrocities perpetrated on their co-religionists who could not escape.

Relations were further complicated by the economic dislocations resulting from partition and the division of the assets of undivided India, including everything from bank accounts to railway cars to office equipment and typewriters. Each problem in Indo-Pakistan relations made the solution of every other problem the more difficult.

On January 13, 1948, Gandhi undertook his last fast, appealing to the nation to remove the ill-will and passions which poisoned its relations with Pakistan. He ended his fast on January 18 when a number of leaders in Delhi promised him that they would banish communalism from their hearts. The Indian Government then handed over to Pakistan Rs. 550 million in cash balances, which it owed Pakistan but had previously withheld. This softening of policy toward Pakistan was resented by many Indians, including the fanatic Godse, who twelve days later assassinated Gandhi. The shock of Gandhi's death brought the worst of the communal mass murders to an end, but fear and suspicion between the two new nations continued.

A major problem in the early years after independence was the division of the essential waters of rivers that have their sources in India but fed the irrigation canals of Pakistan before independence. When India temporarily cut off the flow of this water into Pakistan in the spring of 1948, the crops of hundreds of thousands of acres of Pakistan land were ruined, and Pakistan feared that India might use the weapon of starvation to compel her to join the Indian Union.

The most serious problem between India and Pakistan has been the dispute over Kashmir—made more complex by the invasion of part of Kashmir by the Chinese in the late 1950's, and by the more vigorous invasion of 1962. With an area of about 84,000 square miles—almost twice the size of the state of New York—Kashmir has a population of only 4.5 million, about half that of New York City. Between two ranges of the Himalayas which run diagonally across the state, lies the beautiful Vale of Kashmir, the very heart of Kashmir and one of the world's loveliest vacation centers (where, instead of a hotel room, the visitor may rent a houseboat anchored on one or another of the many canals and lakes in which are mirrored the white peaks towering over the fertile green valley).

The eastern part of the state is Ladakh, the section invaded by the Chinese. The northeastern bulge—the Aksai Chin—is high, rugged, arid, and uninhabited. The rest of Ladakh is inhabited (but sparsely) by Buddhists of a racial stock closely akin to the Tibetans, with little in common with the people of the rest of Kashmir, who are predominantly Muslim.

Before independence, Kashmir was one of the semiautonomous princely states. Despite its predominantly Muslim population, its ruler was a Hindu Maharajah. At the time of independence, when the rulers of all the other princely states (except Hyderabad and Junagadh) acceded either to Pakistan or India, this Maharajah postponed his decision. In the autumn of 1947, unorganized but well-armed Muslim tribesmen from Pakistan invaded Kashmir, penetrating deep into the Vale and looting and burning villages. The Maharajah hastily acceded to India, and Indian troops were then promptly flown in to oppose the tribesmen. India appealed to the Security Council of the United Nations, which sent a Commission to investigate the facts and make recommendations—the United Nations Commission on India and Pakistan (UNCIP). By 1948, regular units of the Pakistan Army had entered Kashmir in support of the tribesmen. Actual warfare lasted for more than a year, until UNCIP succeeded in arranging a cease-fire in January, 1949. The western and northern portion of the state—about a third of its total area—fell on the Pakistan side of the cease-fire line. The remaining portions, including Ladakh and the all-important Vale, remained on the Indian side. In places, no precise cease-fire line was marked out because of high altitudes and snow.

As early as April 21, 1948, the U.N. Security Council recommended that a plebiscite be held to determine the inhabitants' preference between India and Pakistan. From the outset, Nehru took the position that the Maharajah's accession had given India sovereignty over Kashmir. Even so, he agreed at first to a plebiscite, but only on condition that it be held after the invading forces were withdrawn and India had set up a system of representative government in Kashmir.

It proved impossible to achieve agreement on the demilitarization considered by the U.N. as an essential prelude to a fair plebiscite. Pakistan would not withdraw her forces unless India at the same time withdrew the Indian forces on her side of the line. India, on the other hand, held that since Pakistan had been the aggressor, the Pakistan withdrawal must occur first. She also took the position that Indian forces could not be withdrawn completely, leaving Kashmir unprotected or ungoverned. When it was suggested in the United Nations that a U.N. force composed of contingents from European or American countries should hold Kashmir pending a plebiscite, Nehru strongly objected that this would be a reversal to European domination. But he indicated his willingness to settle the Kashmir question by the partition of the state along the existing cease-fire line. Hoping to get the majority vote of the Muslim population if a fair plebiscite were held, Pakistan refused to agree to this compromise.

In a speech made during his tour of India in December, 1955, Khrushchev made a statement welcome to Indian ears—that a plebiscite was unnecessary. Thereafter, for the first time Nehru explicitly rejected the possibility of a plebiscite, saying that U.S. military aid to Pakistan had altered the situation completely.[6]

Meanwhile, India had gone ahead with a number of expensive development projects in Indian-held Kashmir and had arranged for the election of a Kashmir constituent assembly. This assembly duly voted for the incorporation of Kashmir into India, to be concluded on January 26, 1957. But was this a true expression of the will of the people of the state? The Kashmiri leader Sheik Abdullah—Prime Minister of Kashmir from 1947 to 1953—was imprisoned in 1953 without trial and held in prison almost continuously thereafter. Though a Muslim, Sheik Abdullah had been a friend of Nehru's before independence and had favored the accession of Kashmir to India. His imprisonment occurred when his position regarding Indian rule wavered and he began to favor either independence or greater autonomy for his state.

Over the years, the U.N. has attempted mediation of the Kashmir dispute at various times, and bilateral negotiations between India and Pakistan have also taken place several times. Nothing has yet come of any of these efforts.

Apart from its strategic location, Kashmir seems to Indian leaders a test of the very basis of the Indian nation. Having declared herself to be a secular state, India insists that she must and can provide democracy and equal opportunity for people of all religions within her boundaries. To admit that the Muslims of Kashmir, just because they are Muslims, might want to join the Islamic state of Pakistan would seem to her a denial of the nation's essential secular principle. If India should yield to the demand for a plebiscite, how many of the Muslims in India would Hindu extremists kill?

Even if widespread slaughter could be prevented, a plebiscite might threaten the Indian nation in another way. It might lead to demands for plebiscites in other areas. Guerrilla warfare on behalf of an independent Naga state in Assam has kept contingents of the Indian Army busy for over a decade. In Madras, the supporters of an independent Dravidian state have grown in numbers in recent years. In the mid-1940's, the Communist Party of India supported the right to self-determination of seventeen supposedly separate nationalities within India. If self-determination were granted in one state—Kashmir—how could this fail to set a dangerous precedent leading to increased demands for self-determination in other Indian states? To many Indian leaders, it has seemed that the very survival of the nation was at stake.

To say this is not to pass judgment on the "merits" of the Kashmir case, but only to indicate that it looks quite different within the world of India from the way it looks in the distant West.

After 1963, when Pakistan reached an agreement with China regarding the borders of Pakistan-held Kashmir, Indo-Pakistan relations deteriorated rapidly. In 1965, mutual charges of border violations grew frequent. Sharp fighting in the Rann of Cutch (at the southernmost end of India's border with West Pakistan) in April, 1965, was halted by a cease-fire in May. But in August and September, even more serious fighting broke out. First, India charged that several thousand armed infiltrators had entered Kashmir. Pakistan claimed that the persons with arms were not infiltrators but dissatisfied Kashmiris rebelling against the pro-Indian regime in control of Indian-held Kashmir. The U.N. observers in Kashmir, however, reported that the men in question had in fact come from across the cease-fire line. To prevent more infiltration, India seized army posts on the Pakistan side of that line. The Pakistan Army retaliated, using Patton tanks it had received as military aid from the United States. India sent planes to destroy the tanks. Pakistan let loose her air force, too, including American-made F-86 Sabre Jets.

Early in September, each nation launched a ground attack across the international boundary, a far more serious matter than merely crossing the disputed cease-fire line within Kashmir itself. Pakistan aimed to cut India's supply route to Kashmir; India aimed to cut Pakistan's supply route to that Pakistan advanced column and also to seize nearby Lahore, Pakistan's second largest city, only fifteen miles from the boundary. Each nation reported the bombing of some of her cities by the air force of the other.

Thus the conflict escalated, creating for India—and the world as a whole—a highly dangerous situation in view of the possibility of another Chinese invasion as well. China, indeed, cautioned India that her action against Pakistan might lead to a "chain of circumstances," and Pakistan claimed to have received assurances of Chinese help. The Chinese, in fact, issued an ultimatum to India regarding certain military installations on the Chinese side of the border between China and the Indian protectorate of Sikkim. And they began massing troops near Sikkim. The Soviet Union, however, remained neutral, even offering its services for mediation, and the Chinese backed down from their threat.

The U.S. Government canceled further military aid to both India and Pakistan, but indicated it believed that Pakistan was the more to blame, though India by reason of her exaggerated response to the infiltration was far from blameless either. President Johnson did give reason to believe, however, that if China should actually invade India again, American military aid would be resumed.

After three weeks of hard fighting, both India and Pakistan yielded to pressure from the United Nations and agreed to a cease-fire. But thereafter both sides charged repeatedly that the other had violated this cease-fire. Sporadic fighting continued, and the underlying issues remained unsolved and seemingly insoluble. The Pakistani demand for a plebescite in Kashmir had grown most insistent, and the Indians' position against a plebescite had stiffened with what they regarded as a military victory.

To India's great satisfaction and elation, the Kashmiris themselves had not helped the infiltrators by rising in general revolt against their Indian-controlled government, as Pakistan had claimed they were doing. But though the Kashmir countryside remained quiet, anti-Indian demonstrations flared up in the capital city of Srinagar. The government responded by arresting more than thirty Kashmir leaders and suppressing all criticism of India.

China and the Northern Border

Until 1959, India followed a consistent policy of all-out friendship with China and made this a major cornerstone of the entire structure of her foreign policy. She repeatedly sponsored the claim of Communist China to the Chinese seat in the United Nations.

Official visits of various kinds were arranged between the two countries. Cultural delegations, delegations of agricultural and other experts and of women leaders went back and forth. Many Indians returning from China spoke with enthusiasm of what they had been shown. Again and again, Indian leaders proclaimed that the Indians and the Chinese were brothers. But there had been increasing signs of trouble with China long before the autumn of 1962, when India could no longer pretend that the Chinese threat was not grave.

The first small sign of trouble came when India discovered, as early as 1950, that Chinese maps included within China's boundaries large areas that India regarded as her own. The Chinese explanation was that these maps antedated the Communist regime in China and that there had not yet been time to re-examine them.

Next, trouble arose over Tibet. The legal status of this high, rugged, uninviting tableland behind the Himalayan barrier had been discussed at various times before independence and was far from clear. Perhaps it is fair to say that it theoretically belonged to China, though it had the right to partial autonomy. But the British, who regarded it as an essential buffer state between Russia, China, and India, had sent an expedition there in 1904 and secured special privileges, including the right to keep military contingents in the town of Gyantse and to maintain political and trade agents in Tibet, as well as postal and telegraph facilities. At independence, the new Indian Government inherited these privileges. Up to 1950, China had made no attempt for a long while to exercise sovereignty over Tibet, but in that year the Chinese Communists sent in an occupying force. This, of course, brought the Chinese much closer to India—a matter of concern to the Indian Government.

Indian anxieties on this score were allayed by a treaty with China, signed in 1954, which recognized the pilgrimage and trading rights important to India, but not the extraterritorial and military rights held by the British Indian Government, which free India did not choose to assert. It also laid down for the first time the famous "Five Principles of Peaceful Coexistence" (Panchsheela): mutual respect for each other's territorial integrity, mutual nonaggression, mutual noninterference in each other's internal affairs, equality and mutual benefit, and peaceful coexistence. These seemed to India a clear solution to the problem of world peace—until they were broken by the Chinese in 1959.

Before then, however—in 1957—the Indian Government discovered that the Chinese had actually built a road across the Aksai Chin tip of Ladakh without India's knowledge. The government lodged an official protest with the Chinese Government, but it apparently was not seriously concerned. The area is so remote, rugged, and uninhabitable that some Indian leaders seem to have regarded it at first as not worth enough to India to risk a real breach with China. Separated by high mountains from the rest of Kashmir, Ladakh seemed to some at least to be part of Tibet. It had been conquered by the Hindu Maharajah of Kashmir in the mid-nineteenth century, but no international agreement on its boundary had ever been reached. The representatives of the British Indian Government and of Tibet and China had held a conference at Simla in 1913–14 to discuss the boundary between Tibet and India in general, but (curiously) their talks were confined to the eastern section. Although the line around Ladakh had been marked on British maps, it seems scarcely to have been discussed; but it was later protested by Tibet.

In the spring of 1958, India, which had previously not attempted to maintain military check posts near what it regarded as the boundary in the difficult Aksai Chin area, sent two detachments there to examine the new Chinese road. One detachment was captured by the Chinese. Again the Indian Government protested. Letters passed back and forth between Nehru and Chou En-lai.

Meanwhile, the Chinese had been gradually tightening their control over Tibet. Following their occupation in 1950, they did not at first assert authority vigorously. They kept their military headquarters well outside the capital city of Lhasa, and recognized the Tibetan Dalai Lama as the supreme temporal and ecclesiastical power of the state. At the time of the Panchsheela agreement, India had understood that China would continue to grant Tibet this autonomy. But Chinese pressure on the people gradually increased. A revolution broke out on March 20, 1959. The Dalai Lama—his life in danger—fled to India, followed by thousands of Buddhist refugees. Many Hindus feel a close bond with Buddhists, and the plight of the Dalai Lama aroused much sympathy. The reception given him in India apparently angered the Chinese. Relations became more strained.

Then, in August, 1959, 300 Chinese troops crossed the eastern section of India's long northern border and captured one significant post, Longju, in India's Northeast Frontier Agency. A centrally controlled military defense zone north of Assam, the Northeast Frontier Agency is administered by the Governor of Assam acting as the agent of the central government. There—from Bhutan to Burma—the Government of India had considered the dividing line between India and Chinese-controlled Tibet to be the MacMahon Line, drawn on a map in 1914 by Sir Arthur MacMahon on behalf of the British Indian Government. At the Simla Conference, the representatives of China and Tibet agreed to this line, which follows the crest of a high Himalayan ridge and is therefore logical geographically. The Chinese Government, however, believed that it should have been drawn farther to the south, down the Indian side of the mountains. It never ratified the Simla agreement, but was at the time too weak to make an effective protest.

The Chinese incursions into the Northeast Frontier area and the much deeper incursions into Ladakh led some members of Parliament, especially members of the Jana Sangh and the Praja Socialists, to demand that India take the strongest possible action to drive China out of all Indian territory. Others, however, advised caution and negotiation. Even after Chou En-lai, on September 8, 1959, denounced the entire boundary as the work of British imperialists and hence not to be respected, Nehru urged moderation. He said: "To imagine that India can push China about is silly. To imagine that China can push India about is equally silly. We must accept things as they are. . . . It is fantastic to talk about war."[7] Faithful to his belief that all disputes can be settled by negotiations, he carried on prolonged discussions with Chou En-lai early in 1960. Finally he admitted publicly that no agreement had proved possible, that the Chinese claimed sovereignty over 52,000 square miles of what he regarded as Indian territory and had occupied 14,000 square miles of the total, most of it in Ladakh.

For the next three years, the situation changed very little, and many Indians seemed to be lulled into the comfortable belief that the Chinese had no further designs against them. Some Indian officers argued that no more than a few stations of advanced pickets would be able to operate at the altitudes in question, that to keep even one combat soldier supplied and fed in the high mountains involved such problems of carrying great loads up steep, narrow, difficult mountain trails that the Chinese would never succeed in massing large forces near the boundary line. Even fuel for cooking and for warmth had to be brought up to the soldiers on muleback or—where the footing was too difficult—on the backs of men. Each winter during those three years, the pickets of both the Chinese and the Indians retreated from the high passes with the coming of the heavy snow. Each spring, they raced back up the slopes to attempt to establish themselves—before the enemy arrived—at their previous posts. To many Indians, it seemed that this kind of warfare was a quasi game that might go on indefinitely.

The new thrusts of the Chinese in October, 1962, were entirely unexpected in their scale and intensity. Most of India's army of about half a million men was still stationed on the Pakistan border. Only 30,000 or 40,000 men guarded the passes, and these were armed largely with World War II weapons. The Indians had probably no more than one division (12,000 to 15,000 men) in Ladakh and perhaps two or three divisions in the Northeast Frontier Agency.[8]

The Chinese troops that overran the Indian outposts may not have been much more numerous, but they were far better equipped and supplied. The Chinese soldiers carried semiautomatic rifles and had Soviet mortars firing 120-mm. shells.[9] The Indians went into battle without automatic weapons and, in some cases, without sufficient winter clothing.[10] But even more telling was the difference in the supply situation. The Chinese soldiers were backed by a host of porters, mules, jeeps, trucks, laborers, and supply services of all kinds.[11] In the Ladakh area, Chinese laborers hastily built roads on which trucks could drive to within a few miles of the forward Chinese positions—while Indian troops had long marches (often a week or more) from their nearest base or airport.[12]

The sheer length of the northern frontier (about 2,600 miles altogether, counting the many indentations in the line) makes its defense extremely difficult. For it is impossible to guard such a long boundary solidly and in depth. The army on the offense has a pronounced advantage since it can choose its own striking point. The defending army must then move contingents and supply services, often from distant locations, to meet the attack. Although India put all the aircraft of her civil-defense lines at the disposal of the army for transport services, and the Indian Air Force had Soviet helicopters and American C-119 transports, many of these planes proved unsuited for the special conditions under which they had to operate. Helicopters had trouble in the turbulent mountain air, and some of India's other airplanes had difficulty taking off and landing on the short, rough improvised airstrips that were hastily made in whatever small valley was available as near as possible to the scene of fighting.

In Ladakh, the Chinese rapidly seized more than even the area they had previously claimed. In the Northeast Frontier Agency, they came far down the mountain slopes in several places, threatening the entire valley of the Brahmaputra River and the all-important oil fields of Assam.

On October 29, Nehru sent an urgent request to the United States and the United Kingdom for military aid. Both responded immediately—the United States with an airlift of $5 million worth of small arms. After a further request, the United States also sent a squadron of twelve U.S. C-130 Hercules transport planes piloted by Americans, to help transport Indian troops, with the understanding that they would not go into battle areas. Nehru continued to hope for aid from the Soviet Union also, but the Soviets urged him to accept the Chinese proposal for a cease-fire, and for a while they delayed delivery of the supersonic MIG fighter planes promised to India earlier. The first of these arrived only the following February. The factories the Soviet Union had promised to help India build for production of MIG fighters had originally been scheduled to be ready by July, 1964; but after the invasion, the Soviet Union delayed more than a year before proceeding with the project.

Suddenly, on November 21, China made a unilateral offer of a cease-fire and said that on December 1 Chinese troops would be pulled back 12.5 miles behind the positions of actual control on November 7, 1959. This meant leaving the Chinese in control of much of the territory they had taken in their autumn thrust in 1959. Nehru preferred withdrawal to the line of September 8, 1962, by which time India had regained some of the territory previously lost in Ladakh. Without any agreement on the matter, both sides stopped fighting, and the Chinese pulled back much as they had promised. There was no assurance, however, that the cease-fire would continue to be observed by the Chinese.

This raises the question of Chinese objectives in India. Does China want possession of large areas of Indian territory? Or did other motives prompt the invasion? The answers to these questions must be largely conjectural, but a few points at least are clear. For one thing, China has felt a real need for a road across the Aksai Chin and for enough territory in Ladakh to ensure the defense of that road. The road provides a link between Tibet and the Chinese province of Sinkiang, especially essential to China because the other (eastern) road linking Tibet and China passes through difficult terrain where the Tibetans, still unreconciled to Chinese rule, have repeatedly tried to ambush or harass Chinese traffic. China may well consider the roundabout route through Ladakh as essential if she is to hold Tibet. One possibility is that her invasion of the other area, far to the east, was partly to gain territory there (more valuable to India than to her) which she could bargain back in exchange for Ladakh.

In any event, a long article published in Peking on October 27, 1962, made it clear that no mere border adjustment would satisfy China. The article accused Nehru of "an attempt to establish an Indian sphere of influence in Asia that would far surpass that of the colonialist system formerly set up in Asia by the British Empire." Indian ruling circles headed by Nehru, it said, have sought to control the economy and trade of countries around India and have demanded their "absolute obedience."[13]

The article clearly revealed a deep feeling of rivalry with India. Nothing less than the leadership of Asia seems to be at stake for the Chinese. Viewed in this light, a successful invasion, especially of areas that matter more to India than Ladakh, could accomplish many purposes more useful to China than the actual possession of land on the far side of the Himalayas. It could undercut India's influence in the border states of Nepal, Bhutan, and Sikkim, which might well hesitate to side with a defeated neighbor against a victorious one. It could doubtless divert India's resources from development to defense, and thus weaken her economically. And—unless the Soviet Union were prepared for an open split with China—it could lead to a cancellation of the promised MIG fighters and the MIG factory in India, perhaps driving a permanent wedge between Russia and India. Any or all of these effects would have a bearing on the relative power positions of India and China.

Although opinions vary as to how strained the relations between the Soviet Union and China may be, certainly the Chinese must have considered the effect of their invasion not only on India's position but also on China's own position within the Communist world. To force the Russians to choose between China and India may itself have seemed a triumph likely to enhance China's influence with other Communist countries. It could even be thought of as a step toward the world domination to which Communist Chinese leaders doubtless aspire.

It is a matter of conjecture as to how long China may pause before striking India again, or whether, indeed, another attack will seem to her the best policy, in view of prompt Western intervention. But Chinese charges of Indian border violations were issued with increasing frequency after the outbreak of the Indo-Pakistan war. China also accused India of aggression against Pakistan and declared publicly that she would aid Pakistan. At the very least, this could result in diverting a substantial part of the Indian Army to defend India's frontiers against Chinese encroachment.

The Buffer States

At the center of India's northern boundary, there is a stretch of about 1,195 miles* where India and China are separated from

* The figure usually given in the press is 800 miles, but this does not take into account the many bends and indentations in the boundary line, which are of real importance in defense. For the figure I have used, I am indebted to Professor John E. Brush, Department of Geography, Rutgers University. He cautions, however, that no figure for any of India's northern boundary

each other by Nepal, Sikkim, and Bhutan. What happens to these buffer states is of vital importance to India's own security.

Nepal is an independent kingdom. Bhutan is a semi-independent state; India recognizes its "independence," but nevertheless controls its external relations. Sikkim is a protectorate of India, but with its own Maharajah. Nehru has clearly stated: "Any aggression against Sikkim and Bhutan will be considered aggression against India."[14]

With an area of 2,800 square miles and a population of only 140,000—Buddhists of Tibetan stock—Sikkim is the smallest of the three border states. But it is of major strategic importance for it would provide the shortest, easiest route between China and the important city of Calcutta. A full-scale invasion along that route would sever Assam and part of West Bengal from the rest of India. Since 1962, India has maintained sizable army detachments in Sikkim. As already mentioned, in 1965, China threatened to use Sikkim as the new invasion route into India.

About six times the size of Sikkim, Bhutan is more closely connected with Tibet than with India—geographically, culturally, and racially. Fourteen mountain passes lead from Tibet into Bhutan, whereas until recently it was almost impossible to enter Bhutan from India directly without going through Tibet. When Nehru paid a state visit to Bhutan in September, 1958, he had to go by way of Tibet—and on donkey back. India has recently undertaken a road-building program to make access easier.

The largest of the buffer states, Nepal has an area of 54,000 square miles, roughly three times the size of Bhutan. It contains not only Mount Everest, but also eight of the next ten highest mountain peaks in the world. It is a rugged and difficult country, but with fertile valleys between the mountains. Until recently, it has had hardly any roads except mountain foot trails over which men and donkeys carried great loads on their backs.

---

can be exact, since the line has never been demarcated on the ground and cannot be accurately measured on maps—because it runs up and down steep slopes. His estimates for the two sections of India's northern boundary that front directly on Chinese territory are 850 miles for the western section (including the Ladakh boundary) and 570 miles for the eastern section (the MacMahon Line)—hence a total of 2,615 miles for the entire northern boundary.

The Nepalese are as proud of their independence as the Indians are of theirs. Even a war with the British in 1814–16 did not subdue them. The British took the western portion of their territory, which now forms the extreme northern portion of the states of Uttar Pradesh and the Punjab, but found the Nepalese such fierce and hardy fighters that it seemed wise not to press the war further. Thereafter, many of the Nepalese warrior class—the Gurkhas—enlisted in the Indian Army as mercenaries. They still form 8 per cent of that army.

From 1845 to 1950, the country was under the control of a hereditary line of prime ministers, the Rana family, who kept the Nepalese royal family and the country as a whole in as much isolation as possible in order to prevent the arrival of any disturbing modern liberal ideas. The Ranas taxed the people unmercifully and accumulated for themselves large palaces and much wealth. Then, in 1950, there was a coup, spearheaded by a discontented branch of the Rana family and backed by the Indian Congress Party. In a speech in Parliament on December 6, 1950, Nehru made no secret of his sympathy with the coup.[15] Its leaders restored liberty to the monarch. Although his powers were nominally limited by a constitution that provided for an elective parliament, he was able to choose a pro-Indian Prime Minister.

With the King of Nepal in debt to India for the restitution of his authority, Indians assumed that Nepal would remain permanently pro-Indian. But five years later, the old King died and was succeeded by his more independent-minded and self-assertive son, the present King Mahendra. The latter promulgated a new constitution in 1959 and called for elections. After these had resulted in a victory for the Nepalese Congress Party, which was critical of the King, he dismissed the Cabinet, only newly formed, and began governing the country himself in 1960. Although Nepal has received aid from India, especially for the building of an important and difficult road over the mountains to India, the King is wary of Indian control and anxious to keep on good terms with Communist China. But in 1965, he canceled an agreement he had reached with China for the building of a road to link Nepal with Tibet. This came as a great relief to India, for if they could control Nepal, the Chinese would have easy access to north India, since the high passes would then be behind them.

Do the Chinese intend sooner or later to press on into the lowlands? Just south of Nepal are the great states of Uttar Pradesh and Bihar, where much of India's industrial development is centered. From Sikkim to the vital port city of Calcutta is only a little over 300 miles, most of it across flat plains. If the Chinese struck in either direction, India would be severely hurt.

The Bomb, or an Atomic Shield?

When the Chinese exploded their first nuclear device, in the autumn of 1963, the Indian Government announced that it would not immediately make an atomic bomb, although it had several nuclear reactors and a number of experienced nuclear physicists. Since India had always opposed the production and testing of nuclear weapons and had urged nuclear disarmament, the government argued that the making of a bomb would mean the abandonment of Indian principles. Doubtless, the government was also concerned over the expense involved in producing not only the bomb but also the means with which to deliver it.

Many Indians even within Shastri's own party, however, had different views. Only after heated debate did the next conference of the Congress Party pass a formal resolution endorsing the government's policy on this matter. There followed much public discussion as to whether the West or the Soviet Union would come to India's aid if the Chinese used the bomb against India. Leaders of the Swatantra Party argued strongly that it was impossible to count on the Soviet Union. Remembering how the shipment of MIG fighter planes had been delayed at the crucial moment in 1962, most Indians were inclined to agree. Members of the Swatantra Party urged Nehru to seek the promises of nuclear protection from the West. Answering that this would be a grave departure from the policy of nonalignment, Nehru refused.

The Communists and left-wing members of the Congress Party continued to press for the manufacture of a bomb by India—and the government continued to resist. In the spring of 1965, the Indian delegation to the U.N. Disarmament Conference urged that the United Nations should provide a nuclear shield for nations attacked by nuclear weapons. Nothing came of this suggestion, and India's future nuclear policy remained a matter of controversy within the country. Following the outbreak of fighting with Pakistan in 1965, the production of the bomb by India was vigorously urged by more than eighty members of Parliament.

Relations Between India and the West

The threat to India's very existence forces the West to decide how vital to the survival of the free world as a whole India may be. Before 1962, India's relations with the West were punctuated with mutual misunderstandings. India could not understand the West's Cold War policies; the West could not understand India's nonalignment, her relations with Pakistan, or her seizure of Goa. The low point was probably reached in 1954, when U.S. military aid to Pakistan began. But it must be underlined that cultural relations between India and the West have been basically stronger at all times than those between India and the Soviet Union, and that India—a member of the British Commonwealth—has remained unexpectedly close to her ex-rulers. An upsurge of mutual confidence between India and the West began in 1957, with greatly increased Western economic aid and with increasing realization in the West that India's foreign policy, like that of any nation, must grow out of its total situation of the moment. The promptness with which the United States rushed small arms and planes to India in 1962 was greatly appreciated. On the other hand, many Indians resented American pressure upon India to make peace with Pakistan. Such a peace would, of course, put India in a much better position to resist any new Chinese aggression. Indeed, President Muhammad Ayub Khan of Pakistan himself had suggested earlier that if outstanding disputes could be settled, the two nations might well reach some arrangement for the joint defense of the subcontinent. (From the American point of view, it made no sense to supply military as well as economic aid to two rivals who might at any moment fight each other.) But even with the need for greater security against China, India considered it impossible to yield to Pakistan, and her position on Kashmir had become so rigid that she resented any suggestion that it be altered. The tussle over Kashmir, it seemed, was more important to her than her stance against Chinese aggression.

Anti-Americanism flared up in the spring of 1965 after President

Johnson informed Prime Minister Shastri that the latter's visit to the United States, scheduled for May, 1965, would have to be postponed. Shastri interpreted this as a deliberate snub and announced that he would cancel the visit completely.

The press reported that the reason for the postponement was President Johnson's desire not to meet with the President of Pakistan, who had been flirting more and more with China, and had been scheduled to visit Johnson that same spring. Not to give clear offense to Pakistan, Johnson had suggested the postponement of Shastri's visit as well. Indians felt hurt not merely by the postponement of Shastri's visit, but more especially by the fact that India and Pakistan had been equated in the Presidential announcement. On this occasion, as on so many others, India seemed to the West to be obsessed with her hostile feelings toward Pakistan.

India was also greatly disturbed that the United States apparently at first tolerated the use by Pakistan of American tanks against India in 1965—although Pakistan had promised not to use them except in self-defense.

As the hostilities between India and Pakistan escalated into war, it became clear that by violating her promises to the United States regarding the use of the military aid she had received, as well as by her apparent courting of the support of China, Pakistan had forfeited American friendship. The United States would not soon give aid to Pakistan again. The policy, long followed, of American neutrality toward Indo-Pakistan rivalries had broken down, it appeared. But because she had escalated the war, India also had lost much of the sympathy felt for her earlier in the West. Meanwhile, many Indians vigorously urged a closer tie with the United States.

Although U.S. military aid to both sides was cut off in September, 1965, informed and thoughtful observers cautioned against any stoppage in economic aid as well. Wherever the major share of blame for the fighting might lie—whether with Pakistan or with India—the West could hardly afford to turn its back on either. For it would be the free world that would be the loser if the Indian subcontinent should be left with nowhere to turn except Communist China or the Soviet Union.

17 • THE DEFENSE FORCES AND THEIR BRITISH BACKGROUND

In 1962, as waves of Chinese soldiers poured over Himalayan passes so high they had previously been considered impassable by large numbers, the attention of India and of much of the free world became riveted on the embattled Indian Army, clearly so unprepared for such an assault. Again, in 1965, when the Chinese threatened another invasion of India, the defense potential of India became a matter of paramount importance to the West.

Having inherited their armed forces from the British Government of India, many Indians had not previously fully realized that these forces were now theirs, that they were the essential safeguard of their own free nation. This fact and Nehru's optimistic hope that nonalignment would keep India free from wars partly accounted for the state of unpreparedness. A further reason, paradoxically, was that the very size of the Chinese Army in relation to that of India made it seem hopeless to plan seriously for defense against China. As late as the winter of 1962, General K. S. Thimayya, former Chief of the Army Staff (and hero of the 1947–48 war against Pakistan in Kashmir), wrote: "I cannot even as a soldier envisage India taking on China in an open conflict on its own. China's present strength in manpower, equipment, and aircraft exceeds our resources a hundredfold with the full support of the U.S.S.R., and we can never hope to match China in the foreseeable future. It must be left to the politicians and diplomats to insure our security."[1]

It must be admitted that the Chinese invasion ended in a military debacle for India. Obviously, the Indian armed forces were not prepared to fight a modern war in difficult terrain or to employ the complex machinery of modern battle groups. The Indians were outgunned and outgeneraled, and they were quickly overrun wherever a stand was attempted.

There were probably many reasons for this debacle, and it is difficult for an outsider to weigh the various factors and determine the share of the blame. Clearly, the lack of modern arms was disastrous, With only vintage Lee-Enfield rifles, even stouthearted Gurkhas cannot fight against a modern army. During Krishna Menon's regime as Defense Minister (1957–62), military advancement may have depended more on an ability to say "yes" to Krishna Menon than on brilliant staffwork and an insistent demand for modern armaments. And it is apparent that India's intense concentration on economic development and the widely held belief in the efficacy of good will and reasonableness made it very difficult to allocate anything like an adequate portion of the budget for military expenditures.

As the following table shows, defense expenditures decreased slightly in 1958–59, and again in 1959–60, then rose again in response to the first small evidences of the Chinese threat. Until 1963–64, they constituted a fairly small percentage of the total national budget—20 per cent in 1955–56, and only 15 per cent in 1961–62, after the progressive increases in the development effort had more than doubled national expenditures.[2] By 1964–65, on the other hand, they constituted 40 per cent of the national budget.

India's Defense Expenditures
(in millions of dollars)

1955–56	$ 401
1956–57	445
1957–58	588
1958–59	585
1959–60	558
1960–61	638
1961–62	656
1962–63	985
1963–64	1,697
1964–65	1,783

SOURCES: *India, 1964,* pp. 177–78. The figures cited here represent the totals of the amounts spent under both the Revenue Account and the Capital Budget.

Perhaps it required as great a shock as the nation received in October–November, 1962, to alert it to the fact that a well-equipped army and air force are essential to the nation's life. As for the Indian Navy—which consists of one aircraft carrier, two prewar cruisers, three destroyers, plus a number of escort vessels, minesweepers, and other ships, mostly purchased from the United Kingdom—it has been vigorously criticized as an unnecessary showpiece, too expensive, too ill-adapted to the realities of Indian geography, and a slavish imitation in miniature of the Royal Navy. According to some strategists, India's coastline is so long that even a navy many times as large could not possibly defend it all from enemy encroachments by sea. A less expensive and more effective defense against such encroachments might be a greatly enlarged air force. Indeed, as Major General E. Habibullah, former Commandant of the National Defense Academy, has asked: Why should India need an aircraft carrier when the very shape of the Indian peninsula, jutting out far into the Indian Ocean, makes the land itself the most effective aircraft carrier that could be desired.[3]

The lack of air power was clearly a significant factor in the defeat India suffered at the hands of the Chinese in 1962. The tiny Indian air force had slight troop-carrying capacity and did not include sufficient bombers to threaten Chinese assembly areas or even to consider bombing the passes through which the Chinese poured a steady stream of men and matériel. And it certainly did not have the masses of helicopters and transport and cargo aircraft needed to back up the frontline troops, who were actually fighting a mountain war.

Before going on to examine India's subsequent defense increases, it may be well to review briefly the history of the Indian Army for a better understanding of her resources and capabilities.

The army's history traces back to those first armed guards hired by the East India Company to protect its warehouses. As the Company grew into a political power after the Battle of Plassey, the sepoys (Indian mercenary soldiers) were organized into military units based on the organizational pattern of the British Army. Their officers were always Britishers or Europeans. Indians rose to be senior noncommissioned officers, taking over much of the drilling and training of the regiments, but they remained subordinate to the youngest British subaltern.

European regiments were also recruited by the Company, and after 1754 regiments of the British Government likewise participated in the Company's wars. But non-Indians formed a minority of the Company's forces. In 1857, at the time of the sepoy revolt, the army consisted of only 45,000 British troops, as against 233,000 Indians. The prolonged war that followed the revolt was put down with great difficulty. Afterward, soldiers who had participated in the revolt were executed; other discontented sepoys retired; and many regiments were disbanded altogether. The army was then completely reorganized, with Europeans placed in sole charge of the artillery. The proportion of European troops was increased so that Indian soldiers never again outnumbered Europeans by more than five to two until 1914.

Before the revolt, a large proportion of the sepoys had been high-caste Brahmans. Afterward, there was an emphasis on recruitment of other castes and creeds, especially the Gurkhas from the independent neighboring kingdom of Nepal, Sikhs and Muslims from the Punjab, and Pathan Muslim tribesmen from the northwest frontier. Because the various peoples recruited had different food habits and languages, they were normally formed into separate regiments or battalions based on religion, language, or geographical origin.

When the Crown took over the Company's empire, the Company's army became part of the Imperial forces. Contingents were repeatedly sent overseas to serve Imperial purposes. In World War I, Indian soldiers fought in France, East Africa, and Mesopotamia. During the course of the war, more than 800,000 combat troops and 400,000 noncombatants were recruited on a voluntary basis.[4] In World War II as well, Indian troops fought in many campaigns: in North Africa, the Middle East, Burma, and Italy. Having had a prewar strength of 182,000 men, the Indian Army had risen to 2 million by 1945. Again, all the recruitment was voluntary. The casualties suffered during the war were 180,000, including about 30,000 killed.[5]

While so many Indians fought gallantly on the Allied side,

other Indians (regarding England as the major enemy) joined a Japanese-sponsored Indian National Army. Their leader, Subhas Chandra Bose, a brilliant, deeply religious and ascetic Hindu, typified the militant tradition within India which has never come to terms with Gandhiism. His career is worth noting in detail—if only because the real strength of the militant tradition in India has always been greatly underestimated in the West. Although he devoted himself to the nationalist movement from the early 1920's with the utmost intensity (he was jailed eleven times), he was always critical of Gandhi's leadership for its moderation and what he regarded as its lack of clarity. Despite his open disagreement with Gandhi, he attained sufficient stature within the Indian National Congress to be elected its President in 1938. But after Subhas' re-election in 1939, "the Mahatma and his followers struck back with the same weapon they had used to confound John Bull: noncooperation. This worked, and Subhas, hesitant to shoulder the responsibility of a wide-open split in Congress at that critical juncture, resigned."[6] Following the outbreak of World War II, Subhas went to Germany, where he made radio broadcasts urging his fellow countrymen to overthrow British rule. Then he went on a German submarine to Tokyo. His appeal to the Axis powers was a step that Nehru, strongly anti-fascist from the very beginning, would never have taken. By July, 1943, with Japanese help, he had raised his Indian National army of 60,000 men from among Indian soldiers taken prisoner by the Japanese and Indians resident in Southeast Asia. In October, he announced the formation of a Provisional Government of Free India and declared war on Great Britain and the United States. His INA invaded Indian territory, but soon had to fall back because of a shortage of supplies. It disintegrated in 1945 just before Subhas, now known as Netaji ("Venerable Leader"), died in a plane crash on the way to Japan. Subhas became a popular hero all over India, his photograph displayed beside those of Gandhi and Nehru, with both of whom he disagreed so fundamentally. A legend sprang up that he had not really died in the plane crash, but would reappear when India most needed him. Some Indians still believe this legend.

When the British attempted to try the officers and enlisted

men of the INA for treason at the end of the war, nationwide demonstrations for their release were held. And so much agitation occurred that most of the sentences were suspended.

The cause of the INA soldiers was sponsored by Indian enlisted men of the Indian Royal Navy, who mutinied in February, 1946, in the harbor of Bombay. This mutiny was no small affair. The mutineers, concerned with their low pay as well as with politics, pulled down the Union Jack on two naval vessels anchored in Bombay Harbor and raised the Congress flag instead. Then they left many ships virtually deserted and stormed into the business section of the city, where they broke the windows of European offices, set fire to buildings, and used machine guns to resist arrest. Bombay, in turmoil, was aflame for several days. In other parts of the country, a thousand Indians in the Indian Royal Air Force staged a sympathetic mutiny, trade unions went on strike, and mobs gathered to protest both the deplorable condition under which the seamen had to live and the larger issue of the pending trials of the members of the INA. After several tense days, they surrendered, but only after Nehru had deplored their use of violence and the British had rushed three regiments to Bombay, a squadron of air-force bombers, and several British naval vessels. The British Commanding General also felt it necessary to promise that he would not press charges against them. This mutiny and the smoldering postwar disaffection in the army (which broke out only in one small area) were important factors in Great Britain's decision to grant India freedom.

The way in which the Indian Army was turned over to the new nation is worth noting. One problem was the officer corps. In the early twentieth century, nationalists had demanded the Indianization of the officer corps of the army. Not until 1918, however, did the British take any steps in this direction. It was then that the first Indian officer candidate received an appointment to Sandhurst (the British equivalent of West Point). Thereafter, a number of Indian officers entered Sandhurst each year and secured the desired King's Commission. In 1932, an Indian military academy was established at Dehra Dun in north India. Its graduates also qualified for the King's Commission. Yet Indianization of the officer corps remained a slow process. At the time of independence, only 25 per cent of the officers were Indian, and only three Indians had risen to the rank of Brigadier.[7]

In January, 1947, a Commission on the Nationalization of the Indian Army stated that it would still take a number of years to nationalize the army—the British members of the Commission estimating fifteen years, the Indian members more optimistically estimating about five years. But six months later, independence had come, and the process was greatly hastened. Although a few British officers stayed on for a few years after independence, the majority left almost immediately, as did all purely European contingents. Junior Indian officers received quick promotions. The lack of pre-independence experience, even in medium-level command, on the part of many officers now of the highest rank remains one of the weaknesses of the army.

The partition of India required the partition of the army also. Muslim regiments went to Pakistan. Officers were given the choice as to which of the new nations they would serve. India received about two-thirds of the native portion of the pre-independence Indian Army, Pakistan the remaining third. The confusion resulting from the simultaneous loss of British and Muslim troops and officers formed part of the background of the terrible bloodshed that accompanied the migrations of millions in 1947. Only a small boundary force—as yet undivided—remained intact to patrol the Punjab.

After independence, the Indian Army was somewhat reorganized, though many of the old regiments retained their names, their flags, and their pride in regimental traditions dating back to British days. At the time of the Chinese invasion of 1962, the army was generally believed to number a little over half a million. Indian officers felt that two world wars had proved that the Indian Army could be a good fighting force when well armed. The Indian enlisted man, they have always said, will obey any order and face any danger, no matter how great. If fighting is his duty, he will do that duty to the death, convinced that he will reap his reward in another incarnation.

Before the 1962 invasion, the army had seen action on a number of occasions, none of them calling for an all-out effort with the most modern weapons. It took over the princely state of

Hyderabad in 1948. It fought the Pakistan Army in Kashmir until a U.N. cease-fire line was established on January 5, 1949; even after that, the bulk of the army remained stationed near the Pakistan boundary. Since 1952, a number of contingents have been used continuously to suppress the insurrection of the Naga tribesmen in Assam—a reminder of the potential importance of the army if any other section of the country should try to secede from the Indian Union or if serious civil disturbances of any kind should break out on the home front.

In 1961, the Indian Army seized Goa in an operation involving the coordination of sizable forces and resulting in a rather impressive display against practically no resistance. It has also accepted a number of international assignments—in the Congo, in Vietnam and Laos, in the Gaza Strip, in Lebanon, and in Korea. Some of these have involved contingents of troops, some only a few selected officers. Although India would not take part in the Allied military intervention in Korea in 1950, it consented to have an Indian serve as Chairman of the Neutral Nations' Repatriation Commission in Korea from 1953 to March, 1954. An Indian custodian force took charge of the prisoners of war while they were questioned as to whether or not they wished to return to their country of origin.

Since independence, the segregation of enlisted men according to religion, caste, and geographical origin has been modified only slightly. Language barriers, food habits, and other such considerations make this necessary. Enlistment has no longer been confined, however, to the particular castes or groups which the British listed as the "martial races" and to which they confined enlistments. The officers are assigned to units without regard to geographical origin, caste, or religion. Fluent in English and national in their outlook, they cement the army together.

Far more Westernized and Western in their habits of thought than even the average educated Indian, the officer group has retained many hallowed regimental customs stemming from British days. The formal regimental mess, with a solemn toast (previously to the King, now to the President of India), the ban on any mention of work or women at the mess, the meticulous performance of formal ceremonies such as "beating retreat" and the unveiling of new flags—all these illustrate the hold of memories stemming from Sandhurst days and from the admiration of British officers. There has been public criticism of this traditionalism as unsuited to the army of a free India. But while officers trained by the British remain in command, it seems likely to persist.

The change in thinking caused by the Chinese invasion of 1962 was dramatic and electric. Nehru himself was prompt to admit that the Indian reliance on peaceful coexistence had been an unrealistic dream. On October 25, 1962, he said: "We were getting out of touch with reality in the modern world and we were living in an artificial atmosphere of our own creation. We have been shocked out it, all of us, whether it is the government or the people." Then, comparing the Indian situation to that of the British after Dunkirk, Nehru said: "A whole British army in France was wiped out. They [the British] were a great people under a great leader, Mr. Winston Churchill. They started building anew . . . and ultimately defeated the enemy. We have to function like that."[8]

Following Nehru's leadership, India set out to build a strong, modern, well-trained defense force. Accordingly, the sums budgeted for defense were almost tripled in the three years following the 1962 invasion. Y. B. Chavan, who replaced V. K. Krishna Menon as Defense Minister at the time of the invasion, announced a six-point defense program:

1) An increase in the size of the army to 825,000 men, and the equipment of the army with modern weapons and matériel.

2) An increase of the air force to 45 squadrons and the acquisition of substantial numbers of transport planes, helicopters, and jet fighters.

3) Rapid improvement of roads in the areas near the Chinese border.

4) A phased program for the replacement of over-age ships in the navy.

5) Development of factories for defense production with the objective of eventually providing all the planes, arms, and ammunition needed through domestic manufacture.

6) Improvement of defense organization and training.

Estimates of the extent to which India had accomplished these objectives by 1965 varied. According to Hanson Baldwin, the well-known military analyst of *The New York Times*, the air force had been increased to about 400–450 combat planes. (The Pakistani air force at that time consisted of 150–200 American-made combat planes, faster and more modern than most of the Indian planes.[9])

Most of the Indian planes were jets, but not supersonic. They included British Canberra tactical bombers, British Hunter fighters, light British Gnat fighters, French Mystère fighters, and 12 recent-vintage supersonic Soviet MIG-21's. India also had acquired perhaps 200 or more transport planes, including 90 American C-119's and 50 American C-47's, an unknown number of Soviet AN-12 heavy transports, some Canadian medium transports, and some Soviet MI-4 helicopters.

In the 1950's, India had begun the "progressive manufacture" of her own air-force planes. She started by assembling imported parts at two airplane factories: at Bangalore in south India and at Kanpur in the Ganges Valley. Since then, components of these planes—mostly British in design—have been produced in India, and several other airplane factories have been erected. But so far, India is able to make only transport planes and lightweight fighters.

In the summer of 1962, the Soviet Union promised to aid India in the manufacture within India of MIG supersonic fighters. After the Chinese invasion that autumn, the Soviet Union delayed further consideration of the matter for about a year and a half, then resumed discussions. By 1965, it had been agreed that three interrelated factories would be needed to produce the MIG's, and that the Soviet Union would proceed to help India build them. But it is doubtful that construction of these factories will be completed before 1968.

As for the expansion of the army, more than enough men volunteered for enlistment, so a draft was unnecessary. Although the target of 825,000 equipped and trained men may not have been quite reached by 1965, well-informed observers believed that the army was very nearly that size at the time of the outbreak of war with Pakistan. (Pakistan enlisted strength was estimated at about 230,000.)

Of India's new divisions, a number (perhaps six) had been

especially equipped and trained for mountain warfare of the type necessary if the Chinese were to be fought again at the Himalayan border. Military aid from the United States and the United Kingdom had helped equip these—for example, with self-loading rifles, machine guns, and light long-range mortars. To accustom the soldiers to mountain conditions, these regiments were kept at high altitudes for extended periods, while their officers had them test out various new tactical concepts of mountain warfare on the actual terrain that would be involved. In short, by 1965, India had made determined and systematic efforts to prepare herself for a new war against the Chinese.

As further military aid from the United States, India had received radar and other air-defense equipment, road-building machinery, the transport aircraft mentioned above, communications equipment, and a grant for the purchase of vehicles. (She did not, however, receive the American supersonic jet fighter planes Defense Minister Chavan had asked for.) But the total value of American military aid actually delivered before the outbreak of the Indo-Pakistan war was estimated at only $80 million, as against $1.5 billion American military aid to Pakistan since 1954.[10]

Although the Indo-Pakistan war broke out over the disputed mountain state of Kashmir, the fighting soon shifted to the flat plains to the south and became largely an engagement of tanks and planes, with each side claiming the destruction of large numbers of the other's tanks and planes. Although analysts considered that the Indian armed forces (on the ground and in the air, and including equipment) probably had a three-to-one or at least a two-to-one superiority over the Pakistan forces,[11] about twelve of her estimated sixteen divisions were believed to be stationed along the Chinese border, and would probably have to remain there.[12] In the first three weeks of fighting, India not only checked Pakistan aggression, but managed to advance into Pakistan territory. Yet it was clear that it would be impossible for India to fight successfully against both her hostile neighbors at once. Hence the popular demand for a still greater increase in the defense forces.

18 • CONCLUSION

THE GROWING realization of the pivotal importance of the Indian subcontinent in world politics makes it more essential to comprehend the underlying factors in the total Indian scene. Whatever the immediate results and long-term effects of the confrontation with Pakistan and China (and they may be great), India will carry with her into the future a cultural personality, a complex individuality formed in the past—in the various ages of the distant past, as well as in more recent years. For a society is truly an organism, as strangely wonderful as that of human beings—body, mind, and soul united in a unique whole—but on a far larger scale.

The innumerable deposits of history (invasions, old empires, regional kingdoms, periods of confusion and other periods of the highest culture), the resilience of Hinduism and the continuing hold of the Hindu way of life, the ever-present reality of six minority religions, the attraction (for some) of Western techniques and ways of thought, the tenacity of the caste system and the evolution of new interrelationships within it, the groping for social equality, the wide gamut of educational levels (from illiteracy to the most modern scientific research), the Western governmental framework, the political background and forces so distinctly non-Western, the proliferation of parties, the poverty and the drive toward national economic development, the bullock carts and the blast furnaces, the tiny villages and the sprawling cities—all these and many more disparate elements, some tangible, some intangible, are elements in India's cultural personality. Within such an inherited culture, the 490 million Indians go on acting and reacting, suffering and striving, choosing and avoiding choices, loving and hating—each in his own way, as do individuals everywhere. But if the individual is always to some extent unpredictable, a society as a whole is even more so.

It may be useful to summarize some of the recent pre-war trends in Indian society while pulling together the threads of this book. The chief trend, of course, has been toward change—from the old, traditional, hierarchical, other-worldly, religion-based view of life toward one which, while still rooted in India's past, will reflect increasingly the whole complex of ideas, values, and technology originally borrowed from the West. How fast will the transition be? How much will be taken from the West permanently, now that India is free to choose? If the contrast between the old and the new were only a matter of technology, the answer would be clear. India is adopting as much of Western industrial technology as she can afford to do and as quickly as possible.

But in agriculture, the old techniques tend to linger, partly because 75 million peasant families are hard to reach and to teach, partly because small peasant holdings do not lend themselves to Western techniques designed for larger-scale farming. Yet science-based methods and tools of a simpler nature, adapted to Indian conditions—with field-well pumps, iron or steel plows, fertilizers, and selected seeds—are gradually replacing India's old, laborious, wasteful agricultural methods. This change, however, will inevitably take far more time than Indian planners expected or hoped. The inertia that must be overcome has deep roots. The belief in fate, in karma, and in reincarnation has obvious attractions for those who are very poor. To place less reliance on such consolations and instead take a more active and inquisitive interest in improving agriculture may be something that only the well-to-do peasants can face doing, until the visible material benefits of better agriculture (as practiced by richer neighbors) outweighs the invisible emotional benefits of a life based on nonattachment to worldly goods.

Thus, perhaps there can be no rapid and significant technological change in the countryside until the old attitudes that underlie the old techniques are vigorously and skillfully attacked. But to make a deliberate attack on a person's beliefs and fundamental attitudes is contrary to the very essence of Hinduism, its wide tolerance and acceptance of various levels of belief. Below the surface, many Indians, even Westernized ones, may perhaps feel a certain reluctance to attempt any major change in rural traditionalism.

While slow but essential changes occur in the countryside, India's educated leaders have been concerned with the basic principles of the very direction of change. Apart from technology, what of the rest of the Western tradition with which British rule put them in contact? How should they choose between or fuse Western and Indian ideas and values? And what, after all, is truly Indian? What are Indians really like as a people? What is their peculiar genius? Countless educated Indians are deeply absorbed in searching for the answers to these questions. Some turn to Indian history, subjecting it to new scrutiny and study. A pioneer in this was Nehru himself, whose famous book *The Discovery of India,* written while he was in jail in 1943, is a broad, colorful, and vivid study of India's history. A leading Muslim essay is that of Humayun Kabir, *The Indian Heritage.*

Besides scholarly works, there has been a proliferation of new histories in which the authors rewrite the past, reflecting in it their own beliefs as to what India should be in the future. Whatever the merit of particular books, this new searching of the past is a natural outgrowth of the deep conviction that under British rule Indians were virtual slaves, unable to be their true selves, required by their British masters to Westernize social customs and learn Western knowledge. According to this line of reasoning, the true nature of India and of Indians must be sought in the history of the centuries before the British conquest.

Other educated Indians, more reconciled to Western influence, argue that for better or worse some part of the Western heritage is now truly theirs. They argue, indeed, that the very essence of Indianness is the ability to assimilate and fuse. They cite the first great fusion of Aryan and Dravidian elements, then point to the many subsequent absorptions of new ethnic strands from outside. They may even argue (particularly if they are Muslims) that India produced a great new synthesis after the Muslim invasions, with Hinduism influenced by Islam and vice versa. (The actual degree of mutual influence between the two religions is a subject of debate among scholars.) Similarly, they hold, it is India's genius to incorporate in Indian life and culture the best of what has been learned from the West, yet to hold fast to the best that India had before the Westerners came.

Among the Western values that seem to have come to India to stay, the foremost is the ideal of social equality. Whatever may happen, no caste or group can any longer make good a claim to have a vested right to superiority. And as long as votes count, the Indian Government will have to pay at least something more than lip service to the principle of social equality in order to stay in office.

Yet this principle continues to rest uneasily side by side with the Hindu concept of hierarchy. Trends resulting from this juxtaposition include the diminishing consciousness of caste barriers among the wealthy and the educated, a decrease in discrimination against the lowest castes or untouchables, but a constant jockeying for position among many middle and lower castes, and the increasing role of caste in politics, as the various castes seek to use the political process to raise their position by developing their economic advantage and power. A prominent British political scientist has made the comment that under the influence of caste and linguistic pressures, Indian politics is taking on much of the nature of the American and Canadian political "pork barrels"—a useful reminder that human nature has much in common the world over, despite great cultural differences.

Besides social equality among castes and other groups, the trend is toward increasing equality of the sexes, but still within the context of the formal recognition of the husband as a highly superior personage—so superior and so close to being godlike that most Indian women, including many Westernized ones, will not even speak his name, referring to him always simply as "he."

Another significant Western idea—that of individualism, individual responsibility and decision-making, as opposed to group or family solidarity—still meets great resistance, although the trend seems to be toward its partial, if reluctant, acceptance. Should the members of the younger generation be self-reliant, or should they accept strict discipline as a matter of course? Should they take it for granted that they will enter the family business or trade and be sheltered by family loyalties, or should they choose their occupation and make their own way in the world? Should they find their own mates, or regard marriage as a rightful concern of the family as a whole? These questions affecting the very core of personal life are naturally the most difficult to decide. Many Indians are ambivalent about them.

The concept of the family as the essential unit still remains, on the whole, far stronger than the concept of the individual, and it is doubtful that Indians will soon give up or lose their close family ties and solidarity. At the same time, however, increasing numbers of young Indians have begun to rebel against authority —against the parent, who has traditionally made every decision for the child and often would not even brook argument, and against the dogmatic, dictatorial teacher, who has required the pupil to memorize and "learn" without questioning. But, while rebelling, young Indians have not yet fully grasped the important fact that true individualism requires also that the individual give up his dependence on the authority and become increasingly self-reliant and responsible for his own life and thoughts. These young Indians may disobey and even defy their parents as an earlier generation would not have done. They may even go on strike in protest against their teachers. Still, they often expect their parents to shelter them indefinitely, and their teachers not only to get them through their examinations with a minimum of effort on their part, but also, in effect, to tell them what to think.

Even when they have become quite mature in years, lower-middle-class Indians seem to retain a certain fear of thinking their own thoughts, of reaching their own conclusions—apparently since these conclusions might differ from those of some imaginary person who might know more and therefore be more of an authority. Yet, an encouraging sign is that at least some Indians have begun to recognize their ambivalence about authority. In a recent issue of the Indian magazine *Seminar*, an expert on education called attention to this fear of thinking.[1] Another writer, in the same issue, expressed the present dilemma of the individual:

> The old joint family security and its traditional authority is fast disappearing but we are not sure of our new function and our exact

place in the sun. . . . Authority now appears like a blundering patriarch who is either obeyed unthinkingly or cursed indiscriminately for failing to please or pamper. The result is . . . impotent anger. . . . One is either a rat or a rebel until one outgrows the psychology of childish dependence and learns to . . . feel secure in risk and responsibility.[2]

Periods of sharp transition are no easier for a society than they are for an individual—perhaps harder. The many members of the society who feel insecurity and anxiety in the face of rapidly changing values are made all the more uncomfortable by the many evidences they see that similar problems are being experienced by those around them. Certainly, many of the Western-educated Indian males of today under thirty or even thirty-five years of age tend to be confused, frustrated, anxious, even angry. Their faces have by no means the serenity either of their elders or of their contemporaries in the villages who have not been so greatly exposed to change, through education or otherwise.

One can scarcely speak of any aspect of Indian life without mentioning problems. They are real and concrete, as well as psychological. Apart from the pressing problem of defense against two hostile neighbors, some of the most acute problems seem to be in the areas of education, language, economics, and politics.

India has aimed at a far more rapid diffusion of education than occurred in any Western country. The quantitative increase since independence has been great. The number of universities and colleges has tripled since independence, and the number of students in higher education has increased sevenfold. Secondary education has also undergone a marked expansion, and the government has still more actively promoted the goal of free primary education for all. The rate of literacy has risen from about 15 per cent to about 25 per cent of the population.

But while educational facilities have expanded, quality has lagged. Teacher-training has been too slow, and teachers' salaries have remained so low that, as one Indian has put it, "The teaching profession has become the last resort of the unemployed."[3]

A complete revaluation of Indian education is now under way, with the aid of foreign experts. This will undoubtedly lead to changes. But three great obstacles to any real improvements remain: One is budgetary, another human, the third linguistic.

India is so poor that the money available for educational improvement cannot fail to be far less than is needed. In 1961–62, only about $200 million was spent on education in the entire nation.[4] (With a population less than half that of India, the United States spends 200 times that amount per year on education.) Yet, this amount included as much as a fifth of the budgets of all the Indian states. It would be hard to increase this budgetary allotment because of the many other urgent programs competing with education for limited government funds: among them, defense, population control, agricultural improvement, industrial development, housing for the unhoused.

The human obstacle to the qualitative improvement of education lies in the fact that the vast majority of teachers are so accustomed to the old sterile, authoritarian method of lecturing, of requiring rote learning, and of discouraging discussion that there is a lack of teachers who can train new teachers how to teach in a more creative way.

The language problem makes better education all the more difficult. As the regional languages have increasingly supplanted English in the secondary schools, more and more young people have entered college ill-equipped to read even slowly the English textbooks still used at the college level or to understand the lectures of their professors.

The decline in the study of English and the political pressures on behalf of the regional languages have been such that in 1965 a general understanding was reached that the regional languages should become the medium of instruction at the college level (as well as the secondary level) as soon as possible. But before this can be done, textbooks must be translated and printed in a dozen languages ill-suited to convey modern technological meanings. This colossal and expensive task will further eat into the limited funds available for education.

Quite apart from its impact on education, the language problem has wider and even more serious implications for the future. More and more young Indians are growing up unable to communicate with Indians of other parts of the country except through interpreters. Some nations, of course, have succeeded in maintaining national unity without a single common language. Trilingual Switzerland is one example; and in Asia, the Philippines, Indonesia, and Ceylon are linguistically diversified. But no nation except the Soviet Union has so complex a language problem as India, and totalitarianism in the Soviet Union has masked linguistic difficulties.

Although English has never been known by more than 1–2 per cent of the Indian population, it has served as a common language at least for the elite. Its deterioration and partial abandonment mean the destruction of an invaluable link. An effort has been made to promote the study of Hindi by people of other language groups, so that in time it might serve as a new common link. But the 1961 census showed that the process had not gone far: Hindi was known to only 1.8 per cent of the people whose mother tongue was not Hindi, and most of this 1.8 per cent consisted of people residing in or near the Hindi-speaking area. In the states of Kerala and Madras, for example, as few as 0.2 per cent could speak Hindi.[5] (According to this 1961 census report on language—not released until 1965—Hindi was known to only 32 per cent of the population, as compared with a figure of 42 per cent generally given previously by Hindi enthusiasts.)

Fear of economic and political domination by the speakers of Hindi is far more serious in south India than the Hindi-speaking north has yet recognized. Secession is not discussed openly—since the government has made the advocacy of secession a criminal offense. But if free discussion of the issue were possible, secession might be a real political issue, at least in Madras, at any time when the nation is not keyed up against some outside power.

On the economic front, some advance has been achieved between 1950 and 1965, but there are danger signals that do not portend well for the future. Still predominantly an agricultural nation, India has made rapid strides toward industrialization, has achieved some growth in agricultural yields, and has managed a 20 per cent increase in the average per capita income. In the various forms of social and economic overhead necessary for growing industrialization—railroads, roads, civilian airplane services, electric power, telephone and telegraph facilities, managerial talent, and skilled labor—India has a distinct advantage over most of the other "underdeveloped" nations, although the further development of all these is necessary if industry is to continue to expand.

While the government has taken a prominent role in economic development, private enterprise has continued to exist and even sometimes to prosper in India's mixed economy. Besides the publicly owned projects, a host of flourishing new privately owned industries have sprung up. And all over the country, on a smaller scale, resourceful individual entrepreneurs, with the simplest machinery and equipment, have found profitable niches for themselves in the over-all pattern of production.

But despite economic progress and the new air of bustle and activity in many centers, widespread poverty remains, and countless millions are truly destitute. The figures of 15 million totally unemployed, and 50 to 60 million man-years wasted per year at present in partial or total unemployment, are most disturbing, particularly in view of the fact that they represent a steady increase in unemployment over the past fifteen years, rather than a decrease.

Although India has plans for a greatly increased drive for family planning, this cannot hope to affect the unemployment situation in the foreseeable future. Even if no children at all were born in India from now on—obviously out of the question—the potential labor force would continue to grow every year until those who are now infants reached working age.

In spite of the best that family planning may achieve, some Indians have begun to wonder how long India can manage to provide the wherewithal even to keep her millions alive. In recent years, she has had to rely on increasing imports of foreign grain. Even if the rate of population growth can be decreased substantially, it is unlikely that it can be held stationary—except, of course, by mass famine, the specter that Indians fear.

As the population grows, there will be increasing dependence on food-grain imports, unless agricultural production can be steadily stepped up. Although there has been proof, in selected areas, that great increases of agricultural output are possible if all the needed "inputs" are brought together at once (fertilizers, better seeds, irrigation, skilled agricultural extension services, and the like), it will be a colossal job to achieve this on a nationwide scale.

For one thing, the manufacture of fertilizers in India is by no means adequate, and the shortage of foreign exchange (growing steadily more acute since 1957) limits the amount of fertilizers that can be bought from outside. This foreign-exchange shortage hampers India in other ways, too. With her reserves so diminished that she cannot afford to deplete them further, India can now buy from abroad no more in value than she exports—indeed, far less than this, since her external debt has grown so large that an increasing percentage of the foreign exchange earned by exports is required just to service her past borrowings. Unless she should receive a moratorium on repayment of the principal, $240 million of debt servicing was due to be subtracted in 1965 from her foreign-exchange earnings, which have run to about $350 million a year.

India's own foreign-exchange earnings have been greatly augmented in recent years by foreign aid. She hopes for the continuance of this aid, but since most of it tends to be in the form of loans, not grants, it has the disadvantage of increasing her total external debt.

Even with foreign aid, India has not had as much foreign exchange as she has needed—even in peacetime—and has constantly faced difficult choices as to how to allocate the foreign exchange available to her. Should she import food to decrease hunger today, or import fertilizers in the hope of decreasing it more tomorrow? Should she try to begin the manufacture within India of substitutes for various other kinds of imports essential to defense or to industry, and thus save foreign exchange in the future? If she does, these new industries will eat up precious foreign exchange today. Caught in such dilemmas, India seems to have no alternative but to go into debt still further—as far as her creditors will allow.

Meanwhile, her efforts to improve her situation through the Five-Year Plans have had certain unfortunate side effects. To finance the plans, she has raised tax rates repeatedly and often. As tax rates have gone up, the incentive to evade taxes has increased. This has been particularly true in the case of income taxes; in India, incomes are received in cash much more often than by check, which makes tax evasion easy. The total undeclared income (known in India as "black money") since 1945 has been estimated at $7 billion.[6] Only about 2 million persons have been paying income taxes, although perhaps five times that number have taxable incomes. (A tax is payable on all nonagricultural incomes over $400 a year for single persons and $700 for couples. Agricultural incomes are exempt from income tax, but there is a land tax that is less easily evaded.)

Unable to finance her plans through taxation, the government has resorted to deficit financing. This has led to serious inflation, which has hurt especially the lower middle classes living on fixed incomes. (Employees in factories and other large establishments often receive "dearness allowances"—i.e., cost-of-living allowances—which tend to lessen but not eliminate the effect of inflation upon them.) Although, statistically, national income rose in fifteen years, those who gained were apparently the peasants with the maximum landholdings permitted by law, and more especially the upper middle classes—entrepreneurs or traders, who used the price trend as an excuse for still greater rises in their own selling prices and whose type of work made tax evasion easy.

Rising prices, rising taxes, rising unemployment have led to widespread dissatisfaction. Hundreds of thousands of office workers, who had been led by the plans to hope for a better life, felt instinctively that something was wrong. What (they asked one another) was happening to all the money, supposedly being spent for economic improvement? It was not benefiting them. Many of them angrily felt it was lining the pockets of high government officials.

Charges of corruption multiplied. In 1964, in the case of three former chief ministers of states, the evidence of corruption seemed clear. (Shastri ordered no formal inquiries or court proceedings against these individuals—partly on the grounds that, since they were now out of office, no useful purpose could be served, and partly on the grounds that in any case a federal government could not interfere in this way in state matters.)

The fact that the government seemed willing to gloss over charges of corruption increased public cynicism—particularly in the big cities—about politicians and the government in general. As the government has assumed greater and greater responsibilities

—not only in the administration and in the regulation of the private sector of the economy, but also in the actual construction and operation of large publicly owned plants and factories—the opportunities for corruption have, of course, multiplied.

In recent years, the power of the central government in relation to the states has continued to grow, partly because of the latter's financial dependence on the Centre and partly as a result of the Centre's increased use of the emergency powers vested in the central executive branch by the Constitution itself. Under special Defense of India Rules announced in 1962 at the time of the Chinese invasion, but not later revoked, the government has imprisoned Communists and other opponents of the existing regime, not only without trial, but also without even the statement of the causes of the arrest which had been required by earlier preventive detention acts.

The government's emergency powers, if ever used to the extreme permitted by the Constitution, could lead to completely authoritarian rule, with all freedoms suspended—though with Parliament at least nominally entitled to call a halt to the use of the emergency powers.

In 1965, two distinguished army generals, one of them a retired commander-in-chief of the Indian Army, openly urged the President of India to use his emergency powers to place the government in the hands of a council not subject to Parliamentary control—in other words to dismiss Parliament indefinitely. They urged this on the grounds that Communism was spreading and needed to be stamped out firmly. They also argued that a council not subject to political pressures would be able to deal with the economic situation more effectively.

Until the general elections of 1967, it will be impossible to know whether Communism is in fact spreading, in terms of popular support, and if it is, whether the left or the right wing of the Communist Party has gained the more thereby. By the autumn of 1965, however, it seemed apparent that the left-wing Communists had decided not to rely on elections alone but rather to embark on an underground campaign to promote disorder, dissatisfaction, and finally insurrection. The violent month-long student strike over language in Madras in 1965 showed signs that well-trained professional agitators had a hand in it somewhere. Then, too, the Home Minister of the Government of India announced that he had proof of Communist plans for insurrection, although he declined to divulge details of the proof. Furthermore, the left-wing Communists themselves announced that the basic units of their organization would be cells consisting of not more than eleven persons each—a form of organization strongly suggestive of secret activities by small, close-knit groups.

So far as elections are concerned, it is doubtful whether either wing of the Communist Party will do as well in the future as the united Party did in the past. The other two chief opposition parties, the Swatantra and the Jana Sangh, have similarly shown no signs of gaining significant ground. The Congress Party still dominates the political scene.

In every national election through 1962, the Congress Party has won more than 70 per cent of the seats in the central Parliament. Indeed, it has been so strong that the Indian Government has functioned almost on a one-party basis. The opposition was, and is, too fragmented to provide the clear-cut check on the ruling party that is taken for granted in the two-party system.

Especially after Nehru's death, the Congress Party seemed for a while badly divided into factions at both the national and the state levels. At least at the national level, much of this factionalism seemed to be wiped out by the almost unanimous enthusiasm for the Indo-Pakistan war. The crucial point to watch is whether this factionalism reasserts itself as the war fever abates.

In the states, divisions within the Congress Party tend to be based on caste or religious rather than ideological differences. (Christians form the backbone of the dissident Congress group within Kerala, while two castes of Hindus dominate the other half of the party.) Control of the party machine in a state means control over lucrative jobs and other forms of patronage. The struggle for party patronage is therefore waged in grim earnest. Each faction seeks to control the nomination of as many candidates for Parliament and for the state assemblies as possible.

When factions within a state cannot themselves compromise their differences regarding candidates, the decision is made at the national headquarters of the party. In all cases, the central election committee of the party has the nominal right to decide who the candidates will be, but it normally exercises this right only when factions cannot agree. This will suggest how greatly Congress politics in the states depend on the national leadership, and how severely they would be affected by any serious rift in that leadership.

In one state, Kerala, the split between factions that occurred in 1964 was so bitter and complete that even the intervention of the Congress "high command" (a handful of the top national leaders) was unable to bridge the gap. In the 1965 state elections, the two factions supported two rival slates of candidates. After the election, the "regular" Congress Party refused to join with the dissident "Kerala Congress Party" to form the government of the state. Together, the two Congress factions had won the election, but because of their antagonism, they in effect lost it, and Kerala was again placed under President's Rule.

Other states where there has been intense factionalism in the party include Gujerat, Madhya Pradesh, Mysore, Orissa, the Punjab, Uttar Pradesh, and West Bengal. But so far, in none of these has the rift become absolute, as it did in Kerala.

Before the war-induced harmony of 1965, the great danger seemed to be that factionalism in the national leadership of the party was reaching a point where one or another national leader, rival to Shastri, might try to mobilize support from within dissident state factions, thus giving factionalism national dimensions.

The central leadership seemed to consist of a left wing, a right wing, and a middle-of-the-road group—the last headed by Shastri. Members of both the left and the right wings were often openly critical of steps proposed by the middle-of-the-road group—that is, by the government their own party had formed. Thus they encouraged, and on certain issues even supported, one opposition party or another. The left-wing group, especially, seemed to differ hardly at all from the right wing of the Communist Party. (On issues such as the language question, which could have an effect on the balance of power between regions, members of Congress in Parliament have tended to line up according to regional interest rather than ideology. And certain sharp personal rivalries within Congress have further confused the picture.)

But, as mentioned above, in the autumn of 1965, this factionalism at the national level seemed to disappear. If it should reappear, and if each faction should seek the support of factions within the states (as would be only natural), the result might be intolerable political instability. No segment of the old Congress Party (or any other of India's many parties) would be likely to win a clear majority. In this case, cabinet rule would necessarily require a coalition of parties, each of which might be constantly tempted to improve its situation by shifting to some new coalition, thus upsetting the rule of the existing cabinet.

In several neighboring Asian countries (including Pakistan), chronic cabinet instability has led to outright military dictatorship. Similarly, in India, any serious condition of political instability (or grave military danger) would probably lead to firm action. Because of the constitutional provisions, this would not necessarily require a military coup (as in Pakistan). It could be achieved by a simple declaration of President's Rule. Army support for such action would, of course, increase the firmness of President's Rule. The Indian Army has traditionally been nonpolitical, but under emergency conditions it would undoubtedly favor authoritarian rule.

But a split within the Congress Party would not be the only road to authoritarian rule. If the party remains undivided and dominant, the continuance of democracy will depend upon the state of mind of its national leaders—specifically, their willingness to let opposition groups or parties in the states exist and express themselves. The jailing of Communist leaders in Kerala before the 1965 elections, though an interference with the democratic process, may be a kind of interference with which Westerners are apt to sympathize—since Communists in so many nations have treated their opponents in the same fashion. But this is by no means the only example of the increasingly tight control of state affairs by the central government. To a greater extent than ever before, the Indo-Pakistan war made dissent seem synonymous with treason, as so often happens in a nation at war. The suppression of civil liberties within Kashmir and the arrest of opposition leaders following the U.N. cease-fire of 1965 suggested that the Congress party itself could be tempted to impose completely authoritarian rule in any parts of India where opposition to its policies gained significant strength.

Even if authoritarian rule should not be instituted, it is doubtful if democracy will ever function in India as it does in nations with quite different historic, religious, economic, social, and political backgrounds. The large number of parties and the overwhelming dominance of the Congress Party are not the only factors that have made democracy in India quite different from Western-style democracy. Poverty, illiteracy, distrust of political leaders (unless they are full-fledged saints that can be worshiped), the persistence of subservience (in the case of many) toward authority, plus other factors already noted affect the situation. Even Nehru, an architect of the present Constitution, once indicated that he had come to wonder whether Western democracy fitted Indian conditions. He said:

> Democracy is something deeper than a political form of government —voting, elections, etc. In the ultimate analysis it is a manner of thinking, a manner of action, a manner of behavior to your neighbor. . . . If the inner content is absent and you are just given the outer shell, well, it may not be successful. I do not know whether I am prepared to say that the same type of democratic institution is suited to every country. . . . In the final analysis, you come back not to political terms, not to economic terms, but to some human terms; or, if you like, spiritual terms.[7]

Nehru's statement contains no indication as to what form of government he then believed suitable for India. Perhaps he was not sure.

In any event, the deterioration of the economy in the mid-1960's, the new militancy of the left-wing Communists, the increasing dissatisfaction of the lower middle classes—many of them, no doubt, easy targets of Communist propaganda—and the critical problem of military defense placed new strains on India's own particular form or degree of democracy. A war situation creates stresses and strains in any country. In 1965, the Indian economy was ill-prepared to bear these strains.

In the long run, the great transition in which the rural masses are beginning to be involved—from an accepting to a striving attitude—is an emotional and psychological revolution of the first magnitude. Can the people on the land pass through that revolution of attitudes and still retain some of their old steadiness—enough steadiness not to turn restive and violent by the millions? The answer to this question is linked to the future growth of the Indian economy as a whole. When the now inarticulate masses begin actively to want and demand a decent living, will the Indian economy be ready and able to provide them with the opportunity to earn at least a little better livelihood than they earn today?

To pass through present dangers successfully, India will need large-scale economic aid from outside, in addition to whatever military aid the international situation may dictate.

In that situation, the unsolved and perhaps insoluble Kashmir problem seems likely to remain a prime explosive. At any moment that Pakistan believes she can count on greater military support from Communist China than she received in 1965—or, alternatively, on a more favorable attitude on the part of the Soviet Union—she would doubtless try again to take Kashmir by force of arms, thereby precipitating a major war. Kashmir has thus become a focal point in the curious triangular struggle between the United States, the Soviet Union, and China.

The West was sadly disillusioned in 1965 by the spectacle of Western military aid being used by Pakistan in the Indo-Pakistan war (and perhaps also by India, though this is not clear). Western nations did not want to choose between India and Pakistan. But such a choice seemed to have been forced by China's antagonism toward India, and by Pakistan's near-alliance with China.

India's need for substantial, perhaps massive, economic and military aid from the West in order to survive as a free non-Communist nation is no greater than the West's need to keep India within the free world. If Chinese armies driving southward should place in power and support a puppet Indian Communist government, or if India should fall behind the Bamboo or the Iron Curtain through any other set of circumstances, the loss to the free world would be at least as great as was that other great loss when the Communist armies overran China in the late 1940's.

In the shock of discovering how much it had suddenly shrunk, the free world would then realize, too late, the extent to which India's destiny is linked with that of the West. The free world cannot afford to let the largest democracy in the world be overrun. It cannot afford to let the South Asian peninsula, jutting deep into the Indian Ocean, fall into hostile hands which could use its location to cut the sea and air routes essential for trade and for the next line of defense against Communist aggression. To let India fall would be to let the rest of Asia fall, and perhaps to start an avalanche totally beyond control. Its cumulative results could scarcely fail to prove fatal to the nations of Western Europe and of North America. The essential line of defense for the West may well be in the high Himalayas. One only needs to glance at a map to see how hopelessly severed the non-Communist world would be if India should fall.

To help India defend herself would be a far more rewarding venture than some other Western interventions. No nation in Asia, Africa, or South America (with the exception of Japan) has as trained, as capable, as resolute a leadership group as has India. No nation around the perimeter of Communist China has as fine a defense force or (again with the exception of Japan) is as industrialized as India—hence as capable of producing at least some of its own defense equipment.

Although India is important to the West from a practical point of view, it has another kind of importance, perhaps equally great in a different way. Just as the fall of China with its centuries of high culture, its Temple of Heaven, and its endless other exquisite creations was an irreparable cultural loss to the free world, so, too, the subtraction of India from our lives would mean loss of contact with one of the greatest cultural traditions of the world.

NOTES

Chapter 1: Introduction

1. Nehru, *Toward Freedom* (New York: The John Day Company, 1941), p. 353.

Chapter 3: The Great Vista of India's Past

1. Nehru, *The Discovery of India* (New York: The John Day Company, 1946), p. 25.
2. *The Dhammapada,* chaps. XV, XVII, translated by F. Max Muller. Quoted in Lin Yutang (ed.), *The Wisdom of China and India* (New York: Random House, 1942), pp. 342, 344, 353.
3. Basham, *The Wonder That Was India* (London: Sidgwick and Jackson, 1954; New York: The Macmillan Co., 1955), p. 8.

Chapter 4: The Nature of the Muslim Period

1. Quoted in Stanley Lane-Poole, *Mediaeval India Under Mohammedan Rule* (Calcutta: Susil Gupta, 1951), I, 14.
2. Vincent A. Smith, *The Oxford History of India* (3d ed., edited by Percival Spear; London and New York: Oxford University Press, 1958), p. 238.
3. Percival Spear, *Twilight of the Mughals* (London: Cambridge University Press, 1951), p. 117.
4. Smith, *op. cit.*, p. 259.
5. Quoted in Lane-Poole, *op. cit.*, I, 148.
6. E. M. Edwardes and H. L. O. Garrett, *Mughal Rule In India* (Delhi: S. Chand & Co., 1956), p. 168.
7. Vincent A. Smith, *Akbar, The Great Mogul* (Oxford: Clarendon Press, 1917), p. 355.
8. Smith, *Oxford History of India,* p. 380.
9. Quoted in Edward Thompson and G. T. Garratt, *The Rise and Fulfillment of British Rule in India* (London: The Macmillan Co., 1934), p. 37.

Chapter 5: The Rise and Consolidation of British Rule

1. Quoted in Smith, *Oxford History of India,* p. 522.
2. *Ibid.*, p. 523.

3. Quoted in Thompson and Garratt, *op. cit.*, p. 199.
4. *Ibid.*
5. Letter of Henry Dundas to Lord Wellesley, dated March 18, 1799, Wimbledon, England. Manuscript in collection of Randall J. LeBoeuf, Jr., New York City.
6. Quoted in Kenneth Ballhatchet, *Social Policy and Social Change in Western India, 1817–1830* (London: Oxford University Press, 1957), p. 37.
7. Quoted in V. P. Menon, *The Integration of the Indian States* (New York: The Macmillan Co., 1956), p. 8.
8. Edward Thompson, *The Other Side of the Medal* (London: Hogarth Press, 1925), pp. 39–42.
9. P. 327.

Chapter 6: Toward Independence—And After

1. Quoted in Reginald Coupland, *The Indian Problem* (New York: Oxford University Press, 1944), p. 26.
2. Norman D. Palmer, "India," in George McTurnan Kahin (ed.), *Major Governments of Asia* (Ithaca, N.Y.: Cornell University Press, 1958), p. 258.
3. Palmer, *The Indian Political System* (Boston: Houghton Mifflin Co., 1961), p. 55.
4. B. R. Nanda, *Mahatma Gandhi* (Boston: Beacon Press, 1958), p. 19.
5. *Ibid.*, p. 20.
6. *Ibid.*, p. 21.
7. M. K. Gandhi, *An Autobiography, or the Story of My Experiments with Truth* (2nd ed.; Ahmedabad: Navajivan Publishing House, 1940), p. 92.
8. *Ibid.*, p. 90.
9. Nanda, *op. cit.*, p. 34.
10. R. C. Majumdar, H. C. Raychaudhuri, and Kalilinkar Datta, *An Advanced History of India* (London: Macmillan and Co., 1950), p. 987.
11. V. P. Menon, *Transfer of Power in India* (Princeton, N.J.: Princeton University Press, 1957), p. 294.
12. Reported to the author by several of Gandhi's friends, including B. G. Kher (in Bombay, on December 6, 1956).

Chapter 7: Hinduism—The Religion of the Majority

1. M. N. Srinivas, "A Note on Sanskritization and Westernization," *Far Eastern Quarterly*, Vol. XV, No. 4 (August, 1956).
2. *Ibid.*
3. The Right Reverend Henry Whitehead, *The Village Gods of South India* (London: Oxford University Press, 1921), p. 47.
4. Unpublished report of Gertrude Woodruff at the Conference of the Association of Asian Studies, March 23, 1959.
5. Stella Kramrish, "Traditions of the Indian Craftsman," in Milton Singer (ed.), *Traditional India: Structure and Change* (Philadelphia: American Folklore Society, 1959), p. 18.
6. Norvin Hein, "The Ram Lila," in Singer (ed.), *op. cit.*, p. 91.
7. See, for example, G. Morris Carstairs, *The Twice Born* (London: Hogarth Press, 1957), p. 158.

8. Radhagovinda Basak, "The Hindu Concept of the Natural World," in Kenneth W. Morgan (ed.), *The Religion of the Hindus* (New York: Ronald Press, 1953), p. 89.
9. Chandogya Upanishad 6.8.6., in *The Thirteen Principal Upanishads,* translated by R. E. Hume (London: Oxford University Press, 1934).
10. Quoted in Gertrude Sen, *Pageant of Indian History* (New York: Longmans, Green & Co., 1948), p. 56.
11. *Bhagavad Gita,* chap. II, verses 38, 71; translated by S. Radhakrishnan. Quoted in Sarvepalli Radhakrishnan and Charles A. Moore, *A Source Book in Indian Philosophy* (Princeton, N.J.: Princeton University Press, 1957), pp. 109, 112.
12. *Ibid.,* chap. VII, verses 6–11, p. 127.
13. In a speech before the Association of Asian Studies, New York, 1960.
14. Khushwant Singh, "India's Star Readers Again Ascend," *The New York Times Magazine,* April 22, 1962.
15. Radhakrishnan, *The Hindu View of Life* (London: George Allen and Unwin, 1927), pp. 70–71.
16. *Ibid.,* p. 71.
17. Northrop, *The Taming of the Nations* (New York: The Macmillan Co., 1952), *passim.*
18. Quoted in John N. Farquhar, *Modern Religious Movements in India* (New York: Macmillan & Co., 1910), p. 32.
19. Gandhi, *Hindu Dharma* (Ahmedabad: Navajivan Publishing House, 1950), p. 16.
20. *Ibid.,* p. 38.
21. *Ibid.,* p. 73.
22. *Ibid.,* p. 379.
23. *Ibid.,* p. 47.
24. *Ibid.,* pp. 102–123.
25. *Ibid.,* p. 43.
26. Sri Aurobindo, *The Life Divine* (Pondicherry: Sri Aurobindo Ashram, 1960), p. 45.
27. *Ibid.,* p. 493.
28. Milton Singer, "The Great Tradition in a Metropolitan Center: Madras," in Singer (ed.), *op. cit.,* p. 152.
29. V. Raghavan, "Introduction to the Hindu Scriptures," in Morgan (ed.), *op. cit.,* p. 275.

Chapter 8: The Religious Minorities

1. Quoted in Majumdar *et al., op. cit.,* p. 406.

Chapter 9: Caste, Family, and Social Change

1. K. M. Panikkar, *Hindu Society at the Crossroads* (Bombay: Asia Publishing House, 1955), p. 10.
2. Irawati Karve, *Hindu Society, An Interpretation* (Poona: Deccan College, 1961), *passim.*
3. John T. Hitchcock, "The Idea of the Martial Rajput," in Milton Singer (ed.), *op. cit.,* p. 14.
4. Robert C. North, "The Indian Council of Ministers: A Study of

Origins," in Richard L. Park and Irene Tinker (eds.), *Leadership and Political Institutions in India* (Princeton, N.J.: Princeton University Press, 1959), p. 110.

5. Dhananjay Keer, *Dr. Ambedkar: Life and Mission* (Bombay: A. V. Keer, 1954), pp. 14–23.
6. Helen Lamb, "The Indian Merchant," in Milton Singer (ed.), *op. cit.*, p. 26.
7. M. N. Srinivas, "A Note on Sanskritization and Westernization," *Far Eastern Quarterly*, XV, No. 4 (August, 1956), *passim.*
8. Indera Singh, "A Sikh Village," in Milton Singer (ed.), *op. cit.*, p. 281.
9. G. S. Ghurye, *Caste and Class in India* (Bombay: Popular Book Depot, 1950), pp. 192–93.
10. M. N. Srinivas, "Caste in Modern India," *The Journal of Asian Studies*, XVI, No. 4 (August, 1957).
11. Kamaladevi Chattopadhyay, "The Struggle for Freedom," in Tara Ali Baig (ed.), *Women of India* (New Delhi: Ministry of Information and Broadcasting, 1958), p. 25.
12. Dr. S. Chandrasekhar, quoted in Margaret Cormack, *She Who Rides a Peacock: Indian Students and Social Change* (New York: Frederick A. Praeger, 1962), p. 177.

Chapter 10: Language Barriers and Cultural Links

1. Summary of the 1965 census paper on language, in *Asian Recorder* (New Delhi), July 30–August 5, 1965.
2. *Young India*, April 21, 1920; quoted in Nirmal Kumar Bose, *Selections from Gandhi* (2nd ed.; Ahmedabad: Navajivan Publishing House, 1957), p. 286.

Chapter 11: Education: Problems and Progress

1. Kabir, *The Indian Heritage* (Bombay: Asia Publishing House, 1955), pp. 125–26.
2. H. Sharp (ed.), *Selections from Educational Records* (Calcutta: Superintendent of Government Printing, 1920), p. 111.
3. Quoted in Thompson and Garratt, *op. cit.*, p. 315.
4. The Earl of Ronaldshay, *Life of Lord Curzon* (New York: Boni and Liveright, 1928), II, 186.
5. Humayun Kabir, *Education in New India* (London: George Allen & Unwin, 1956), p. 16.
6. Author's interview in 1965 with Prem Kirpal, Secretary of Indian Ministry of Education.
7. John T. Reid, "A Dozen Problems of Indian Higher Education" (mimeographed; New Delhi, 1961), p. 41.
8. Government of India, *India, 1962*, p. 77.
9. Reid, *op. cit.*, p. 15.
10. Cormack, *op. cit.*, p. 194.
11. Reid, *op. cit.*, p. 18.
12. *Hindu Weekly Review* (Madras), XI, No. 43 (October 22, 1962), 6.
13. Government of India, *India, 1964*, p. 67; and Government of India, *Review of Education in India (1947–61)* (New Delhi: Ministry of Education, 1961), p. 916.

14. *India, 1962*, p. 77.
15. *Review of Education*, p. 792.
16. *Ibid.*, p. 802.
17. *Ibid.*, p. 808.
18. *India, 1962*, p. 77; and U.S. Department of Commerce, *Statistical Abstract of the United States, 1961*, p. 105.
19. *Review of Education*, p. 794.
20. *Ibid.*, p. 818.
21. *Ibid.*, p. 823.

Chapter 12: Nehru and India's Western-Type Government

1. Nehru, *Toward Freedom*, p. 56.
2. *Ibid.*, p. 126.
3. Quoted in Michael Brecher, *Nehru: A Political Biography* (London and New York: Oxford University Press, 1959), p. 138.
4. *Ibid.*, p. 275.
5. *Ibid.*, p. 227.
6. For a detailed account of Nehru's victory within his party, see Michael Brecher, *Nehru: A Political Biography* (New York and London: Oxford University Press, 1959), pp. 432–35.
7. Sharokh Sabavala, in *The Christian Science Monitor*, November 17, 1960.
8. Sham Lal, in *Seminar* (New Delhi), No. 63 (November, 1964).
9. Quoted in M. V. Pylee, *Constitutional Government in India* (New York: Asia Publishing House, 1960), p. 16.
10. Quoted in Hugh Tinker, "Tradition and Experiment in Forms of Government," in C. H. Philips (ed.), *Politics and Society in India* (New York: Frederick A. Praeger, 1963), p. 159.
11. *Ibid.*
12. G. N. Joshi, *The Constitution of India* (London: The Macmillan Co., 1952), p. 333.
13. Tinker, *loc. cit.*, p. 164.
14. David H. Bayley, "The Indian Experience with Preventive Detention," *Pacific Affairs* (Vancouver), XXXV, No. 2 (Summer, 1962), pp. 104, 105.
15. *Journal of the National Academy of Administration* (Government of India), July, 1960.
16. Government of India, *Report of the Team for the Study of Community Projects and National Extension Service* (New Delhi: Committee on Plan Projects, 1957), Vol. I, *passim*.
17. Palmer, *Indian Political System*, p. 153.
18. Myron Weiner, "The Struggle for Equality in India," *Foreign Affairs*, Vol. 40, No. 4 (July, 1962).

Chapter 13: The Indian Nature of Indian Politics

1. *India, 1962*, pp. 144 and 173.
2. *India, 1964*, p. 131.
3. *India, 1962*, p. 173.
4. *Symposium* (New Delhi), No. 22 (June, 1961).
5. *India News* (Embassy of India, Washington, D.C.), April 27, 1962.

6. Margaret W. Fisher and Joan D. Bondurant, *Indian Experience with Democratic Elections* (Indian Press Digests, Monograph Series, No. 3; Berkeley, Calif.: University of California, December, 1956), p. 6.
7. *Ibid.*, p. 4.
8. Palmer, *The Indian Political System*, p. 9.
9. Coupland, *op. cit.*, p. 87.
10. Sharokh Sabavala, in *The Christian Science Monitor*, November 2, 1960.
11. Cormack, *op. cit.*, p. 215.
12. S. L. Poplai (ed.), *National Politics and the 1957 Elections in India* (New Delhi: Diwan Chand Information Center, 1957), p. 1; Poplai (ed.), *1962 General Elections in India* (Bombay: Allied Publishers, 1962), pp. 410–13.
13. *India News*, April 27, 1962.
14. *Ibid.*
15. Poplai (ed.), *1962 General Elections*, p. 413; and *India News*, April 27, 1962.
16. Quoted in Fisher and Bondurant, *Indian Approaches to a Socialist Society* (Indian Press Digests, Monograph Series, No. 2; Berkeley, Calif.: University of California, July, 1956), p. 38.
17. *India News*, April 27, 1962; and Poplai (ed.), *1962 General Elections*, p. 413.
18. Gene D. Overstreet and Marshall Windmiller, *Communism in India* (Berkeley and Los Angeles, Calif.: University of California Press, 1959), p. 120.
19. *Ibid.*, p. 210.
20. *The New York Times*, May 1, 1962.
21. *India News*, April 27, 1962.
22. *Ibid.*
23. Poplai (ed.), *1962 General Elections*, p. 22.
24. *Hindu Weekly Review* (Madras), March 24, 1965.
25. Poplai (ed.), *1962 General Elections*, pp. 379–401.
26. *India News*, April 27, 1962.
27. Richard D. Lambert, "Hindu Communal Groups in Indian Politics," in Park and Tinker (eds.), *Leadership and Political Institutions in India*, p. 211–24.
28. Poplai (ed.), *1962 General Elections*, pp. 51–59.
29. *Ibid.*, p. 144.
30. *India News*, April 27, 1962.
31. *Ibid.*
32. *Ibid.*
33. Quoted in *The New York Times*, May 6, 1962.
34. *Hindu Weekly Review*, April 5, 1965.

Chapter 14: Villages and Cities

1. Information supplied to the author in February, 1965, by the Indian Ministry of Information and Broadcasting.
2. Government of India, *Third Five-Year Plan*, p. 673.
3. *India, 1964*, p. 318.
4. Nair, *Blossoms in the Dust* (New York: Frederick A. Praeger, 1962), pp. 194–95.

5. John E. Brush, "The Morphology of Indian Cities," in Roy Turner (ed.), *India's Urban Future* (Berkeley, Calif.: University of California Press, 1962), p. 64.
6. D. K. Rangnekar, *Poverty and Capital Development in India* (London: Oxford University Press, 1958), p. 181.
7. Government of India, *Report of the Ministry of Works, Housing, and Supply, Report for 1960–61*, November 1, 1961.

Chapter 15: Toward Economic Development

1. Government of India, *Third Five-Year Plan* (New Delhi, 1961), p. 55.
2. *Ibid*, pp. 1–19.
3. Government of India, *Pocketbook of Economic Information* (Ministry of Finance, 1961), p. 11.
4. Information supplied in January, 1957, by P. N. Thapar, then Secretary of the Ministry of Agriculture.
5. *India, 1962*, p. 230.
6. Government of India, *Report on India's Food Crisis and Steps to Meet It by the Agricultural Team Sponsored by the Ford Foundation* (Ministry of Food and Agriculture, 1959).
7. *Third Five-Year Plan*, p. 382.
8. Kusum Nair, *op. cit.*, p. 196.
9. *India, 1962*, p. 163.
10. *Ibid.*, p. 373.
11. Milton Friedman, quoted in P. T. Bauer, *Indian Economic Policy and Development* (New York: Frederick A. Praeger, 1961), pp. 83–84.
12. V. B. Karnik, *Indian Trade Unions: A Survey* (Bombay: Allied Publishers Private, 1960), p. 123.
13. Government of India, *Monthly Abstract of Statistics*, April, 1965, p. 69.
14. Information supplied to the author in March, 1965, by the Indian Ministry of Information and Broadcasting.
15. Information supplied to the author in February, 1965, by Robert Park, Ford Foundation, New Delhi.
16. *Second Five-Year Plan*, pp. 43–50.
17. *First Five-Year Plan*, p. 21; *Third Five-Year Plan*, p. 28.
18. G. L. Mehta (Chairman of the Governing Body, Indian Investment Centre), in a speech delivered in New York City, October 2, 1961.
19. U.S. Information Service, New Delhi, "Fact Sheet on U.S. Economic Assistance to India," mimeographed paper, February 8, 1965.
20. Eugene Black, "The World Bank's Role in India's Development," *India News* (Washington, D.C.: Embassy of India), January 26, 1963, p. 4.
21. Author's interview with John P. Lewis, U.S. AID Administrator in New Delhi, March 30, 1965.

Chapter 16: Foreign Policy and the Chinese Threat

1. Nehru, *India's Foreign Policy* (Indian Ministry of Information and Broadcasting, 1961), pp. 114–15.
2. *The New York Times*, December 3, 1955.
3. Phillips Talbot and S. L. Poplai, *India and America* (New York: Harper & Brothers, 1958), p. 41.

4. Nehru, *India's Foreign Policy,* p. 89.
5. Hector Abhayawardhana, "Ceylon," in *Seminar* (New Delhi), No. 37 (September, 1962) pp. 32–36.
6. *The New York Times,* April 3, 1956.
7. Nehru, *India's Foreign Policy,* p. 352.
8. Hanson Baldwin, in *The New York Times,* October 27, 1962.
9. *The New York Times,* November 7, 1962.
10. *Ibid.,* October 29, 1962.
11. Hanson Baldwin, *loc. cit.*
12. *The New York Times,* October 22, 1962.
13. *Ibid.,* November 4, 1962.
14. Nehru, *India's Foreign Policy,* p. 339.
15. *Ibid.,* p. 435.

Chapter 17: The Defense Forces and Their British Background

1. "Adequate 'Insurance,'" in *Seminar* (New Delhi), No. 35 (July, 1962), p. 14.
2. *India, 1962,* pp. 72, 202, and 204.
3. "Facing Facts," in *Seminar,* No. 35 (July, 1962), p. 28.
4. Majumdar *et al., op. cit.,* p. 930.
5. *Ibid.,* p. 969.
6. Chattar Singh Samra, "Subhas Chandra Bose: An Indian National Hero," in Park and Tinker (eds.), *op. cit.,* pp. 76–77.
7. Nandan Prasad, *Expansion of the Armed Forces and Defense Organization* (Calcutta: Orient Longmans, 1956), p. 187.
8. Quoted in *The Hindu* (Madras), October 26, 1962.
9. *The New York Times,* September 9, 1965.
10. *Ibid.,* September 8, 1965.
11. *The Christian Science Monitor,* September 10, 1965.
12. *The New York Times,* September 10, 1965.

Chapter 18: Conclusion

1. L. Chatterjee, "Text Books," in *Seminar* (New Delhi), No. 71 (July, 1965).
2. M. Y. Ghorpade, "A Change of Approach," in *ibid.*
3. *Ibid.*
4. *India, 1964,* p. 64.
5. *Asian Recorder* (New Delhi), July 30–August 5, 1965.
6. *The New York Times,* June 4, 1965.
7. Quoted in Hugh Tinker, "Tradition and Experiment in Forms of Government," in Philips, *op. cit.,* p. 177.

BIBLIOGRAPHY*

Chapter 2: The Indian Setting

Davies, C. Collins. *An Historical Atlas of the Indian Peninsula.* London: Oxford University Press, 1949.

Panikkar, K. M. *Geographical Factors in Indian History.* Bombay: Bharatiya Vidya Bhavan, 1955.

Platt, Raye R. (ed.). *India: A Compendium.* New York: American Geographical Society, 1962.

Spate, O. H. K. *India and Pakistan: A General and Regional Geography.* New York: E. P. Dutton & Co., 1954.

U.S. Army Area Handbook for India, Dept. of the Army Pamphlet No. 550–21 (Washington, D.C.: Government Printing Office, 1964).

Chapter 3: The Great Vista of India's Past

Basham, A. L. *The Wonder That Was India.* London: Sidgwick and Jackson, 1954. New York: The Macmillan Co., 1955. New York: Grove Press, 1959 (paperback ed.).

Kabir, Humayun. *The Indian Heritage.* London: Meridian Books, 1947. Bombay: Asia Publishing House, 1955.

Majumdar, R. C.; Raychaudhuri, H. C.; and Datta, Kalilinkar. *An Advanced History of India.* London: The Macmillan Co., 1950.

Nehru, Jawaharlal. *The Discovery of India.* New York: The John Day Company, 1946. Calcutta: Signet Press, 1948. New York: Anchor Books, 1960 (paperback ed.).

Rapson, E. J. (ed.). *The Cambridge History of India.* Vol. I. London: Cambridge University Press, 1922. New York: The Macmillan Co., 1922. Delhi: S. Chand & Co., 1958.

Sen, Gertrude Emerson. *The Pageant of Indian History.* New York: Longmans, Green & Co., 1948.

Smith, Vincent A. *Asoka.* Oxford: Clarendon Press, 1901. Delhi: S. Chand & Co., 1957.

* Editor's note: The original British or American editions of some of the titles listed here are no longer in print; in such cases, wherever possible, Indian reprint editions are listed as well. Paperback editions, when available, are also listed.

———. *The Oxford History of India.* 3d ed. Edited by Percival Spear. New York: Oxford University Press, 1958. Oxford: Clarendon Press, 1958.

SPEAR, PERCIVAL. *India, A Modern History.* Ann Arbor, Mich.: University of Michigan Press, 1961.

Chapter 4: The Nature and Legacy of the Muslim Period

BINYON, SIR LAURENCE. *Akbar.* New York: D. Appleton and Co., 1932.

CHAND, TARA. *Influence of Islam on Indian Culture.* Allahabad: The Indian Press, 1954.

EDWARDES, E. M., and GARRETT, H. L. O. *Mughal Rule in India.* Delhi: S. Chand & Co., 1956.

HAIG, SIR WOLLESLEY (ed.). *The Cambridge History of India.* Vols III and IV. London: Cambridge University Press, 1937. New York: The Macmillan Co., 1937. Delhi: S. Chand & Co., 1958.

KABIR, HUMAYUN. *The Indian Heritage.*

LANE-POOLE, STANLEY. *Mediaeval India Under Mohammedan Rule.* 2 vols. London: Ernest Benn, 1903. New York: G. P. Putnam's Sons, 1903. Calcutta: Susil Gupta, 1951.

MAJUMDAR, R. C.; RAYCHAUDHURI, H. C.; and DATTA, KALILINKAR. *An Advanced History of India.*

NEHRU, JAWAHARLAL. *The Discovery of India.*

SARKAR, SIR JADUNATH. *Mughal Administration.* Calcutta: M. C. Sarkar & Sons, 1935.

SHARMA, S. R. *The Crescent in India: A Study in Medieval History.* Revised ed. Bombay: Hind Kitabs, 1954.

SMITH, VINCENT A. *Akbar, The Great Mogul.* Oxford: Clarendon Press, 1917. Delhi: S. Chand & Co., 1958.

———. *The Oxford History of India.*

SPEAR, PERCIVAL. *India, A Modern History.*

———. *Twilight of the Mughals.* London: Cambridge University Press, 1951.

Chapter 5: The Rise and Consolidation of British Rule

DODWELL, H. H. (ed.). *The Cambridge History of India.* Vols. V and VI. London: Cambridge University Press, 1929 and 1932. New York: The Macmillan Co., 1929 and 1932. Delhi: S. Chand & Co., 1958.

GRIFFITHS, SIR PERCIVAL. *The British Impact on India.* London: Macdonald, 1953.

MAJUMDAR, R. C.; RAYCHAUDHURI, H. C.; and DATTA, KALILINKAR. *An Advanced History of India.*

MOON, PENDEREL. *Strangers in India.* London: Faber and Faber, 1944.

NEHRU, JAWAHARLAL. *The Discovery of India.*

PANIKKAR, K. M. *Asia and Western Dominance.* Rev. ed. New York: Hillary House Publishers, 1959.

Report of the Indian Statutory Commission. London: His Majesty's Stationery Office, Cmd. 3568, 1930.

ROBERTS, P. E. *History of British India.* 3d ed. New York and London: Oxford University Press, 1952.

SANDERSON, GORHAM D. *India and British Imperialism.* New York: Bookman Associates, 1951.

SMITH, VINCENT A. *The Oxford History of India.*

SPEAR, PERCIVAL. *India: A Modern History.*

———. *The Nabobs: A Study of the Social Life of the English in Eighteenth Century India.* London: H. Milford, 1932.

STOKES, ERIC. *The English Utilitarians and India.* Oxford: Clarendon Press, 1959.

THOMPSON, EDWARD. *The Other Side of the Medal.* London: Hogarth Press, 1925.

———, and GARRATT, G. T. *Rise and Fulfillment of British Rule in India.* London: The Macmillan Co., 1934. Allahabad: Central Book Depot, 1958.

WOODRUFF, PHILIP. (pseud. for Philip Mason). *The Men Who Ruled India.* Vol. I: *The Founders of Modern India.* Vol. II: *The Guardians.* New York: St. Martin's Press, 1954.

Chapter 6: Toward Independence—And After

ALEXANDER, HORACE. *New Citizens of India.* London: Oxford University Press, 1951.

ANDREWS, C. F., and MOOKERJI, G. *The Rise and Growth of the Congress in India.* London: George Allen and Unwin, 1938.

AZAD, MAULANA ABUL KALAM. *India Wins Freedom: An Autobiographical Narrative.* Bombay: Orient Longmans, 1959.

BOLITHO, HECTOR. *Jinnah: Creator of Pakistan.* New York: The Macmillan Co., 1955.

BONDURANT, JOAN. *Conquest of Violence: The Gandhian Philosophy of Conflict.* Princeton, N.J.: Princeton University Press, 1958.

BROWN, D. MACKENZIE. *The Nationalist Movement: Indian Political Thought from Ranade to Bhave.* Berkeley, Calif.: University of California Press, 1961.

COUPLAND, R. *The Indian Problem.* New York: Oxford University Press, 1944.

DESAI, A. R. *Social Background of Indian Nationalism.* 3d ed. Bombay: Popular Book Depot, 1959.

FISCHER, LOUIS. *Gandhi, His Life and Message for the World.* New York: New American Library of World Literature, 1954 (paperback ed.).

———. *The Life of Mahatma Gandhi.* New York: Harper & Brothers, 1950. New York: Collier Books, 1962 (paperback ed.).

GANDHI, M. K. *Gandhi's Autobiography: The Story of My Experiments With Truth.* Boston: Beacon Press, 1957 (paperback ed.).

GOPAL, RAM. *Indian Muslims: A Political History, 1858–1947.* New York: Asia Publishing House, 1959.

GOVERNMENT OF INDIA. *Report of the States Reorganization Commission.* New Delhi: 1955.

MAJUMDAR, R. C.; RAYCHAUDHURI, H. C.; and DATTA, KALILINKAR. *An Advanced History of India.*

MENON, V. P. *The Integration of the Indian States.* New York: The Macmillan Co., 1956.

———. *Transfer of Power in India.* Princeton, N.J.: Princeton University Press, 1957.

MOON, PENDEREL. *Divide and Quit.* Berkeley, Calif.: University of California Press, 1961.

MOSLEY, LEONARD. *The Last Days of the British Raj.* New York: Harcourt, Brace and World, 1962.

NANDA, B. R. *Mahatma Gandhi.* Boston: Beacon Press, 1958.

———. *The Nehrus: Motilal and Jawaharlal.* Boston: Beacon Press, 1963.

NEHRU, JAWAHARLAL. *Toward Freedom.* New York: The John Day Company, 1941. Boston: Beacon Press, 1958 (paperback ed.).

SITARAMAYYA, P. B. *The History of the Indian National Congress (1885–1935).* 2 vols. Bombay: Padma Publications, 1946–47.

SMITH, VINCENT A. *The Oxford History of India.*

SMITH, WILFRED CANTWELL. *Modern Islam in India: A Social Analysis.* 2d ed. Lahore: Ripon Printing Press, 1947.

SYMONDS, RICHARD. *The Making of Pakistan.* London: Faber and Faber, 1949.

WOLPERT, STANLEY A. *Tilak and Gokhale.* Berkeley, Calif.: University of California Press, 1962.

Chapter 7: Hinduism—The Religion of the Majority

ARCHER, W. G. *The Loves of Krishna.* New York: Grove Press, 1958 (paperback ed.).

BONDURANT, JOAN V. *Conquest of Violence: The Gandhian Philosophy of Conflict.*

ELIOT, SIR CHARLES. *Hinduism and Buddhism: An Historical Sketch.* 3 vols. London: Routledge & Kegan Paul, 1921; reprinted in 1954.

FARQUHAR, JOHN N. *Modern Religious Movements in India.* New York: The Macmillan Co., 1910.

FISCHER, LOUIS. *The Life of Mahatma Gandhi.*

GANDHI, M. K. *Gandhi's Autobiography: The Story of My Experiments With Truth.*

———. *Hindu Dharma*. Ahmedabad: Navajivan Publishing House, 1950.

GARRATT, G. T. (ed.). *The Legacy of India*. Oxford: Clarendon Press, 1937. New York: Oxford University Press, 1937.

LIN YUTANG (ed.). *The Wisdom of China and India*. New York: Random House, 1942.

MORGAN, KENNETH W. (ed.). *The Religion of the Hindus*. New York: Ronald Press, 1953.

NANDA, B. R. *Mahatma Gandhi*.

NATARAJAN, S. *A Century of Social Reform in India*. Bombay: Asia Publishing House, 1959.

PITT, MALCOLM. *Introducing Hinduism*. New York: Friendship Press, 1955.

RADHAKRISHNAN, S. *Eastern Religions and Western Thought*. London: Oxford University Press, 1939. New York: Oxford University Press, n.d. (paperback ed.).

———. *The Hindu View of Life*. London: George Allen and Unwin, 1927. New York: The Macmillan Co., n.d. (paperback ed.).

———, and CHARLES A. MOORE (eds.). *A Source Book in Indian Philosophy*. Princeton, N.J.: Princeton University Press, 1957.

SARMA, D. S. *Hinduism Through the Ages*. Bombay: Bharatiya Vidya Bhavan, 1956.

Seminar (New Delhi). No. 64 (December, 1964). Special issue: "Our Changing Values."

SEN, GERTRUDE EMERSON. *Pageant of India's History*.

SINGER, MILTON (ed.). *Traditional India: Structure and Change*. Philadelphia: American Folklore Society, 1959.

VYAS, K. C. *The Social Renaissance in India*. Bombay: Vora & Co., 1957.

WHITEHEAD, THE RIGHT REVEREND HENRY. *The Village Gods of South India*. London: Oxford University Press, 1921.

Chapter 8: The Religious Minority Groups

MORGAN, KENNETH W. *Islam: The Straight Path*. New York: The Ronald Press Co., 1958.

POTHACAMURY, ARCHBISHOP THOMAS. *The Church in Independent India*. New York: Maryknoll Publications, 1958.

SINGH, KHUSHWANT. *The Sikhs*. London: George Allen and Unwin, 1953.

SMITH, WILFRED CANTWELL. *Modern Islam in India: A Social Analysis*.

Chapter 9: Caste, Family, and Social Change

AIYAPPAN, A., and BALA RATNAM, L. K. (eds.). *Society in India*. Madras: Social Science Association, 1956.

AMBEDKAR, B. R. *The Untouchables.* New Delhi: Amrit Book Co., 1948.

BAIG, TARA ALI (ed.). *Women of India.* New Delhi: Ministry of Information and Broadcasting, 1958.

CHAUDHURI, NIRAD C. *The Autobiography of an Unknown Indian.* New York: The Macmillan Co., 1951.

CORMACK, MARGARET. *The Hindu Woman.* Bombay: Asia Publishing House, 1961. New York: Teacher's College, Bureau of Publications, 1953.

———. *She Who Rides a Peacock: Indian Students and Social Change.* New York: Frederick A. Praeger, 1962.

DESAI, I., and DAMLE, Y. B. "A Note on the Change in the Caste," in K. M. Kapadia (ed.), *Professor Ghurye Felicitation Volume.* Bombay: Popular Book Depot, 1954. Reprinted in *Introduction to the Civilization of India.* Chicago: University of Chicago Press, Syllabus Division, September, 1957.

ELWIN, VERRIER. *Nagaland.* Shillong, Assam: Published by P. Dutta, for the Research Department, Adviser's Secretariat, 1961.

GHURYE, G. S. *Caste and Class in India.* Bombay: Popular Book Depot, 1950.

GOVERNMENT OF INDIA. *The Law Relating to Hindu Marriages.* Delhi: Ministry of Law, 1956.

———. *The Law Relating to Hindu Succession.* Delhi. Ministry of Law, 1956.

HARRISON, SELIG S. "Caste and the Andhra Communists," *American Political Science Review.* Vol. I, No. 2 (June, 1956).

HAZARI. *An Indian Outcaste: The Autobiography of an Untouchable.* London: Bannisdale Press, 1951.

HEINRICH, J. C. *The Psychology of a Suppressed People.* London: George Allen and Unwin, 1937.

HUTTON, J. H. *Caste in India,* 3d ed. New York: Oxford University Press, 1961.

IYER, K. V. SUNDARESA. *Democracy and Caste.* Madurai: The Minerva Printers, 1956. Reprinted in Myron Weiner (ed.). *Introduction to the Civilization of Developing India.* Chicago: University of Chicago Press, Syllabus Division, Vol. II, April, 1961.

KARVE, IRAWATI. *Hindu Society: An Interpretation.* Poona: Deccan College, 1961.

———. *Kinship Organization in India.* Poona: Deccan College, Monograph Series, 1953.

KEER, DHANANJAY. *Dr. Ambedkar: Life and Mission.* Bombay: A. V. Keer, 1954.

LAM, MITHAN J. *Women in India.* New Delhi: All-India Women's Conference, 1956.

Majumdar, D. N. *Caste and Communication in an Indian Village.* Bombay: Asia Publishing House, 1958.

Mandelbaum, David G. "The Family in India," *Southwestern Journal of Anthropology.* Vol. IV, No. 2 (1948).

Marriot, McKim. *Village India: Studies in the Little Community.* Chicago: University of Chicago Press, 1955.

Mayer, Adrian C. *Caste and Kinship in Central India.* Berkeley, Calif.: University of California Press, 1960.

Nanavati, M. B., and Vakil, C. N. (eds.). *Group Prejudices in India.* Bombay: Vora, 1951.

O'Malley, L. S. S. *India's Social Heritage.* Oxford: Clarendon Press, 1934.

Panikkar, K. M. *Hindu Society at the Crossroads.* Bombay: Asia Publishing House, 1955. New York: Taplinger Publishing Co., 1961 (2d ed.).

Rao, M. S. A. *Social Change in Malabar.* Bombay: Popular Book Depot, 1957.

Rice, Stanley. *Hindu Customs and Their Origins.* London: George Allen and Unwin, 1937.

Seminar (New Delhi). No. 70 (June, 1965). Special issue: "Caste and the Future."

Srinivas, M. N. "Caste in Modern India," *Journal of Asian Studies.* Vol. XVI, No. 4 (August, 1957).

———. "The Nature of Indian Unity," *Economic Weekly.* Bombay: April 26, 1958. Reprinted in Myron Weiner (ed.). *Introduction to the Civilization of Developing India.*

———. "A Note on Sanskritization and Westernization," *The Far Eastern Quarterly.* Vol. XV, No. 4 (August, 1956).

———. "Varna and Caste," in S. Radhakrishnan *et al.* (eds.). *Essays in Philosophy.* Baroda: University of Baroda, 1954. Reprinted in *Introduction to the Civilization of India.* Chicago: University of Chicago Press, Syllabus Division, September, 1957.

——— (ed.). *India's Villages.* 2d ed. New York: Asia Publishing House, 1960.

Wiser, W. H. *Hindu Jajmani System.* Lucknow: Lucknow Publishing House, 1958.

Zinkin, Taya. *Caste Today.* New York and London: Oxford University Press, 1962.

———. *India Changes.* New York: Oxford University Press, 1958.

Chapter 10: Language Barriers and Cultural Links

Chatterjee, S. K. *Languages and the Linguistic Problem.* London: Oxford Pamphlets on Indian Affairs, No. 11, 1945.

Choubey, Jagdish Narain. *Problems of National Integration.* Delhi: National Integration Council, 1961.

Gandhi, M. K. *Thoughts on National Language.* Ahmedabad: Navajivan Press ,1956.

Government of India. *Report of the Official Language Commission.* New Delhi: Official Language Commission, 1956.

———. *Report of the States Reorganization Commission.*

Gumperz, John J. "Language Problems in the Rural Development of North India," *Journal of Asian Studies,* Vol. XVI, No. 2 (February, 1957).

———. "Some Remarks on Regional and Social Language Differences in India," *Introduction to the Civilization of India.* Chicago: University of Chicago Press, Syllabus Division, September, 1957.

Harrison, Selig S. *India: The Most Dangerous Decades.* Princeton, N.J.: Princeton University Press, 1960.

Seminar (New Delhi). No. 68 (April, 1965). Special issue: "Language."

Chapter 11: Education: Problems and Progress

Cormack, Margaret. *She Who Rides a Peacock: Indian Students and Social Change.*

Government of India. *Report of the Secondary Education Commission (October, 1952–June, 1953).* New Delhi: Ministry of Education, 1953.

———. *Report of the University Education Commission (December, 1948–August, 1949).* Vol. I. Government of India Press, 1950.

———. *Report of the University Grants Commission.* New Delhi: University Grants Commission, 1960.

———. *Review of Education in India (1947–61).* New Delhi: Ministry of Education, 1961.

Kabir, Humayun. *Education in New India.* London: George Allen and Unwin, 1956.

Nurullah, Syed, and Naik, J. P. *A History of Education in India.* Bombay: The Macmillan Co., 1951.

Rawat, P. L. *History of Indian Education.* 3d ed. Agra: Bharat Publications, 1956.

Reid, John T. "A Dozen Problems of Indian Higher Education." New Delhi: American Embassy, 1961.

Seminar (New Delhi). No. 71 (July, 1965). Special issue: "At School."

Sharp, H. (ed.). *Selections from Educational Records.* Calcutta: Government Printing Office, 1920.

Useem, John, and Useem, Ruth Hill. *The Western Educated Man in India.* New York: Dryden Press, 1955.

Chapter 12: Nehru and India's Western-Type Government

ALEXANDROWICZ, C. H. *Constitutional Developments in India.* New York and London: Oxford University Press, 1957.

APPLEBY, PAUL H. *Public Administration in India: Report of a Survey.* New Delhi: Government of India, Cabinet Secretariat, 1953.

———. *Re-examination of India's Administrative System.* New Delhi: Government of India, Cabinet Secretariat, 1956.

BAYLEY, DAVID H. "The Indian Experience with Preventive Detention," *Pacific Affairs.* Vol. XXXV, No. 2 (Summer, 1962).

BRECHER, MICHAEL. *Nehru: A Political Biography.* New York and London: Oxford University Press, 1959.

BROWN, D. MACKENZIE. *Indian Political Thought from Ranade to Bhave: The Nationalist Movement.*

———. *The White Umbrella: Indian Political Thought from Manu to Gandhi.* Berkeley, Calif.: University of California Press, 1953, 1959 (paperback ed.).

DEAN, VERA M. *New Patterns of Democracy in India.* Cambridge, Mass.: Harvard University Press, 1959.

JENNINGS, SIR WILLIAM IVOR. *Some Characteristics of the Indian Constitution.* New York: Oxford University Press, 1953.

JOSHI, G. N. *The Constitution of India.* London: The Macmillan Co., 1952. New York: St. Martin's Press, 1953 (3d ed.).

MORRIS-JONES, W. H. *Parliament in India.* Philadelphia: University of Pennsylvania Press, 1957.

———. *The Government and Politics of India.* London: Hutchinson University Library, 1964.

PALMER, NORMAN D. "India," in George McT. Kahin. *Major Governments of Asia.* Ithaca, N.Y.: Cornell University Press, 1963 (2d ed.).

———. *The Indian Political System.* Boston: Houghton Mifflin Company, 1961

PYLEE, M. V. *Constitutional Government in India.* New York: Asia Publishing House, 1960.

Report of the Team for the Study of Community Projects and Extension Service. 3 vols. New Delhi: Committee on Plan Projects, 1957.

RETZLAFF, RALPH H. *Village Government in India.* New York: Asia Publishing House, 1962.

Seminar (New Delhi). No. 22 (June, 1961). Special issue: "Administration."

Seminar. No. 63 (November, 1964). Special issue: "Nehru and the Ism."

———. No. 66 (February, 1965). Special issue: "Parliament."

SMITH, DONALD E. *India as a Secular State.* Princeton, N.J.: Princeton University Press, 1963.

Chapter 13: The Indian Nature of Indian Politics

BONDURANT, JOAN V. *Regionalism Versus Provincialism: A Study in Indian National Unity*. Berkeley, Calif.: University of California, Indian Press Digests, Monograph Series No. 4, December, 1958.

CURRAN, J. A., JR. *Militant Hinduism in Indian Politics: A Study of the R.S.S.* New York: Institute of Pacific Relations, 1951.

DEAN, VERA M. *New Patterns of Democracy in India*.

FISHER, MARGARET W., and BONDURANT, JOAN V. *Indian Approaches to a Socialist Society*. Berkeley, Calif.: University of California, Indian Press Digests, Monograph Series, No. 2, July, 1956.

———. *The Indian Experience with Democratic Elections*. Berkeley, Calif.: University of California, Indian Press Digests, Monograph Series, No. 3, December, 1956.

Government of India. *Report of the Second General Elections in India, 1957*. 2 vols. New Delhi: Election Commissioner of India, 1958.

KOGEKAR, S. V., and PARK, RICHARD L. (eds.). *Reports on the Indian General Elections, 1951–52*. Bombay: Popular Book Depot, 1956.

MASANI, M. R. *The Communist Party of India: A Short History*. New York: The Macmillan Co., 1954.

MEHTA, ASOKA. *The Political Mind of India: An Analysis of the Results of the General Elections*. Bombay: Socialist Party, 1952.

———. "The Political Mind of India," *Foreign Affairs*. July, 1957.

NARAYAN, JAYAPRAKASH. *Swaraj for the People*. New Delhi: Rajghat, 1961.

OVERSTREET, GENE D., and WINDMILLER, MARSHALL. *Communism in India*. Berkeley and Los Angeles, Calif.: University of California Press, 1959.

PALMER, NORMAN D. "India," in George McT. Kahin. *Major Governments of Asia*.

———. *The Indian Political System*.

PARK, RICHARD L., and TINKER, IRENE, (eds.). *Leadership and Political Institutions in India*. Princeton, N.J.: Princeton University Press, 1959.

PHILIPS, C. H. (ed.). *Politics and Society in India*. New York: Frederick A. Praeger, 1963.

———. (ed.). *1962 General Elections in India*. Bombay: Allied Publishers, 1962.

POPLAI, S. L. *National Politics and the 1957 Elections in India*. Delhi: Metropolitan Book Co., 1957.

RUDOLPH, LLOYD I., and RUDOLPH, SUZANNE H. "The Political Role of India's Caste Associations," *Pacific Affairs*. March, 1960.

Seminar (New Delhi). No. 67 (March, 1965). Special issue: "Secularism."

SMITH, DONALD E., *op. cit.*

TALBOT, PHILLIPS. *Second General Elections: Voting in the States.* New York: American Universities Field Staff, 1957.

TINKER, HUGH. *India and Pakistan: A Political Analysis.* New York: Frederick A. Praeger, 1962.

WEINER, MYRON. *Party Politics in India: The Development of a Multi-Party System.* Princeton, N.J.: Princeton University Press, 1957.

———. *The Politics of Scarcity.* New York and Bombay: Asia Publishing House, 1963.

Chapter 14: Villages and Cities

AGGARWAL, S. C. *Recent Developments in Housing.* New Delhi: Jain Book Agency, 1958.

BADEN-POWELL. *The Indian Village Community.* New Haven, Conn.: Graf Press, 1957.

BEIDELMAN, THOMAS O. *A Comparative Analysis of the Jajmani System.* Locust Valley, N.Y.: J. J. Augustin Co., 1959.

DUBE, S. C. *India's Changing Villages.* Ithaca, N.Y.: Cornell University Press, 1958.

Government of India. *Evaluation Report on the Working of Community Projects and N.E.S. Blocks.* New Delhi: Programme Evaluation Organization, Planning Commission, 1957.

Government of India, Planning Commission. *The New India: Progress Through Democracy.* New York: The Macmillan Co., 1958.

———. *Report of the Team for the Study of Community Projects and National Extension Service.*

LEWIS, OSCAR. *Village Life in Northern India: Studies in a Delhi Village.* Urbana, Ill.: University of Illinois Press, 1958.

MAMORIA, C. B., and DOSHI, S. L. *Labour Problems and Social Welfare in India.* Allahabad: Kitab Mahal, 1958.

MARRIOT, MCKIM. *Village India: Studies in the Little Community.*

MAYER, ALBERT, and Associates. *Pilot Project, India.* Berkeley, Calif.: University of California Press, 1958.

NAIR, KUSUM. *Blossoms in the Dust: The Human Element in Indian Development.* New York: Frederick A. Praeger, 1962.

OPLER, MORRIS E. "The Extensions of an India Village," *Journal of Asian Studies.* Vol. XVI, No. 1 (November, 1956).

SINGH, RUDRA DATT. "The Unity of an Indian Village," *Journal of Asian Studies.* Vol. XVI, No. 1 (November, 1956).

TURNER, ROY. *India's Urban Future.* Berkeley, Calif.: University of California Press, 1962.

WISER, W. H. *Hindu Jajmani System.*

WISER, WILLIAM AND CHARLOTTE. *Behind Mud Walls, 1930–1960.* Berkeley, Calif.: University of California Press, 1963.

Chapter 15: Toward Economic Development

ANSTEY, VERA. *The Economic Development of India.* 4th ed. New York: Longmans, Green & Co., 1952.

BAUER, P. T. *Indian Economic Policy and Development.* New York: Frederick A. Praeger, 1961.

DAVIS, KINGSLEY. *The Population of India and Pakistan.* Princeton, N.J.: Princeton University Press, 1951.

DUTT, ROMESH. *The Economic History of India: Under Early British Rule.* London: Routledge & Kegan Paul, 1956.

———. *The Economic History of India in the Victorian Age.* London: Routledge & Kegan Paul, 1956.

FISHER, MARGARET W., and BONDURANT, JOAN V. *Indian Approaches to a Socialist Society.*

GADGIL, D. R. *Economic Policy and Development.* Poona: Gokale Institute, 1955.

———. *Planning and Economic Policy in India.* New York: Asia Publishing House, 1962.

GOVERNMENT OF INDIA. *First Five-Year Plan.* New Delhi: Planning Commission, 1952.

———. *India, 1961.* New Delhi: Ministry of Information and Broadcasting, 1961.

———. *India, Pocket Book of Economic Information.* New Delhi: Ministry of Finance, Department of Economic Affairs, 1961.

———. *The Indo-U.S. Technical Cooperation Program: Report 1961.* New Delhi: Ministry of Finance, Department of Economic Affairs, 1961.

———. *Outline Report of the Study Group on Educated Unemployed.* New Delhi: Planning Commission, 1956.

———. *Report of the Food Grains Enquiry Commission.* New Delhi: Ministry of Food and Agriculture, 1957.

———. *Report on India's Food Crisis and Steps to Meet It, by the Agricultural Team sponsored by the Ford Foundation.* New Delhi: Ministry of Food and Agriculture, 1959.

———. *Second Five-Year Plan.* New Delhi: Planning Commission, 1956.

———. *Third Five-Year Plan.* New Delhi: Planning Commission, 1961.

———. Planning Commission. *The New India: Progress Through Democracy.*

HART, HENRY C. *New India's Rivers.* Bombay: Orient Longmans, 1956.

HERMAN, CELIA I. *Investment in India.* Washington, D.C.: U.S. Department of Commerce, 1961.

KARNIK, V. B. *Indian Trade Unions: A Survey.* Bombay: Allied Publishers Private, 1960.

LEWIS, JOHN P. *Quiet Crisis in India: Economic Development and American Policy*. Washington, D.C.: Brookings Institution, 1962.

MALENBAUM, WILFRED. *East and West in India's Development: The Economics of Competitive Coexistence*. Washington, D.C.: National Planning Association, 1959.

———. *Prospects for Indian Development*. London: George Allen and Unwin, 1962. New York: The Free Press of Glencoe, 1962.

MAMORIA, C. B. *Agricultural Problems of India*. Allahabad: Kitab Mahal, 1958.

RANGNEKAR, D. K. *Poverty and Capital Development in India*. London: Oxford University Press, 1958.

TATA INDUSTRIES. *Statistical Outline of India, 1961*. Bombay: Tata Industries, 1961.

The United States Contribution to Indian Development. New Delhi: U.S. AID Mission to India, December 31, 1961.

VAKIL, C. N. *Economic Consequences of Divided India: A Study of the Economy of India and Pakistan*. Bombay: Vora & Co., 1950.

VENKATASUBBIAH, H. *Indian Economy Since Independence*. Bombay: Asia Publishing House, 1958.

VERGHESE, B. G. *A Journey Through India: A Times of India Survey*. New Delhi: Times of India, 1959.

Chapter 16: Foreign Policy and the Chinese Threat

BERKES, ROSS N., and BEDI, MOHINDER S. *The Diplomacy of India*. Palo Alto, Calif.: Stanford University Press, 1958.

CHAKRAVARTY, P. C. *India's China Policy*. Bloomington, Ind.: Indiana University Press, 1962.

DAS GUPTA, J. B. *Indo-Pakistan Relations (1947–1955)*. Amsterdam: 1958.

FISHER, MARGARET W., and BONDURANT, JOAN V. *Indian Views of Sino-Indian Relations*. Berkeley, Calif.: University of California Press, February, 1956.

HARRISON, SELIG (ed.). *India and the United States*. New York: The Macmillan Co., 1961.

JAIN, GIRILAL. *Panchsheel and After*. Bombay: Asia Publishing House, 1960.

KORBEL, JOSEF. *Danger in Kashmir*. Princeton, N.Y.: Princeton University Press, 1954.

KUNDRA, J. C. *Indian Foreign Policy, 1947–1954*. Bombay: Vora & Co., 1955.

NEHRU, JAWAHARLAL. *India's Foreign Policy*. Publication Division, Ministry of Infonnation and Broadcasting, Government of India, 1961.

PALMER, NORMAN D. *South Asia and United States Policy*. Boston: Houghton Mifflin Company, 1965.

Seminar (New Delhi). No. 37 (September, 1962). Special issue: "Our Neighbors."

———. No. 58 (May, 1964). Special issue: "Kashmir."

———. No. 65 (January, 1965). Special issue: "The Bomb."

———. No. 69. (May, 1965). Special issue: "Goa"

TALBOT, PHILLIPS, and POPLAI, S. L. *India and America.* New York: Harper & Brothers, 1958.

WARD, BARBARA. *India and the West.* New York: W. W. Norton & Company, 1961.

Chapter 17: The Defense Forces and Their British Background

The Army in India and its Evolution. Calcutta: Superintendent of Government Printing, 1924.

CHATTAR, SINGH SAMRA. "Subhas Chandra Bose: An Indian National Hero," in Richard L. Park and Irene Tinker (eds.). *Leadership and Political Institutions in India.*

EVANS, HUMPHREY. *Thimayya of India: A Soldier's Life.* New York: Harcourt, Brace & Co., 1960.

PANIKKAR, K. M. *Problem of Indian Defense.* Bombay: Asia Publishing House, 1960.

PRASAD, BISHESHWAR (ed.). *Official History of the Indian Armed Forces in the Second World War, 1939–45.* Calcutta: Orient Longmans, 1956.

PRASAD, NANDAN. *Expansion of the Armed Forces and Defense Organization.* Calcutta: Orient Longmans, 1956.

Seminar (New Delhi). No. 35 (July, 1962). Special issue: "National Defense."

SINGH, BRIGADIER RAJENDRA. *Organization and Administration in the Indian Army.* Aldershot: Hampshire Gale and Polden, 1952.

INDEX